The Anglo-Saxon Chronicle is the most important single source for the pre-Conquest history of England, but it is a complicated record, which cannot be accurately or fully used without an understanding of the relationship of the various versions and a knowledge whether an individual entry is in all manuscripts or is confined to one branch, or even to a single manuscript. Without such knowledge one cannot usually find out the date at which the entry was written, or judge its historical validity. This is the only translation of the Chronicle which makes the position clear. While full acknowledgement should be made to the great pioneer work of Charles Plummer, it should be noted that these particulars cannot be gathered from his text, nor from translations based on it, since it prints in full only two manuscripts. Moreover, anyone who has attempted to use the various versions (often with wrong annal dates) for the reign of the Confessor will appreciate the clarity of their setting out in this volume in parallel columns beside the true date. Though Plummer laid the foundation for all subsequent Chronicle study, important advances have been made since. Professor Whitelock's introduction embodies the advances made by herself and other scholars, and hints at lines on which a solution to outstanding problems may be sought. The footnotes not only elucidate points of difficulty, but include citations from Latin authors and the Anglo-Norman Gaimar who had access to versions of the Chronicle which have since been lost.

This edition of the Chronicle is based upon the translations which were included in the first two volumes of *English Historical Documents* edited by Professor Whitelock, and by Professor Douglas and G. W. Greenaway. The setting out of the parts taken from the two volumes has been made completely uniform, some alterations have been made to take account of the most recent scholarship and the text has been completely reset. A number of new and useful notes have been added.

The Anglo-Saxon Chronicle

The
Anglo-Saxon Chronicle

A REVISED TRANSLATION

EDITED BY

DOROTHY WHITELOCK

LITT.D., F.B.A.

Elrington and Bosworth Professor of Anglo-Saxon,
University of Cambridge

WITH

DAVID C. DOUGLAS

M.A., F.B.A., Professor of History, University of Bristol

AND

SUSIE I. TUCKER

M.A., Senior Lecturer in English,
University of Bristol

INTRODUCTION
BY DOROTHY WHITELOCK

LONDON
EYRE AND SPOTTISWOODE
22 HENRIETTA STREET WC2

This edition first published 1961
Copyright © 1961 by Dorothy Whitelock and David Douglas
Printed in Great Britain by Jarrold & Sons Ltd, Norwich
Cat. No. 6/2391

Contents

Foreword

MANY persons have expressed appreciation of the system of arrangement of the Anglo-Saxon Chronicle adopted in *English Historical Documents* (vol. I, 1955, edited by D. Whitelock; vol. II, 1954, edited by D. C. Douglas and G. W. Greenaway, with translation by S. I. Tucker), since this enables the reader easily to compare the various versions and to assess the degree of authority of the individual entries. It seems, therefore, that a separate edition, combining the two parts of this record hitherto divided between volume I and volume II, will meet a need. Moreover, Chronicle studies have not stood still since 1955. The introduction in the present work incorporates new material; and, in order to support and illustrate the conclusions there drawn, the practice previously confined to volume I, of including in the footnotes relevant material from Latin authors, has been extended to the rest of the Chronicle. The translation has been revised and alterations have been made in the interests of a consistent treatment throughout. The bibliography has been brought up to date, and an index of proper names has been added, together with some new genealogical tables. It is hoped that the material here presented will give scholars an opportunity for considering some unsolved problems concerning the transmission of this important source.

Introduction

The Anglo-Saxon Chronicle, the most important source for the political history of the period, has come down to us in seven manuscripts (one known mainly from a sixteenth-century transcript) and two fragments. For long stretches these manuscripts are versions of the same work, but some entries are confined to a group of manuscripts while others are peculiar to a single manuscript. The arrangement adopted in the present translation is intended to make it easy for the reader to distinguish the common stock of the Chronicle from the individual additions, and is explained in detail in the note before the commencement of the translation.[1]

The versions of the Chronicle

The extant manuscripts[2] are as follows: Corpus Christi College, Cambridge, MS. 173, cited as 'A', which is often called the Parker MS. after its donor, Matthew Parker, archbishop of Canterbury, 1559–1575. It is the oldest manuscript, being written up to almost the end of 891 in one hand of the late ninth or very early tenth century. After that it is continued in a series of hands, and the scribe who added annals 925–955,[3] probably not long after the latter year, was certainly writing at Winchester. He enters some events of purely local interest. In annal 964 the word *ceaster*, 'the city', means Winchester. It is possible that the manuscript was from the first written at the Old Minster, Winchester.[4] This manuscript gives a detailed account of events up to 920, and, apart from a copy of it, 'G',[5] contains the only record of the later wars of Edward the Elder. Then it shares in the general decay in historical writing and is the scantiest of our texts, for it uses neither the Mercian Register nor the northern annals. It contains tenth-century poems and royal obits which are in other versions, and some local entries of its own, but it did not receive the excellent record of the reign of Ethelred the Unready found in 'C', 'D', and 'E'.

[1] The most commonly used edition, that of J. Earle and C. Plummer (*Two of the Saxon Chronicles Parallel*, 2nd ed., 1952), gives the complete text of only two manuscripts, 'A' and 'E'. In the introduction to vol. II, however, Plummer discussed the whole problem of the relationship of the various versions and of the transmission of the Chronicle. Though the account in this present work differs in some respects from that of Plummer, his monumental work forms the basis of all Chronicle study.

[2] For a fuller description, see N. R. Ker, *Catalogue of Manuscripts containing Anglo-Saxon*, Oxford, 1957, on which the palaeographical information given below is based.

[3] In J. Earle and C. Plummer, *op. cit.*, II, p. xxv, he is called the eighth scribe, but I agree with Mr Ker that older palaeographers distinguished too many changes of hand, and that the second scribe, who begins with the last paragraph of 891, continues until 924 (excluding two and a half lines on f. 23 v and four on f. 24, which are in different and inferior hands). This second

hand is very close to that of the Tollemache Orosius (Brit. Mus. Addit. MS. 47967). The next scribe, who wrote annals 925–955, also inserted annal 710. He wrote also *Bald's Leechbook* (Brit. Mus. Royal MS. 12 D. xvii) and probably most of the Old English version of Bede's *Ecclesiastical History* in Brit. Mus. Cott. Otho B. xi. A late-tenth-century scribe added annals 958–967, and another scribe annals 975–1001. Only a few short annals were added after the manuscript was moved to Canterbury, except for a longer one at 1070 in a late-eleventh-century hand; but many alterations and additions were made to the existing text, mainly by the scribe who wrote version 'F' of the Chronicle.

[4] The accession of Bishop Frithustan to Winchester in 909 is specially marked (see p. 61, n. 2). His name occurs at the head of the first folio of the *Epistula Sedulii* which is bound up with this manuscript.

[5] See below, p. xii.

Instead, it has an independent entry of some length at 1001, but otherwise only a few scrappy entries after 975. At some time in the eleventh century it was removed to Christ Church, Canterbury, certainly being there by c. 1075. Here the scribe of 'F', who had before him the archetype of 'E', made many interpolations, some from this source, and a few entries were made by other scribes. To make room for these interpolations certain passages in 'A' were erased, but fortunately a copy of 'A' had been made before it left Winchester. Only fragments of this copy survived the Cottonian fire of 1731,[1] but it had previously been transcribed by Laurence Nowell, dean of Lichfield, a friend of Archbishop Parker and, like him, a collector of manuscripts.[2] This copy of 'A', which I shall call 'G',[3] is chiefly important as evidence for the state of 'A' before it was tampered with at Canterbury. 'A' is shown to have remained at Christ Church by the mention of it in later catalogues of the library of that house. It is the only surviving manuscript old enough for us to be able to distinguish palaeographically the stages of growth, and to separate the original text from later interpolations. It should warn us to be on our guard when examining versions which survive only in eleventh- or twelfth-century copies, where such accretions are hidden from our sight. In spite of its importance as our oldest manuscript, the value of 'A', even for the period in which it is a full record, must not be overstressed, for it is rather carelessly written, and is at least two removes from the original work. The support of Latin writers who had access to early versions of the Chronicle which have since been lost sometimes proves the superiority of readings in the manuscripts later than 'A'.

Manuscripts Brit. Mus. Cott. Tiber. A. vi, cited as 'B', and Cott. Tiber. B. i, cited as 'C', are very closely connected, having many features in common which separate them from other versions. Their annal for 977 shows a connexion with Abingdon, and the events of 971 would be known at that house. But there is no trace of a special interest in Abingdon previous to this annal. Neither manuscript mentions the refoundation of the monastery nor the consecration of Æthelwold, its first abbot, as bishop of Winchester in 963. It seems unlikely, therefore, that the version of the Chronicle which lies behind these two manuscripts was originally an Abingdon production, nor, in fact, is it probable that Abingdon would possess a copy of the Chronicle before the mid-tenth-century refoundation of the abbey.

'B' ends in 977. A detached leaf, Brit. Mus. Cott. Tiber. A. iii, f. 178, in the same handwriting, has been shown by Mr Ker to have originally followed the Chronicle in this manuscript. It contains the West Saxon genealogy and regnal list which forms the preface of 'A', and it continues the regnal list up to the accession of Edward the Martyr. As it breaks off with the words 'and he held', as if the

---

[1] Brit. Mus. Cott. Otho B. xi, ff. 39–47+Addit. MS. 34652, f. 2. In this manuscript the Chronicle was preceded by the Old English version of Bede's *Ecclesiastical History* (Otho B. xi+Otho B. x, ff. 55, 58, 62), mainly written by the scribe responsible for annals 925–955 in 'A'. The Chronicle portion, including Addit. MS. 34652, f. 2 (a detached leaf containing the West Saxon genealogy and regnal list which forms the preface in 'A'), is in the hand of the scribe who wrote Bede's autobiographical note at the end of the *Ecclesiastical History*, and can be

dated early eleventh century. Nowell's transcript is Brit. Mus. Addit. MS. 43703.

[2] On him, see R. Flower, 'Laurence Nowell and the Discovery of England in Tudor Times', *Proc. Brit. Acad.*, xxi, pp. 47–73.

[3] Thorpe calls it 'G', but Plummer, who uses a special form of 'A' to denote the Parker MS., refers to the Otho MS. as 'A'. He objects to 'G' as implying a date later than 'F'; but 'F' is itself earlier than 'E'.

writer did not know the length of the reign, it is reasonable to assume that he was writing before Edward's death on 18 March 978. 'B' has the peculiar feature that after 652 it usually omits the annal numbers, and there is nothing in the manuscript to account for this, for such annal numbers as are given are obviously being entered by the scribe himself as he goes on, and hence their absence in other places cannot be explained as the failure of a rubricator to complete his work. Apparently, therefore, it was the condition of the exemplar he was using that caused the scribe of 'B' to stop entering the annal numbers. Joscelyn, Archbishop Parker's secretary, refers to this manuscript as the Saxon History of St Augustine's, Canterbury, but there is no evidence before this sixteenth-century statement that it belonged to this house. Since Mr Ker has shown that the list of popes in it is in the hand of the scribe who added this same list to 'A' about 1100, it is probable that 'B' was at Christ Church, Canterbury, in the late eleventh century, not at St Augustine's,[1] though it may have been transferred there later.

'C' is written in hands of the mid eleventh century. It continues up to the end of annal 1056, when half a page is left blank. Then, beginning on a new folio, annals 1065 and 1066 are added, but with blanks instead of annal numbers. Annal 1066 breaks off at the end of a gathering in the middle of the account of the battle of Stamford Bridge, though a late-twelfth-century scribe has added a few lines on the first of two added leaves, the rest of which remain blank. It is, therefore, not possible to ascertain how far 'C' originally extended. It has several references to Abingdon affairs and was doubtless the product of that house, where it seems to have remained. Besides continuing further, 'C' differs from 'B' in omitting the West Saxon genealogy and regnal list. The scribe seems to have regarded the two texts which precede the Chronicle in his manuscript as forming an introduction to it. They are the *Menologium*, i.e. an Old English poem on the Church festivals, and a set of gnomic verses.

It is normally assumed that 'B' and 'C' are independent copies of a common archetype, but the history of 'C' may be rather more complicated. Mr Ker has pointed out that from 491, where a new scribe begins in 'C', to 652 the agreement of 'C' with 'B' is so close, even including certain letter-forms, that 'C' appears to be a direct copy of 'B'. There is certainly a change in the relationship of the two manuscripts from 653 on. Up till 652 there is no reading which suggests that 'C' had access to any other manuscript than 'B'. But after this date 'C' is not solely dependent on 'B'; in innumerable places a comparison with other versions shows 'C' to have better readings than 'B'. It can hardly be accidental that this change in the relationship comes at the exact point where 'B' stops inserting the annal numbers. If the scribe of 'C' were copying 'B', he would now have to find some other authority for his dates;[2] and he might then sometimes prefer the readings of this other authority. Nevertheless, he did not discard 'B' at this point. 'B' and 'C' continue to share readings against those of other manuscripts, and, as Mr Ker has noted, the relationship from about 945 to 977, when 'B' ends, is again very close.

---

[1] Ker, *op. cit.*, p. 250. See also p. 472, where Mr Ker suggests that a lost version of a forged letter purporting to be from Pope Boniface IV to Ethelbert of Kent in 611 once stood at the beginning of 'B', since Joscelyn says it was 'set before a saxon historye once belonging to the monastery of S. Austines in Canterberye'. The text given by Joscelyn is in the form otherwise found at Christ Church, Canterbury.

[2] This would be necessary even if he were copying the exemplar of 'B' rather than 'B' itself, if, as I have suggested above, this exemplar did not supply the annal numbers after 652.

In addition to sharing many minor readings, and annals 957, 971, and 977, which do not occur elsewhere, 'B' and 'C' agree in entering the Mercian Register without any attempt to dovetail its annals into those of the Chronicle. They insert it in a block after a puzzling list of blank annals which follows the Chronicle entry for 915. In 'B' this list reads DCCCXVI–DCCCXIX (presumably for DCCCCXVI–DCCCCXIX, to follow the last entry, 915), then DCCC, DCCCI; 'C' starts the list with DCCCXCVI, and follows with DCCCXCVII, etc., until it reaches DCCCC; it then has DCCCI (an obvious error for DCCCCI), after which comes the first annal of the Mercian Register, DCCCCII. It looks as if a list of blank annals beginning 916 in the exemplar has been partially altered in 'B' to make a better introduction to the Mercian Register, whereas 'C' has improved it further for this purpose. 'C' is not solely dependent on 'B' for its text of the Mercian Register, for it has annal 921 which 'B' omits. Apart from the Mercian Register, 'B' and 'C' have no entries between 915 and 934.

Brit. Mus. Cott. Tiber. B. iv, cited as 'D', and Laud Misc. 636 in the Bodleian Library, cited as 'E', must also be linked together. Both differ from the versions hitherto discussed in their inclusion in the early part of the Chronicle of much material of northern interest, drawn from Bede and from northern annals which were also available to the author of the twelfth-century work *The History of the Kings* which is ascribed to Simeon of Durham. They agree also in having a rhythmical passage in the style of Archbishop Wulfstan II of York at 959; in giving a prose instead of a verse account of Edgar's coronation in 973; in inserting a lengthy passage on the murder of Edward the Martyr; and in innumerable minor matters. Together they form what is known as the northern recension of the Chronicle, and I have little doubt that the common archetype from which both are derived was compiled at York. This would be the most likely place for such activity in the tenth and eleventh centuries, and the author of this recension refers to York as *ceaster*, 'the city', a circumstance which rules out the see of St Cuthbert, whether before or after this was moved to Durham from Chester-le-Street, for there an unqualified *ceaster* would surely refer to the latter place. Plummer suggested Ripon as the place of origin, but on slender evidence.[1]

The close agreement between 'D' and 'E' continues until 1031, after which for a long time each manuscript has a separate history. But even during the early sections there are important differences between the two manuscripts. 'D' contains a large amount of material which is also in 'A', 'B', and 'C', but which is missing from 'E', including the later events of Alfred's reign (891, 893–900), the wars of Edward the Elder (901–914), and the poems entered at 937 and 942. 'D' also uses the Mercian Register, though it is not inserted *en bloc* as in 'B' and 'C', but dovetailed into the annals of the main Chronicle. 'D' has also a number of tenth-century annals, dealing mainly with northern affairs, which are peculiar to it, and it has a passage at 975 in the style of Archbishop Wulfstan II which has been replaced in 'E' by a short statement.

Since Plummer's edition it has been customary to account for the absence from 'E' of sections which 'D' shares with 'A', 'B', and 'C' by assuming that the northern recension split early into two versions,

---

[1] For arguments against Ripon and in favour of York, see D. Whitelock, *The Peterborough Chronicle* (Early English Manuscripts in Facsimile, IV), pp. 29f.

and that the passages in question reached the ancestor of 'D', but not that of 'E'. Yet it is difficult to explain on this theory the close relationship, which extends to points of detail, between 'D' and 'E' for a long time after this alleged separation. It is easier to believe that the material missing from 'E' was originally foreign to the northern recension, and was not added to 'D' until later on, after the connexion with 'E' had ceased. This supposition receives support from a close examination of the existing state of 'D', for this reveals several places where two versions of the Chronicle have been conflated in 'D'. This is very clear in annal 855, where 'D' adds the genealogy, as found in 'A', 'B', and 'C', although it has already given the matter which follows the genealogy, as if, like 'E', 'D' originally omitted the genealogy. As 'D' then follows the genealogy with a repeat of this matter, it is not merely a question of rearrangement of the annal, but of the clumsy combination of two sources.[1] As the oldest hand in 'D' is not earlier than the second half of the eleventh century, there is no palaeographical obstacle to the supposition that 'D' is the result of a conflation of the northern recension with another text of the Chronicle at some date after the ancestor of 'E' had split off and moved south. The task of conflating the two texts cannot have been easy, and it would not be surprising if the compiler occasionally omitted parts of the northern recension, either by accident, or to make room for other matter. Such an inference would explain the absence from 'D' of the northern annals 949, 952 'E', while annals 1023 and 1025 in 'E' seem to have been ousted from 'D' by a long account of the translation of St Ælfheah. It should be noted that if 'D' did arise as here postulated, there is no longer any reason to assume that a version of the Chronicle reached the North in Alfred's reign, for Plummer's view that it did depends on the assumption that the northern copy had split into two versions before the account of Alfred's later campaigns, 892–896, was received. There is no evidence that any version of the Chronicle reached the North early, and it may well have first come there in the later part of the tenth century, when the see of York was held by archbishops of southern education.

'D' preserves a strong interest in northern affairs after the date of its separation from 'E', and was probably still being kept up at York. As the manuscript was at Worcester in the sixteenth century, and as it contains from 1033 on several entries concerning the diocese of Worcester, the theory that its eleventh-century portion was composed in this diocese has received wide currency. The prominence given to northern affairs is then attributed to the holding of the sees of York and Worcester in plurality from 972 to 1016, and from 1060 to 1062. Yet this argument will work the opposite way also, and can be used to explain the interest of a York writer in events in the diocese of Worcester. This version of the Chronicle shows so much interest in Archbishop Aldred of York that it has been suggested that in its later section it originates from a member of his household. In striking contrast is its total disregard of Aldred's successor at Worcester, no less a person than St Wulfstan, whose doings occupy a prominent place in the work of Worcester writers. If 'D' originated in Worcester, its failure to mention Wulfstan would be strange. Plummer suggested that it was the product of the rival house of Evesham, but Sir Ivor Atkins has shown that there is little to support this view, and that some of the references to Evesham are unlikely to proceed from a member of that monastery.[2]

---

[1] For other signs of conflation, see D. Whitelock, *op. cit.*, pp. 28 f.   [2] See *Eng. Hist. Rev.*, LV, pp. 8–26, and cf. p. 108, n. 5 below

'D' is greatly interested in Margaret of Scotland, adding to annal 1057 particulars of her father's marriage and of his offspring and to 1067 an account of her herself which reads like an extract from some Life of this saint. It expands annal 1075 (for 1074) with a long account of the reception of the atheling Edgar by Margaret and her husband Malcolm, and deals in annal 1078 with an action of Malcolm's against the rival house of Moray. In view of this interest in internal Scottish affairs, Sir Frank Stenton has suggested that 'D' was destined for a Scottish court. Plummer,[1] relying on Warner's opinion that the latest hands in 'D' need not be earlier than 1100, claims that the anxiety of the compiler to trace Margaret's ancestry shows that the insertions made to this end were not added before the marriage of her daughter Edith-Matilda to Henry I in 1100. This is not certain, for if this version were intended for a Scottish court, an interest in the queen's ancestry might well be shown earlier. Yet the interpolator of the passage in annal 1067 concerning the queen could hardly have access to a Life of her before her death in 1093. Hence the date suggested by Mr Ker for the hand which wrote ff. 83/11–86 (1071–1079), the 1070's or 1080's, seems too early. Apart from a short and much later entry, 'D' extends to 1079. It ends imperfectly, as the bottom half of a folio has been cut away, but not much has been lost, for the verso was blank until it received, in late-twelfth-century script and language, an entry which shows that even at this late date the interest in the struggle between the Scottish kings and the house of Moray was maintained. This records the slaying of Angus, earl of Moray, in 1130, though in order to make this follow directly on the previous annal, 1079, it is dated 1080. Florence of Worcester used a manuscript very like 'D', but he has none of these Scottish entries. Even if it could be shown that he had actually our manuscript 'D', it would not follow that this was a product of Worcester, for it could have been brought there, perhaps for Florence's use, from the North.

The archetype of 'E' ceases to be a northern version when it separates from 'D' about 1031. By about the middle of the eleventh century it appears to have reached St Augustine's, Canterbury, for from 1045 (wrongly dated 1043) until 1061 it has several entries concerning the abbots of that monastery. At Canterbury it was available to the Christ Church scribe of 'F', who used it as the basis of his bilingual chronicle, and who inserted some of its readings into 'A'.[2] Some of the Latin entries in 'E' must have been added to this archetype at Canterbury for they are in 'F' as well. Their purpose is to supply some facts of Norman history and of universal Church history to an insular chronicle. Eventually this archetype of 'E', or a copy of it, reached Peterborough, perhaps in order to replace a chronicle lost in the fire of 1116. 'E' is a copy made at Peterborough, and is written at one stretch up to 1121, with several interpolations relating to Peterborough. Then the same scribe added at intervals annals 1122–1131.[3] Finally, in or after 1155, the section dealing with events from 1132 to the early part of 1155 was added by another scribe who can only rarely assign them to their proper year.[4] 'E' is thus the version

---

[1] *Op. cit.*, II, pp. xxxiii f., lxxviii.

[2] See above, p. xii.

[3] This view, which differs from that of Plummer, who ends the first scribe's work at 1121 and assigns annals 1122–1131 to four or five scribes, is supported by Wanley, *Thesaurus*, II, p. 64, and by Ker, *op. cit.*, pp. 424 f.

[4] His hand appears in other Peterborough MSS. See C. Clark, 'Notes on MS. Laud Misc. 636', *Med. Æv.*, XXIII, pp. 71 f., and T. A. M. Bishop, 'Notes on Cambridge MSS.', *Trans. Camb. Bibl. Soc.*, I, pt. V, p. 440.

of the Chronicle which continues longest, being, apart from the fragment 'H', the sole vernacular version after 'D' comes to an end.[1] The *Waverley Annals* show that the writer of 'E' had a source extending to 1121, for they give a Latin translation of annals 1000–1121 of the Chronicle, and they cannot be basing it on 'E', since they give annal 1070 in the form in which it occurs in 'D', before it was altered and expanded at Peterborough. There is also evidence for a source behind 'E' even later, for the work ascribed to Florence of Worcester and his continuators, which has connexions with the Anglo-Saxon Chronicle even after 'D' has come to an end in 1079, shares a passage with 'E' as late as 1130. The final section in 'E', annals 1132–1154, is unconnected with any Latin writer except the Peterborough author Hugh Candidus,[2] and the similarities may point merely to the use of 'E' by Hugh.

Besides being the only surviving manuscript of the last part of the Chronicle, 'E' is important as the best representative of the northern recension, before it was expanded by 'D' from a text of a different type; from 286 until the middle of 693 it is the sole representative of this recension, as 'D' has lost several folios at this point.

We have already had occasion to mention 'F', i.e. Brit. Mus. Cott. Domit. viii, the bilingual chronicle produced at Christ Church, Canterbury, in the late eleventh or early twelfth century, by a scribe who used the archetype of 'E' as his base, but also had 'A' before him. He occasionally drew on other sources, mainly relating to Canterbury. 'F' is no doubt the *Cronica latine et anglice* in the medieval catalogue of Christ Church. Mr Ker has recently suggested that it is the *Historia Angliæ Sax.* which once followed Ælfric's Grammar and Glossary in Camb. Univ. Lib. MS. Hh. i. 10, according to the list of Archbishop Parker's gifts to the University of Cambridge. It disappeared from this manuscript and was considered lost.

'G', i.e. Brit. Mus. Cott. Otho B. xi, a copy of 'A', made fairly early in the eleventh century, has been considered above.[3] Finally, there is the fragment, Brit. Mus., Cott. Domit. ix, f. 9, known as 'H'. It deals with the years 1113–1114 and is independent of 'E', the only other text to continue so late. It originates from some centre where a more classical Old English could still be written. Its errors suggest that it is a copy, and not the author's autograph.[4]

The interrelationships of 'C', 'D', and 'E' in the eleventh century present a complicated problem. The agreement of all three of these manuscripts, which begins at 983, lasts until 1022,[5] and is found again in the brief entry for 1028. 'D' and 'E', as we have seen, remain connected until the annal which they date 1031,[6] but they are then independent of one another until 1057,[7] the archetype of 'E' being now at St Augustine's, while that of 'D' retains its northern interests. But from 1057 until 'D' ends in 1079

---

[1] Yet 'E' is not quite the swan-song of vernacular historical writing, for Mr Ker, *op. cit.*, has drawn attention to some marginalia in Brit. Mus. Royal MS. 10 C. v, where short entries of events of 1193 and 1194 are entered in English in the manner of the Anglo-Saxon Chronicle.

[2] Unless the verbal similarities with William of Malmesbury's *Historia Novella* in the account of the violence of Stephen's reign are more than coincidence. See p. 119, n. 2.

[3] See p. xii.

[4] See p. 183, n. 7.

[5] Each manuscript makes alterations in 1020.

[6] Cnut's journey to Rome recorded in this annal took place in 1027.

[7] In annals where similarity is confined to the recording of the same obits in the formulae usual for such entries, the resemblance may well be accidental, and such connexions (e.g. in 1034 and 1053) have been ignored in this discussion.

they are again closely related, perhaps because they share a common source. 'E' is independent of either of the other versions from 1032 to 1042 (dated 1041 'E'), and from 1048 (dated 1046 'E') to 1052, perhaps to 1056, for the slight resemblances to the other manuscripts in annals 1053 to 1055 may be accidental. Rather surprisingly, 'E' is identical with 'C' in 1043 and 1044, and may be connected with this version in 1045 and 1047. Meanwhile 'D', in the sections where it is independent of 'E', is often closely linked with 'C', i.e. in 1035–1038, 1040 to the end of the first sentence in 1043, 1045, 1049, 1052, and 1054–1056. Then 'C' has no entries until 1065, while 'D', as stated above, has affiliations with 'E' from 1057 on. When 'C' resumes with annals 1065 and 1066, 'D' produces a conflated text combining the versions of 'C' and 'E'. Each manuscript has in addition material peculiar to it, both complete annals and additions to annals shared with one of the other manuscripts. As has often been noted, the three versions show different sympathies in describing the political controversies of the reign of Edward the Confessor. 'C' tends to be hostile towards the house of Godwine, which, as Professor Douglas notes,[1] is notable, seeing that Godwine seems on the whole to have been friendly to Abingdon. He suggests that this attitude may perhaps be attributed to independent criticism on the part of the writer, or may be connected with the appointment in 1051 of a certain Rothulf, described as a kinsman of the king, as abbot of Abingdon. 'D' displays a somewhat impartial attitude to the political disputes, whereas 'E' has a strong bias in favour of Godwine and his family. 'E' was at this date a Kentish chronicle, and Godwine was earl of Kent.

Lost versions of the Anglo-Saxon Chronicle

In addition to the surviving versions, something can be learnt of copies which have not survived but were available to Latin writers. Behind the twelfth-century work known as the *Annals of St Neots* lies a version free from the chronological error from 756 to 845, which is in all extant versions and in those used by other Latin writers. The West Saxon ealdorman, Æthelweard, a descendant of Alfred's elder brother, who wrote at the end of the tenth century a Latin chronicle[2] for the benefit of his continental kinswoman, Matilda, abbess of Essen, had a version of the Chronicle which, while it had this error in chronology, was in some respects closer to the original than any extant manuscript. For example, it had not lost by homœoteleuton a whole sentence from annal 885, as all our surviving manuscripts, and the one used by Asser, as well as those available to later writers, have done. Æthelweard's chronicle has authentic details of its own, especially in relation to south-western affairs, and it becomes completely independent of the Anglo-Saxon Chronicle for its account of Alfred's last years after the autumn of 893. There would appear to have been annalistic writing going on somewhere in the South-west. Moreover, it would be interesting to know where Æthelweard obtained his precise information about events in

---

[1] *E.H.D.* II, p. 107.

[2] Only fragments of the burnt manuscript remain. The text, as printed by Savile in 1596, ends at 975, but E. E. Barker has shown (*Bull. Inst. Hist. Research*, XXIV, pp. 46–62) that the chapter headings in the fragments of Brit. Mus. Cott. Otho A. x include the reigns of Edward the Martyr and Ethelred. The work must, therefore, have been continued later in this version. The manuscript is in a hand of the early eleventh century. On Æthelweard, see K. Sisam, 'Anglo-Saxon Royal Genealogies', *Proc. Brit. Acad.*, XXXIX, p. 320n., where it is suggested that some of the peculiar features of this work, e.g. its strange Latin and its misunderstandings of the Old English, may point to the employment of a Celtic-trained secretary.

Northumbria, such as the death and burial at York in 895 of Guthfrith, the Danish king of Northumbria. His work should warn us against assuming that the Anglo-Saxon Chronicle was the only instance of historical writing in the time of Alfred.

Asser, who was writing his *Life of King Alfred* in 893, can be shown by a comparison with the *Annals of St Neots* and Æthelweard's chronicle to have used a version of the Anglo-Saxon Chronicle which already at this early date was at least two removes from the original text. He shows no knowledge of the Chronicle after annal 887, an annal which could not have been composed before 889. The text he used sometimes supports the readings of the other manuscripts against 'A', though there are places where his text, and the version used by Æthelweard, and 'A', all agree against the combined evidence of 'B', 'C', 'D', and 'E', to an extent which suggests that these four manuscripts all descend from a common version which contained several new features.

The version of the Chronicle which Henry of Huntingdon mainly used is very similar to our 'E'. It could have been this very manuscript, though the fact that he does not use it after 1121 suggests rather that he had a copy of it made before any continuation had been added, or else had a previous version from which 'E' was copied. He had also access to another version, which Plummer thought was our manuscript 'C';[1] but this is improbable, for when Henry adds the genealogies omitted by 'E' to the annals which originally contained them, his forms of the names are not those of 'C', but those of 'G', which were probably once in 'A' also.[2] Moreover, Henry includes Essex in Ethelbert's kingdom in annal 855, when 'C' has accidentally omitted it.[3]

A version like 'E', but lacking the Peterborough interpolations and alterations, lies behind the *Waverley Annals*,[4] while Gaimar, the author of a mid-twelfth-century *History of the English* in French verse, had access to a better text of the northern recension than that in 'E' or 'F', for he avoids the errors common to these two manuscripts. Hence his reading often agrees with the other representative of the northern recension, 'D'. Yet it is clear that the text he used lacked those sections of 'D' which are missing from 'E' and 'F' and which we have suggested above were a later addition to the 'D' version.[5] Though Gaimar sometimes refers to his authority as 'chronicles', his phrase in l. 2331 'chronicles, a big book', shows that his plural does not necessarily refer to more than one version. When in ll. 3451–3454 he attributes to Alfred an English book 'of adventures and of laws and of battles in the land and of kings who made war', he could be describing either 'A' or 'G', in both of which the Chronicle was followed by laws; but he betrays no knowledge of the readings peculiar to these manuscripts. This makes one suspect that when he declares that there was in Winchester in the cathedral 'the true history of the kings', which King Alfred had bound with a chain, so that those who wished could read it, but not remove it,[6] his statement may be based on nothing stronger than a reminiscence

---

[1] J. Earle and C. Plummer, *op. cit.*, II, pp. lviif.

[2] They were erased from 'A' to make room for Canterbury additions. Henry could have gone to a separate set of genealogies for these forms, but why should he have troubled to do so rather than use the Chronicle text in front of him?

[3] Henry could not get this from 'E' which omits the whole sentence.

[4] See p. xvii above.

[5] It apparently lacked also the entries on tenth-century affairs peculiar to 'D'. It had annal 949, now only in 'E' and 'F', which we suggested above to have been accidentally omitted from 'D' when this was being compiled from two versions of the Chronicle.

[6] ll. 2331–2340.

of Alfred's instructions regarding his translation of Gregory's *Cura Pastoralis*. He refers also to 'an English book of Washingborough',[1] but as he says it contained an account of the emperors of Rome who had tribute from the English and of the kings who held of them, this does not sound like a text of the Chronicle.[2] For his account of eleventh-century history, Gaimar draws largely on legendary matter, but in the parts which seem to come from the Chronicle he is closest to 'D'. He has also matter, especially relating to northern affairs, which sounds authentic but is in no surviving manuscript of the Chronicle. It is tempting to suppose that his version of the Chronicle had been kept up in the North and there received this extra material, but it could come from some separate source.

The author of the early twelfth-century work which goes under the name of Florence of Worcester[3] had more than one version of the Chronicle. He used a manuscript of the northern recension, retaining much of the northern material peculiar to this, and as he uses entries which are in 'D' alone, it is reasonable to suppose that he knew this recension in a manuscript of the 'D' type. If it was our 'D' manuscript itself, he must deliberately have omitted the references to Margaret of Scotland and other Scottish affairs. He also had a text close to 'A', for he has the later annals of Edward the Elder's reign which have come down only in this manuscript and its copy 'G'.[4] Yet there are other places where Florence's readings agree with 'C', and he knows annal 977, now in 'B' and 'C' only, and annals 980–982, which are in 'C' alone. He uses the Mercian Register, dovetailing its annals into those of the main Chronicle, but in a different way from 'D', and he uses more of it than is in 'D'. In the eleventh-century part of his work, he drew on a text very like 'D', but sometimes prefers the readings of 'C'. He has no sign of the peculiarities of 'E'; yet, after 1079, when 'D' ends and 'E' remains our sole representative of the Chronicle, Florence and his continuators continue to use the Chronicle. Verbal similarities prove a connexion with this work as late as 1130.

William of Malmesbury several times acknowledges his debt to an English chronicle, or chronicles. He had access to a version very like 'E', which he uses up to about 1120; yet it is unlikely that his text was 'E' itself, for this remained at Peterborough for some time after William was writing. Moreover, he shows no knowledge of the Peterborough additions. Presumably he had a copy of 'E''s archetype, if not the archetype itself. He seems to have had neither 'C' nor 'D', for he remarks that the chronicles are silent about the murder of the atheling Alfred in 1036, which is fully treated in both these versions. One might suspect that when he is nearer to 'D' than to 'E' he is using a form of the latter version in which a closer connexion with 'D' was preserved than in the Peterborough copy, but it is possible that he derives the information he gives from the work of Florence of Worcester. In the early portions of his work William may have used a version of the Chronicle not quite identical with any that survive.

---

[1] l. 6469.

[2] This seems a more likely view of Gaimar's relation to the Chronicle than that which I expressed in 1955.

[3] This consists of long additions to a series of annals on world history compiled by Marianus Scotus in the eleventh century. The attribution to Florence, who died in 1118, depends on a reference to him in what used to be regarded as a continuation of his work by John of Worcester, as the man whose 'acute observation and laborious and diligent studies have made this

chronicle from chronicles excel all others'. Professor Darlington has suggested that the whole work up to 1141 is by John, who might speak thus of an older monk who had helped him. For practical convenience, however, I cite this work by its familiar designation.

[4] It was not 'G' which he used, for he has the correct *Mameceaster* 'Manchester' in his annal 920, as in 'A', where 'G' reads *manige ceaster* 'many cities'.

But as he also used Æthelweard, genealogies, and regnal tables, and makes great efforts to reconcile his various sources, it is difficult to pronounce with certainty on his versions of the Chronicle. His chief addition that may come from a lost version is a reference to a battle fought by Cenwealh against the Britons at *Wirtgernesburg*.[1] He makes no reference to the battle of Bradford-on-Avon fought by this king in 652 (Æthelweard says it was a civil war), which is recorded in 'A', 'B', and 'C' but omitted in 'E';[2] this fact confirms the impression that he was mainly dependent on a chronicle of the 'E' type.

Simeon of Durham's *History of the Kings* quotes, from what he calls 'the history or chronicle of this country', the accession of Cuthbert to the see of Canterbury and of Dunn to that of Rochester under the year 740,[3] the date in which this is entered in 'C', 'D', 'E', and 'F', when 'A' has 741. He does not make enough use of the Chronicle for one to ascertain closely what version he had. The entries on northern affairs which he shares with 'D' and 'E' are to be attributed to his use of a common source, i.e. some sets of Northumbrian annals which he inserts much more fully than the Chronicle does. Besides annal 740, he uses the main Chronicle in his annals 888, 890, 893, and 894, and in the last two, where the original dates of 'A' differ from all other manuscripts, he agrees with 'A'. His dating of Alfred's death in 899, and of the killing of Brehtsig (i.e. Brihtsige, at the battle of the Holme) in 902, must, however, come from some source – possibly a version of the Chronicle – which did not begin the year on 24 September, as all extant manuscripts of the Chronicle do in these annals. An old catalogue of the library of Durham lists *cronica duo Anglica*, which may have been those used by Simeon.[4]

Finally, the Peterborough chronicler Hugh Candidus makes use of 'E', though it is possible that there was at Peterborough a history of the abbots which he and the writer of the last section of 'E' both used.[5] Hugh has fuller information in many places than has 'E', but he could have obtained it from the oral traditions of his house.

The composition and circulation of the Chronicle

The fact that Asser, writing in 893, had a manuscript of the Chronicle reaching at least up to 887, which was already two removes from the original text; that the Parker MS. is copied in one handwriting up to the year 891, and is at a similar remove from the original; that the text used by Æthelweard seems to have lacked the annals from 893 to 915 which record in detail Alfred's last campaigns and those of his son Edward; and that 'E' similarly comes from a version with these annals lacking, all seems to point to a copying and circulation of manuscripts soon after 890. Some of the manuscripts then circulated apparently remained barren, others were continued with later material, in some cases added soon after the events described, in others probably copied in at various later periods by comparison with copies that contained it. For there are various indications that we must reckon with a good deal of collation of different texts and later alteration. The movements of the various versions that have survived have already been discussed.

---

[1] See p. 20, n. 2.
[2] 'D' has lost several folios at this place.
[3] Ed. Arnold, II, p. 38.

[4] Cf. J. Earle and C. Plummer, *op. cit.*, p. lxxii, n. 1, where it is suggested that *Elfledes Boc* in the same catalogue may refer to the Mercian Register.
[5] On this question, see D. Whitelock, *op. cit.*, p. 33.

With even our oldest manuscript in one hand up to 891, it is difficult to ascertain the previous history of the work. Many scholars have taken the elaborate genealogy of King Æthelwulf, entered in 855 after the statement that the king died two years after his return from Rome (i.e. 858), to mark the conclusion of an earlier stage of the compilation. But this is by no means certain.[1] It is likely that a compiler writing in Alfred's reign might think that this was a good place to insert the family tree of the reigning house, for there is reason to believe that this compiler was himself the author of the annals which deal with the latter years of Æthelwulf's reign, annals which have a retrospective tone and which introduce a new method of commencement of the year.[2] It would doubtless have been more logical to put the genealogy at the accession of Egbert, the first king of this dynasty, but it is probable that there was available a set of earlier annals dealing with his reign and the early part of Æthelwulf's. On this view, the compiler put the genealogy at the first suitable place in the part of the record he was himself composing.

The materials the compiler had at his disposal included some epitome of universal history which has not been identified, Bede's *Ecclesiastical History*, the chronological summary at the end being especially useful to him, a few northern annals, some genealogies,[3] lists of regnal years, and episcopal lists. He probably also had some sets of earlier West Saxon annals, including one for the first half of the eighth century and another for the reign of Egbert and the early years of his successor. Some of these may have been entered in the margins of Easter tables, i.e. the lists drawn up for a series of years to show the date on which Easter would fall, which were then found convenient for the entering of outstanding events, and which sometimes have wide margins left for this purpose. The English missionaries took such tables with annals to the Continent in the eighth century, so we cannot doubt that they were familiar in the homeland also. It cannot be proved that any of these written sources were in the vernacular; certain archaic forms noted by Stevenson are confined to place-names and prove nothing about the original language of the annals.

The events prior to the adoption of Christianity would not be entered on Easter tables; where they are not from Bede, they must go back eventually to oral tradition, perhaps handed down in verse, and the assignment to particular years can have been little more than guesswork. The artificial arrangement of the incidents of the English settlement has often been commented on, and Sir Frank Stenton[4] has shown that one set of incidents has probably been duplicated.

Another type of source seems implied by annal 755, in which the circumstantial account of the feud between Cynewulf and Cyneheard has plainly been added to an annal that once existed without it; its rather archaic prose suggests that it had an earlier written source, though the incident may have been handed down by oral narrative for some time before it was put in writing.

Since Sir Frank Stenton has argued from indications in the surviving text and in Æthelweard that the chronicler was particularly interested in the south-western counties and their nobles, and has postulated some Somerset ealdorman or thegn as patron of the work,[5] the confident attribution of the

---

[1] See K. Sisam, *op. cit.*, p. 332.
[2] See A. J. Thorogood in *Eng. Hist. Rev.*, XLVIII, pp. 353–363.
[3] See K. Sisam, *op. cit.*

[4] *Anglo-Saxon England*, pp. 22 f.
[5] *Essays in Medieval History presented to T. F. Tout*, pp. 15–24.

work to Alfred's instigation cannot be upheld. It is impossible that he should himself have mistaken the ceremony that took place at Rome when he was a child, when he was invested with the insignia of a Roman consul, as a coronation ceremony, as the chronicler does.[1] The rapid dissemination of the work may owe something to his encouragement, but we must not forget that Alfred's own words in the preface to his translation of the *Pastoral Care* imply that there was a reading public for vernacular works. That the Chronicle does not stand entirely apart from the works produced by Alfred, however, is shown by its referring to the Emperor Titus in almost identical words with those used of him in the Alfredian translation of Orosius. There are other correspondences between that work and the Chronicle, but unfortunately we have too little early West Saxon prose apart from Alfred's writings to be able to decide whether they are anything more than the natural correspondences in phraseology of contemporary writers on similar themes. The translator of Orosius may have been familiar with the Chronicle.

Plummer considered that the absence of any influence from the Old English translation of Bede's *Ecclesiastical History* suggests that the latter was later than the compilation of the Chronicle about 892, and he thought that the translator of Bede omitted the chronological epitome because much of it was already in the Anglo-Saxon Chronicle.[2] Dr Sisam points out that, if the two works had the same literary and linguistic background, one would expect likenesses of expression, whichever was the earlier.[3] Nevertheless, he suggests that the pedigrees of the early kings of Kent were omitted from the Chronicle because they were available in two of the most important chapters of Bede. He takes this fact, together with the omission of the epitome from the Old English Bede, as evidence that the two works were regarded as complementary, and considers that further evidence of a plan to avoid overlapping is provided by the almost negligible use by the Chronicle of the text, as opposed to the epitome, of Bede.[4] He concludes: 'If the *OE. Bede* was not earlier than the Chronicle of 892, it must have been a related project carried out at the same time.'

Chronology

The chronology of the Chronicle causes many complications. Mechanical dislocations arise easily out of the habit of numbering a series of years in advance, for it was easy to make an entry against a wrong number, or to take too much space for an entry and fail to adjust the numbers of the subsequent annals; or a copyist might fail to notice a blank annal and so pre-date events for a considerable stretch. Already in pre-Conquest times annal numbers were sometimes altered by a later corrector attempting to get rid of contradictions and inconsistencies. Detailed studies have been made of the alterations to the numbers in 'A'; but 'C' has also been tampered with, while in 'B' the scribe more often than not leaves blanks instead of putting in annal numbers. In all our extant manuscripts there is a dislocation of two, and even three, years from the mid eighth to the mid ninth century; in 'C', an entry of seven blank annals,

---

[1] See p. 43, cf. *English Historical Documents*, I, No. 219.
[2] *Op. cit.*, II, p. cviii and n. 6.
[3] *Op. cit.*, pp. 335 f.

[4] Taken alone, this is not a strong argument, for the epitome was obviously so much more convenient for an annalist's use that the compiler of the Chronicle may have mainly confined himself to it to save time and trouble.

846–852, where 'A', 'D', and 'E' have only five, throws the chronology out of line, and though a little later the discrepancy was narrowed by the omission of a blank annal, 'C' remains a year in advance until at least 900. And many other instances of dislocation could be given.

Where there is a difference of a single year between the dating of an event in different texts, it is not always possible to decide if one text is in error, or if they are using different styles of beginning the year. The early annals contain no data for deciding this question, but it is clear that annal 794[1] begins at Christmas, as do the additions made into this section of the Chronicle in the northern recension. Christmas seems also the style in 822 and 823,[2] and there is no clear indication of any other usage until 851, which begins in the autumn, presumably on 24 September with the Caesarean Indiction. The change may have begun about 840, when the Alfredian compiler probably began to compose the annals, as we have suggested above. A beginning in the autumn continues at least as far as 889, and is again clear in 900 and 912 'A'.[3] A reversion to Christmas dating for 891–896 has been suggested, though personally I think that the writer of these annals is thinking rather in campaigning years than in calendar years. The Mercian Register begins its year at Christmas, and so undoubtedly does the main Chronicle from 917 'A'.[4] In fact, after this time the only suggestion of a commencement on 24 September comes in the recording of certain obits, where the Chronicle may be using lists drawn up on this system. The clearest instance is the dating of Athelstan's death on 27 October 939 as 940. But in the eleventh century another method competes with Christmas, dating from the Annunciation on 25 March. This is certainly used by 'C' from 1044 to 1053, and again in 1065 and 1066, when 'C' comes to an end. 'D' has it also in these last two years, and, I believe, continued to the end to use this style, which is also visible in 'E' in the first few years after the Conquest. By 1094, however, 'E' has clearly reverted to Christmas dating.[5]

---

[1] For 796.
[2] For 824 and 825.
[3] =913 'C', 'D'.

[4] =915 'C', 'D'.
[5] For a detailed discussion, see J. Earle and C. Plummer, *op. cit.*, pp. cxxxix–cxlii *d*.

Select Bibliography

(a) *The Anglo-Saxon Chronicle*

The sole edition to give the various versions of the Chronicle is *The Anglo-Saxon Chronicle*, ed. by B. THORPE (R.S., London, 1861), vol. I containing the text, vol. II a translation. The edition now most used, *Two of the Saxon Chronicles Parallel*, ed. by C. PLUMMER on the basis of an edition by J. EARLE (Oxford, I, 1892, II, 1899, reprinted 1952, with a bibliographical note and a note on the commencement of the year by D. WHITELOCK), is a complete text only of two versions, 'A' and 'E'. Neither of these editions gives the Otho version ('G'), of which the only edition is that of ABRAHAM WHELOCK, in his *Venerabilis Bedae Historia Ecclesiastica* (Cambridge, 1644). Manuscript 'F' is inadequately represented in Thorpe, and has recently been edited by F. P. MAGOUN, Jr, *Annales Domitiani Latini: an Edition* (Mediaeval Studies of the Pontifical Institute of Mediaeval Studies, IX, 1947, pp. 235–295). Separate editions of the other manuscripts are available as follows: a facsimile edition of 'A', *The Parker Chronicle and Laws*, ed. by ROBIN FLOWER and HUGH SMITH (Early English Text Society, O.U.P., 1941); 'D' in *An Anglo-Saxon Chronicle from British Museum Cotton MS., Tiberius B. iv*, ed. by E. CLASSEN and F. E. HARMER (Manchester, 1926); 'C' in *The C-Text of the Old English Chronicle*, ed. by H. A. ROSITZKE (*Beiträge z. engl. Phil.*, XXXIV, Bochum-Langendreer, 1940); a facsimile edition of 'E', *The Peterborough Chronicle*, ed. by D. WHITELOCK (Early English Manuscripts in Facsimile, IV, Copenhagen, 1954). Part of 'A' is edited by A. H. SMITH, *The Parker Chronicle (832–900)* (Methuen's Old English Library, London, 2nd ed., 1939), part of 'E' by C. CLARK, *The Peterborough Chronicle, 1070–1154* (Oxford English Monographs, O.U.P., 1958), and the reign of Ethelred from 'C' by M. ASHDOWN, in *English and Norse Documents relating to the Reign of Ethelred the Unready* (Cambridge, 1930), pp. 38–71. The *Monumenta Historica Britannica*, ed. by H. PETRIE (London, 1848), pp. 291–466, has the portion up to 1066. The poem on the battle of *Brunanburh* has been frequently edited, best by A. CAMPBELL, *The Battle of Brunanburh* (London, 1938). The regnal list which occurs in 'A', 'B', and 'G' is edited by B. DICKINS, *The Genealogical Preface to the Anglo-Saxon Chronicle* (Occasional Papers of the Department of Anglo-Saxon, Cambridge, No. II, 1952).

Modern English translations occur in the above editions by Thorpe, Ashdown, Petrie, and Campbell. For separate translations see E. E. C. GOMME, *The Anglo-Saxon Chronicle* (London, 1909), G. N. GARMONSWAY, *The Anglo-Saxon Chronicle* (Everyman's Library, corrected edition, 1955) and, for the 'E' text, H. A. ROSITZKE, *The Peterborough Chronicle* (New York, 1951).

The standard discussion of the origin and transmission of the Anglo-Saxon Chronicle is that by C. PLUMMER, forming the introduction to vol. II of the above-mentioned *Two of the Saxon Chronicles Parallel*. It should be supplemented by pp. 679–684 of F. M. STENTON, *Anglo-Saxon England* (Oxford, 2nd ed., 1947); chapter 2 of H. M. CHADWICK, *The Origin of the English Nation* (Cambridge, 1907, reprinted 1924); pp. 16–24 of J. ARMITAGE ROBINSON, *The Times of St Dunstan* (Oxford, 1923);

F. M. STENTON, 'The South-western Element in the Old English Chronicle' (*Essays in Medieval History presented to T. F. Tout*, Manchester, 1925), which is an extremely important study; pp. 624–629, 745–747 of vol. II of R. H. HODGKIN, *A History of the Anglo-Saxons* (Oxford, 3rd ed., 1952); ROBIN FLOWER, 'Laurence Nowell and the Discovery of England in Tudor Times' (*Proc. Brit. Acad.*, XXI, 1935); SIR IVOR ATKINS, 'The Origin of the Later Part of the Saxon Chronicle known as D' (*Eng. Hist. Rev.*, LV, 1940); K. JOST, 'Wulfstan und die angelsächsische Chronik' (*Anglia*, XLVII, 1923); N. R. KER, 'Some Notes on the Peterborough Chronicle' (*Medium Aevum*, III, 1934); F. P. MAGOUN, Jr, 'The Domitian Bilingual of the *Old-English Annals*: The Latin Preface' (*Speculum*, XX, 1945); id. 'The Domitian Bilingual of the *Old-English Annals*: Notes on the F-text' (*Mod. Lang. Quarterly*, VI, 1945); introduction by D. WHITELOCK to the above-mentioned facsimile edition of *The Peterborough Chronicle*.

Of works dealing with individual parts of the Chronicle the following should be noted: on the genealogical tables, K. SISAM, 'Anglo-Saxon Royal Genealogies' (*Proc. Brit. Acad.*, XXXIX, 1953), which supersedes earlier studies; on annal 755 (for 757), F. P. MAGOUN, Jr, 'Cynewulf, Cyneheard, and Osric' (*Anglia*, LVII, 1933), C. L. WRENN, 'A Saga of the Anglo-Saxons' (*History*, XXV, 1940–1941); on the poems in the Chronicle, A. MAWER, 'The Redemption of the Five Boroughs' (*Eng. Hist. Rev.*, XXXVIII, 1923), F. HOLTHAUSEN, 'Zu dem ae. Gedichte von Aelfreds Tode (1036)' (*Anglia Beiblatt*, L, 1939); on the annals of the mid tenth century, M. L. R. BEAVEN, 'King Edmund I and the Danes of York' (*Eng. Hist. Rev.*, XXXIII, 1918), A. CAMPBELL, 'Two Notes on the Norse Kingdoms in Northumbria' (*ibid.*, LVII, 1942).

A great number of works deal with the chronology. The principal are W. H. STEVENSON, 'The Date of King Alfred's Death' (*Eng. Hist. Rev.*, XIII, 1898); R. L. POOLE, 'The Beginning of the Year in the Anglo-Saxon Chronicles' (*ibid.*, XVI, 1901); M. L. R. BEAVEN, 'The Regnal Dates of Alfred, Edward the Elder, and Athelstan' (*ibid.*, XXXII, 1917) and 'The Beginning of the Year in the Alfredian Chronicle' (*ibid.*, XXXIII, 1918); R. H. HODGKIN, 'The Beginning of the Year in the English Chronicle' (*ibid.*, XXXIX, 1924); A. J. THOROGOOD, 'The Anglo-Saxon Chronicle in the Reign of Ecgberht' (*ibid.*, XLVIII, 1933); W. S. ANGUS, 'The Chronology of the Reign of Edward the Elder' (*ibid.*, LIII, 1938) and 'The Eighth Scribe's Dates in the Parker Manuscript of the Anglo-Saxon Chronicle' (*Medium Aevum*, X, 1941); F. T. WAINWRIGHT, 'The Chronology of the "Mercian Register"' (*Eng. Hist. Rev.*, LX, 1945); D. WHITELOCK, 'On the Commencement of the Year in the Saxon Chronicles' (pp. cxxxix–cxlii d of vol. II of the 1952 reprint of *Two of the Saxon Chronicles Parallel*); R. VAUGHAN, 'The Chronology of the Parker Chronicle 890–970' (*Eng. Hist. Rev.*, LXIX, 1954). In two articles in *Leeds Studies in English*, VI, 1937, 'The day of Byrhtnoth's death and other obits from a twelfth-century Ely kalendar' and 'The day of the battle of *Æthelingadene*', B. DICKINS shows how calendar evidence can supplement knowledge drawn from chronicles.

The publications of the English Place-Name Society and E. EKWALL's *The Concise Oxford Dictionary of English Place-Names* (Oxford, revised ed. 1960) should be used to check identifications of places. Articles dealing specifically with the place-names in the Chronicle are A. MAWER, 'Some Place-Name

Identifications in the Anglo-Saxon Chronicles' (*Palaestra*, CXLVII, 1925) and F. P. MAGOUN, Jr, 'Territorial, Place- and River-Names in the Old English Chronicle, A-Text' (*Harvard Stud. and Notes in Phil. and Lit.*, XVIII, 1935), 'D-Text' (*ibid.*, XX, 1938).

(b) *Latin (and Anglo-Norman) authors who used the Anglo-Saxon Chronicle*
Asser's *Life of King Alfred* is edited by W. H. STEVENSON (Oxford, 1904, reprinted with an article by D. WHITELOCK on recent work on Asser, 1959); it is translated by L. C. JANE, *Asser's Life of King Alfred* (London, 1926). Æthelweard still awaits a modern editor. As the MS. is lost, the earliest form of this work is the edition by H. SAVILE in *Rerum Anglicarum Scriptores post Bedam* (London, 1596). It is also in *Monumenta Historica Britannica*, ed. H. PETRIE (London, 1848). There is no reliable translation of this difficult text, though it is included in *Six Old English Chronicles*, ed. J. A. GILES (Bohn's Antiquarian Library, London, 1891). The *Annals of St Neots* are edited by W. H. STEVENSON along with *Asser's Life of King Alfred*. The chronicle which goes by the name of Florence of Worcester is edited by B. THORPE, *Florentii Wigorniensis Monachi Chronicon ex Chronicis* (London, 1848) and translated by J. STEVENSON in *The Church Historians of England*, vol. II, pt. i (London, 1853) and by T. FORESTER (Bohn's Antiquarian Library, 1854); for the later section see J. R. H. WEAVER, *The Chronicle of John of Worcester, 1118–1140* (Anecdota Oxoniensia, 1908). The works by or attributed to Simeon of Durham are edited by T. ARNOLD, *Symeonis Monachi Opera Omnia* (R.S., 1882–1885), vol. I including his *Historia Ecclesiæ Dunhelmensis*, vol. II the *Historia Regum*; both works are translated by J. STEVENSON in *The Church Historians of England*, vol. III, pt. ii (London, 1855). William of Malmesbury's *De Gestis Regum Anglorum* and his *Historia Novella* are edited by W. STUBBS (R.S., 1887–1889), and translated by JOHN SHARPE (London, 1815) and by J. A. GILES (Bohn's Antiquarian Library, 1876); the *Historia Novella* is edited with translation by K. R. POTTER (Medieval Texts, ed. by V. H. GALBRAITH and R. A. B. MYNORS, London, etc., 1955). For Henry of Huntingdon's *Historia Anglorum* see the edition by T. ARNOLD (R.S., 1879) and the translation by T. FORESTER (Bohn's Antiquarian Library, 1909). For the *Waverley Annals* see *Annales Monastici*, II, ed. by H. R. LUARD (R.S., 1865). For Hugh Candidus, see *The Chronicle of Hugh Candidus, a Monk of Peterborough*, ed. by W. T. MELLOWS (O.U.P., 1949). Gaimar's *Lestorie des Engles* is edited with translation by SIR THOMAS DUFFUS HARDY and C. TRICE MARTIN (R.S., 1888–1889).

The *Monumenta Historia Britannica* (see above) includes Asser, Æthelweard, and the sections up to 1066 of Florence of Worcester, Simeon's *Historia Regum*, Henry of Huntingdon, and Gaimar.

Little of value has been published on Asser since Stevenson's edition, but one should note an article by MARIE SCHÜTT on 'The Literary Form of Asser's "Vita Alfredi"' (*Eng. Hist. Rev.*, LXXII, 1957). The importance of Æthelweard is demonstrated by F. M. STENTON in three articles, 'The South-western Element in the Old English Chronicle' (see above), 'Æthelwerd's Account of the Last Years of Alfred's Reign' (*Eng. Hist. Rev.*, XXIV, 1909), and 'The Danes at Thorney Island in 893' (*ibid.*, XXVII, 1912). E. E. BARKER, 'The Cottonian Fragments of Æthelweard's Chronicle' (*Bulletin of the Institute of Historical Research*, XXIV, 1951) not only gives a new reading of the surviving fragments of this work, but shows that there must have been a continuation into Ethelred's reign.

On the post-Conquest historians the chapter by W. LEWIS JONES, 'Latin Chroniclers from the Eleventh to the Thirteenth Centuries', in vol. I of the *Cambridge History of English Literature* (Cambridge, 1907), may be consulted; also R. L. POOLE, *Chronicles and Annals* (Oxford, 1926), and R. R. DARLINGTON, *Anglo-Norman Historians* (Inaugural Lecture at Birkbeck College, London, 1947). On Florence of Worcester see also W. H. STEVENSON, *Asser's Life of King Alfred*, pp. 107–109. On Simeon of Durham, besides the introduction to the edition cited above, that to W. STUBB's edition of Roger of Hoveden (R.S., 1868) is important, as also is P. HUNTER BLAIR, 'Symeon's History of the Kings' (*Arch. Aeliana*, 4th series, XVI, 1939); see also *English Historical Documents*, I, pp. 118f., on the relationship between northern sources.

(c) The Principal Modern Works on English History between the English Settlement and 1154

The indispensable modern works on the period covered by the Anglo-Saxon Chronicle are F. M. STENTON, *Anglo-Saxon England* (Oxford, 2nd ed., 1947) and A. L. POOLE, *From Domesday Book to Magna Carta* (Oxford, 1951). A large selection of other sources for the period, along with introductions dealing with their interpretation and with the general history of the period, is contained in the two first volumes of *English Historical Documents*, general editor D. C. DOUGLAS (vol. I, *c.* 500–1042, ed. by D. WHITELOCK, 1955; vol. II, 1042–1189, ed. by D. C. DOUGLAS and G. W. GREENAWAY, 1953). All these works contain extensive bibliographies.

Other general works that may be consulted are: R. H. HODGKIN, *A History of the Anglo-Saxons*, 2 vols. (Oxford, 1935; 3rd ed., 1952), for the period up to the death of Alfred; P. HUNTER BLAIR, *An Introduction to Anglo-Saxon England* (Cambridge, 1956); E. A. FREEMAN, *History of the Norman Conquest* (5 vols. and index, Oxford, 1867–1879), which needs to be used with caution, but which includes, especially in its appendices, a mass of detail; D. JERROLD, *An Introduction to the History of England* (London, 1949); H. W. C. DAVIS, *England under the Normans and Angevins* (11th ed., London, 1937). The following chapters contributed by W. J. CORBETT in the *Cambridge Medieval History* are relevant to this period: vol. II, 1913, 'England (to *c.* 800) and English Institutions', vol. III, 1922, 'The Foundation of the Kingdom of England' and 'England from A.D. 954 to the Death of Edward the Confessor', vol. V, 1926, 'The Development of the Duchy of Normandy and the Norman Conquest of England' and 'England, 1087–1154'.

On the relations of England with Wales SIR JOHN E. LLOYD, *A History of Wales from the Earliest Times to the Edwardian Conquest* (2 vols., 3rd ed., London, 1939), should be consulted; on relations with Scotland see W. F. SKENE, *Celtic Scotland* (3 vols., Edinburgh, 1876–1880); R. L. GRAEME RITCHIE, *The Normans in Scotland* (Edinburgh, 1954); the collection of sources in A. O. ANDERSON, *Scottish Annals from English Chroniclers* (London, 1908), and *Early Sources of Scottish History A.D. 500 to 1286* (Edinburgh, 1922).

On the Viking settlements and relations with Scandinavia see A. MAWER, *The Vikings* (Cambridge

Manuals of Science and Literature, 1913); T. D. KENDRICK, *A History of the Vikings* (London, 1930); F. M. STENTON, 'The Scandinavian Colonies in England and Normandy' (*Trans. R. Hist. Soc.*, 4th Series, XXVII, 1945) and 'The Danes in England' (*Proc. Brit. Acad.*, XIII, 1927); F. T. WAINWRIGHT, 'Ingimund's Invasion' (*Eng. Hist. Rev.*, LXIII, 1948) and 'The Submission to Edward the Elder' (*History*, XXXVII, 1952).

M. DE BOUARD, *Guillaume le Conquérant* (Paris, 1958), is an excellent short summary of William's career as Duke and King, and both F. M. STENTON, *William the Conqueror* (London, 1908), and E. A. FREEMAN, *The Reign of William Rufus* (2 vols., Oxford, 1882), may still be consulted with profit. A. J. MACDONALD, *Lanfranc* (Oxford, 1926, 2nd ed. 1944), is indispensable for the ecclesiastical politics of the period, and it should be read in connexion with Z. N. BROOKE, *The English Church and the Papacy* (Cambridge, 1931). *Regesta Regum Anglo-Normannorum* (vol. I, ed. H. W. C. DAVIS, Oxford, 1913; vol. II, ed. C. JOHNSON and H. A. CRONNE, Oxford, 1956), contains a mass of information relating to the period 1066–1100, whilst J. H. ROUND, *Geoffrey de Mandeville* (London, 1892), remains perhaps the best general account of the reign of Stephen. The feudal background to the history of this period is admirably depicted in F. M. STENTON, *The First Century of English Feudalism* (Oxford, 1932).

Important works and monographs dealing with individual periods and topics include the following: W. LEVISON, *England and the Continent in the Eighth Century* (Oxford, 1946); C. PLUMMER, *The Life and Times of Alfred the Great* (Oxford, 1902); B. A. LEES, *Alfred the Great, the Truth Teller* (New York, 1915); E. S. DUCKETT, *Alfred the Great and his England* (London, 1957), which is a popular survey; J. ARMITAGE ROBINSON, *The Times of St Dunstan* (Oxford, 1923); DOM DAVID KNOWLES, *The Monastic Order in England* (Cambridge, 2nd ed. 1949); D. V. J. FISHER, 'The Anti-Monastic Reaction in the Reign of Edward the Martyr' (*Camb. Hist. Journ.*, X, pt. iii, 1952); L. M. LARSON, *Canute the Great* (New York, 1912); B. WILKINSON, 'Freeman and the Crisis of 1051' (*Bull. John Rylands Library*, XXII, 1938) and 'Northumbrian Separatism in 1065 and 1066' (*ibid.*, XXIII, 1939); D. WHITELOCK, 'The Dealings of the Kings of England with Northumbria in the Tenth and Eleventh Centuries' (*The Anglo-Saxons: Studies in some Aspects of their History and Culture presented to Bruce Dickins*, ed. P. CLEMOES, 1959); R. R. DARLINGTON, 'The Last Phase of Anglo-Saxon History' (*History*, XXII, 1937).

The early history of the Duchy of Normandy and its connexion with England may be examined in H. PRENTOUT, *Étude critique sur Dudon* (Paris, 1916); in D. C. DOUGLAS, 'The Rise of Normandy' (*Proc. Brit. Acad.*, XXXIII, 1947), and in M. DE BOUARD, 'La Duché de Normandie', which is chapter I of vol. I of *Histoire des Institutions françaises au Moyen Age*, edited by F. LOT and R. FAWTIER (Paris, 1957). Anglo-Norman politics in the period 1066–1155 are illustrated in C. H. HASKINS, *Norman Institutions* (Harvard, 1918); in C. W. DAVID, *Robert Curthose* (Harvard, 1920); and in F. M. POWICKE, *The Loss of Normandy* (Manchester, 1913). The Flemish impact upon English history is considered in P. GRIERSON, 'The Relations between England and Flanders before the Norman Conquest' (*Trans. R. Hist. Soc.*, 4th Series, XXIII, 1941).

Plan of the present edition

The Anglo-Saxon Chronicle is a complicated record. It is not the aim of this edition to set out in full all the textual variants, for it would be impossible in a translation to make clear the transmission of the text, which can be fully seen only from the Old English texts, and to attempt to do so would only detract from the use of the translation to historians. What is aimed at is an arrangement to make it easier for the reader to distinguish the information common to all or several manuscripts from those additions peculiar to single versions. To have set out in columns (or otherwise) all the manuscripts would not only have entailed a great amount of useless repetition, but, what is more serious, would have obscured from the reader what a lot is common to all or most versions. Where matter is essentially the same in many versions, it is given once only, with significant variations at the foot of the page; but where there are important entries in single versions, use is made of an arrangement in two or more columns. Post-Conquest additions of no historical importance, such as the Canterbury additions in 'A' and 'F', or the Peterborough additions to 'E', are not included, unless there is reason to believe that they are drawn from pre-Conquest sources and thus have an importance for Anglo-Saxon history.

Unfortunately, the nature of this record varies so greatly in different sections that it is not feasible to adopt precisely the same arrangement throughout. In the sections from 814 to 900, 985 to 1018, the versions are so closely in unison that it is possible to give one only; but from the beginning to 806, the additions made in the tenth century in the northern recension are so important that an arrangement in columns is necessary. Again, during most of the tenth century, and from 1019 to 1079, it is rare that any two manuscripts are sufficiently close for them to be treated as a single version. Even where they contain annals which share the same base, there are usually variant readings of too great importance to be relegated to footnotes, and therefore the various texts are set out in columns. After 1079 only 'E' survives, except for one late entry in 'D' and for the fragment 1113–1114 'H'.

In those sections where all manuscripts contain almost identical passages, this common stock can easily be distinguished here from the annals peculiar to single versions, because it reads straight across the page without any distinguishing letter before the date. The basis chosen for this common stock is manuscript 'C', for the earlier manuscripts 'A' and 'B' come to an end too soon; but where these have better readings, this is put in the text, with a footnote to draw attention to it. 'D' is chosen as the better version of the northern recension, though one has to depend on 'E' at the point where some folios have been lost from 'D'. In the headings, the manuscript which has been taken as the basis is put first; e.g. C (A, B) means that the annal is in these three versions, but the translation is based on 'C'.

A further complication is caused by the Mercian Register, a series of consecutive annals from 902 to 924 which 'B' and 'C' insert in a block quite arbitrarily after a set of blank annals perhaps extending to 919, while the compiler of 'D' tries to dovetail them into the main Chronicle. He is not very success-ful, however, and I have therefore placed each annal beside that of the same year in the main Chronicle. For it seems to me that this is most convenient for the reader wishing to compare these two complemen-tary sources for Edward the Elder's reign.

The date in the left-hand margin is the actual date of the events described,[1] wherever it can be ascertained, so that the reader is relieved of the necessity of correcting chronological dislocations in the manuscripts. Where the date in any manuscript differs from the date in the margin, it is placed in brackets at the beginning of the annal. It may be assumed that a manuscript not mentioned to have a different date has the true one, except in the case of 'B', which usually has no date at all. My dates for 'C' often differ from those in Thorpe, for I give the original dating, recovered in some places by ultra-violet ray. I give the original, and not the corrected, dates of 'A'.

'G'[2] has mainly been ignored, as being only a late copy of 'A', and similarly I have rarely troubled to note the readings and omissions of 'F', for this alone would have required a bulky set of footnotes of no practical value for my purpose – to make accessible the historical information contained in the Chronicle. The question what the compiler of 'F' chose to extract has its own interest, but no bearing on this issue. Hence his readings are usually given only when they shed light on the condition of the archetype of 'E'. Minor variations, obvious errors, and accidental omissions in texts not used as the base of the translations have frequently been ignored, as too heavy a critical apparatus would defeat the purpose of this volume.

In the footnotes I have referred to passages in Latin writers who had access to copies of the Chronicle now lost. I have sometimes quoted such passages in full. But by the time we reach the reign of Cnut the additional material in the Chronicle which goes under the name of Florence of Worcester has become very bulky, and I have given only a selection, where he may have been using a lost manuscript of the Chronicle or where his information helps to explain the text. From time to time, it has also been necessary to refer in the footnotes to other sources of information necessary for the elucidation of passages in the Chronicle.

---

[1] Except for the annals taken from an epitome of world history, which are not concerned with English history.

[2] Brit. Mus. Cott. Otho B. xi.

THE ANGLO-SAXON CHRONICLE

The Anglo-Saxon Chronicle

Preface to manuscripts 'A' and 'G'

[The regnal list and genealogy prefixed to the Chronicle in 'A' exists elsewhere as a separate work. A fragment from the second half of the ninth century (British Museum Additional MS. 23211) is printed by Sweet, *The Oldest English Texts*, p. 179, to which I refer in the following notes as Sw. On the other versions of this text, see Napier in *Mod. Lang. Notes*, XII, pp. 106–114; B. Dickins, *The Genealogical Preface to the Anglo-Saxon Chronicle*; K. Sisam, 'Anglo-Saxon Royal Genealogies', in *Proc. Brit. Acad.*, XXXIX, pp. 294–297, 332–334.

A single leaf, now folio 178 of Brit. Mus. Cott. Tiber. A. iii (called β by Plummer), has been shown to have originally followed the text of 'B'. It is printed at pp. 232–233 of Thorpe's edition of the Chronicle. It was presumably written in the reign of Edward the Martyr, for it brings the regnal list up to that point, and does not add the length of his reign. It is not a copy of 'A', for its variant readings are sometimes supported by Sw. The scribe of 'A' seems himself to be responsible for some alterations that bring the information given in the genealogies and list more into line with that in the first paragraph and in the annals themselves. The writer of β seems to have been content to let some of the discrepancies stand.

I give the text of 'A' as far as it goes, calling attention to the variants in Sw. and β; and I then subjoin the continuation to the reign of Edward the Martyr in β.]

In the year when 494[1] years had passed from Christ's birth, Cerdic and his son Cynric landed at *Cerdicesora* with five ships; and Cerdic was the son of Elesa, the son of Esla, the son of Gewis, the son of Wig, the son of Freawine, the son of Frithugar, the son of Brand, the son of Bældæg, the son of Woden.

And six years[2] after they had landed they conquered the kingdom of the West Saxons, and they were the first kings who conquered the land of the West Saxons from the Britons. And he held the kingdom for 16 years, and when he died, his son Cynric succeeded to the kingdom and held it [for 26 years. When he died, his son Ceawlin succeeded and held it][3] for 17[4] years. When he died, Ceol succeeded to the kingdom, and held it for six[5] years. When he died, his brother Ceolwulf succeeded and he reigned 17 years, and their descent goes back to Cerdic. Then Cynegils, the son of Ceolwulf's brother, succeeded to the kingdom and reigned 31[6] years, and he was the first of the kings of the West Saxons to receive baptism. And then Cenwealh succeeded, and held it for 31 years, and Cenwealh was Cynegils's son. And then his queen Seaxburh held the kingdom for a year after him. Then Æscwine, whose descent goes back to Cerdic, succeeded to the kingdom, and held it for two years. Then Centwine,

---

[1] The annals date this 495.
[2] Æthelweard's version dated the conquest of Wessex, six years after the landing, 500.
[3] From β, the omission in 'A' being clearly accidental.

[4] All MSS. place his accession in 560 and his expulsion 592.
[5] Five, β.
[6] Twenty, β, but 31 in the text of annal 611, all MSS.

the son of Cynegils, succeeded to the kingdom of the West Saxons and reigned for seven[1] years. Then Ceadwalla, whose descent goes back to Cerdic, succeeded to the kingdom and held it for three years. Then Ine, whose descent goes back to Cerdic, succeeded to the kingdom of the [West][2] Saxons and held it for 37 years. Then Æthelheard, whose descent goes back to Cerdic, succeeded and held it for 14 years.[3] Then Cuthred, whose descent goes back to Cerdic, succeeded and held it 17 years. Then Sigebriht, whose descent goes back to Cerdic, succeeded and held it one year. Then Cynewulf, whose descent goes back to Cerdic, succeeded to the kingdom and held it 31 years. Then Brihtric, whose descent goes back to Cerdic, succeeded to the kingdom, and held it 16 years. Then Egbert succeeded to the[4] kingdom and held it for 37 years and seven months; and then his son Æthelwulf succeeded and held it for 18 and a half years.

Æthelwulf was the son of Egbert, the son of Ealhmund, the son of Eafa, the son of Eoppa, the son of Ingild, the son of Cenred. And Ine was the son of Cenred, and Cuthburh the daughter of Cenred, and Cwenburh the daughter of Cenred.[5] Cenred was the son of Ceolwold, the son of Cuthwulf, the son of Cuthwine, the son of Ceawlin,[6] the son of Cynric,[7] the son of Cerdic.

And then his son Æthelbald succeeded to the kingdom and held it for five years. Then his brother Ethelbert succeeded and held it for five years. Then their[8] brother Ethelred succeeded to the kingdom and held it for five years.[9] Then their brother Alfred succeeded

A (Sw.)	β
to the kingdom, and then 23 years of his life were passed, and 396 years[11] from when his race first conquered the land of the West Saxons from the Britons.	and held it one and a half years less than thirty. Then Edward, son of Alfred, succeeded, and held it for 24 years.[10] When he died, his son Athelstan succeeded and held it for 14 years, seven weeks and three days.[12] Then his brother Edmund succeeded and held it for six and a half years all but two days.[13] Then his brother Eadred succeeded and held it for nine years and six weeks.[14] Then Eadwig, the son of King Edmund, succeeded and held it for three years and 36 weeks,

[1] Nine, corrected from eight, β.

[2] From β.

[3] Sixteen, β. In the annals 'A' dates his reign 728–741, the other MSS. 726–740.

[4] At this point the fragment Sw. begins.

[5] This whole sentence does not occur in the fragment Sw.

[6] 'A' and β have Celm, a misreading of Celin, an Anglian form of the name Ceawlin. Sw. has Ceaulin.

[7] Both β and Sw. have another link here, adding the name of Crioda (Creoda) as father of Cynric and son of Cerdic. 'A' has brought the genealogy into line with its first paragraph, and with the annals. Similarly 'A' omits Creoda from the genealogy given in annal 855 below.

[8] His, Sw.

[9] β omits this sentence.

[10] Nearly correct if reckoned from his coronation 8 June 900. He died 17 July 924.

[11] This figure must be wrong. Whether we reckon from the conquest of Wessex, i.e. 500, as given above, or from the 'Coming of the English' in 449, we do not arrive at the year of Alfred's accession, 871.

[12] Reckoned from his coronation, 4 September 925. He died 27 October 939.

[13] This appears to be reckoned from about 29 November 939.

[14] From Edmund's murder on 26 May 946, to Eadred's death on 23 November 955 is nine years and almost six months.

Florence says Eadred was crowned on 16 August 946, but a reign reckoned from this date would be nine years and ten weeks.

β

all but two days.[1] When he died, his brother Edgar succeeded, and held it for 16 years, eight weeks and two days.[2] When he died, Edward, Edgar's son, succeeded and held it . . .[3]

Preface to manuscripts 'D', 'E', and 'F'

[It is not possible to know whether the version of the Chronicle which reached the North contained the genealogical preface found in 'A' and originally in 'B'. If it did, the writer who added to the annals a lot of new matter, drawn from Bede and northern annals, preferred to substitute the following preface, which is based on Bede's *Ecclesiastical History*, Book I, chap. 1.]

The island of Britain is 800 miles long and 200 miles broad, and here in the island there are five languages, English, British, Scottish,[4] Pictish, and Latin. At first the inhabitants of this island were Britons, who came from Armenia[5] and first occupied southern Britain. Then it happened that the Picts came from the south, from Scythia,[6] with a few warships, and landed first in North Ireland. They asked the Scots to allow them to dwell there, but they would not permit them, for they said that they could not all dwell there together. And then the Scots said: 'We can, however, give you advice. We know of another island, east from here, where you can settle if you wish; and if anyone resists you, we will help you to conquer it.' The Picts then went away and conquered the north of this land, the Britons, as we have said before, holding the south. The Picts asked for wives from the Scots, [receiving them] on condition that they should always choose their royal line on the female side,[7] and they kept to this for a long time afterwards. Then it happened in the passage of years that a certain portion of the Scots came from Ireland to Britain and conquered a part of the land, and their leader was called Reoda, and from him they are named the people of Dal Riada.[8]

The annals

C (A, B)	D (E)
Sixty years before Christ's incarnation, the emperor, Gaius Julius, came to Britain, as the first of the Romans, and defeated the Britons by a battle and overcame	Sixty years before Christ was born, Gaius Julius, emperor of the Romans, came to Britain with 80 ships. There at first he was harassed with cruel fighting and he led to destruction a great part of his army. Then he let his army remain among the Scots and went south to Gaul and collected there 600 ships, with which he returned

[1] As he died on 1 October 959, this would make his coronation *c.* 26 January 956.

[2] This reign seems calculated neither from the date of his precedessor's death nor from Edgar's acceptance as king by the Mercians and Northumbrians. If the compiler of the table knew the date of Edgar's delayed coronation in 973, i.e. 11 May, and assumed that it took place in the year of his accession, 959, the length given would be correct. He died 8 July 975.

[3] *β* breaks off here.

[4] As in Bede and all texts before the tenth century, the words

Scots and Scottish usually refer to the inhabitants of Ireland, though sometimes the Irish colony in the west of Scotland is meant.

[5] This arose from a misreading of Bede's *Armoricano*, i.e. Brittany.

[6] Bede does not place Scythia in the south, and in one place seems to use it of Scandinavia.

[7] A legend that has grown up to explain the Pictish matriarchal system of succession.

[8] Approximately equivalent to the modern Argyle.

C (A, B)

them, and nevertheless could not win the kingdom there.

D (E)

to Britain. And in the first clash, the emperor's reeve, who was called Labienus, was killed. Then the Britons held the ford of a certain river and staked it all with stout sharp posts below water. That river is called the Thames. When the Romans discovered that, they would not cross the ford. Then the Britons fled to the wild woodlands,[1] and the emperor took very many chief towns, with much fighting, and returned to Gaul.

C (A, B, D, E)

1 Octavian reigned 66[2] years and in the 52nd[3] year of his reign Christ was born.

2 The three astrologers came from the East in order to worship Christ, and the children in Bethlehem were slain because of the persecution of Christ by Herod.

3 (4 C; 2 E) In this year Herod died, stabbed by his own hand, and his son Archelaus succeeded to the kingdom.

6 (7 C; 11 E) Five thousand and two hundred years had passed from the beginning of the world to this year.[4]

12 Philip and Herod divided Lycia and Judea into tetrarchies.

16 (15 C) In this year Tiberius succeeded to the throne.

26 (25 C; 27 A[5]) In this year Pilate obtained the rule over the Jews.

30 (29 C) In this year Christ was baptized, and Peter and Andrew converted, and James and John and Philip and the twelve Apostles.

33 In this year Christ was crucified, five thousand two hundred and twenty-six years from the beginning of the world.

34 In this year St. Paul was converted and St. Stephen stoned.

35 In this year the blessed Apostle Peter occupied the see of the city of Antioch.

39 In this year Gaius succeeded to the throne.

44 (45 A, D, E) In this year the blessed Apostle Peter occupied the see of Rome.

45 (46 A, D, E) In this year died Herod, who had killed James one year before his own death.

---

[1] 'E': 'the wood-fastnesses'.
[2] 56, altered from 66, in 'A'.
[3] 42nd in 'B', 'D', 'E', corrections in 'A'; 62nd in 'G'.
[4] An annal on the accession in 11 of Herod, son of Antipater, was added to 'A' at Canterbury.
[5] This annal in 'A' is a Canterbury addition.

C (A, B)	D (E)
47 In this year Claudius came to Britain, the second of the kings of the Romans to do so, and obtained the greater part under his control, and likewise subjected the island of Orkney to the rule of the Romans.	In this year Claudius, king of the Romans, went with an army into Britain, and conquered the island and subjected all the Picts and Britons to the power of the Romans. He fought this war in the fourth year of his reign. And in that year occurred the great famine in Syria, which was foretold in the Acts of the Apostles by the prophet Agabus.[1] Then after Claudius Nero succeeded to the throne, who finally abandoned the island of Britain because of his sloth.

F47 Mark the Evangelist begins to write the gospel in Egypt.

48 In this year was a very severe famine.

49 In this year Nero began to rule.

50 In this year Paul was sent to Rome in chains.

62 In this year James the brother of the Lord suffered martyrdom.

63 In this year Mark the Evangelist died.

69 (68 D) In this year Peter and Paul suffered martyrdom.

70 In this year Vespasian succeeded to the throne.

71 In this year Titus, Vespasian's son, killed 111,000 Jews in Jerusalem.

81 In this year Titus succeeded to the throne – he who said that he lost the day on which he did no good act.[2]

83 (84 D, E) In this year Domitian, Titus's brother, succeeded to the throne.

85 (87 A, D, E; 84 F) In this year John the Evangelist wrote the book of the Apocalypse on the island of Patmos.

100 (99 A[3]) In this year the Apostle Simon was hanged and on that day John the Evangelist went to his rest in Ephesus.

101[3] In this year Pope Clement died.

---

[1] This last sentence was copied into 'A' in a modified form at Canterbury in the eleventh century.

[2] Almost identical words are used of Titus in King Alfred's translation of Orosius (ed. Sweet, p. 264).

[3] In 'A' these annals are Canterbury additions.

110 (109 C) In this year Bishop Ignatius suffered martyrdom.

F116 In this year the Emperor Hadrian began to reign.
137 In this year Antoninus began to reign.

C (A, B)	D (E)
155[1]	In this year Marcus Antonius and his brother Aurelianus[2] succeeded to the throne.
167 In this year Eleutherius received the bishopric of Rome and held it gloriously for 15 years. To him Lucius, king of Britain, sent letters asking that he might be made Christian, and he carried out what he asked.	In this year Eleutherius received the bishopric of Rome and held it with honour for 15 years. To him Lucius, king of the Britons, sent men and asked for baptism, and he at once sent it to him. And they afterwards remained in the true faith until Diocletian's reign.[3]
189 In this year Severus succeeded to the throne, and he ruled for 17 years. He enclosed the land of Britain with a dike from sea to sea.	In this year Severus succeeded to the throne and journeyed with an army to Britain and conquered a great part of the island by fighting, and then made a wall of turves, with a palisade on top, from sea to sea, as a protection for the Britons. He ruled 17 years and then died in York. His son Bassianus succeeded to the throne.[4] His other son, who perished, was called Geta.[5]

F200 In this year the Holy Cross was found.

	E
286	In this year St. Alban suffered martyrdom.[1]

F343 In this year St. Nicholas died.

	E
379	In this year Gratian succeeded to the throne.[1]

[1] These annals were added to 'A' in Canterbury.
[2] 'E': Aurelius.
[3] The last sentence was added to 'A' in Canterbury.

[4] The last two sentences were added to 'A' in Canterbury.
[5] From this point there is a gap in 'D' until 693.

C (A, B)	E
381 In this year the emperor Maximus[1] succeeded to the throne. He was born in the land of Britain, and he went from there into Gaul.[2]	(380) In this year Maximus succeeded to the throne. He was born in the land of Britain and he went from there into Gaul and there he killed the emperor Gratian and drove his brother, who was called Valentinian, from his homeland. And Valentinian again collected a force and killed Maximus and succeeded to the throne. In those times the heresy of Pelagius arose throughout the world.
410 (409) In this year the Goths stormed Rome and the Romans never afterwards reigned in Britain.[3]	(409) In this year Rome was destroyed by the Goths, eleven hundred and ten years after it was built. Then after that the kings of the Romans no longer reigned in Britain. Altogether they had reigned there 470 years since Gaius Julius first came to the land.

418 In this year the Romans collected all the treasures which were in Britain, and hid some in the ground, so that no one could find them afterwards, and took some with them into Gaul.

C (A, B)	E
423	In this year Theodosius the younger succeeded to the throne.[4]
430 In this year Bishop Palladius was sent by Pope Celestine to the Scots, that he might strengthen their faith.	In this year Patrick[5] was sent by Pope Celestine to preach baptism to the Scots.
446	(443) In this year the Britons sent across the sea to Rome and begged for help against the Picts, but they got none there, for the Romans were engaged in a campaign against Attila, king of the Huns. And they then sent to the Angles, and made the same request of the chieftains of the English.

F444 In this year St. Martin died.
448 In this year John the Baptist revealed his head in the place which once was Herod's dwelling to two monks who had come from the East to pray in Jerusalem.

449 In this year Mauritius[6] and Valentinus succeeded to the throne and ruled for seven years.

---

[1] 'A': Maximianus.
[2] The rest of the annal in 'A' is a Canterbury addition, and is exactly as in 'E'.
[3] A Canterbury addition in 'A' continues the annal as in 'E'.
[4] This was added to 'A' in Canterbury.

[5] In the absence of 'D', it is unknown how early this change was made. 'F' has Palladius, but may have taken it from 'A', where 'or Patricius' is written over Palladius by the Canterbury glossator.
[6] 'A', 'B', 'C' only. 'E', 'F' have correctly Martianus, and this has been added in 'A', above Mauritius, at Canterbury.

C (A, B)	E
In their days Hengest and Horsa, invited by Vortigern, king of the Britons, came to Britain at the place which is called Ebbsfleet, first to the help of the Britons, but afterwards fought against them.[1]	And in their days Vortigern invited the English hither, and they then came in three ships to Britain at the place Ebbsfleet. King Vortigern gave them land in the south-east of this land on condition that they should fight against the Picts. They then fought against the Picts and had the victory wherever they came. They then sent to Angeln, bidding them send more help, and had them informed of the cowardice of the Britons and the excellence of the land. They then immediately sent hither a greater force to the help of the others. Those men came from three tribes of Germany; from the Old Saxons, from the Angles, from the Jutes. From the Jutes came the people of Kent and of the Isle of Wight, namely the tribe which now inhabits the Isle of Wight and that race in Wessex which is still called the race of the Jutes. From the Old Saxons came the East Saxons, the South Saxons, and the West Saxons. From Angeln, which ever after remained waste, between the Jutes and the Saxons, came the East Angles, the Middle Angles, the Mercians, and all the Northumbrians. Their leaders were two brothers, Hengest and Horsa, who were sons of Wihtgils. Wihtgils was the son of Witta, the son of Wecta, the son of Woden. From that Woden has descended all our royal family, and that of the Southumbrians also.[2]

455 In this year Hengest and Horsa fought against King Vortigern at the place which is called *Ægelesthrep*, and his brother Horsa was killed there; and after that Hengest and his son Æsc succeeded to the kingdom.

456 (457 A) In this year Hengest and his son Æsc fought against the Britons in the place which is called *Creacanford*[3] and killed 4,000 men;[4] and the Britons then deserted Kent and fled with great fear to London.

465 (461 B, C; 466 F) In this year Hengest and Æsc fought against the Britons near *Wippedesfleot*, and there slew twelve British chiefs, and a thegn[5] of theirs was slain there whose name was Wipped.

473 In this year Hengest and Æsc fought against the Britons and captured countless spoils and the Britons fled from the English as from fire.[6]

---

[1] There follows a long Canterbury addition in 'A', much as in 'E'.

[2] A clear indication that this addition was made in Northumbria.

[3] 'A', 'E': *Crecganford*. Neither form fits the common identification with Crayford.

[4] 'E', 'F': 'four troops'.

[5] This word supplied from 'A', 'E', 'F'. It is accidentally omitted in 'B', 'C'.

[6] Instead, 'E' has 'very grievously'.

477   In this year Ælle and his three sons, Cymen, Wlencing, and Cissa, came into Britain with three ships at the place which is called *Cymenesora*,[1] and there they killed many Britons and drove some into flight into the wood which is called *Andredeslea*.[2]

F482   In this year the blessed Abbot Benedict shone with the glory of miracles for the benefit of this world, as the blessed Gregory relates in the book of 'Dialogues'.

485   In this year Ælle fought against the Britons near the bank of *Mearcredesburna*.

488   In this year Æsc succeeded to the kingdom and was king of the people of Kent for 24 years.

491   (490 F) In this year Ælle and Cissa besieged *Andredesceaster*,[3] and killed all who were inside, and there was not even a single Briton left alive.

495   In this year two chieftains,[4] Cerdic and his son Cynric, came with five ships to Britain at the place which is called *Cerdicesora*, and they fought against the Britons on the same day.[5]

501   In this year Port and his two sons Bieda and Mægla came to Britain with two ships at the place which is called Portsmouth;[6] and there they killed a [young][7] British man of very high rank.

508   In this year Cerdic and Cynric killed a British king, whose name was Natanleod, and 5,000 men with him; and the land right up to Charford was called Netley after him.

F508   In this year St. Benedict the abbot, father of all monks, went to heaven.

514   In this year the West Saxons came into Britain with three ships at the place which is called *Cerdicesora*; and Stuf and Wihtgar fought against the Britons and put them to flight.

519   In this year Cerdic and Cynric succeeded to the kingdom;[8] and in the same year they fought against the Britons at a place called Charford.[9]

---

[1] A place now covered by the sea, south of Selsea Bill.
[2] The Weald.
[3] The Roman *Anderida*, near Pevensey.
[4] 'Ealdormen', but it is uncertain whether the chronicler is using it in its technical sense.
[5] Æthelweard adds, 'and finally were victorious', and then gives an important annal that was probably in his text of the Chronicle: 'In the sixth year after their arrival they conquered the western part of Britain which is now called Wessex.'
[6] 'E' adds: 'and immediately seized the land'.
[7] 'B', 'C' omit 'young'.
[8] 'E' and additions to 'A' add: 'of the West Saxons'.
[9] 'E' and additions to 'A' add: 'and princes of the West Saxons ruled from that day onwards'.

527 In this year Cerdic and Cynric fought against the Britons in the place which is called *Cerdicesleag*.[1]

530 In this year Cerdic and Cynric captured the Isle of Wight and killed a few[2] men in *Wihtgarabyrig*.

534 In this year Cerdic died; and his son Cynric ruled for 27[3] years. And they gave the Isle of Wight to their two kinsmen,[4] Stuf and Wihtgar.

538 In this year there was an eclipse of the sun on 16 February from daybreak until nine o'clock in the morning.

540 In this year there was an eclipse of the sun on 20 June, and stars were visible for nearly half an hour after nine o'clock in the morning.

544 In this year Wihtgar died and he was buried in *Wihtgarabyrig*.

547 In this year Ida, from whom the royal family of the Northumbrians took its rise, succeeded to the kingdom.

C (B *and originally* A)	E
Ida was the son of Eoppa, the son of Esa, the son of Ingui, the son of Angenwit, the son of Aloc, the son of Benoc, the son of Brand, the son of Bældæg, the son of Woden, the son of Freotholaf,[5] the son of Freothowulf, the son of Finn, the son of Godwulf, the son of Geat.	And he reigned twelve years; and he built Bamburgh, which was first enclosed with a hedge and afterwards with a wall.[6]

552 In this year Cynric fought against the Britons in the place which is called Salisbury,[7] and put the Britons to flight.[8] Cerdic was Cynric's father. Cerdic was the son of Elesa, the son of Esla, the son of Gewis, the son of Wig, the son of Freawine, the son of Freothogar, the son of Brand, the son of Bældæg, the son of Woden.

556 In this year Cynric and Ceawlin fought against the Britons at Barbury.[9]

560 (559 F) In this year Ceawlin succeeded to the kingdom in Wessex and Ælle to the kingdom of the Northumbrians,

---

[1] 'E', erroneously, has Charford.

[2] This was the original reading of 'A', as well as of 'B', 'C', Asser, and Æthelweard. 'E' and additions to 'A' wrongly have 'many'.

[3] This is the number in 'B', 'C' 'F', and Æthelweard. 'A' and 'E' have 26.

[4] The word used can mean both 'grandsons' and 'nephews'. Asser calls Cerdic their *avunculus* and Cynric their *consobrinus*. They were probably sons of Cerdic's daughter.

[5] 'A', judging by its copy in 'G', omitted this link. The genealogy was erased from 'A' later.

[6] This was added to 'A' at Canterbury to replace the genealogy.

[7] It is believed that references to *Searoburh* apply to Old Sarum, rather than the present Salisbury.

[8] 'E' omits the genealogy. 'F' has the first clause of this annal followed by a mutilated entry of the birth of Ethelbert of Kent.

[9] Barbury Castle, Wilts.

C (B, *originally* A)	E
and held it for 30 years. Ælle was the son of Yffe, the son of Uscfrea, the son of Wilgils, the son of Westerfalca, the son of Sæfugel, the son of Sæbald, the son of Sigegeat, the son of Swefdæg, the son of Sigegar, the son of Wægdæg, the son of Woden.	Ida having died; and each of them ruled for 30 years.

565 In this year the priest Columba came from Ireland to Britain, to instruct the Picts, and built a monastery on the island of Iona.

In this year Ethelbert succeeded to the kingdom of the people of Kent[1] and held it for 53 years. In his days Gregory sent us baptism. And the priest Columba came to the Picts and converted them to the faith of Christ. They are the dwellers[2] north of the moors. And their king gave him the island which is called Iona, where, by what men say, there are five hides. There this Columba built a monastery, and he was abbot there 32 years, and died there when he was 77. His heirs still hold that place. The South Picts had been baptized a long time before. Bishop Ninian had preached baptism to them. He was educated in Rome, and his church and monastery is at Whithorn, dedicated in St. Martin's name, and he lies buried there with many holy men. Now in Iona there must always be an abbot, not a bishop, and all the bishops of the Scots must be subject to him, for Columba was an abbot, not a bishop.[3]

C (A, B, E, F)

568 In this year Ceawlin and Cutha[4] fought against Ethelbert, and drove him in flight into Kent, and killed[5] two ealdormen, Oslaf[6] and Cnebba, at *Wibbandun*.

C (A, B, E)

571 In this year Cuthwulf[7] fought against the Britons at *Biedcanford*,[8] and captured four towns, Limbury, Aylesbury, Bensington, and Eynsham; and in the same year he died.[9]

---

[1] Bede dates his accession 560; 53 is an error for 56. See p. 16, n. 3.

[2] The unusual word *wærteres* used here seems to be taken from the place-name *Wertermorum* which occurs in Simeon of Durham. See *E.H.D.*, I, p. 252.

[3] This was added to 'A' at Canterbury to replace the original annal.

[4] 'F' adds: 'Ceawlin's brother'.

[5] This word is omitted by 'B' and 'C', and supplied from 'A', 'E', and 'F'.

[6] 'E' and 'F': Oslac.

[7] 'E': Cutha.

[8] The form of the name does not support identification with Bedford.

[9] 'E' adds: 'This Cutha was Ceawlin's brother.'

C (A, B, E)

577 In this year Cuthwine and Ceawlin fought against the Britons and killed three kings, Conmail, Condidan, and Farinmail, at the place which is called Dyrham; and they captured three of their cities, Gloucester, Cirencester, and Bath.

E

583   In this year Mauricius[1] succeeded to the rule of the Romans.

584 In this year Ceawlin and Cutha fought against the Britons at the place which is called *Fethanleag*,[2] and Cutha was killed there; and Ceawlin captured many villages and countless spoils,[3] and in anger returned to his own land.

588 In this year King Ælle died and Æthelric reigned after him for five years.

591 In this year Ceol[4] reigned for five[5] years.

E

592   In this year Gregory succeeded to the papacy at Rome.[6] And In this year there occurred a great slaughter at 'Woden's barrow',[7] and Ceawlin was driven out.

593 In this year Ceawlin, Cwichelm, and Crida perished. And Æthelfrith succeeded to the kingdom

E

in Northumbria. He was the son of Æthelric, son of Ida.

596[8] In this year Pope Gregory sent Augustine to Britain with a good number of monks, who preached God's word to the English people.

597 In this year Ceolwulf began to reign in Wessex, and he continually fought and contended either against the English, or the Britons, or the Picts, or the Scots.[9] He was the son of Cutha, the son of Cynric, the son of Cerdic, the son of Elesa, the son of Esla, the son of Gewis, the son of Wig, the son of Freawine, the son of Freothogar, the son of Brand, the son of Bældæg, the son of Woden.

601 In this year Gregory sent the *pallium* to Britain to Archbishop Augustine, and many religious teachers to his assistance; and Bishop Paulinus [who][10] converted Edwin, king of the Northumbrians, to baptism.

---

[1] This annal was added to 'A' at Canterbury. 582 is the date usually given for the accession of the eastern emperor, Mauricius Flavius Tiberius.

[2] A place of this name is mentioned in a twelfth-century document relating to Stoke Lyne in north-east Oxfordshire.

[3] 'E' omits the rest of the annal.

[4] 'E' and a late correction in 'A' have Ceolric.

[5] 'E' and additions to 'A': six.

[6] This was added at Canterbury to 'A' at the end of annal 592.

[7] Now called Adam's Grave, in Alton Priors, Wilts. 'E' adds 'in Britain'.

[8] In 'A' this is dated 595 and written in a later hand over an erasure which probably had the same statement dated 596.

[9] 'E' omits the genealogy.

[10] The relative pronoun has probably been omitted by the archetype of all our versions. 'F' supplied 'and among them was Paulinus'.

C (B, *and originally* A)	E
603 In this year was a battle at *Degsastan*.[2]	In this year Aedan,[1] king of the Scots, fought along with the people of Dal Riada against Æthelfrith,[3] king of the Northumbrians, at *Degsastan*, and almost all his army was slain.[4] There Theodbald, Æthelfrith's brother, was slain with all his troop. No king of the Scots dared afterwards lead an army against this nation. Hering, son of Hussa, led the army thither.[5]
604 In this year the East Saxons, under King Sæberht[6] and Bishop Mellitus, received the faith and the baptismal bath.	In this year Augustine consecrated two bishops, Mellitus and Justus. He sent Mellitus to preach baptism to the East Saxons where the king was called Sæberht, the son of Ricule, Ethelbert's sister, and Ethelbert had set him as king there. And Ethelbert gave to Mellitus an episcopal see in London, and he gave to Justus Rochester, which is 24 miles from Canterbury.[7]
604 (606) In this year Gregory died, ten years after he sent us baptism.[9] His father was called Gordianus and his mother Sylvia.	(605) In this year Pope Gregory died; and Æthelfrith led his army to Chester[8] and there killed a countless number of Britons. And thus was fulfilled Augustine's prophecy, by which he said: 'If the Britons do not wish to have peace with us, they shall perish at the hands of the Saxons.' There also were killed 200 priests who had come there to pray for the army of the Britons. Their leader was called Brocmail,[10] and he escaped with 50 men.[11]

607 In this year Ceolwulf fought against the South Saxons.

611 In this year Cynegils succeeded to the kingdom in Wessex, and held it for 31 years.[12] Cynegils was the son of Ceola, the son of Cutha, the son of Cynric.

---

[1] Aedan mac Gabrain, king of the Irish settlement in Argyle from 574 to about 608.

[2] Corruptly given as *Egesan stan* in 'B', 'C', and originally in 'A'. The identification with Dawston in Liddesdale, which has been doubted on philological grounds, has recently been defended by Max Förster, *Der Flussname Themse und seine Sippe*, pp. 796–811.

[3] Correcting the manuscript corruption, which reads: 'fought against the people of the Dal Riada and Æthelfrith'.

[4] This was added to 'A' at Canterbury, to replace the original annal.

[5] This is one of the few places where the northern recension has had access to material not in Bede. Nothing further is known of Hering. Hussa, king of Bernicia, occurs in Nennius; see *E.H.D.*, I, p. 237.

[6] Æthelweard has Sigebyrht (wrongly).

[7] This was added to 'A' at Canterbury to replace the original annal.

[8] Bede does not date the battle of Chester, but it must have occurred between 613 and 616.

[9] He died 12 March.

[10] 'E': Scromail. I have corrected from Bede.

[11] The Old English idiom 'one of fifty' means literally 'with forty-nine'; but from the ninth century it was no longer used precisely, and the chronicler is here translating Bede's fifty.

[12] 'E' omits the genealogy.

614 In this year Cynegils and Cwichelm fought at *Beandun*, and killed 2,045[1] Britons.[2]

616 In this year Ethelbert, king of the people of Kent, died,[3] and his son Eadbald succeeded to the kingdom.

C (B, *and originally* A)	E
And that same year 5,800[4] years had passed from the beginning of the world.[5]	He abandoned his baptismal faith and lived by heathen customs, so that he had his father's widow as his wife. Then Laurence, who was then archbishop in Kent, intended to go south across the sea and abandon everything; but the Apostle Peter came to him in the night and scourged him violently, because he wished thus to desert God's flock, and bade him go to the king and preach the true faith to him. He did so, and the king submitted and was baptized. In the days of this king, Laurence, who was archbishop in Kent after Augustine, died, and was buried next to Augustine on 2 February. Then after him Mellitus, who had been bishop of London, succeeded to the archbishopric. Then the people of London, which had been Mellitus's see, became heathen. And five years later in Eadbald's reign, Mellitus departed to Christ. After that Justus succeeded to the archbishopric, and he consecrated Romanus for Rochester, where he had been bishop.
	(617) In this year Æthelfrith, king of the Northumbrians, was killed by Rædwald, king of the East Angles, and Edwin, the son of Ælle, succeeded to the kingdom and conquered all Britain except the people of Kent alone, and drove out the athelings, Æthelfrith's sons, namely Eanfrith, Oswald, Oswiu, Oslac, Oswudu, Oslaf, and Offa.

F619 In this year Archbishop Laurence died.

C (A, B)	E
624	In this year Archbishop Mellitus died.
625 In this year Paulinus was consecrated as bishop for the Northumbrians by Archbishop Justus.	In this year Archbishop Justus consecrated Paulinus as bishop on 21 July.

---

[1] 'A' and 'E': 2,065; 'G': 2,046; Æthelweard: 2,040 and more.

[2] Instead of this annal, 'F' has a mutilated entry of the accession of Archbishop Laurence.

[3] 'E' adds: 'and he had reigned 56 years'.

[4] 'G': 5,616.

[5] This sentence was replaced in 'A' by the annal in 'E'.

C (A, B)

626 In this year Eanflæd, King Edwin's daughter, was baptized on the holy eve of Pentecost; and Penda held his kingdom for 30 years, and he was 50 years old when he succeeded to the kingdom.[1] Penda was the son of Pybba, the son of Creoda, the son of Cynewold, the son of Cnebba, the son of Icel, the son of Eomær, the son of Angeltheow, the son of Offa, the son of Wærmund, the son of Wihtlæg, the son of Woden.[3]

627 In this year King Edwin was baptized with his people at Easter.

E

626 In this year Eomær came from Cwichelm, king of the West Saxons, intending to stab to death King Edwin, but he stabbed his thegns Lilla and Forthhere, and wounded the king. And that same night was born Edwin's daughter, who was called Eanflæd. Then the king promised Paulinus that he would give his daughter to God, if he would by his prayers obtain from God that he might destroy his enemy who had sent the assassin thither. And he then went into Wessex with an army and destroyed there five kings, and killed many of that people. And Paulinus baptized his daughter and twelve[2] people with her at Pentecost. And within a twelvemonth, the king was baptized at Easter with all his following. Easter was then on 12 April. This took place at York, where he had ordered a church to be built of wood, which was consecrated in St. Peter's name. The king gave Paulinus an episcopal see there, and afterwards ordered a bigger church to be built there of stone. And in this year Penda succeeded to the kingdom and reigned for 30 years.

627 In this year King Edwin was baptized by Paulinus, and the same Paulinus also preached baptism in Lindsey, where the first to believe was a powerful man named Blæcca, with all his following. And at this time Honorius[4] succeeded to the papacy after Boniface,[5] and sent hither the *pallium* to Paulinus. And Archbishop Justus died on 10 November, and Honorius was consecrated by Paulinus in Lincoln.[6] The pope sent the *pallium* also to this Honorius. And he sent a letter to the Scots, that they should turn to the right Easter.

628 In this year Cynegils and Cwichelm fought against Penda at Cirencester, and afterwards came to terms.

627–8 (632) In this year Eorpwold[7] was baptized.

---

[1] This would make him eighty when he was killed, but must have arisen from some misunderstanding, for he left two sons who were minors, nor would he, if so old, have been likely to have a sister young enough to marry Cenwealh of Wessex who reigned from about 642 to 673. The date 626 for his accession is also doubtful. Bede implies that he was not king until 632.

[2] Literally 'one of twelve', but see p. 15, n. 11. Some Bede MSS. say eleven, some twelve companions.

[3] This genealogy has been erased from 'A'.

[4] Honorius I.

[5] Boniface V.

[6] 'F' adds: 'as archbishop of Canterbury'.

[7] King of East Anglia.

	C (A, B)	E

633 In this year Edwin was slain, and Paulinus returned to Kent and occupied the see of Rochester there.

In this year King Edwin was slain by Cadwallon and Penda at Hatfield[1] on 14 October, and he had reigned for 7[2] years, and his son Osfrith also was slain with him. And then Cadwallon and Penda afterwards advanced and laid waste all the land of the Northumbrians. When Paulinus saw that, he took Æthelburh, Edwin's widow, and went away by ship to Kent, and Eadbald and Honorius received him with great honour and gave him an episcopal see in Rochester, and he stayed there until his death.

634 In this year Bishop Birinus preached baptism to the West Saxons.

In this year Osric, whom Paulinus had baptized, succeeded to the kingdom of the Deirans. He was the son of Ælfric, Edwin's paternal uncle. And Æthelfrith's son Eanfrith succeeded to Bernicia. And also Birinus first preached baptism to the West Saxons under King Cynegils. This Birinus came there by the advice of Pope Honorius, and he was bishop there until the end of his life. And also in this year Oswald succeeded to the kingdom of the Northumbrians, and he reigned for nine years. The ninth year is counted to him because of the heathenism practised by those who reigned the one year between him and Edwin.

635 In this year King Cynegils was baptized by Bishop Birinus in Dorchester,[3] and Oswald[4] stood sponsor to him.

636 In this year Cwichelm was baptized in Dorchester, and he died that same year, and Bishop Felix preached the faith of Christ to the East Angles.[5]

639 In this year Birinus baptized King[6] Cuthred in Dorchester, and also received him as his godson.

	C (A, B)	E

640 In this year Eadbald, king of the people of Kent, died, and he had reigned 25 years.[7]

(639) In this year Eadbald, king of the people of Kent, who had been king for 24 years, died. Then his son Eorcenberht succeeded to the kingdom, and he demolished all the idols in his kingdom and was

---

[1] Somewhere in Hatfield Chase.
[2] An error for 17.
[3] Dorchester-on-Thames, Oxfordshire.
[4] 'E' adds: 'king of the Northumbrians'.
[5] Felix was preaching there in 630–631.
[6] This title only in 'B', 'C', and 'F'.

[7] The additions to 'A' add: 'He had two sons, Eormenræd and Eorcenberht, and Eorcenberht reigned there after his father, and Eormenræd begat two sons who were afterwards murdered by Thunor.' This is a reference to a late Canterbury legend.

C (A, B)   E

the first of the English kings to establish the Easter fast. His daughter was called Eormengota,[1] a holy virgin and a wonderful person, whose mother was Seaxburh,[2] daughter of Anna, king of the East Angles.

641 (642 A[3]) In this year Oswald, king of the Northumbrians, was slain. (643 A) And Cenwealh succeeded to the kingdom of the West Saxons, and held it for 31[6] years.

In this year Oswald, king of the Northumbrians, was slain by Penda, the Southumbrian, at *Maserfeld*[4] on 5 August, and his body was buried at Bardney. His holiness and miracles were afterwards made known in manifold ways throughout this[5] island, and his hands are undecayed in Bambrugh. In this year Cenwealh succeeded to the kingdom of the West Saxons and held it for 21[6] years. The same Cenwealh had the church of Winchester built and he was the son of Cynegils. And the same year that Oswald was killed, his brother Oswiu succeeded to the kingdom of the Northumbrians, and he reigned two years less than thirty.

642 (643 A) The same Cenwealh had the Old[7] Minster built at Winchester.

644 (643 B, C) In this year Paulinus, who had been archbishop of York and was afterwards bishop of Rochester, died.

(643) In this year Archbishop Paulinus died in Rochester on 10 October. He had been bishop one year less than twenty, and two months and 21 days. And Oswine, [Edwin's][8] cousin's son, the son of Osric, succeeded to the kingdom of the Deirans, and ruled seven years.

645 (644, B, C, E) In this year King Cenwealh was driven out by King Penda.

646 (645 B, C, E) In this year Cenwealh was baptized.

648 (647 B, C) In this year Cenwealh gave to his kinsman Cuthred[9] three thousand hides[10] of land near Ashdown. This Cuthred was the son of Cwichelm, the son of Cynegils.[11]

---

[1] Abbess of Brie in Gaul.
[2] Abbess of Ely.
[3] From here to 650 'A' is one year in advance of the other versions.
[4] Usually identified with Oswestry (Oswald's tree), Shropshire.
[5] The MS. has 'his'.

[6] The regnal lists also give 31. His death is entered under 672 below.
[7] Only 'B' and 'C' add the word 'old', after the foundation of the New Minster in the early tenth century.
[8] Accepting Earle and Plummer's correction.
[9] Eadred, 'E'.
[10] 'Hides' inserted in 'B', 'C' only.
[11] 'E' omits the genealogy.

F648 In this year the minster in Winchester was built, which Cenwealh caused to be made and consecrated in St. Peter's name.

650 (649 B, C, E) In this year Agilbert from Gaul received the bishopric in Wessex[1] after the Roman bishop Birinus.

C (A, B)	E
651 In this year King Oswine was slain and Bishop Aidan died.	(650) In this year King Oswiu had King Oswine slain on 20 August, and twelve days later Bishop Aidan died on 31 August.

652 In this year Cenwealh fought at Bradford-on-Avon.[2]

653 (652 E) In this year the Middle Angles,[3] under Ealdorman Peada,[4] received the true faith.

654 (653 E) In this year King Anna was slain, and Botwulf began to build the minster at *Icanho*.[5]

C (A, B)	E
	And in this year Archbishop Honorius died on 30 September.
655 In this year Penda perished and the Mercians became Christians.	(654) In this year Oswiu killed Penda at *Winwædfeld*, and 30 princes with him, and some of them were kings. One of them was Æthelhere, brother of Anna, king of the East Angles.

Then five thousand, eight hundred and fifty[6] years had passed from the beginning of the world. And Peada, the son of Penda, succeeded to the kingdom of the Mercians.[7]

E

(655) In this year Ithamar, bishop of Rochester, consecrated Deusdedit to Canterbury on 26 March.

657 (656 E, F) In this year Peada died,[8] and Wulfhere, son of Penda, succeeded to the kingdom of the Mercians.[9]

---

[1] 'E': 'of the Saxons'.

[2] William of Malmesbury seems to have had access to other matter here, for he makes no mention of Bradford-on-Avon, but speaks of a battle against the Britons at 'Vortigern's *burg*', of which nothing further is known. Æthelweard calls the campaign of 652 'civil war'.

[3] 'A': 'Middle Saxons'.

[4] Son of Penda.

[5] This is not, as often suggested, Boston, for the *Life of Ceolfrith* proves that it was in East Anglia. It may have been at Iken, Suffolk. See F. S. Stevenson, *Proc. Suff. Inst. Arch.*, XVIII, pp. 29–52.

[6] 'E': 5,800.

[7] Here 'E' has a Peterborough insertion relating to the founding of the abbey.

[8] 'E' says more specifically 'was slain'.

[9] A long Peterborough insertion about the consecration and endowment of the monastery occurs here in 'E'.

658 In this year Cenwealh fought against the Britons at *Peonnan*,[1] and put them to flight as far as the Parret. This was fought after he came from East Anglia, and he had been in exile there for three years. Penda had driven him out and deprived him of his kingdom because he deserted his sister.

660 In this year Agilbert[2] left Cenwealh, and Wine held the bishopric for three years, and this Agilbert received the bishopric of the Parisians, by the Seine in Gaul.

661 In this year Cenwealh fought at Easter at *Posentesbyrig*;[3] and Wulfhere, the son of Penda, harried on[4] Ashdown; and Cuthred, son of Cwichelm, and King Cenberht died in one and the same year. And Wulfhere, the son of Penda, harried in the Isle of Wight, and gave the people of the Isle of Wight to Æthelwold,[5] king of the South Saxons, because Wulfhere had stood sponsor to him at baptism. And the priest Eoppa was the first man to bring baptism to the people of the Isle of Wight, by the commands of Wilfrid[6] and King Wulfhere.[7]

	C (A, B)	E
664	In this year there was an eclipse of the sun, and Eorcenberht, king of the people of Kent, died. And Colman went with his companions to his own land.[8] And the same year there was a great pestilence. And Ceadda and Wilfrid were consecrated.[11] And that same year Deusdedit died.	In this year there was an eclipse of the sun on 3 May; and in this year a great pestilence came to the island of Britain, and in that pestilence Bishop Tuda[9] died, and was buried at *Wagele*.[10] And Eorcenberht, king of the people of Kent, died, and his son Egbert succeeded to the kingdom. And Colman went with his companions to his own land. And Ceadda and Wilfrid were consecrated, and in the same year Archbishop Deusdedit died.
667		In this year Oswiu and Egbert sent the priest Wigheard to Rome, that he might be consecrated archbishop, but he died immediately he came there.
668	In this year Theodore was consecrated as archbishop.	In this year Pope Vitalian consecrated Theodore as archbishop and sent him to Britain.

[1] Usually identified as Penselwood, Somerset. Rositzke suggests Pen Pits, Wiltshire, W. G. Hoskins, *The Western Expansion of Wessex* (Leicester, 1961), pp. 15 f., either Pinn Beacon or Pinhoe, Devon.

[2] Bishop of the West Saxons.

[3] Hoskins, *op. cit.*, p. 14, suggests Posbury, Devon.

[4] So 'B', 'C', 'E'; but 'A' reads 'as far as'. Ashdown means the line of the Berkshire Downs.

[5] Bede calls him Æthelwealh.

[6] Bishop of Northumbria, in exile.

[7] The three oldest manuscripts ('A', 'B', 'C') have Wulfhere in the nominative instead of the required genitive case.

[8] This is the only hint the Chronicle gives of the important synod at Whitby held this year. Colman left after its decisions.

[9] Of Northumbria.

[10] The *W* is an error for *P*, the letters being similar in Anglo-Saxon script. Bede has *Pægnalaech*. It cannot be identified.

[11] Both to the see of Northumbria, in succession, Ceadda being appointed when Wilfrid delayed abroad.

669 In this year King Egbert gave Reculver to the priest Bass, to build a minster in it.

670 In this year Oswiu, king of the Northumbrians, died,[1] and Ecgfrith[2] reigned after him; and Leuthere, Bishop Agilbert's nephew, succeeded to the bishopric over the land of the West Saxons, and held it for seven years, and Bishop Theodore consecrated him.[3] Oswiu was the son of Æthelfrith, the son of Æthelric, the son of Ida, the son of Eoppa.

671 In this year there was the great mortality of birds.

672 In this year Cenwealh died, and his queen Seaxburh reigned one year after him.

673 In this year Egbert, king of the people of Kent, died; and in the same year there was a synod[4] at Hertford, and St. Æthelthryth[5] began the monastery at Ely.

674 In this year Æscwine succeeded to the kingdom of Wessex.[3] He was the son of Cenfus, the son of Cenferth, the son of Cuthgils, the son of Ceolwulf, the son of Cynric, the son of Cerdic.

675 In this year Wulfhere, the son of Penda, and Æscwine[6] fought at *Biedanheafde*; and in the same year Wulfhere died[7] and Ethelred succeeded to the kingdom.[8]

676 In this year Æscwine died. And Hædde succeeded to the bishopric,[9] and Centwine succeeded to the kingdom.[10] And Centwine was the son of Cynegils, the son of Ceolwulf. And Ethelred, king of the Mercians, ravaged Kent.

C (A, B)	E
678 In this year the star called 'comet' appeared; and Bishop Wilfrid was driven from his bishopric by King Ecgfrith.	In this year the star called 'comet' appeared in August, and shone every morning for three months, like a sunbeam. And Bishop Wilfrid was driven from his bishopric by King Ecgfrith, and two bishops were consecrated in his place, Bosa for Deira and Eata for Bernicia. And Eadhæd was consecrated bishop for the people of Lindsey. He was the first bishop of Lindsey.

---

[1] 'E' adds: 'on 15 February'.
[2] 'E' adds: 'his son'.
[3] 'E' omits the genealogy.
[4] 'E', 'F': 'Archbishop Theodore assembled a synod'.
[5] 'B', 'C' (wrongly): 'St Æthelbyrht'.
[6] 'E' adds: 'son of Cenfus'.

[7] Probably in 674, after 23 September, and so recorded in Bede as 675.
[8] 'B' has accidentally omitted this annal. 'E' has a long Peterborough insertion at this point, with Pope Agatho's privilege.
[9] Of Wessex.
[10] 'E' adds: 'of the West Saxons' and omits the genealogy.

C (A, B)	E

679 In this year Ælfwine[1] was slain, and St. Æthelthryth[2] died.

In this year Ælfwine was slain near the Trent, where Ecgfrith and Ethelred were fighting. And St. Æthelthryth died; and Coldingham was burnt by divine fire.

680 In this year Archbishop Theodore presided over a synod in Hatfield, because he wished to correct the faith in Christ; and the same year the Abbess Hilda [of Whitby][3] died.

E

681 In this year Trumberht was consecrated bishop of Hexham and Trumwine for the Picts, because these then were subject to this country.[4]

682 (683 C) In this year Centwine put the Britons to flight as far as the sea.

C (A, B)	E

684

In this year Ecgfrith sent an army into Ireland,[5] and with it Briht his ealdorman, and they miserably injured and burnt God's churches.

685 In this year Ceadwalla began to contend for the kingdom.[6] Ceadwalla was the son of Cenberht, the son of Ceadda, the son of Cutha, the son of Ceawlin, the son of Cynric, the son of Cerdic; and Mul, who was afterwards burnt in Kent, was Ceadwalla's brother. And that same year King Ecgfrith was slain. Ecgfrith was the son of Oswiu, the son of Æthelfrith, the son of Æthelric, the son of Ida, the son of Eoppa. And Hlothhere died that same year.

In this year King Ecgfrith ordered that Cuthbert be consecrated bishop, and Archbishop Theodore consecrated him at York on the first day of Easter[7] as bishop of Hexham,[8] because Trumberht had been deposed from the bishopric. And that same year King Ecgfrith was slain north of the sea[9] on 20 May, and a great army with him. He had been king for 15 years; and his brother Aldfrith succeeded to the kingdom after him. And in this year Ceadwalla began to contend for the kingdom. And that same year Hlothhere, king of the people of Kent, died. And John[10] was consecrated bishop of Hexham, and was there until Wilfrid was restored. Then John succeeded to the bishopric of the city,[11] for Bishop Bosa had died. Then afterwards his priest Wilfrid[12] was consecrated bishop of the city and [John] went to his monastery in *Derawudu*.[13]

---

[1] Brother of Ecgfrith of Northumbria.
[2] Abbess of Ely.
[3] 'A', 'E', 'F'.
[4] Literally 'hither', i.e. to Northumbria.
[5] Literally 'among the Scots'.
[6] Of Wessex.
[7] 26 March

[8] Later he exchanged sees with Eata, bishop of Lindisfarne.
[9] The Firth of Forth.
[10] John of Beverley.
[11] York. This indicates that the writer is a Northumbrian.
[12] Wilfrid II, 718–732.
[13] 'The wood of the Deirans.' The monastery was at Beverley.

F685 In this year there occurred in Britain bloody rain, and milk and butter were turned to blood.[1]

686 In this year Ceadwalla and Mul[2] ravaged Kent and the Isle of Wight.[3]

687 In this year Mul was burnt in Kent, and twelve other men with him, and that year Ceadwalla again ravaged Kent.

C (A, B)	E
688 In this year Ine succeeded to the kingdom of the West Saxons, and held it for 37 years.[4] And the same year Ceadwalla went to Rome, and received baptism from the pope, and the pope called him Peter. Seven days later he died. Now Ine was the son of Cenred, the son of Ceolwold. Ceolwold was the brother of Cynegils, and they both were the sons of Cuthwine, the son of Ceawlin, the son of Cynric, the son of Cerdic.	In this year King Ceadwalla went to Rome and received baptism from Pope Sergius, and he gave him the name of Peter; and seven days afterwards he died on 20 April, wearing the baptismal robes,[5] and was buried in St. Peter's church. And Ine succeeded to the kingdom of the West Saxons after him. He reigned 27[6] years, and afterwards went to Rome and lived there until the day of his death.
690 In this year Archbishop Theodore died, and Brihtwold succeeded to the bishopric.[7] Hitherto there had been Roman bishops; afterwards they were English.	In this year Archbishop Theodore died. He had been bishop for 22 years, and he was buried in Canterbury.
692	In this year Brihtwold was elected archbishop on 1 July. He had been abbot of Reculver. Hitherto there had been Roman bishops; afterwards they were English. Then there were two kings in Kent, Wihtred[8] and Swæfheard.[9]

D (E)

693[10]   In this year Brihtwold was consecrated archbishop by Godwine,[11] bishop of the Gauls, on 3 July. Meanwhile Bishop Gefmund[12] had

---

[1] This portent is mentioned in *Annales Cambrenses* 689. 'F' continues with a brief reference to Cuthbert's consecration.

[2] 'E' adds: 'his brother'.

[3] 'E' has a short Peterborough addition, recording an alleged grant to the monastery by Ceadwalla.

[4] 'A' (marginal entry in an early hand) and 'G': 'And he built the minster at Glastonbury.'

[5] Literally 'Christ's clothes'.

[6] An error for 37.

[7] The other recension is correct in putting his election two years later.

[8] 'E': Nihtred; 'F': Wihtred.

[9] 'E': Wæbheard; 'F': Webheard.

[10] Near the beginning of this annal 'D' is resumed.

[11] Archbishop of Lyons. I have corrected to the form of his name in most MSS. of Bede. But the Namur MS. has *Gudune*, which is nearer to the forms here, 'D': *Guodune*; 'E', 'F': *Godune*.

[12] Of Rochester.

D (E)

died, and Brihtwold consecrated Tobias in his place. And Dryht-helm[1] was escorted from this life.

694 In this year the people of Kent made terms with Ine, and paid him thirty thousand [pence][2] because they had burnt Mul. And Wihtred succeeded to the kingdom of the people of Kent, and held it for 33 years.[3] Wihtred was the son of Egbert, the son of Eorcenberht, the son of Eadbald, the son of Ethelbert.

D (E)

697 In this year the Southumbrians slew Osthryth, Ethelred's queen and Ecgfrith's sister.

698 (699) In this year the Picts killed Ealdorman Briht[red].[4]

702 (?) In this year Cenred succeeded to the kingdom of the Southum-brians.[5]

705 (703)[6] In this year Bishop Hædde died, and he had held the bishopric of Winchester for 27 years.

704 In this year Ethelred, son of Penda, king of the Mercians, became a monk. And he had held the kingdom 29 years. Then Cenred succeeded.

C (A, B)	D (E)
705 In this year died Aldfrith, king of the Northumbrians, and Bishop Seaxwulf.[7]	In this year Aldfrith, king of the Northumbrians, died on 14 December, at Driffield. Then Osred his son succeeded to the kingdom.

[1] A man who had a vision of the other world, told by Bede, *Eccles. Hist.*, v, 12. 'E' wrongly calls him Brihthelm.

[2] The text does not name the unit, but pence is certainly meant. 'B' and 'C' replace 'thousands' by 'pounds', 'G' by 'men'.

[3] 'F' has a late Canterbury insertion, on Wihtred's donation to churches at the council of Bapchild. 'E' and 'F' omit the genealogy.

[4] Bede shows that this was his name. The chronicles call him here Berht, which is the same name as that of the leader of Ecgfrith's force to Ireland in 684.

[5] This seems to be recording the same event as 704, from a source two years out, but it is just possible, as Plummer suggests, that Cenred was associated with Ethelred in the kingship two years before the latter's abdication.

[6] An episcopate of 27 years from 676 would bring Hædde's death to 703, but as Bede shows that he was alive in 705, either the date of his accession or the length of his episcopate as given in the Chronicle must be wrong. 'B' and 'C' have 37; the others have 27.

[7] A wrong date: Seaxwulf was dead by 692. He was bishop of the Mercians.

709 (708 C)[1] In this year Aldhelm, who was bishop west of the wood,[2] died. Early in Daniel's time the land of the West Saxons had been divided into two dioceses, whereas it had previously been one. Daniel held the one and Aldhelm the other. Forthhere succeeded Aldhelm. And Ceolred succeeded to the kingdom of the Mercians, and Cenred went to Rome, and Offa[3] with him.

<table>
<tr><td>C (B)</td><td>D (E)</td></tr>
</table>

C (B)	D (E)

And Cenred was there until the end of his life. And that same year Bishop Wilfrid died in Oundle, and his body was taken to Ripon. He was bishop for 45 years, and King Ecgfrith previously drove him to Rome.

710 In this year Ealdorman Briht-ferth fought against the Picts.[4] And Ine and Nunna fought against Geraint the king.

In this year Acca, Wilfrid's priest, succeeded to the bishopric which Wilfrid had held. And that year Ealdorman Brihtferth fought against the Picts between the Avon and the Carron. And Ine and his kinsman Nun fought against Geraint, king of the Britons. And that same year Sigbald[5] was killed.

A710 In this year Ealdorman Brihtferth fought against the Picts. And Ine and his kinsman Nun fought against Geraint, king of the Britons.[6]

714 In this year the holy Guthlac died.

715 In this year Ine and Ceolred fought at 'Woden's barrow'.[7]

716 (717[8] (?) C) In this year Osred, king of the Northumbrians, was slain.[9] He held the kingdom for seven[10] years after Aldfrith. Then Cenred succeeded to the kingdom and held it for two years; then Osric, and he held it for eleven years. And in that year Ceolred,[11] king of the Mercians, died, and his body lies in Lichfield, and that of Ethelred, son of Penda, in Bardney. And then Æthelbald succeeded to the kingdom in Mercia, and held it for 41 years. Æthelbald was the son of Alweo, the son of Eawa, the son of Pybba,

---

[1] 'C' is one year behind here, but from 710 to 715 it was originally in line with the other MSS., though the numbers have since been tampered with. I restore the original dates.

[2] Selwood, which divides East and West Wessex.

[3] King of Essex.

[4] 711, according to Bede's summary.

[5] Hygebald in 'E', but Gaimar supports 'D''s reading. He is unknown.

[6] This annal was originally omitted in 'A', and was copied in at Winchester in the mid-tenth century, from a text like that in

'D' and 'E', only without their additions. Geraint ruled the Cornish Britons.

[7] Now Adam's Grave, in Alton Priors, Wilts.

[8] Though in the printed text 'C' appears to be in line with the other texts, it seems originally to have been a year in advance, and to have been altered by subsequent erasure. The annal numbers assigned by Thorpe to 'B' have no authority.

[9] 'D' and 'E' add: 'south of the border'.

[10] 'D': Eight.

[11] 'B' and 'C' have wrongly Ceolwold.

whose ancestry is given above.[1] And the venerable man Egbert induced the monks on the island of Iona to observe Easter correctly and the ecclesiastical tonsure.[2]

718 In this year Ingild, Ine's brother, died. Their sisters were Cwenburh and Cuthburh. And Cuthburh founded the monastery at Wimborne. She had been married to Aldfrith, king of the Northumbrians, and they separated during their lifetime.

721 In this year Daniel[3] went to Rome; and in the same year Ine slew Cynewulf

D (E)

the atheling. And in this year the holy Bishop John died, who had been bishop for 33 years, eight months and 13 days; and his body lies in Beverley.

722 In this year Queen Æthelburh demolished Taunton, which Ine had built; and the exile Ealdberht went away into Surrey and Sussex, and Ine fought against the South Saxons.[4]

C (A, B)	D (E)
725 In this year, Wihtred, king of the people of Kent, died.[5] [And Ine fought against the South Saxons and there slew Ealdberht].[8]	In this year Wihtred, king of the people of Kent, died on 23 April. He had ruled 34 years. And Ine fought against the South Saxons, and there slew the atheling Ealdberht[6] whom he had banished.[7]

726 (728 A) In this year Ine went to Rome,[9] and Æthelheard[10] succeeded to the kingdom of the West Saxons, and held it for 14 years.[11] And the same year Æthelheard and the atheling Oswald fought. Oswald was the son of Æthelbald, the son of Cynebald, the son of Cuthwine, the son of Ceawlin.

D (E)

727 In this year Bishop Tobias of Rochester died, and in his place Archbishop Brihtwold consecrated Ealdwulf bishop.

---

[1] 'D', 'E' omit the genealogy.
[2] 'St Peter's tonsure', 'D', 'E', 'F'. 'F' has only Æthelbald's accession, and the last sentence.
[3] Bishop of Winchester.
[4] The last phrase is omitted by 'D', 'E', and 'F'.
[5] 'A' adds: 'whose ancestry is give above'.
[6] 'D': Eadberht (wrongly).
[7] 'F' omits the last sentence. Both it and the Canterbury additions to 'A' add that Wihtred was succeeded by Eadberht.

[8] The bracketed portion is not in 'B' or 'C', but as it is in 'A' as well as in 'D' and 'E', it must have been in the original chronicle.
[9] Interlined in 'A' is 'and there gave up his life'. It is also in 'G'.
[10] 'D' and 'E' add: 'his kinsman'.
[11] 'E' and 'F' omit the rest of this annal.

C (A, B)

729 In this year the star called 'comet' appeared and St. Egbert[1] died.

730 [In this year the atheling Oswald died.] [2]

C (A, B)

731 [4] In this year Osric, king of the Northumbrians, was slain, and Ceolwulf succeeded to the kingdom, and held it for eight years. And Ceolwulf was the son of Cutha, the son of Cuthwine, the son of Leodwold, the son of Ecgwold, the son of Aldhelm, the son of Ocga, the son of Ida, the son of Eoppa. And Archbishop Brihtwold died, and the same year Tatwine was consecrated as archbishop.

D (E)

In this year two comets appeared; and the same year Osric, who had been king eleven years, died, and the holy Egbert died in Iona. Then Ceolwulf succeeded to the kingdom and held it eight years.

E (D)[3]

In this year Archbishop Brihtwold died on 13 January. He was bishop 37 years and six months and 14 days.[5] And the same year Tatwine was consecrated as archbishop. He had been priest at Breedon in Mercia.[6] He was consecrated by Daniel, bishop of Winchester, and Ingwold, bishop of London, and Ealdwine, bishop of Lichfield, and Ealdwulf, bishop of Rochester, on 10 June.

733 In this year Æthelbald occupied Somerton,[7] and there was an eclipse of the sun.[8]

D (E)

And Acca was driven from his bishopric.[9]

734 In this year the moon looked as if it were suffused with blood, and Tatwine and Bede died.[10]

D (E)

And Egbert was consecrated bishop.[11]

735

In this year Bishop Egbert received his *pallium* from Rome.

---

[1] On him, see annal 716. He was a Northumbrian who lived in Ireland.

[2] Though omitted in 'B' and 'C', this annal, being in 'A', 'D', and 'E', must have been in the original.

[3] 'E' gives the best text of the northern recension. See n. 5 below.

[4] 731 is right for Brihtwold's death, but Osric died in 729.

[5] 'D' inserts at this place almost the whole of the annal as in 'A', 'B', and 'C', including the death of Brihtwold. It thus

refers to this twice, and repeats the death of Osric, already given under 729.

[6] Breedon-on-the-Hill, Leics.

[7] In Somerset. Æthelweard calls it a royal vill.

[8] 'F' adds: 'and all the circle of the sun became like a black shield'.

[9] Hexham. The true date is probably 731.

[10] 735 is probably the true date of Bede's death.

[11] Of York. The true date was 732.

736 In this year Archbishop Nothhelm[1] received the *pallium* from the bishop of the Romans.

737 In this year Bishop Forthhere and Queen Frithugyth[2] went to Rome,

D (E)

and King Ceolwulf received St. Peter's tonsure[3] and gave his kingdom to Eadberht, the son of his paternal uncle, and Eadberht reigned 21 years. And Bishop Æthelwold[4] and Acca[5] died, and Cynewulf was consecrated bishop.[6] And the same year King Æthelbald[7] ravaged Northumbria.

738 In this year Eadberht, son of Eata, son of Leodwold, succeeded to the kingdom of the Northumbrians and held it for 21 years. And his brother was Archbishop Egbert, son of Eata; and they are both buried in the city of York, in the same chapel.

740 (741 A) In this year King Æthelheard died, and Cuthred[8] succeeded to the kingdom of the West Saxons, and held it 16 years.[9] And he fought stoutly against King Æthelbald.[10] And Cuthbert[11] was consecrated archbishop and Dunn bishop of Rochester.

D (E)

741   In this year York was burnt down.

F742 In this year a great synod was collected at *Clofesho* which was attended by Æthelbald, king of the Mercians, and Archbishop Cuthbert and many other wise men.[12]

743 In this year Æthelbald[10] and Cuthred[13] fought against the Britons.

744 In this year Daniel resigned in Winchester, and Hunfrith succeeded to the bishopric.

---

[1] Of Canterbury.
[2] Wife of King Æthelheard of Wessex.
[3] i.e. took clerical vows.
[4] Of Lindisfarne. Simeon of Durham dates his death and Acca's 740.
[5] Deposed bishop of Hexham.
[6] Of Lindisfarne.
[7] Of Mercia. 'E': Æthelwald (wrongly).

[8] 'D', 'E' add: 'his kinsman'.
[9] This is the figure in 'A', 'D', and 'E'; 'B' and 'C' have 26, wrongly.
[10] 'D', 'E', add: 'king of the Mercians'.
[11] 'E': Eadberht (wrongly).
[12] It is uncertain whether this entry can be relied on. The charter which follows it is dubious.
[13] 'D', 'E', add: 'king of the West Saxons'.

D (E)

And shooting stars were frequent. And Wilfrid the younger, who had been bishop of York, died on 29 April. He had been bishop for 30 years.

745 In this year Daniel died. Forty-three[1] years had then passed since he succeeded to the bishopric.

746 In this year King Selred[2] was slain.

748 (747 C) In this year Cynric, an atheling of the West Saxons, was slain, and Eadberht, king of the people of Kent, died.[3]

750 In this year King Cuthred[4] fought against the arrogant ealdorman Æthelhun.

752 In this year, in the twelfth year of his reign, Cuthred[4] fought at *Beorhford* against Æthelbald,

D (E)

king of the Mercians, and put him to flight.

753 In this year Cuthred[4] fought against the Britons.

756 (754)[5] In this year Cuthred[4] died. And Cyneheard succeeded to the bishopric of Winchester after Hunfrith. And Canterbury was burnt down that year. And Sigeberht[6] succeeded to the West Saxon kingdom and held it for one year.

757 (755) In this year Cynewulf[7] and the councillors of the West Saxons deprived Sigeberht[6] of his kingdom because of his unjust acts, except for Hampshire; and he retained that until he killed the ealdorman who stood by him longest; and then Cynewulf drove him into[8] the Weald, and he lived there until a swineherd stabbed him to death by the stream at Privett, and he was avenging Ealdorman Cumbra. And Cynewulf often fought with great battles against the Britons. And when he had held the kingdom 31[9] years, he wished to drive out an atheling who was called Cyneheard, who was brother of the

[1] 'E': 46. It should be 40.
[2] King of the East Saxons.
[3] A Canterbury addition to 'A' adds that he was succeeded by Ethelbert, King Wihtred's son.
[4] 'D', 'E', add: 'king of the West Saxons'.
[5] At this point begins the dislocation of chronology mentioned on pp. xviii and xxiii, by which all extant versions are dated two – or further on even three – years too early up to the

annal for 845. The error must therefore have been present in the archetype of all surviving texts, and Æthelweard has it also.
[6] 'D', 'E', add: 'his kinsman'.
[7] On him, see *E.H.D.*, I, pp. 23 f.
[8] 'C' has wrongly 'from'.
[9] Thus MSS. 'A', 'B', 'C', though the length of the reign was 29 years, as given in the *Annals of St Neots*. 'D' has 21, 'E' has 16.

aforesaid Sigeberht. And Cyneheard discovered that the king was at *Meretun* visiting his mistress with a small following, and he overtook him there and surrounded the chamber[1] before the men who were with the king became aware of him.

Then the king perceived this and went to the doorway, and nobly defended himself until he caught sight of the atheling [and thereupon he rushed out against him and wounded him severely].[2] Then they all fought against the king until they had slain him. Then by the woman's outcry, the king's thegns became aware of the disturbance and ran to the spot, each as he got ready [and as quickly as possible].[3] And the atheling made an offer to each of money and life; and not one of them would accept it. But they continued to fight until they all lay dead except for one British hostage, and he was severely wounded.

Then in the morning the king's thegns who had been left behind heard that the king had been slain. Then they rode thither – his ealdorman Osric and his thegn Wigfrith and the men he had left behind him – and discovered the atheling in the stronghold where the king lay slain – and they had locked the gates against them[4] – and they went thither. And then the atheling offered them money and land on their own terms, if they would allow him the kingdom, and told[5] them that kinsmen of theirs, who would not desert him, were with him. Then they replied that no kinsman was dearer to them than their lord, and they would never serve his slayer; and they offered their kinsmen that they might go away unharmed. Their kinsmen said that the same offer had been made to their comrades who had been with the king. Moreover they said that they would pay no regard to it, 'any more than did your comrades who were slain along with the king'. And they proceeded to fight around the gates until they broke their way in, and killed the atheling and the men who were with him, all except one, who was the ealdorman's godson. And he saved his life, though he was often wounded. And Cynewulf reigned 31 years, and his body is buried at Winchester and the atheling's at Axminster; and their true paternal ancestry goes back to Cerdic.

And in the same year[6] Æthelbald, king of the Mercians, was slain at Seckington, and his body is buried at Repton.[7] And Beornred succeeded to the kingdom and held it for but a little space and unhappily. And that same year Offa[8] succeeded to the kingdom and held it for 39 years, and his son Ecgfrith held it for 141 days. Offa was the son of Thingfrith,[9] the son of Eanwulf, the son of Osmod, the son of Eawa, the son of Pybba, the son of Creoda, the son of Cynewold, the son of Cnebba, the son of Icel, the son of Eomær, the son of Angeltheow, the son of Offa, the son of Wærmund, the son of Wihtlæg, the son of Woden.

---

[1] So 'A', 'D', and 'E'. 'B', 'C' have wrongly altered *bur* to *burh*, 'fortress'.

[2] From other MSS.; omitted by 'C'.

[3] Omitted in 'B', 'C'.

[4] Or 'on themselves'; but the instances of the idiom are ambiguous. Æthelweard translates *ex adverso*.

[5] 'A' and 'C' have a plural verb here, which would refer to the atheling's party, with an abrupt change of subject. But it is possibly an accidental repetition of the plural ending of the preceding verb, and 'B', 'D', and 'E' may be right to emend to the singular.

[6] 757, the date of the events at the beginning of the annal, not those immediately preceding. The death of Cynewulf has been recorded out of place.

[7] 'D', 'E' add: 'And he reigned 41 years.'

[8] 'D', 'E' add: 'put Beornred to flight and'.

[9] The rest of the genealogy is omitted in 'D', 'E', 'F'.

D (E)

758

(757) In this year Eadberht, king of the Northumbrians, received the tonsure, and his son Oswulf succeeded to the kingdom, and ruled for one year, and the men of his household slew him on 24 July.[1]

760 (758) In this year Archbishop Cuthbert died.[2]

761 (759) In this year Bregowine was consecrated archbishop at Michaelmas.[3]

D (E)

759[4]

And Moll Æthelwold succeeded to the kingdom of the Northumbrians, and reigned six years and then lost it.

762 (760) In this year Ethelbert, king of the people of Kent,[5] died,

D (E)

and Ceolwulf died also.[6]

763 (762 C, 761 A, D, E, F) In this year occurred the great winter.

D (E)

761[7]

And Moll, king of the Northumbrians, killed Oswine at 'Edwin's cliff' on 6 August.[8]

765 (763 A, C; 762 D, E, F) In this year Jænberht[9] was consecrated archbishop on the 40th day after Christmas Day.

D (E)

763[7]

(762) And Frithuwold, bishop of Whithorn, died on 7 May. He had been consecrated in the city[10] on 15 August in the sixth year of Ceolwulf's reign, and was bishop 29 years.[11] Then Pehtwine was consecrated bishop of Whithorn at Elvet on 17 July.[12]

---

[1] So in 'E'; 'D' has '25 July'.

[2] 'F' adds: 'And he held the bishopric 18 years.'

[3] 'F' adds: 'and held it for four years'.

[4] The parts of these annals peculiar to the northern recension come from a source without the chronological dislocation of the Chronicle, and are therefore usually two years earlier than the events in the parts of the annal common to all versions.

[5] 'F' calls him 'son of Wihtred, king of the people of Kent'.

[6] He had formerly been king of Northumbria. The exact date of his death is uncertain.

[7] See n. 4 above.

[8] cf. Simeon of Durham, who, in his annal 759, says the battle took place at Eildon.

[9] 'B', 'C': Eadbriht (wrongly).

[10] York. See p. 23, n. 11.

[11] This would put his accession in 734, and 15 August was a Sunday in that year.

[12] This was a Sunday in 763. Elvet is part of Durham.

C (A, B)	D (E)

766 (764) In this year Jænberht[1] received the *pallium*.

765[2]

> In this year Alhred succeeded to the kingdom of the Northumbrians, and ruled nine years.[3]

766

> In this year Egbert, archbishop of York, who had been bishop 37[4] years, died on 19 November; and Frithuberht, of Hexham, who had been bishop 34[5] years, died. And Ethelbert was consecrated for York and Alhmund for Hexham.

768

> In this year Eadberht, son of Eata, died on 20 August.[6]

774 (772) In this year Bishop Mildred[7] died.

D (E)

774

> In this year the Northumbrians drove their king Alhred from York at Easter, and took as their lord Ethelred, Moll's son, and he reigned for four years.

776 (774 C, D, E, F, G; 773 A) In this year a red cross appeared in the sky after sunset. And that year the Mercians and the people of Kent fought at Otford. And marvellous adders were seen in Sussex.

D (E)

776[8]

> In this year Bishop Pehtwine died on 19 September; he had been bishop for 14 years.

779 (777) In this year Cynewulf and Offa fought around[9] Bensington and Offa captured the town.

D (E)

777

> And that same year Ethelbert was consecrated bishop of Whithorn at York on 15 June.[10]

---

[1] 'B': Eanbriht; 'C': Eadbriht (wrongly).
[2] See p. 32, n. 4.
[3] 'E': Eight.
[4] 'E': 36. Both are wrong; it should be 34.
[5] 'E': 33.

[6] This statement was added to 'A' at Canterbury. 'E' has 19 August.
[7] Of Worcester.
[8] Simeon: 777.
[9] 'D', 'E': 'contested about'.
[10] 'E' has an addition about donations to Peterborough.

D (E)

778
In this year Æthelbald and Heardberht killed three high-reeves, Ealdwulf, son of Bosa, at Coniscliffe, Cynewulf and Ecga at *Helathirnum*, on 22 March.[1] And then Ælfwold succeeded to the kingdom and drove Ethelred from the country;[2] and he reigned for ten years.

782 (780 A, C; 779 D, E) In this year the Old Saxons and the Franks fought.[3]

D (E)

779[4]
And the high-reeves of the Northumbrians burnt Ealdorman Beorn in *Seletun* on 25[5] December. And Archbishop Ethelbert, in whose place Eanbald had previously been consecrated, died in the city;[6] and Bishop Cynewulf[7] of Lindisfarne resigned.

780[8]
In this year Alhmund, bishop of Hexham, died on 7 September, and Tilberht was consecrated in his place on 2 October. And Higbald was consecrated bishop of Lindisfarne at Sockburn; and King Ælfwold sent to Rome for the *pallium* and made Eanbald an archbishop.

782[9]
In this year Werburh, Ceolred's queen, and Cynewulf, bishop of Lindisfarne, died. And there was a synod at *Aclea*.

F (Lat.) 784 At this time King Ealhmund reigned in Kent. (F English) This King Ealhmund was Egbert's father. Egbert was Æthelwulf's father.

786 (784 A, D, E; 783 C) In this year Cyneheard killed King Cynewulf,[10] and was himself slain there and 84 men with him. And then Brihtric succeeded to the kingdom of the West Saxons; and he reigned 16 years, and his body is buried at Wareham; and his true paternal ancestry goes back to Cerdic.

---

[1] Simeon, who does not distinguish two events, gives the date as 29 September.

[2] The MSS. read: 'into the country'. Simeon dates this event 779.

[3] The Saxons defeated the Franks in the Süntel Hills in 782, and Charles took his revenge by the massacre at Verden on the Aller.

[4] Simeon: 780.

[5] 'E': 24.

[6] York.

[7] 'E': Cynebald (wrongly).

[8] Simeon, *History of the Kings*, 781, *History of the Church of Durham*, 780. 2 October was not a Sunday in either year.

[9] Simeon: 783.

[10] cf. annal 757.

D (E)

786?   (785) In this year Abbot Botwine of Ripon died.

787 (785) In this year there was a contentious synod at Chelsea, and Archbishop Jænberht lost a certain part of his province,[1] and Hygeberht was chosen by King Offa. And Ecgfrith was consecrated king.[2]

D (E)

786   (785) And at this time messengers were sent by Pope Hadrian from Rome to England to renew the faith and the friendship which St. Gregory sent us through Bishop Augustine, and they were received with great honour and sent back in peace.[3]

789 (787) In this year King Brihtric married Offa's daughter Eadburh. And in his days there came for the first time three ships of Northmen[4] and then the reeve[5] rode to them and wished to force them to the king's residence, for he did not know what they were; and they slew him. Those were the first ships of Danish men which came to the land of the English.

D (E)

787[6]   (788) In this year a synod was assembled in Northumbria at *Pincanheale* on 2 September. And Abbot Ealdberht of Ripon died.[7]

788[8]   (789) In this year Ælfwold, king of the Northumbrians, was killed by Sicga on 23 September, and a heavenly light was often seen where he was killed, and he was buried inside the church at Hexham. And a synod was assembled at *Aclea*. And Osred, Alhred's son, who was Ælfwold's nephew, succeeded to the kingdom after him.

792 (790) In this year Archbishop Jænberht[9] died, and Abbot Æthelheard[10] was elected archbishop the same year.

---

[1] i.e. Lichfield was made an archbishopric.

[2] Offa's son was consecrated in his father's lifetime. This is the first reference to the 'consecration' of a king in England.

[3] See the report of this mission, *E.H.D.*, I, No. 191. The last clause of the annal is in 'D' only.

[4] 'A' omits 'of Northmen' but it was in the archetype, for it is also in the *Annals of St Neots*, which gives the additional information that they landed in Portland. 'D', 'E', and 'F' add: 'from Hörthaland' (in Norway).

[5] Æthelweard, whose additions to this annal sound authentic and may be drawn from the early copy of the Chronicle used by him, calls him Beaduheard, and says he was staying in the town of Dorchester. He says that he rode to the harbour with a few men, thinking the strangers to be traders rather than enemies; and that his men were killed with him.

[6] Simeon: 787.

[7] Only 'D' mentions Ripon.

[8] Simeon: 788.

[9] 'B', 'C': Eadbriht (wrongly).

[10] 'F' adds: 'of the monastery of Louth'.

D (E)

790[1] And Osred, king of the Northumbrians, was betrayed and driven from the kingdom, and Ethelred, Æthelwold's son, again succeeded to the kingdom.

791 In this year Badwulf[2] was consecrated bishop of Whithorn by Archbishop Eanbald and by Bishop Ethelbert[3] on 17 July.

794 (792) In this year Offa, king of the Mercians, had Ethelbert[4] beheaded.

D (E)

792[1] And Osred, who had been king of the Northumbrians, was captured after he had returned home from exile, and killed on 14 September, and his body is buried at Tynemouth. And King Ethelred took a new wife, who was called Ælfflæd,[5] on 29 September.

793 In this year dire portents appeared over Northumbria and sorely frightened the people. They consisted of immense whirlwinds[6] and flashes of lightning, and fiery dragons were seen flying in the air. A great famine immediately followed those signs, and a little after that in the same year, on 8 June,[7] the ravages of heathen men miserably destroyed God's church on Lindisfarne, with plunder and slaughter. And Sicga died on 22 February.

796 (794) In this year Pope Hadrian and King Offa died;[8] and Ethelred, king of the Northumbrians, was killed by his own people.[9] And Bishop Ceolwulf[10] and Bishop Eadbald[11] left the country. And Ecgfrith succeeded to the kingdom of the Mercians and died the same year. And Eadberht, whose other name was Præn, succeeded to the kingdom in Kent.

D (E)

794[1] And Ealdorman Æthelheard died on 1 August. And the heathens ravaged in Northumbria, and plundered Ecgfrith's monastery at

---

[1] See p. 34, n. 4.
[2] Or perhaps Baldwulf. The sources vary as to his name.
[3] Of Hexham.
[4] King of East Anglia. He was afterwards regarded as a saint, Hereford Cathedral being one of the places dedicated to him.
[5] She was a daughter of Offa of Mercia.
[6] Omitted in 'E'.
[7] The MSS. have by mistake January for June.
[8] Hadrian died on 25 December 795, Offa on 29 July 796.
[9] 'D', 'E' add: 'on 19 April'.
[10] Of Lindsey.
[11] Of London.

D (E)

Donemuthan;[1] and one of their leaders was killed there, and also some of their ships were broken to bits by stormy weather, and many of the men were drowned there. Some reached the shore alive and were immediately killed at the mouth of the river.

796   (795) In this year there was an eclipse of the moon between cock-crow and dawn on 28 March, and Eardwulf succeeded to the kingdom of the Northumbrians on 14 May; and he was afterwards consecrated and enthroned on 26 May in York, by Archbishop Eanbald, and Ethelbert, Higbald, and Badwulf.[2]

796[3]   In this year Offa, king of the Mercians, died on 29 July.[4] He had reigned 40 years. And Archbishop Eanbald died on 10 August of the same year, and his body is buried in York. And that same year Bishop Ceolwulf[5] died, and Eanbald the second was consecrated in place of the other Eanbald on 14 August.

798 (796) In this year Cenwulf,[6] king of the Mercians, ravaged the people of Kent and of the Marsh,[7] and they seized Præn their king and brought him in fetters into Mercia.

F796 . . . and they had his eyes put out and his hands cut off. And Æthelheard, archbishop of Canterbury, arranged a synod, and established and confirmed at the command of Pope Leo[8] all the things relating to God's monasteries which were appointed in the days of King Wihtred and of other kings.[9]

799 (797) In this year the Romans cut out Pope Leo's tongue and put out his eyes and banished him from his see; and then immediately afterwards he could, with God's help, see and speak and was again pope as he had been before.

---

[1] i.e. 'the mouth of the Don'. Simeon's *History of the Church of Durham* identifies it as Jarrow. It cannot in that case be the *Donaemutha* of Pope Paul I's letter (*E.H.D.*, I, No. 184), for this had belonged to an abbess and was in lay hands in the mid eighth century.

[2] Bishops of Hexham, Lindisfarne, and Whithorn, respectively.

[3] The northern recension, drawing from a correctly dated source, here duplicates the entries taken from the Chronicle, with its error of two years.

[4] 'E', having 'ides' in mistake for 'kalends', gives the date as 10 August.

[5] Of Lindsey.

[6] So, correctly, 'B' and 'C'. All other MSS. have Ceolwulf.

[7] Romney Marsh. 'A' reads 'as far as the Marsh', but all other MSS. and Æthelweard have 'the people of the Marsh'.

[8] Leo III.

[9] A passage purporting to be the archbishop's speech is then added.

D (E)

797[1] And Eanbald received the *pallium* on 8 September, and Bishop
       Ethelbert[2] died on 16 October, and Heardred was consecrated
       bishop in his place on 30 October.

798   In this year there was a great battle in Northumbria in spring, on
       2 April, at Whalley, and Alric, Heardberht's son, was killed and
       many others with him.

F798 And Bishop Ælfhun[3] died in Sudbury and was buried in Dunwich, and Tidfrith was elected to
     succeed him. And Sigeric, king of the East Saxons, went to Rome. In the same year the body of
     Wihtburh[4] was found all sound and undecayed in Dereham, 55 years after she departed from
     this life.

801 (799) In this year Archbishop Æthelheard and Cyneberht, bishop of the West Saxons, went to Rome.

D (E)

800   In this year there was an eclipse of the moon in the second hour of
       the eve of 16 January.

802 (800) In this year King Brihtric and Ealdorman Worr died, and Egbert succeeded to the kingdom of
     the West Saxons. And that same day Ealdorman Æthelmund rode from the province of the Hwiccians
     across the border at Kempsford. And Ealdorman Weohstan with the people of Wiltshire met him, and
     a great battle took place, and both ealdormen were killed and the people of Wiltshire had the victory.

D *only*

804   (801) In this year Beornmod was consecrated bishop of Rochester.

D (E)

802   In this year there was an eclipse of the moon in the dawn on
       20 May.[5]

804 (802)[6] In this year Beornmod was consecrated bishop of Rochester.

---

[1] 'F' has this annal, dated 798. His chronology is one year
ahead till 802. But note that the 30 October was a Sunday in
798, not 797.

[2] Of Hexham.

[3] Of Dunwich.

[4] She was sister of St Æthelthryth of Ely.

[5] Assuming that the manuscripts, which have the 13th of the
kalends of January (20 December) have written January for
June. There was an eclipse on 21 May.

[6] From here to 824, the numbers in 'C' have been tampered
with, and are now a year behind the other MSS., though
originally 'C' was in line with the others. I have given the
original dating. In the MS. one minim has been erased where
possible, and where numbers end in v or x this has usually been
erased, without anything been added to complete the number.
For example, DCCCV now reads DCCC, with a blank; it was
meant to be completed as DCCCIIII.

D (E)

803   In this year Higbald, bishop of Lindisfarne, died on 25 May,[1] and Egbert was consecrated in his place on 11 June.

805 (803) In this year Archbishop Æthelheard died and Wulfred was consecrated archbishop; and Abbot Forthred died.[2]

806 (804) In this year Archbishop Wulfred received the *pallium*.

807 (805) In this year King Cuthred died in Kent, and Abbess Ceolburh[3] and Ealdorman Heahberht.[4]

D (E)

806   In this year there was an eclipse of the moon on 1 September. And Eardwulf, king of the Northumbrians, was driven from his kingdom.[5] And Eanberht, bishop of Hexham, died.

F806   Also in the same year on 31 May the sign of the cross was revealed in the moon, on a Wednesday at dawn. And again in this year on 30 August a wonderful circle was revealed round the sun.

809   In this year there was an eclipse of the sun at the beginning of the fifth hour of the day on 16 July, the second day of the week, the twenty-ninth day of the moon.[6]

814 (812 A, C, D, E; 814 F) In this year King Charles[7] died, and he had reigned 45 years. And both Archbishop Wulfred and Wigberht, bishop of the West Saxons, went to Rome.

815 (813 A, C, D, E; 815 F) In this year Archbishop Wulfred with Pope Leo's[8] blessing returned to his own bishopric. And that year King Egbert ravaged in Cornwall, from east to west.

816 (814 A, C, D, E; 816 F) In this year the noble and holy Pope Leo died, and after him Stephen[9] succeeded to the papacy.

817 (815 E; 816 A, C, D; 817 F) In this year Pope Stephen died, and Paschal[10] was consecrated pope after him; and that same year the English quarter[11] at Rome was burnt down.

---

[1] Reading *Iunii* for *Iulii*, which would give 24 June.
[2] 'D', 'E', 'F' omit the last clause.
[3] Of Berkeley. See *E.H.D.*, I, No. 81.
[4] 'D', 'E': Heardberht.
[5] In 808 according to Roger of Wendover and the *Annals of the Frankish Kingdom*. See *E.H.D.*, I, Nos. 4 and 21. The Northumbrian annals used by the 'D' and 'E' versions seem to have ended here.
[6] 'F''s Latin, 'on Sunday, the twelfth day of the moon'.
[7] Charles the Great.

[8] Leo III.
[9] Stephen IV.
[10] Paschal I.
[11] Literally 'school', but not in any modern sense of the word. It was first applied to the contingent supplied to the Roman militia by Englishmen in Rome, but by this time had also acquired a local sense. It was on the Vatican hill and was inhabited by ecclesiastics, pilgrims, and others whose business took them to Rome.

821 (819 A, C, D, E; 822 F) In this year Cenwulf, king of the Mercians, died,[1] and Ceolwulf succeeded to the kingdom. And Ealdorman Eadberht died.

823 (821) In this year Ceolwulf was deprived of his kingdom.

824 (822) In this year two ealdormen, Burghelm and Muca, were killed. And there was a synod at *Clofesho*.

825 (823) In this year there was a battle between the Britons and the men of Devon at Galford.[2] And the same year Egbert[3] and Beornwulf, king of the Mercians, fought at Wroughton,[4] and Egbert had the victory and a great slaughter was made there.[5] Then he sent from the army his son Æthelwulf and his bishop Ealhstan[6] and his ealdorman Wulfheard to Kent, with a large force, and they drove King Bealdred north across the Thames; and the people of Kent and of Surrey and the South Saxons and the East Saxons submitted to him because they had been wrongfully forced away from his kinsmen. And the same year the king of the East Angles and the people appealed to King Egbert for peace and protection, because of their fear of the Mercians. And that same year the East Angles killed Beornwulf, king of the Mercians.[7]

827 (825) In this year Ludeca, king of the Mercians, was killed, and his five ealdormen with him; and Wiglaf succeeded to the kingdom.

829 (827) In this year there was an eclipse of the moon on Christmas eve.[8] And that year King Egbert conquered the kingdom of the Mercians, and everything south of the Humber; and he was the eighth king who was 'Bretwalda'.[9] The first who had so great authority was Ælle, king of the South Saxons,[10] the second was Ceawlin, king of the West Saxons, the third was Ethelbert, king of the people of Kent, the fourth was Rædwald, king of the East Angles, the fifth was Edwin, king of the Northumbrians, the sixth was Oswald who reigned after him, the seventh was Oswiu, Oswald's brother, the eighth was

---

[1] Gaimar says he died at Basingwerk, Flintshire. See F. M. Stenton, *Anglo-Saxon England*, p. 228.

[2] A Winchester writer who composed or interpolated two charters (Birch, Nos. 389, 390), probably after the Norman Conquest, had some other source of information about this campaign, for he assigns it to its true date and adds matter not in the extant Chronicle. He writes: 'The beginning of this document was written in the army when Egbert, king of the *Gewissi* [=West Saxons] advanced against the Britons at the place called *Creodantreow*, in the year of our Lord's incarnation 825, indiction 3, on 19 August. . . . Then the charter of privilege of this estate was written at Southampton on 26 December.'

[3] 'D', 'E', add: 'king of the West Saxons'.

[4] This name has replaced the old *Ellendun*.

[5] Æthelweard's addition is doubtless authentic: 'And there was killed Hun, ealdorman of the province of Somerset, and he now rests in the city of Winchester.'

[6] Of Sherborne.

[7] Florence of Worcester says Beornwulf was killed when invading the East Angles, and that Ludeca's death the following year was when he led an army against them to avenge his predecessor.

[8] It was in the early morning of 25 December.

[9] This is the form that is familiar in history books. It means 'ruler of Britain'. But it is in 'A' (and its copy 'G') only, so that the variant *Brytenwalda* (*Bretenanwealda*, 'C') must go back to the archetype of all the other MSS. and have replaced *Bretwalda* very early. *Brytenwalda* could mean 'mighty ruler'. It is the form used also in some spurious documents. On the power it implied, see F. M. Stenton, *Anglo-Saxon England*, pp. 34f.

[10] Corrected from 'A', 'D', 'E'. 'B', 'C': 'of the West Saxons'.

Egbert, king of the West Saxons. And Egbert led an army to Dore,[1] against the Northumbrians, and they offered him submission and peace there, and on that they separated.

830 (828) In this year Wiglaf again obtained the kingdom of the Mercians. And Bishop Æthelwold[2] died. And that same year King Egbert led an army among the Welsh, and he reduced them all to humble submission to him.

832 (829) In this year Archbishop Wulfred died.

F829 And Abbot Feologild was elected after him to the archiepiscopal see on 25 April, and he was consecrated on Sunday, 9 June,[3] and he died on 30 August.

833 (830) In this year Ceolnoth was elected bishop and consecrated, and Abbot Feologild died.

834 (831) In this year Archbishop Ceolnoth received the *pallium*.

835 (832) In this year heathen men ravaged Sheppey.

836 (833) In this year King Egbert fought against the crews of 35 ships[4] at Carhampton, and a great slaughter was made there, and the Danes had possession of the battle-field. And two bishops, Herefrith and Wigthegn,[5] and two ealdormen, Duda and Osmod, died.

838 (835) In this year a great naval force arrived among the West Welsh[6] and the latter combined with them and proceeded to fight against Egbert, king of the West Saxons. When he heard that, he then went thither with his army,[7] and fought against them at Hingston Down, and put both the Welsh and the Danes to flight.

839 (836) In this year King Egbert died. Earlier, before he became king, Offa, king of the Mercians, and Brihtric, king of the West Saxons, had driven him from England to France for three years. Brihtric had helped Offa because he had married his daughter.[8] Egbert reigned 37 years and 7 months, and then Æthelwulf, son of Egbert, succeeded to the kingdom of the West Saxons; and he gave to his son[9] Athelstan the kingdom of the people of Kent and the kingdom of the East Saxons[10] and of the people of Surrey and of the South Saxons.

---

[1] In North Derbyshire, near the Northumbrian boundary.
[2] Of Lichfield. 'D', 'E', 'F': Æthelbald (wrongly).
[3] This was a Sunday in 832.
[4] 'D', 'E', 'F': 25.
[5] Both occur in the Winchester lists, in succession.
[6] Of Cornwall.
[7] There was probably a minor error in the original here.

I use the text of 'B', as doubtless representing best the author's intention. 'A' supplies a redundant 'and', 'C' reads 'that' for 'thither'. 'D', 'E', reword the clause.
[8] This explanatory clause is omitted in 'D', 'E', 'F'.
[9] 'D', 'E', 'F', wrongly read 'his other son', thus giving rise to the view that Athelstan was Egbert's son, not Æthelwulf's.
[10] 'The East Saxons' accidentally omitted in 'D', 'E', 'F'.

840 (837) In this year Ealdorman Wulfheard fought at Southampton against the crews of 33[1] ships, and made a great slaughter there and had the victory; and Wulfheard died that year.[2] And the same year Ealdorman Æthelhelm with the people of Dorset fought against the Danish army at Portland, and for a long time he put the enemy to flight;[3] and the Danes had possession of the battle-field and killed the ealdorman.[4]

841[5] (838) In this year Ealdorman Hereberht[6] was killed by heathen men and many men with him in the Marsh;[7] and later in the same year [many men][8] in Lindsey, East Anglia, and Kent, were killed by the enemy.

842 (839) In this year there was a great slaughter in London and Quentavic[9] and in Rochester.

843? (840 A, D, E, F; 841 C) In this year King Æthelwulf fought against the crews of 35 ships at Carhampton, and the Danes had possession of the battle-field.

845?[10] In this year Ealdorman Eanwulf[11] with the people of Somerset and Bishop Ealhstan and Ealdorman Osric with the people of Dorset fought against the Danish army at the mouth of the Parret, and there made a great slaughter and had the victory.

851 (853 C)[12] In this year Ealdorman Ceorl[13] with the contingent of the men of Devon fought against the heathen army at *Wicganbeorg*,[14] and the English made a great slaughter there and had the victory. And for the first time, heathen men stayed through the winter on Thanet.[15] And the same year 350 ships came into the mouth of the Thames and stormed Canterbury and London[16] and put to flight Brihtwulf, king of the Mercians, with his army, and went south across the Thames into Surrey. And King Æthelwulf and his son Æthelbald fought against them at *Aclea* with the army of the West Saxons, and there inflicted the greatest slaughter [on a heathen army][17] that we ever heard of until this present day,[18] and had the victory there.

---

[1] 'C': 34.

[2] Æthelweard, adds: 'in peace'.

[3] 'D', 'E', 'F' omit this clause.

[4] 'D', 'E', 'F' omit these last four words; Æthelweard adds: 'and his companions with him'.

[5] 'E', 'F' omit this annal.

[6] 'D': Ecgbryht.

[7] Romney Marsh. 'D' has *Myrc*, 'boundary', in error for *Mersc*, 'marsh'. Hereberht signs Kentish charters.

[8] Supplied from 'A'.

[9] Near Étaples. 'C' alters to Canterbury.

[10] Either here or by the next annal the dating of most MSS. is correct.

[11] 'D', 'E', 'F': Earnulf.

[12] With two additional blank annals, 'C' gets two years ahead. The lead is reduced to one in 853 by 'C''s omission of a blank annal; but it retains this dating one year in advance of the true date at least for the rest of the century.

[13] Asser adds: 'of Devon'.

[14] Perhaps, as Magoun suggests, Wigborough, near South Petherton, Somerset; but this is not very near the Devon border, and the name Wicga is so common in Devon names that a 'Wicga's hill' may well once have existed there.

[15] 'A' omits 'on Thanet'; Asser has instead 'Sheppey'. Probably his MS. of the Chronicle agreed with 'A' in omitting the name, and he supplied a different one. Æthelweard has Thanet.

[16] 'D', 'E', 'F' omit the mention of London; so did the MS. of Asser, but accidentally, for its next words are descriptive of London.

[17] These words, being in 'A', 'D', 'E', 'F', must have been in the original version.

[18] 'D', 'E', 'F' omit 'until this present day'.

And the same year, King Athelstan and Ealdorman Ealhhere fought in ships[1] and slew a great army at Sandwich in Kent, and captured nine[2] ships and put the others to flight.[3]

C (A, B)   D (E)

53 (854 C) In this year Burgred, king of the Mercians, and his council asked King Æthelwulf to help him to bring the Welsh under subjection to him. He then did so, and went with his army across Mercia against the Welsh, and they made[4] them all submissive to him. And that same year King Æthelwulf sent his son Alfred to Rome. The lord Leo was then pope of Rome, and he consecrated him king[6] and stood sponsor to him at confirmation.

(852 E) in this year Burgred, king of the Mercians, subjected to himself the Welsh with King Æthelwulf's help.[5]

Then the same year Ealhhere with the people of Kent and Huda with the people of Surrey fought in Thanet[7] against the heathen army, and at first had the victory;[8] and many men on both sides were killed and drowned there, and both the ealdormen killed.[9]

C (A, B)   D (E)

And afterwards, after Easter, King Æthelwulf gave his daughter in marriage to King Burgred,[10] from Wessex to Mercia.

And Burgred, king of the Mercians, married the daughter of Æthelwulf, king of the West Saxons.

855–858[11] (855 A, D, E; 856 C, F) In this year heathen men for the first time stayed in Sheppey over the winter. And the same year King Æthelwulf conveyed by charter the tenth part of his land throughout all his kingdom to the praise of God and his own eternal salvation. And he went to Rome the same year with great state,[12] and remained there a twelvemonth, and then went homewards. And Charles, king

---

[1] 'A' and Asser omit 'fought in ships and'.

[2] From 'A', 'D', 'E', 'F', Asser and Æthelweard. 'B', 'C' have eight.

[3] This paragraph is in its present place in 'B', 'C', 'D', 'E', 'F', and Asser; 'A' puts it earlier in the annal, after the battle of Wicganbeorg, and Æthelweard puts it in his preceding annal, which he dates seven years previously. It looks as if it were a marginal addition in the original, inserted into the text differently by the various copies. After this annal, 'E' adds a notice of a benefaction to Peterborough.

[4] In 'B' and 'C' the verb is singular, thus allowing Burgred no share in the campaign, but Asser mentions his presence.

[5] Note the varying sympathies betrayed by the different emphasis of the two versions.

[6] On this error and its significance for the origin of the Chronicle, see p. xxiii.

[7] Asser adds that its British name was *Ruim*.

[8] 'D', 'E' omit this clause.

[9] 'A' and Æthelweard omit this last clause.

[10] Asser adds: 'in the royal residence which is called Chippenham'.

[11] The annal form is temporarily laid aside and the events of four years related. For these events, see Asser (*E.H.D.*, I, pp. 264 f.) and the *Annals of St Bertin's* (*ibid.*, No. 23).

[12] Asser says that he took Alfred with him.

of the Franks, gave him his daughter as his queen. And afterwards he came home to his people, and they were glad of it.[1] And two years[2] after he had come from France, he died, and his body is buried in Winchester,[3] and he had reigned 18 years and a half.[4] And Æthelwulf was the son of Egbert,[5] the son of Ealhmund, the son of Eafa, the son of Eoppa, the son of Ingild. Ingild was the brother of Ine, king of the West Saxons, who held the kingdom for 37 years[6] and afterwards went to St. Peter's and ended his life there. And they were sons of Cenred. Cenred was the son of Ceolwold, the son of Cutha,[7] the son of Cuthwine, the son of Ceawlin, the son of Cynric, the son of Creoda,[8] the son of Cerdic. Cerdic was the son of Elesa, the son of Esla,[9] the son of Gewis, the son of Wig, the son of Freawine, the son of Freothogar, the son of Brand, the son of Bældæg,[10] the son of Woden, the son of Frealaf,[11] the son of Finn, the son of Godwulf, the son of Geat, the son of Tætwa, the son of Beaw, the son of Sceldwa,[12] the son of Heremod, the son of Itermon, the son of Hathra,[13] the son of Hwala, the son of Bedwig, the son of Sceaf,[14] i.e. the son of Noah.[15] He was born in Noah's ark. Lamech, Methuselah, Enoch, Jared, Mahalaleel, Cainan,[16] Enos, Seth, Adam the first man and our father, i.e. Christ.[15] [Amen.][17]

And then Æthelwulf's two sons succeeded to the kingdom, Æthelbald to the kingdom of the West Saxons and Ethelbert to the kingdom of the people of Kent [and the kingdom of the East Saxons],[18] and of the people of Surrey, and to the kingdom of the South Saxons, and then Æthelbald reigned five years.[19]

---

[1] Instead of this clause, 'D', 'E', 'F' have merely 'and came home safe'.

[2] As Æthelwulf was still in France on 1 October 856, and according to Florence of Worcester he died 13 January 858, Æthelweard, who has 'one year', is nearer the truth than the Chronicle.

[3] The *Annals of St Neots* have Steyning, which may come from the copy of the Chronicle they used. If so, Æthelwulf's body was moved to Winchester later.

[4] 'E': 9; 'F': 20.

[5] 'E' omits the rest of the genealogy; 'D' similarly reads from the death of Æthelwulf to the notice about his successors at the end of the annal, but then, unlike 'E', 'D' has the genealogy, as in 'A', 'B', 'C'. As it then follows on with the account of the successors, it has this twice, though only its second entry is complete.

[6] The clause giving the length of the reign is not in 'A' or Æthelweard.

[7] Æthelweard omits Cutha.

[8] 'A' and Æthelweard omit Creoda.

[9] 'D' omits Esla.

[10] Balder in Æthelweard.

[11] 'A' and Æthelweard have two extra names: Frithuwald and Frithuwulf, one before and one after Frealaf.

[12] Æthelweard has Scyld, the form of the name as it occurs in *Beowulf*. He then omits all the names until Sceaf (Scef), again as in *Beowulf*.

[13] Hrawa, 'A', which then omits the next three names, thus making Hrawa born in the ark.

[14] Æthelweard here adds the story of the mysterious arrival of Scef in a ship on the island of Skåne as a child, and his acceptance as king – a story which the *Beowulf* poet applied to Scyld. Æthelweard takes the genealogy no farther.

[15] This explanation is in Latin.

[16] Camon in all texts.

[17] This is in 'A' only. Some have seen the end of an older version of the Chronicle here. But see p. xxii.

[18] In 'A', 'B', and 'D''s second version; the omission in 'C' is therefore an error. 'E' omits all between 'kingdom of the West Saxons' and 'and of the people of Surrey', thus omitting all reference to the second son; so does 'D', in its first version, drawn from the same source as 'E', and it also omits 'the kingdom of the West Saxons'. 'E' omits also 'the kingdom of the South Saxons'. 'F', however, fills in the lacuna, from 'A'. Asser omits Essex.

[19] The *Annals of St Neots* add: 'Æthelbald his son reigned two and a half years after him, and he previously reigned two and a half years with his father.' 'F' adds: 'He had sent Alfred his third son to Rome, and when Pope Leo heard that he had died . . . he then consecrated Alfred as king and stood sponsor to him at confirmation, just as his father Æthelwulf asked when he sent him there.'

860 (861 C, F) In this year King Æthelbald died, and his body is buried at Sherborne. And then his brother Ethelbert succeeded to the whole kingdom and held it in good harmony [and in great peace].[1] And in his time a great naval force came inland and stormed Winchester; and[2] Ealdorman Osric[3] with the men of Hampshire and Ealdorman Æthelwulf with the men of Berkshire fought against that army, and they put the army to flight and had possession of the battle-field.[4] And Ethelbert reigned five years, and his body is buried in Sherborne.

F861 In this year St. Swithin died.

865 (866 C) In this year the heathen army encamped on Thanet and made peace with the people of Kent. And the people of Kent promised them money for that peace. And under cover of that peace[5] and promise of money the army stole away inland by night and ravaged all eastern Kent.[6]

866 (867 C) In this year Ethelbert's brother Ethelred succeeded to the kingdom of the West Saxons. And the same year a great heathen army[7] came into England and took up winter quarters in East Anglia; and there they were supplied with horses, and the East Angles made peace with them.

867 (868 C) In this year the army went from East Anglia to Northumbria, across the Humber estuary to the city of York.[8] And there was great civil strife going on in that people,[9] and they had deposed their king Osbert and taken a king with no hereditary right, Ælla. And not until late in the year did they unite sufficiently to proceed to fight the raiding army;[10] and nevertheless they collected a large army and attacked the enemy in York,[11] and broke into the city; and some of them got inside,[12] and an immense slaughter was made of the Northumbrians, some inside and some outside, and both kings were killed, and the survivors made peace with the enemy.[13] And the same year[14] Bishop Ealhstan died,

[1] From 'A'. 'D', 'E', 'F' omit not only this, but 'in good harmony' as well. It is freedom from internal dissension that is meant, as we can gather from Asser, but the later versions of the Chronicle may have felt that the remark about peace was contradicted by the next sentence in the annal.

[2] Asser adds: 'when they were returning to the ships with immense booty'.

[3] So 'A', 'D', 'E', Asser, and Æthelweard. 'B' and 'C' unaccountably have 'Wulfweard', though this ealdorman died in 840.

[4] This is the engagement mentioned in the Annals of St Bertin's. See E.H.D., I, No. 23.

[5] 'D', 'E' omit this phrase.

[6] Asser adds: 'for they knew that they would seize more money by secret plunder than by peace'.

[7] This is generally known as the 'Great Danish Army', and tradition said it was led by the sons of Ragnar Lothbrok. One of these is mentioned as leader in Æthelweard's version of this annal, namely Igwar (i.e. Ivar).

[8] Simeon, History of the Church of Durham, says they took it on 1 November.

[9] Asser adds: 'as always happens to a people which has incurred the wrath of God'.

[10] The general sense is clear, but the wording ambiguous. A. H. Smith renders: 'They resolved upon this, that they would continue fighting.'

[11] The anonymous History of St Cuthbert and Roger of Wendover both date it Palm Sunday (23 March), Simeon, 21 March.

[12] Asser explains: 'For that city had not as yet in those times strong and stout walls.'

[13] Simeon says the Northumbrians were led by eight earls as well as the kings.

[14] Æthelweard adds: 'Eanwulf, ealdorman of the province of Somerset, died.'

and he had held the bishopric of Sherborne for 50 years, and his body is buried in the cemetery there.[1]

868 (869 C) In this year the same army went into Mercia to Nottingham and took up winter quarters there. And Burgred, king of the Mercians, and his councillors asked Ethelred, king of the West Saxons, and his brother Alfred to help him to fight against the army. They then went with the army of the West Saxons into Mercia to Nottingham, and came upon the enemy in that fortress and besieged them there.[2] There occurred no serious battle there, and the Mercians made peace with the enemy.

869 (870 C) In this year the raiding army returned to the city of York, and stayed there one year.

870 (871 C) In this year the raiding army rode across Mercia into East Anglia, and took up winter quarters at Thetford. And that winter King[3] Edmund fought against them,[4] and the Danes had the victory, and killed the king[5] and conquered all the land.[6] And the same year Archbishop Ceolnoth died.[7]

871 (872 C) In this year the army came into Wessex to Reading,[8] and three days later two Danish earls rode farther inland.[9] Then Ealdorman Æthelwulf encountered them at Englefield, and fought against them there and had the victory, and one of them, whose name was Sidroc, was killed there.[10] Then four days later King Ethelred and his brother Alfred led a great army to Reading[11] and fought against the army; and a great slaughter was made on both sides and Ealdorman Æthelwulf was killed, and the Danes had possession of the battle-field.[12]

And four days later King Ethelred and his brother Alfred fought against the whole army at

---

[1] Æthelweard adds: 'and that of the above-mentioned ealdorman in the monastery which is called Glastonbury'.

[2] 'A' omits all reference to this siege. Asser adds: 'Since the pagans, defended by the protection of the fortress, refused to give battle, and the Christians could not break the wall, peace was made between the Mercians and the pagans, and the two brothers Ethelred and Alfred returned home with their forces.'

[3] 'E': 'Saint'.

[4] Æthelweard: 'For a short time.'

[5] Æthelweard adds: 'and his body lies buried in the place which is called *Beadoriceswyrth*' (Bury St Edmunds).

[6] 'F' names the leaders Ingware and Ubba. 'E' has a Peterborough addition, which is not so exclusively local in its interest as most others: 'and they destroyed all the monasteries they came to. In this same time they came to *Medeshamstede* (Peterborough), burnt and destroyed it, killed the abbot and the monks and all they found there, and brought it to pass that it became nought that had been very mighty'. Æthelweard adds: 'and their king Ivar died the same year'.

[7] Asser and Æthelweard mention his burial at Canterbury; 'D' in error has 'went to Rome' for 'died'; a Canterbury addition to 'A' has: 'and Ethelred, bishop of Wiltshire, was elected archbishop of Canterbury'; 'F' has a long spurious insertion, about the replacement of clerics by monks.

[8] Asser, 'a royal residence'.

[9] Asser adds: 'the remainder making a rampart between the two rivers Thames and Kennet, on the right-hand (i.e. southern) side of this same royal residence'.

[10] 'A', 'F', and Æthelweard do not mention the death of this earl. Asser does, but he does not name him. It is probable that the name was added in the archetype of the other four MSS. of the Chronicle in error, anticipating the account of the battle of Ashdown.

[11] Asser has details that look like mere embroidery.

[12] Æthelweard has an interesting addition: 'Truly the body of the aforesaid ealdorman was stealthily removed and taken into the province of the Mercians to the place which is called *Northworthig*, but Derby in the Danish tongue.' Berkshire had been a Mercian area until the reign of King Æthelwulf, and retained its Mercian ealdorman after it came into West Saxon hands.

Ashdown;[1] and the Danes were in two divisions: in the one were the heathen kings[2] Bagsecg and Healfdene, and in the other were the earls. And then King Ethelred fought against the kings' troop, and King Bagsecg was slain there; and Ethelred's brother Alfred fought against the earls' troop, and there were slain Earl Sidroc the Old,[3] and Earl Sidroc the Younger[4] and Earl Osbearn, Earl Fræna, and Earl Harold; and both enemy armies were put to flight and many thousands were killed, and they continued fighting until night.

And a fortnight later King Ethelred and his brother Alfred fought against the army at Basing, and there the Danes had the victory. And two months later, King Ethelred and his brother Alfred fought against the army at *Meretun*,[5] and they were in two divisions; and they put both to flight and were victorious far on into the day; and there was a great slaughter on both sides; and the Danes had possession of the battle-field. And Bishop Heahmund[6] was killed there and many important men. And after this battle a great summer army came to Reading.[7] And afterwards, after Easter,[8] King Ethelred died, and he had reigned five years, and his body is buried at Wimborne[9] minster.

Then his brother Alfred, the son of Æthelwulf, succeeded to the kingdom of the West Saxons. And a month later King Alfred fought with a small force against the whole army at Wilton[10] and put it to flight far on into the day; and the Danes had possession of the battle-field. And during that year nine[11] general engagements were fought against the Danish army in the kingdom south of the Thames, besides the expeditions which the king's brother Alfred and [single][12] ealdormen and king's thegns often rode on, which were not counted. And that year nine[13] (Danish) earls were killed and one king. And the West Saxons made peace with the army that year.

872 (873 C) In this year the army went from Reading to London, and took up winter quarters there; and then the Mercians made peace with the army.

C (A, B)	D (E)
873 (874 C) In this year the army went into Northumbria,[14] and it took up winter quarters at Torksey in Lindsey; and then the Mercians made peace with the army.	In this year the army took up winter quarters at Torksey.

[1] Asser has a fuller account of this battle than he could have got from the Chronicle. He says that Alfred had to begin the battle alone, since his brother was hearing Mass and refused to leave until it was over; that the Danes had the higher ground, and that the battle raged round a thorn-tree which he had himself seen. Æthelweard, on the other hand, abbreviates the Chronicle account, though when speaking of the Danish losses he adds: 'Never before or since has such a destruction been heard of, from the time when the people of the Saxons obtained Britain by war.'

[2] Nothing is known of Bagsecg. Healfdene was reputed to be a son of Ragnar Lothbrok.

[3] 'D' accidentally omits the first Sidroc.

[4] So in 'B', 'C'. The rest have 'the Young'.

[5] Asser omits this battle.

[6] Bishop of Sherborne. Æthelweard adds that he was buried at Keynsham.

[7] 'A' and Asser omit this reference to Reading, but it is in 'B', 'C', 'D', 'E', and in Æthelweard.

[8] 15 April.

[9] 'C': Sherborne.

[10] Æthelweard does not mention this battle by name. He speaks of a battle lost by the smallness of the English force when King Alfred was attending his brother's funeral; but the Chronicle says Alfred was at the battle of Wilton. Asser describes in some detail the flight of the Danes and their turning on their pursuers.

[11] Asser, who omitted *Meretun*, has eight.

[12] In 'A' only.

[13] Æthelweard has eleven.

[14] Because of a Northumbrian revolt. See *E.H.D.*, I, p. 256.

874 (875 C) In this year the army went from Lindsey to Repton and took up winter quarters there, and drove King Burgred across the sea, after he had held the kingdom 22 years. And they conquered all that land. And he went to Rome and settled there; and his body is buried in the church of St. Mary in the English quarter.[1] And the same year they gave the kingdom of the Mercians to be held by Ceolwulf,[2] a foolish king's thegn; and he swore oaths to them and gave hostages, that it should be ready for them on whatever day they wished to have it, and he would be ready, himself and all who would follow him, at the enemy's service.

875 (876 C) In this year the army left Repton: Healfdene went with part of the army into Northumbria and took up winter quarters by the River Tyne. And the army conquered the land and often ravaged among the Picts and the Strathclyde Britons; and the three kings, Guthrum, Oscetel, and Anwend, went from Repton to Cambridge with a great force, and stayed there a year. And that summer King Alfred went out to sea with a naval force, and fought against the crews of seven ships, and captured one ship and put the rest to flight.

876 (877 C) In this year the enemy army[3] slipped past the army of the West Saxons into Wareham;[4] and then the king made peace with the enemy and they gave him hostages, who were the most important men next to their king in the army,[5] and swore oaths to him on the holy ring[6] – a thing which they would not do before for any nation – that they would speedily leave his kingdom. And then under cover of that, they – the mounted army – stole by night away from the English army to Exeter.

And that year Healfdene shared out the land of the Northumbrians, and they proceeded to plough and to support themselves.

877 (878 C) In this year the enemy army from Wareham came to Exeter; [and the naval force sailed west along the coast][7] and encountered a great storm[8] at sea, and 120 ships were lost at Swanage. And King Alfred rode after the mounted army with the English army as far as Exeter, but could not overtake them [before they were in the fortress where they could not be reached].[9] And they gave him hostages[10] there, as many as he wished to have,[11] and swore great oaths and then kept a firm peace. Then in the harvest season[12] the army went away into Mercia[13] and shared out some of it, and gave some to Ceolwulf.

---

[1] See p. 39, n. 11.

[2] 'A' omits the name, but all other MSS., as well as Asser and Æthelweard, have it.

[3] Æthelweard adds: 'which was in Cambridge'.

[4] As usual, Asser describes the location more fully, telling us that it was a nunnery, between the rivers Frome and Tarrant, with a very secure situation except where, on the west, it joined the mainland.

[5] This passage about hostages is not in 'A', but in all the other MSS. It clearly belongs to the original Chronicle, for both Asser and Æthelweard refer to hostages here.

[6] A sacred ring, normally kept in the inner sanctuary of the heathen temples, and worn by the chief at assemblies, is mentioned in the saga literature of Iceland. According to *Eyrbyggja Saga*, chap. IV, all oaths were sworn on it.

[7] Omitted by 'B', 'C'.

[8] From 'A', 'E', 'D'; 'B', 'C': 'mist'.

[9] Omitted by 'B', 'C'.

[10] 'A', 'D', 'E' read: 'preliminary hostages'.

[11] Æthelweard: 'More than were asked for.'

[12] Asser says: 'in the month of August'. Harvest began on 7 August.

[13] Æthelweard supplies the additional information that they built booths in the town of Gloucester.

878 (879 C) In this year in midwinter after twelfth night the enemy army came stealthily to Chippenham,[1] and occupied the land of the West Saxons and settled there, and drove a great part of the people across the sea, and conquered most of the others; and the people submitted to them,[2] except King Alfred.[3] He journeyed in difficulties through the woods and fen-fastnesses with a small force.[4]

And the same winter the brother of Ivar and Healfdene[5] was in the kingdom of the West Saxons [in Devon],[6] with 23 ships.[7] And he was killed there and 840[8] men of his army with him.[9] And there was captured the banner which they called 'Raven'.[10]

And afterwards at Easter,[11] King Alfred with a small force made a stronghold at Athelney, and he and the section of the people of Somerset which was nearest to it[12] proceeded to fight from that stronghold against the enemy. Then in the seventh week after Easter he rode to 'Egbert's stone'[13] east of Selwood, and there came to meet him all the people of Somerset and of Wiltshire and of that part of Hampshire which was on this side of the sea,[14] and they rejoiced to see him. And then after one night he went from that encampment to Iley,[15] and after another night to Edington, and there fought against the whole army and put it to flight, and pursued it as far as the fortress,[16] and stayed there a fortnight. And then the enemy gave him preliminary hostages and great oaths[17] that they would leave his kingdom, and promised also that their king should receive baptism, and they kept their promise. Three weeks later King Guthrum with 30[18] of the men who were the most important in the army came [to him] at Aller, which is near Athelney, and the king stood sponsor to him at his baptism there; and the unbinding

---

[1] Asser: 'A royal residence.' He says that the Danes wintered there.

[2] This clause is omitted in 'D', 'E'.

[3] 'A' and 'B': 'and conquered and subjected to them most of the others, except King Alfred'. 'D' and 'E' simplify by omission of 'and subjected to them'.

Æthelweard, often well informed on the ealdormen of Somerset, adds: 'Also Æthelnoth, ealdorman of the province of Somerset, stayed with a small force in a certain wood.'

[4] Asser elaborates this. He places the woods and fens in Somerset, and explains the difficulties: 'For he had nothing to live on except what he could seize by frequent raids, either secretly or openly, from the pagans and even from the Christians who had surrendered to the rule of the pagans.'

[5] Gaimar, a twelfth-century writer, assumes that this brother is Ubba, whom tradition associated with Hingwar (Ivar) in the killing of St Edmund.

[6] Omitted by 'B', 'C'.

[7] Both Asser and Æthelweard have further information. Asser says he had come from Dyfed (South Wales), where he had spent the winter and massacred many Christians, and gives details of the defence and sortie of the English from a fort he calls Cynwit (Countisbury). Æthelweard also refers to the siege of a fort. He names Odda, ealdorman of Devon, as the English leader. Strangely enough, he assigns the victory to the Danes.

[8] 'B', 'C': 860.

[9] This is strangely worded in all MSS. as '800 men with him and 40 [60] men of his army'. B. Dickins suggests that here,

'army', was an error for hired, 'retinue', but if so, already the archetype was wrong. M. Hoffmann-Hirtz would read '40 headmen of his army'. Asser has 1,200, Æthelweard 800.

[10] The capture of the raven banner is in 'B', 'C', 'D', 'E', but not in 'A', 'F', Asser, or Æthelweard. The Annals of St Neots have it also, but it is not certain that they took it from the version of the Chronicle they used, for they add later legendary matter, e.g. that the banner was woven by the daughters of Ragnar Lothbrok, and the raven fluttered before victory, drooped before defeat; 'and this has often been proved'.

[11] 23 March.

[12] Æthelweard says he had no helpers but the members of his household.

[13] This cannot be identified.

[14] Probably this means Hampshire west of Southampton Water, though some scholars follow Asser in interpreting it to mean the men of Hampshire who had not fled abroad. But was it only the people of Hampshire who fled?

[15] Iley Oak (now lost) near Warminster, Wilts.

[16] Asser adds: 'and seized all things which he found outside the fort, men and horses and cattle, and slew the men at once'. Cf. annal 893. In the end, the Danes surrendered in desperation, from hunger, cold, and terror.

[17] Asser is fuller: 'They sought peace on these terms, that the king should receive from them distinguished hostages, as many as he wished, and should not give one to them. Never before, indeed, had they made peace with anyone on such terms.'

[18] Literally 29, but see p. 15, n. 11.

of the chrism[1] took place at Wedmore. And he was twelve days with the king, and he honoured him and his companions greatly with gifts.

879 (880 C) In this year the army went from Chippenham to Cirencester, and stayed there for one year. And the same year a band of vikings assembled[2] and encamped at Fulham by the Thames. And the same year there was an eclipse of the sun for one hour of the day.[3]

880 (881 C) In this year the army went from Cirencester into East Anglia, and settled there and shared out the land. And the same year the army which had encamped at Fulham went overseas into the Frankish empire to Ghent and stayed there for a year.

881 (882 C) In this year the army went farther inland into the Frankish empire, and the Franks fought against them;[4] and the Danish army provided itself with horses after that battle.

882 (883 C) In this year the army went farther[5] into the Frankish empire along the Meuse,[6] and stayed there a year. And the same year King Alfred went out with ships to sea and fought against four crews of Danish men, and captured two of the ships – and the men were killed[7] who were on them – and two crews surrendered to him. And they had great losses in killed or wounded before they surrendered.

883 (884 C) In this year the army went up the Scheldt to Condé,[8] and stayed there for a year.[9] And Pope Marinus sent some wood of the Cross to King Alfred. And that same year Sigehelm and Athelstan took to Rome the alms [which King Alfred had promised thither],[10] and also to India[11] to St. Thomas and St. Bartholomew, when the English were encamped against the enemy army at London; and there, by the grace of God, their prayers were well answered after that promise.

884 (885 C) In this year the army went up the Somme to Amiens, and stayed there a year.

[1] For eight days after baptism, white robes were worn and a white cloth, bound round the head after the anointment with the chrism. The ceremony of its removal is what is meant here. Æthelweard gives Ealdorman Æthelnoth a share in this ceremony.

[2] Asser says that it joined the former army, but nevertheless wintered in Fulham.

[3] Asser adds: 'between nones and vespers, but nearer to nones'. It is probably the eclipse of 29 October 878.

[4] Probably the Frankish victory of Saucourt, August 881. Æthelweard says that the Franks had the victory, and put the Danes to flight.

[5] 'A' and Asser have 'far'.

[6] Æthelweard says they camped in Escelun (i.e. Elsloo).

[7] By a change of the auxiliary verb, 'B', 'C' suggest that the men were killed after the capture, whereas in 'A' and Asser it is clear that they were dead before it. 'D', 'E', 'F' go still further and say, 'and they slew the men'.

[8] Asser adds that there was a nunnery there.

[9] The rest of this annal is not in 'A', Asser, or Æthelweard. It has suspicious features. We know of no occasion in or before 883 when the English were encamped against London. Yet as it is in all the MSS. except 'A', it must be an early addition, perhaps misplaced. For what may be meant by India, see Stevenson's edition of Asser, pp. 286–290.

[10] From 'D', 'E'. Something is required to complete the sense in 'B', 'C', but it does not follow that the reading in 'D', 'E' represents the original, rather than an attempt of their common source to make sense of a corrupt passage.

[11] From 'D', 'E', 'F'. 'B', 'C': 'Judea'.

85 (886 C) In this year the aforesaid army divided into two [one part going east],[1] the other part to Rochester, where they besieged the city and made other fortifications round themselves.[2] And nevertheless the English defended the city until King Alfred came up with his army.[3] Then the enemy went to their ships and abandoned their fortification, and they were deprived of their horses there, and immediately that same summer they went back across the sea.[4] That same year King Alfred sent a naval force from Kent[5] into East Anglia. Immediately they came into the mouth of the Stour[6] they encountered 16 ships of vikings and fought against them, and seized all the ships and killed the men. When they turned homeward with the booty, they met a large naval force of vikings[7] and fought against them on the same day, and the Danes had the victory.

That same year before Christmas, Charles,[8] king of the Franks, died. He was killed by a boar, and a year previously his brother,[9] who had also held the western kingdom, had died. They were both sons of Louis,[10] who died in the year of the eclipse of the sun.[11] He was the son of that Charles[12] whose daughter Æthelwulf, king of the West Saxons, had married.[13] That same year a large naval force[14] assembled among the Old Saxons and twice in the year there occurred a great battle, and the Saxons had the victory, and with them there were the Frisians.

That same year Charles[15] succeeded to the western kingdom and to all the kingdom on this side of the Mediterranean and beyond this sea,[16] as his great-grandfather[17] had held it, except for Brittany. This Charles was the son of Louis,[18] the brother of the Charles who was the father of Judith whom King Æthelwulf married; and they were sons of Louis.[19] This Louis was the son of the old Charles.[20] This Charles was Pippin's son.

---

[1] From 'A', 'D', 'E'. Æthelweard says that they went to Louvain.

[2] The last clause is omitted by 'D', 'E'.

[3] Asser's account is fuller and sounds genuine: 'And then the pagans left their fortifications and abandoned all the horses which they had brought with them from the Frankish empire, and also left the greater number of their prisoners in the fort, for the king had come there suddenly; and they fled instantly to the ships, and the Saxons at once seized the prisoners and the horses abandoned by the pagans.'

[4] Æthelweard's account of this year is extremely important. See F. M. Stenton, in *Essays presented to T. F. Tout*, pp. 20–21. One can see from it that the original Chronicle must have had two consecutive sentences ending 'went across the sea', and all our extant MSS. go back on a text which has accidentally lost the second of them, the scribe having continued after the second, instead of the first occurrence of the words. Unfortunately Æthelweard's Latin is particularly obscure in this annal; yet it is clear that only some of the invaders went back across the sea at this moment. The others came to terms with Alfred, but twice broke them by raiding the country south of the Thames. They received aid from the Danes settled in East Anglia, and they encamped at Benfleet, on the north bank of the Thames estuary. There, however, some sort of quarrel occurred and they went across the sea. This passage, accidentally omitted from the extant versions of the Chronicle, explains Alfred's attack on East Anglia.

[5] 'A' omits 'from Kent'.

[6] Erroneously written *Stufe* for *Sture* by 'A', 'B', 'C', and Æthelweard. The correct form is in 'D', 'E', and Asser.

[7] Asser adds that it was collected by the pagans inhabiting East Anglia.

[8] Carloman, correctly given by Asser. Also the *Annals of Fulda* call him Charles. He died 12 December 884.

[9] Asser adds his name, Louis. He died 5 August 882.

[10] 'A' adds: 'who also had held the western kingdom'.

[11] Louis the Stammerer died 10 April 879.

[12] Charles the Bald.

[13] 'E' omits from this point until after 'Pippin's son'.

[14] Asser adds: 'from Germany'.

[15] The Fat, deposed in 887. Asser calls him 'king of the Germans'.

[16] Possibly the English Channel. Asser has: 'the arm of the sea that lies between the Old Saxons and the Gauls'. But it may refer back to the Mediterranean, the lands beyond being in Italy.

[17] Charles the Great.

[18] The German, died 876.

[19] The Pious.

[20] The Great.

That same year there died the good pope, Marinus,[1] who had freed from taxation the English quarter[2] at the request of Alfred, king [of the West Saxons].[3] And he had sent him great gifts, including part of the Cross on which Christ suffered.

And that same year the Danish army in East Anglia[4] violated their peace with King Alfred.

886 (887 C) In this year the Danish army which had gone east went west again, and then up the Seine, and made their winter quarters there at the town of Paris.[5]

That same year King Alfred occupied[6] London; and all the English people that were not under subjection to the Danes submitted to him. And he then entrusted the borough to the control of Ealdorman Ethelred.[7]

887 (888 C) In this year the Danish army went up past the bridge at Paris, then up along the Seine to the Marne, and then up the Marne as far as Chézy, and stayed there and in the Yonne area, spending two winters[8] in those two places.

And the same year Charles,[9] king of the Franks, died; and six weeks before he died his brother's son Arnulf had deprived him of the kingdom.[10] The kingdom was then divided into five, and five kings were consecrated to it. It was done, however, with Arnulf's consent and they said that they would hold it under him, for not one of them was born to it in the male line but him alone. Arnulf then lived in the land east of the Rhine, and Rudolf[11] succeeded to the middle kingdom and Odo[12] to the western portion; and Berengar[13] and Guido[14] to Lombardy and the lands on that side of the Alps; and they held it with much discord and fought two general engagements,[15] and ravaged[16] the land again and again, and each repeatedly drove out the other.

And the same year in which the army went up beyond the bridge at Paris, Ealdorman Æthelhelm[17] took to Rome the alms of King Alfred and the West Saxons.[18]

---

[1] He died 15 May 884.

[2] See p. 39, n. 11.

[3] From 'A', 'D', and 'E'.

[4] 'E' has: 'went and violated their peace'.

[5] 'A' and Æthelweard omit the mention of Paris. Asser has it and more detail: 'They pitched a camp on both sides of the river near the bridge, to prevent the citizens from crossing the bridge – for that city is situated on a small island in the middle of the river – and besieged the city all that year. But since God compassionately befriended them and the citizens defended themselves manfully, they could not break through the fortifications.'

[6] It is clear from Asser's addition, that it was 'after the burning of cities and the massacre of people', that Alfred obtained London by warfare, and it is probably implied by Florence of Worcester, using some lost source, when he says: 'After his (the last Mercian king, Ceolwulf's) death, Alfred, king of the West Saxons, in order to expel completely the army of the pagan Danes from his kingdom, recovered London with the sur-

rounding areas by his activity, and acquired the part of the kingdom of the Mercians which Ceolwulf had held' (ed. Thorpe, I, p. 267).

[7] The lord of the Mercians, who married Alfred's daughter Æthelflæd. Under their rule, Mercia preserved its autonomy.

[8] The winters of 886–887, 887–888.

[9] Charles the Fat, who died in January 888.

[10] On 11 November 887.

[11] Count of Upper Burgundy.

[12] Count of Paris.

[13] Margrave of Friuli.

[14] Duke of Spoleto.

[15] If the battles of Brescia, autumn 888, and Trebbia, spring 889, are meant, this annal cannot have been composed until some way on in the latter year. It does not say they took place in 887.

[16] 'C': 'burnt'.

[17] Asser: 'of Wiltshire'.

[18] This is the last annal to be used by Asser.

888 (889 C) In this year Ealdorman Beocca took to Rome the alms of the West Saxons and of King Alfred. And Queen Æthelswith, who was King Alfred's sister, died,[1] and her body is buried in Pavia. And the same year Archbishop Ethelred and Ealdorman Æthelwold died in the same month.

889 (890 C) There was no expedition to Rome in this year, but King Alfred sent two couriers with letters.

890 (891 C) In this year Abbot Beornhelm took to Rome the alms of the West Saxons and of King Alfred. And the northern king, Guthrum, whose baptismal name was Athelstan, died.[2] He was King Alfred's godson, and he lived in East Anglia and was the first[3] to settle that land.

And the same year the Danish army went from the Seine to St. Lô, which lies between Brittany and France; and the Bretons fought against them and had the victory, and drove them into a river and drowned many of them.

F890 In this year Plegmund was elected by God and all the people to the archbishopric of Canterbury.[4]

891 (891 A, F; 892 C, D)[5] In this year the Danish army went east, and King Arnulf with the East Franks, the Saxons, and Bavarians fought against the mounted force before the ships arrived, and put it to flight.[6]

And three Scots came to King Alfred in a boat without any oars from Ireland, which they had left secretly, because they wished for the love of God to be in foreign lands, they cared not where. The boat in which they travelled was made of two and a half hides, and they took with them enough food for seven days. And after seven days they came to land in Cornwall, and went immediately to King Alfred.[7] Their names were as follows: Dubslane, Machbethu, and Maelinmum. And Swifneh, the best scholar among the Scots, died.

(892 A)[8] And the same year after Easter,[9] at the Rogation days[10] or before, there appeared the star which is called in Latin *cometa*. Some men say that it is in English the long-haired star, for there shines a long ray from it, sometimes on one side, sometimes on every side.[11]

---

[1] By a minor alteration, 'D', 'E' suggest that she was on her way to Rome, and 'F' says so expressly, but it may be only inference. She was wife of Burgred of Mercia.

[2] The *Annals of St Neots* say he was buried at the royal residence at Hadleigh.

[3] i.e. of the Danes.

[4] The compiler of 'F' added Plegmund's election into 'A'. It is entered in Latin in 'E'.

[5] 'E' omits this annal. 'C' continues one year ahead. 'D' and 'E' both have a blank annal 891, then 'D' puts this annal under 892 and continues to be in advance of the true date until 914.

[6] This is the great victory on the River Dyle. It used to be held that it occurred in November, in which case the chronicler is no longer beginning his year in September, for November 891 would have been entered under 892. But it is not certain that the battle was so late in the year, one continental opinion putting it in September, or even late August.

[7] Æthelweard says that then they went towards Rome, intending to go to Jerusalem.

[8] The first scribe in the Parker MS. ('A') ends with this annal number. The second scribe, with something to add to the annal, did not delete the number 892, though he begins his next annal 892. This repeat was got rid of later by someone who added one to the original dates of 'A' up to (and including) the blank annal 929. Possibly he compared a text like 'C' that was already one year ahead. As a result of this, 'A', 'C', and 'D' are all, for different reasons, one year in advance. 'E' and 'F' alone are correct for 892, but do not contain the subsequent annals. 'B' has no dates. I give the original dates of 'A', not the corrected ones.

[9] 4 April.

[10] 10–12 May.

[11] 'D' omits the last four words.

892 (892 A, E, F; 893 C, D)[1] In this year the great Danish army, which we have spoken about before, went back from[2] the eastern kingdom westward to Boulogne, and they were provided with ships there, so that they crossed in one journey, horses and all, and then came up into the estuary of the Lympne with 200 [and 50][3] ships. That estuary is in East Kent, at the east end of that great[4] wood which we call *Andred*.[5] The wood is from east to west 120 miles long, or longer, and 30 miles broad. The river, of which we spoke before, comes out of the Weald. They rowed their ships up the river as far as the Weald, four miles from the mouth of the estuary, and there they stormed a fortress. Inside that fortification[6] there were a few peasants, and it was only half made.

Then immediately afterwards Hæsten[7] came with 80 ships up the Thames estuary and made himself a fortress at Milton,[8] and the other army made one at Appledore.[9]

893[10] (894 C, D) In this year, that was twelve months after the Danes had built the fortress in the eastern kingdom, the Northumbrians and East Angles had given King Alfred oaths, and the East Angles had given six preliminary hostages; and yet, contrary to those pledges, as often as the other Danish armies went out in full force, they went either with them or on their behalf.[11] And then King Alfred collected his army, and advanced to take up a position between the two enemy forces, where he had the nearest convenient site with regard both to the fort in the wood and the fort by the water,[12] so that he could reach either army, if they chose to come into the open country. Then they went afterwards along the Weald in small bands and mounted companies, by whatever side it was then undefended by the English army. And also they were sought by other bands,[13] almost every day, either by day or by night, both from the English army and from the boroughs. The king had divided his army into two, so that always half its men were at home, half on service, apart from the men who guarded the boroughs. The enemy did not all come out of those encampments more than twice: once when they first landed, before the English force was assembled, and once when they wished to leave those encampments.[14] Then they captured much booty, and wished to carry it north across the Thames into Essex, to meet the ships. Then the English army intercepted them and fought against them at Farnham, and put the enemy to flight and recovered the booty. And the Danes fled across the Thames where there was no ford, and

---

[1] On these dates, see p. 53, n. 5.

[2] 'C' writes, 'into'.

[3] Omitted by 'B', 'C', 'D'. The *Annals of St Neots* have 350.

[4] So in 'A', 'E', 'F'; 'B', 'C', 'D': 'the same wood'.

[5] The Weald. See p. 11, n. 2.

[6] This is the reading of 'B', 'C', 'D'. 'A', 'E', 'F' read: '. . . stormed a fortress in the fen; inside were a few peasants.'

[7] Old Norse Hásteinn (*Hastingus*), a viking leader first heard of on the Loire in 866, who afterwards had an active career on the Continent.

[8] Milton Royal, or Regis, or King's Milton, near Sittingbourne, Kent.

[9] After this annal begins the long gap in 'E'. See p. xivf. 'E', 'F' have a Latin entry: 'In this year died Wulfhere, archbishop of the Northumbrians.'

[10] This annal is not in 'E'. On the dates, see p. 53, n. 5. In this

and the next six annals the word *Her* is not used to introduce the annals.

[11] 'C' has, wrongly, 'on the other side', but even the correct reading is not free from ambiguity. I take it to mean that they either joined the invading armies or made raids of their own to assist them. But some scholars would render 'or on their own behalf'.

[12] This is the usual interpretation, but one could render: 'where he had the nearest site affording him the protection of wood and water'.

[13] From 'A'. 'B', 'C', 'D' have an inferior reading, 'peoples'.

[14] Here Æthelweard, who has had nothing corresponding to the first part of this annal, supplies some information. He says that after Easter they raided as far as Wessex, and ravaged Hampshire and Berkshire, and that the army which intercepted them at Farnham was led by Alfred's son Edward.

up the Colne on to an islet.[1] Then the English forces besieged them there for as long as their provisions lasted; but they had completed their term of service and used up their provisions, and the king was then on the way there with the division which was serving with him. When he was on his way there and the other English army was on its way home, and the Danes were remaining behind there because their king had been wounded in the battle, so that they could not move him,[2] those Danes who lived in Northumbria and East Anglia collected some hundred ships, and went south round the coast. [And some 40 ships went north around the coast][3] and besieged a fortress on the north coast of Devon, and those who had gone south besieged Exeter.

When the king heard that, he turned west towards Exeter with the whole army, except for a very inconsiderable portion of the people (who continued) eastwards. They went on until they came to London, and then with the citizens and with the reinforcements which came to them from the west, they went east to Benfleet. Hæsten had then come there with his army which had been at Milton, and the large army which had been at Appledore on the estuary of the Lympne had then also come there. Hæsten had previously built that fortress at Benfleet; and he was then out on a raid, and the large army was at home. Then the English went there and put the enemy to flight, and stormed the fortress and captured all that was within, both goods, and women and also children, and brought all to London; and they either broke up or burnt all the ships, or brought them to London or to Rochester. And Hæsten's wife and two sons were brought to the king; and he gave them back to him, because one of them was his godson, and the other the godson of Ealdorman Ethelred. They had stood sponsor to them before Hæsten came to Benfleet,[4] and he had given the king oaths and hostages, and the king had also made him generous gifts of money, and so he did also when he gave back the boy and the woman. But immediately they came to Benfleet and had made that fortress, Hæsten ravaged his kingdom, that very province which Ethelred, his son's godfather, was in charge of; and again, a second time, he had gone on a raid in that same kingdom when his fortress was stormed.[5]

When the king had turned west with the army towards Exeter, as I have said before, and the Danish army had laid siege to the borough, they went to their ships when he arrived there. When he was occupied against the army there in the west, and the (other) two Danish armies were assembled at Shoebury in Essex, and had made a fortress there, they went both together up along the Thames, and a great reinforcement came to them both from the East Angles and the Northumbrians. [They then

---

[1] Æthelweard calls it Thorney, which has been identified by Sir Frank Stenton as an island near Iver, Bucks.

[2] The chronicler never makes it clear what happened next to these survivors of the great army. We find them a little later with Hæsten at Benfleet. Æthelweard allows us to fill in this gap. He says that Ealdorman Ethelred (whom he wrongly calls king) brought help from London to Edward, who was in charge of the eastward part of the English forces, and that the Danes came to terms, gave hostages, and swore to leave Alfred's kingdom; they then joined the ships from the Lympne at Mersea Island.

[3] From 'A'. It is omitted in the other MSS.

[4] Presumably, therefore, Alfred had been in negotiation during the period earlier in the year while he camped between the two armies; but it is just possible that these events took place in 885, where the original Chronicle no doubt had a reference to the sojourn of vikings at Benfleet, though owing to an accidental omission, we have only Æthelweard's garbled version to go by (see p. 51, n. 4). There is, however, no evidence that Hæsten was leading the army in England in that year.

[5] Is it from misunderstanding, or additional information, that the Annals of St Neots have instead of this last sentence: 'But when Hæsten came again to Benfleet he repaired there the fortress, which had been destroyed'?

went up along the Thames until they reached the Severn, then up along the Severn.]¹ Then Ealdorman Ethelred and Ealdorman Æthelhelm and Ealdorman Æthelnoth and the king's thegns who then were at home at the fortresses assembled from every borough east of the Parret, and both west and east of Selwood, and also north of the Thames and west of the Severn, and also some portion of the Welsh people. When they were all assembled, they overtook the Danish army at Buttington on the bank of the Severn, and besieged it on every side in a fortress. Then when they had encamped for many weeks on the two sides of the river, and the king was occupied in the west in Devon against the naval force, the besieged were oppressed by famine, and had eaten the greater part of their horses and the rest had died of starvation. They then came out against the men who were encamped on the east side of the river, and fought against them, and the Christians had the victory. And the king's thegn Ordheah and also many other king's thegns were killed, and a very great [slaughter]² of the Danes was made, and the part that escaped were saved by flight.

When they came to Essex to their fortress and their ships, the survivors collected again before winter a large army from the East Angles and Northumbrians, placed their women and ships and property in safety in East Anglia, and went continuously by day and night till they reached a deserted city in Wirral, which is called Chester. Then the English army could not overtake them before they were inside that fortress. However, they besieged the fortress for some two days, and seized all the cattle that was outside, and killed the men whom they could cut off outside the fortress, and burnt all the corn, or consumed it by means of their horses, in all the surrounding districts. And that was twelve months after they had come hither across the sea.³

894 (895 C, D)⁴ And then in this year, immediately after that, the Danish army went into Wales from Wirral, because they could not stay there. That was because they were deprived both of the cattle and the corn which had been ravaged. When they turned back from Wales with the booty they had captured there, they went, so that the English army could not reach them, across Northumbria and into East Anglia, until they came into east Essex on to an island called Mersea, which is out in the sea.

And when the Danish army which had besieged Exeter turned homewards, they ravaged up in Sussex near Chichester, and the citizens put them to flight and killed many hundreds of them, and captured some of their ships.

Then that same year in early winter⁵ the Danes who were encamped on Mersea rowed their ships up the Thames and up the Lea. That was two years after they came hither across the sea.⁶

---

¹ Supplied from 'A'. 'D' has the same statement in more concise wording.

² Supplied from 'D'. 'A' has omitted the whole clause, but it it is necessary for the sense.

³ Æthelweard makes no reference to the raid on Chester. Instead, after speaking of the capture of Benfleet and the battle of Buttington, he tells us that the pirate Sigeferth came with a fleet from Northumbria and twice ravaged the coast, and then returned home.

⁴ On the dates, see p. 53, n. 5. 'E' omits this annal.

⁵ So in all MSS. except 'A', which has 'before winter'.

⁶ Æthelweard says that when two years were completed from the arrival at Lympne, Ealdorman Æthelnoth went from Wessex to York against the enemy, who laid waste a large stretch of country in Mercia west of Stamford, between the Welland and the wood called Kesteven. This is probably to be connected with the raids of Sigeferth which he has just mentioned. On the importance of this information, see F. M. Stenton, in *Eng. Hist. Rev.*, XXIV (1909), pp. 79–84.

895 (896 C, D)[1] And in the same year[2] the aforesaid army made a fortress by the Lea, 20 miles above London. Then afterwards in the summer a great part of the citizens and also of other people marched till they arrived at the fortress of the Danes, and there they were put to flight and four king's thegns were slain. Then later, in the autumn, the king encamped in the vicinity of the borough while they were reaping their corn, so that the Danes could not deny them that harvest. Then one day the king rode up along the river, and examined where the river could be obstructed, so that they could not bring the ships out. And then this was carried out: two fortresses were made on the two sides of the river. When they had just begun that work [and had encamped for that purpose],[3] the enemy perceived that they could not bring the ships out. Then they abandoned the ships and went overland till they reached Bridgnorth on the Severn and built that fortress. Then the English army rode after the enemy, and the men from London fetched the ships, and broke up all which they could not bring away, and brought to London those which were serviceable. And the Danes had placed their women in safety in East Anglia before they left that fortress. Then they stayed the winter at Bridgnorth.[4] That was three years after they had come hither across the sea into the estuary of the Lympne.[5]

896 (897 C, D)[1] And afterwards in the summer of this year the Danish army divided, one force going into East Anglia and one into Northumbria; and those that were moneyless got themselves ships and went south across the sea to the Seine.

By the grace of God, the army had not on the whole afflicted the English people very greatly;[6] but they were much more seriously afflicted in those three years by the mortality of cattle and men, and most of all in that many of the best king's thegns who were in the land died in those three years. Of those, one was Swithwulf, bishop of Rochester, and Ceolmund, ealdorman of Kent, and Brihtwulf, ealdorman of Essex [and Wulfred, ealdorman of Hampshire],[7] and Ealhheard, bishop of Dorchester, and Eadwulf, a king's thegn in Sussex, and Beornwulf, the town-reeve of Winchester, and Ecgwulf, the king's marshal, and many besides them, though I have named the most distinguished.

In the same year the armies in East Anglia and Northumbria greatly harassed Wessex along the south coast with marauding bands, most of all with the warships which they had built many years before. Then King Alfred had 'long ships' built to oppose the Danish warships. They were almost twice as long as the others. Some had 60 oars, some more. They were both swifter and steadier and also higher than the others. They were built neither on the Frisian nor the Danish pattern, but as it seemed to him himself that they could be most useful. Then on a certain occasion of the same year, six ships came to the Isle of Wight and did great harm there, both in Devon and everywhere along the coast. Then the king ordered (a force) to go thither with nine of the new ships, and they blocked the

---

[1] On the dates, see p. 53, n. 5. 'E' omits this annal.

[2] The first sentence of this annal would have been better placed at the end of the previous one.

[3] 'C' omits this clause.

[4] This is given its full name, *Cwatbrycg*, at this point, only by 'A'. The others call it simply 'Bridge'.

[5] Æthelweard assigns to this year, on St Bartholomew's day (24 August), the death of Guthfrith, king of the Northumbrians, and says he was buried at York Minster.

[6] So 'B', 'C', 'D'; 'A': 'too greatly'.

[7] From 'A'; omitted by the other MSS.

estuary from the seaward end. Then the Danes went out against them with three ships, and three were on dry land farther up the estuary; the men from them had gone up on land. Then the English captured two of those three ships at the entrance to the estuary, and killed the men, and the one ship escaped. On it also the men were killed except five. These got away because the ships of their opponents ran aground. Moreover, they had run aground very awkwardly: three were aground on that side of the channel on which the Danish ships were aground, and all [the others]¹ on the other side, so that none of them could get to the others. But when the water had ebbed many furlongs from the ships, the Danes from the remaining three ships went to the other three which were stranded on their side, and they then fought there. And there were killed the king's reeve Lucuman, Wulfheard the Frisian, Æbba the Frisian, Æthelhere the Frisian, Æthelfrith the king's *geneat*,² and in all 62 Frisians and English and 120 of the Danes. Then, however, the tide reached the Danish ships before the Christians could launch theirs, and therefore they rowed away out. They were then so wounded that they could not row past Sussex, but the sea cast two of them on to the land, and the men were brought to Winchester³ to the king, and he ordered them to be hanged. And the men who were on the one ship reached East Anglia greatly wounded. That same summer no fewer than 20 ships, men and all, perished along the south coast. That same year died Wulfric, the king's marshal, who was [also]⁴ the Welsh-reeve.⁵

897 (898 C, D)⁶ In this year, nine days before midsummer, Æthelhelm, ealdorman of Wiltshire, died; and in this year died Heahstan,⁷ who was bishop of London.

	C (A, B)	D (E, F)
900	(901 C)⁸ in this year Alfred the son of Æthelwulf died, six days before All Saints' day. He was king over the whole English people except for that part which was under Danish rule, and he had held the kingdom for one and a half years less than thirty; and then his son Edward succeeded to the kingdom.	(901 D, E, F)⁸ In this year King Alfred died on 26 October; and he had held the kingdom 28 years and half a year; and then his son Edward succeeded to the kingdom.⁹

Then the atheling Æthelwold, his father's brother's son,¹⁰ rode and seized the residence at Wimborne¹¹ and at *Twinham*,¹² against the will of the king and his councillors.¹³ Then the king rode with the army

---

¹ From 'A'; omitted by the other MSS.

² A member of the king's household. See *E.H.D.*, I, p. 366, n. 3.

³ 'D': *Wiltunceastre*.

⁴ Supplied from 'A'.

⁵ It is uncertain what this term implies.

⁶ On the dates, see p. 53, n. 5. The annals now begin again with *Her*. 'E' omits this annal.

⁷ From 'A'; all other MSS. make the mistake of calling him Ealhstan.

⁸ On the dates, see p. 53, n. 5. Æthelweard records in 899, before Alfred's death, a great discord because of the hosts of

the Northumbrians, especially among the places still belonging to the English.

⁹ 'E' and 'F' end the annal here. 'D' continues with the other events, as in 'A', 'B', 'C'.

¹⁰ He was son of King Ethelred, Alfred's elder brother and predecessor.

¹¹ This was where his father was buried and probably belonged to his branch of the family.

¹² Now Christchurch, Hampshire.

¹³ 'A' reads: 'without the permission of the king and his councillors'.

till he encamped at Badbury[1] near Wimborne, and Æthelwold stayed inside the residence with the men who had given allegiance to him; and he had barricaded all the gates against him, and said that he would either live there or die there. Then meanwhile the atheling rode away[2] by night, and went to the Danish army in Northumbria, and they accepted him as king and gave allegiance to him.[3] Then the woman was seized whom he had taken without the king's permission and contrary to the bishops' orders – for she had been consecrated a nun.

And in this same year Ethelred, who was ealdorman of Devon, died four weeks before King Alfred.[4]

01[5] (902 A; 903 B, C, D) In this year Ealdorman Æthelwulf, the brother of Ealhswith, King Edward's mother,[6] died, and Virgilius, an abbot among the Scots, and the priest Grimbald.

02[7] (903 A; 904 B, C, D) In this year Æthelwold[8] came hither across the sea with all the fleet he could procure, and submission was made to him in Essex.[9]

Main Chronicle (A, B, C, D)	*Mercian Register*[10]
03[11] (904 A; 905 B, C, D) In this year Æthelwold induced[12] the army in East Anglia to break the peace so that they harried over all Mercia until they reached Cricklade. And they went then across the Thames, and carried off all that they could seize both in and round about Braydon, and turned then homeward. Then King Edward went after them as soon as he could collect his army, and harried all their land between the Dykes and the Ouse,[14] all as far north as the fens. When he wished to go back from there he had it announced over the whole army that they were all to set out together. Then the men	(902) In this year Ealhswith died,[13] and in the same year occurred the battle of the Holme between the people of Kent and the Danes.

[1] Badbury Rings, a prehistoric earthwork.
[2] 'A': 'He stole away.'
[3] It is interesting to note that our most West Saxon version, 'A', omits all reference to Æthelwold's acceptance as king. Instead, it says merely: 'And the king ordered them to pursue him, and then he could not be overtaken.'
[4] Æthelweard, who has no reference to the atheling's rebellion, says that in this year Æthelbald was consecrated archbishop of York, in London.
[5] This annal is not in 'E'. The chronology of this reign is confused. From 901 to 905, 'B', 'C', 'D', and the corrected dates in 'A' are two years ahead, the original dates in 'A' one year. Then 'A' dates 905, 'C', 'D', 906, the peace of Tiddingford, which, judging by Simeon, took place in 906. From then until 912, 'A' is correct, but from 913 to 920 it is three years ahead. 'C', 'D' are one year in advance from 908 to 914, and omit the later annals of Edward's reign. The insertion of the Mercian Register, in a block after a series of blank annals in 'B', 'C' (see p. xiv), piecemeal in 'D', causes further compli-

cation. I have given its annals under their true years, and I give the original dates of 'A'.
[6] 'A' omits 'King Edward's mother'.
[7] Probably the autumn of 901. 'E' omits this annal.
[8] *Annals of St Neots* add: 'king of the Danes'.
[9] 'A' merely says, 'came to Essex with the fleet with which he was'; 'D', 'came, with all the fleet which he could procure and which was subject to him, to Essex'.
[10] On this document, see p. xiv.
[11] The events of this annal probably took place at the end of 902, which was reckoned as 903, in a chronicle beginning its year 24 September.
[12] 'A' has 'seduced'. The *Annals of St Neots* call Æthelwold 'king of the pagans'.
[13] 5 December.
[14] The Dykes are the Devil's Dyke and Fleam Dyke. Ekwall thinks the river is the Wissey, but see *The Place-Names of Cambridgeshire*, pp. 12–14.

Main Chronicle (A, B, C, D)

of Kent lingered behind there against his command – and he had
sent seven messengers to them. Then the Danish army overtook
them there, and they fought there. And there were killed Ealdorman Sigewulf and Ealdorman Sigehelm,[1] and the king's thegn
Ealdwold, and Abbot Cenwulf, and Sigeberht, Sigewulf's son, and
Eadwold, Acca's son, and many besides them, though I have named
the most distinguished. And on the Danish side King Eohric[2] was
killed, and the atheling Æthelwold, whom they had chosen as their
king,[3] and Brihtsige, son of the atheling Beornoth,[4] and Ysopa the
hold[5] and Oscetel the *hold* and also very many with them, whom we
cannot name now. And a great slaughter was made on both sides,
but more of the Danes were killed, though they remained in
possession of the battle-field. And Ealhswith died in that same year.

F903 In this year Grimbald the priest died, and in the same year the New Minster at Winchester was
consecrated, and (there occurred) St. Judoc's arrival.[6]

Main Chronicle (A, B, C, D)   *Mercian Register*

904   In this year there was an eclipse
                                             of the moon.

905   In this year a comet appeared.[7]

906? (905 A; 906 C, D). In this year Alfred, who was reeve at Bath,
died. And that same year the peace was established at Tiddingford,[8]
just as King Edward decreed, both with the East Angles and the
Northumbrians.

E906 In this year King Edward, from necessity, established peace both with the army of the East Angles
and the Northumbrians.

---

[1] King Edward's father-in-law.
[2] King of East Anglia.
[3] 'A', which consistently ignores Æthelwold's kingship, has
instead of this clause: 'who enticed him to that war'.
[4] The names suggest that these were descendants of ninth-
century kings of Mercia.

[5] A Scandinavian title, applied to a class of noblemen in the
Danelaw, which had a wergild double that of a thegn.
[6] i.e. of some relics of this seventh-century Breton saint.
[7] 'D' puts this entry at the beginning of the annal it dates 905,
adding that it was on 20 October.
[8] Near Leighton Buzzard.

Main Chronicle (A, B, C, D)	Mercian Register

907

In this year Chester was restored.

908 (909 C, D) In this year Denewulf, who was bishop of Winchester, died.[1]

909 (910 C, D) In this year Frithustan[2] succeeded to the bishopric in Winchester, and after that Asser, who was bishop of Sherborne, died. And that same year King Edward sent an army both from the West Saxons and from the Mercians, and it ravaged very severely the territory of the northern army, both men and all kinds of cattle, and they killed many men of those Danes, and were five weeks there.

In this year St. Oswald's body was brought from Bardney into Mercia.[3]

910 (911 C, D) In this year the army in Northumbria broke the peace, and scorned every privilege[4] that King Edward and his councillors offered them, and ravaged over Mercia. And the king had collected about 100 ships, and was then in Kent, and the ships were on their way east along the south coast towards him. Then the Danish army thought that the greater part of his forces was on the ships, and that they could go unopposed wherever they wished. Then the king learnt that they had gone on a raid. He then sent his army both from the West Saxons and Mercians, and they overtook the Danish army when it was on its way home and fought against it and put the army to flight and killed many thousands of its men.[6] And there

In this year the English and Danes fought at Tettenhall, and the English were victorious. And that same year Æthelflæd built the borough at *Bremesbyrig*.[5]

[1] 'F' enters his death 909. Æthelweard records the dedication by Archbishop Plegmund of a 'high tower' in Winchester newly founded in honour of St Mary, and Plegmund's journey to Rome with the alms of the people and of King Edward.

[2] This name is marked with a small cross in the text of 'A', and there is a red frame round the beginning of the entry, and a large cross in the margin.

[3] 'D' places this at the beginning of the annal it dates 906.

[4] 'A': 'peace'.

[5] 'D' puts this entry at the beginning of the annal it dates 909. It has recorded the battle three times, from the Main Chronicle, from the Mercian Register, and in the annal dated 910 which it shares with 'E'. It adds to the Mercian Register the date, 6 August.

[6] Æthelweard has fuller information on this battle, which he seems to date 909. 'After one year the barbarians break their pact with King Edward and with Ethelred, who then ruled the districts of Northumbria and Mercia. The fields of the Mercians are wasted on all sides by the aforesaid disturbance, right up to the River Avon, where begins the boundary of the West Angles (i.e. Saxons) and the Mercians. Thence they cross over the River Severn into the western districts, and there obtained by plunder no little booty. But when, exulting in their rich spoils, they withdrew homewards, they crossed a bridge on the eastern side of the Severn, which is commonly called *Cantbrycg*. A battle-line was formed, and the troops of the Mercians and the West Saxons suddenly went against them. A battle ensued and the English without delay obtained the victory at Wednesfield (near Tettenhall), and the army of the Danes was put to flight, overcome by weapons. These things are said to have been done on the fifth day of the month of August. And it may rightly be said that in that turmoil or encounter three of their kings fell, namely Healfdene and Eywysl, and also Ivar lost his sovereignty and hastened to the court of hell, and with them their more distinguished leaders and nobles.'

Both Florence and the *Annals of St Neots* have the name Wednesfield.

Main Chronicle (A, B, C, D)

were killed King Eowils[1] and King Healfdene[2] and Earl Ohter and Earl Scurfa, and Othulf the *hold*,[3] and Benesing the *hold*, and Olaf the Black and Thurferth the *hold*, and Osfrith Hlytta,[4] and Guthfrith the *hold*,[5] and Agmund the *hold* and Guthfrith.

D, E 910[6] In this year the English army and the Danish army fought at Tettenhall, and Ethelred, lord of the Mercians, died, and King Edward succeeded to London and Oxford and to all the lands which belonged to them; and a great naval force came hither from the south from Brittany, and ravaged greatly by the Severn, but they almost all perished afterwards.

Main Chronicle (A, B, C, D)

911 (912 C, D) In this year Ethelred, ealdorman of the Mercians, died,[7] and King Edward succeeded to London and Oxford and to all the lands which belonged to them.

912 (913 C, D) In this year about Martinmas, King Edward ordered the northern borough at Hertford to be built, between the Maran,[8] the Beane, and the Lea, and then after that in the summer, between Rogation days and midsummer,[9] King Edward went with some of his forces into Essex to Maldon, and camped there while the borough was being made and constructed at Witham,[11] and a good number of the people who had been under the rule of the Danish men submitted to him. And meanwhile some of his forces made the borough at Hertford on the south side of the Lea.[13]

913 (916 A; 914 C, D) In this year the army from Northampton and Leicester rode out after Easter[14] and broke the peace, and killed many

Mercian Register

Then the next year Ethelred, lord of the Mercians, died.

In this year Æthelflæd, lady of the Mercians, came on the holy eve of the Invention of the Cross[10] to *Scergeat*, and built the borough there, and in the same year that at Bridgnorth.[12]

In this year, by the grace of God, Æthelflæd, lady of the Mercians,

---

[1] 'A' omits the rest of this annal.

[2] Florence calls them 'brothers of King Hinguar' (Ivar).

[3] 'D' omits the rest of the annal except 'and Agmund the *hold*'. On this title, see p. 60, n. 5.

[4] G. Tengvik, *Old English Bynames*, p. 347, renders this 'diviner, soothsayer'.

[5] The *Annals of St Neots* add Eagellus.

[6] This annal, which stands alone in 'E', but in 'D' is added to that from the Main Chronicle which 'D' dates 910, records the events of several years, 910, 911, 914.

[7] Æthelweard, who dates this 910, adds that he was buried in Gloucester.

[8] This name occurs in two forms, (i) 'A', 'G', Florence, *Annals of St Neots*: *Memeran*; Henry of Huntingdon: *Mimran*; (ii) 'B', 'C': *Meran*; 'D': *Mæran*.

[9] i.e. between 18 May and 24 June. The order of events in this annal, beginning about Martinmas (11 November), suggests that the year is beginning in September.

[10] 2 May.

[11] The *Annals of St Neots* add: 'about the feast of John the Baptist' (presumably the Nativity, 24 June).

[12] This annal is not in 'D'.

[13] Æthelweard has nothing for this year except that he records the death of Eadwulf, who was high-reeve of Bamburgh, in Northumbria. The *Annals of Ulster*, which call him 'king of the North Saxons', enter it at 912 (913).

[14] 28 March.

Main Chronicle (A, B, C, D)

men at Hook Norton and round about there. And then very soon after that, as the one force came home, they met another raiding band[1] which rode out against Luton. And then the people of the district became aware of it and fought against them and reduced them to full flight and rescued all that they had captured and also a great part of their horses and their weapons.

914 (917 A; 915 C, D) In this year a great naval force came over here from the south from Brittany, and two earls, Ohter and Hroald, with them. And they then went west round the coast so that they arrived at the Severn estuary and ravaged in Wales everywhere along the coast where it suited them. And they captured Cyfeiliog, bishop of Archenfield,[5] and took him with them to the ships; and then King Edward ransomed him for 40 pounds. Then after that all the army went inland, still wishing to go on a raid towards Archenfield. Then the men from Hereford and Gloucester and from the nearest boroughs met them and fought against them and put them to flight and killed the earl Hroald and the brother of Ohter, the other earl, and a great part of the army, and drove them into an enclosure and besieged them there until they gave them hostages, (promising) that they would leave the king's dominion. And the king had arranged that men were stationed against them on the south[6] side of the Severn estuary, from the west, from Cornwall, east as far as Avonmouth, so that they dared not attack the land anywhere on that side. Yet they stole inland by night on two occasions – on the one occasion east of Watchet, on the other occasion at Porlock. Then on both occasions they were attacked, so that few of them got away – only those who could swim out to the ships. And then they remained out on the island of Steepholme[7] until they became very short of food and many men had died of hunger because they could not obtain any food. Then they went from there to Dyfed, and from there to Ireland; and this was in the autumn.[8]

Mercian Register

went with all the Mercians to Tamworth, and built the borough there in the early summer, and afterwards, before Lammas,[2] that at Stafford;[3]

then afterwards in the next year, that at Eddisbury in the early summer, and later in the same year, in the early autumn, that at Warwick;[4]

---

[1] 'C' has wrongly 'band of people'.

[2] 1 August.

[3] 'D' enters a brief version of this annal at the beginning of its annal for 913 (real date 912).

[4] 'D' has a brief reference to the building of Warwick at the beginning of its annal 915 (real date 914).

[5] In Herefordshire. The name survives as that of a deanery.

[6] 'C' omits 'south'.

[7] So 'B', 'C', 'D'; 'A' has Flatholme.

[8] Æthelweard refers briefly to these events, which he dates 913. He merely speaks of the arrival of a fleet, of the absence of any heavy engagement, and of its departure for Ireland.

Main Chronicle (A, B, C, D)

Mercian Register

And then after that in the same year, before Martinmas,[1] King Edward went to Buckingham with his army, and stayed there four weeks, and made both the boroughs, on each side of the river, before he went away. And Earl Thurcetel came and accepted him as his lord, and so did all the earls[2] and the principal men who belonged to Bedford, and also many of those who belonged to Northampton.[3]

A *only*[4]

915 (918) In this year King Edward went with his army to Bedford, before Martinmas, and obtained the borough; and almost all the citizens, who dwelt there before, submitted to him. And he stayed there four weeks, and before he went away ordered the borough on the south side of the river to be built.

then afterwards in the next year after Christmas, that at Chirbury and that at *Weardbyrig*; and in the same year before Christmas, that at Runcorn.

916 (919) In this year, before midsummer,[5] King Edward went to Maldon and built and established the borough before he went away. And that same year Earl Thurcetel went across the sea to France, along with the men who were willing to serve him, with King Edward's peace and support.

In this year Abbot Egbert, though innocent, was killed before midsummer on 16 June – that same day was the festival of St. Ciriacus the martyr – with his companions. And three days later Æthelflæd sent an army into Wales and destroyed *Brecenanmere*,[6] and captured the king's wife and 33[7] other persons.

917 (920) In this year before Easter[8] King Edward ordered the borough at Towcester to be occupied and built; and then after that in the same year at the Rogation days[9] he ordered the borough at *Wigingamere* to be built. That same summer, between Lammas and midsummer,[10] the army from Northampton and Leicester and north of these places broke the peace, and went to Towcester, and fought all

In this year, Æthelflæd, lady of the Mercians, with the help of God, before Lammas obtained the borough which is called Derby, with all that belongs to it; and there also four of her

---

[1] 11 November.

[2] So 'B', 'C', 'D'; 'A': *holds*.

[3] Æthelweard has entered the invasion of this year in 913. He then comments on the peacefulness of the winter of 914, when Christmas Day fell on a Sunday.

[4] The account of the later campaigns of Edward is in 'A' only.

[5] 24 June.

[6] Langorse Lake, near Brecon. See J. E. Lloyd, *A History of Wales*, 3rd ed., p. 331, n. 41.

[7] The idiom, 'one of thirty-four', may perhaps be meant literally when no round figures are involved. But see p. 15, n. 11.

[8] 13 April.

[9] 19–21 May.

[10] 24 June–1 August.

A

day against the borough, intending to take it by storm, but yet the people who were inside defended it until more help came to them, and the enemy then left the borough and went away. And then very quickly after that, they again went out with a marauding band by night, and came upon unprepared men, and captured no small number of men and cattle, between Bernwood Forest and Aylesbury. At the same time the army came from Huntingdon and East Anglia and made the fortress at Tempsford, and took up quarters in it and built it, and abandoned the other fortress at Huntingdon, thinking that from Tempsford they would reach[2] more of the land with strife and hostility. And they went till they reached Bedford; and the men who were inside went out against them, and fought against them and put them to flight, and killed a good part of them. Yet again after that a great army assembled from East Anglia[3] and Mercia, and went to the borough at *Wigingamere* and besieged and attacked it long into the day, and seized the cattle round about; and yet the men who were inside defended the borough. And then the enemy left the borough and went away.

Then after that during the same summer a great host assembled in King Edward's dominions from the nearest boroughs which could manage it[4] and went to Tempsford and besieged the borough and attacked it until they took it by storm; and they killed the king and Earl Toglos and his son Earl Manna, and his brother and all those who were inside and chose to defend themselves; and they captured the others and everything that was inside.

And afterwards, very soon after that, a great (English) host assembled in autumn, both from Kent, from Surrey, from Essex and from the nearest boroughs on all sides; and they went to Colchester and besieged the borough and attacked it until they took it and killed all the people and seized everything that was inside – except the men who fled there over the wall.

Then after that, still in the same autumn, a great army from East Anglia collected, consisting both of the army of the district and of the vikings whom they had enticed to their assistance, and

Mercian Register

thegns, who were dear to her, were killed within the gates.[1]

---

[1] 'D' has this annal, with the true date.

[2] Or perhaps 'recover' as in Florence.

[3] Florence: 'and Essex'.

[4] Assuming that the singular verb is an error. At this point begin three lines by a very poor scribe. An alternative rendering is: '. . . which could reach it' (Tempsford or the place of assembly?).

A

they intended to avenge their injury. And they went to Maldon and besieged the borough and attacked it until more troops came to the help of the citizens from outside; and the army left the borough and went away. Then the men from the borough, and also those who had come to their assistance from outside, went out after them and put the army to flight, and killed many hundreds of them, both of the shipmen and of the others.

Then very soon afterwards in the same autumn King Edward went with the army of the West Saxons to Passenham, and stayed there while the borough of Towcester was provided with a stone wall. And Earl Thurferth and the *holds*[1] submitted to him, and so did all the army which belonged to Northampton, as far north as the Welland, and sought to have him as their lord and protector. And when that division of the English army went home, the other division came on service and captured the borough at Huntingdon, and repaired and restored it by King Edward's command where it had been broken; and all the people of that district who had survived submitted to King Edward and asked for his peace and protection.

Moreover, after that during the same year, before Martinmas, King Edward went with the army of the West Saxons to Colchester, and repaired and restored the borough where it had been broken. And many people who had been under the rule of the Danes[2] both in East Anglia and in Essex submitted to him; and all the army in East Anglia swore agreement with him, that they would (agree to) all that he would, and would keep peace with all with whom the king wished to keep peace, both at sea and on land. And the army which belonged to Cambridge chose him especially as its lord and protector, and established it with oaths just as he decreed it.

918 (921) In this year, between Rogation days and midsummer,[3] King Edward went with the army to Stamford, and ordered the borough on the south side of the river to be built; and all the people who belonged to the more northern borough submitted to him and sought to have him as their lord. Then during the stay he made there, his sister Æthelflæd died at Tamworth twelve days before

In this year, with God's help, she peacefully obtained control of the borough of Leicester, in the early part of the year; and the greater part of the army which belonged to it was subjected.

---

[1] See p. 60, n. 5.   [2] Florence adds: 'for nearly 30 years'.   [3] 11 May–24 June.

A

midsummer. And then he occupied the borough of Tamworth, and all the nation in the land of the Mercians which had been subject to Æthelflæd submitted to him; and the kings in Wales, Hywel, Clydog, and Idwal,[1] and all the race of the Welsh, sought to have him as lord.

Then he went from there to Nottingham, and captured the borough and ordered it to be repaired and manned both with Englishmen and Danes. And all the people who had settled in Mercia, both Danish and English, submitted to him.

Mercian Register

And also the people of York had promised her – and some had given pledges, some had confirmed it with oaths – that they would be under her direction. But very soon after they had agreed to this, she died twelve days before midsummer[2] in Tamworth, in the eighth year in which with lawful authority she was holding dominion over the Mercians. And her body is buried in Gloucester in the east chapel of St. Peter's church.[3]

E918 In this year died Æthelflæd, lady of the Mercians.

A

919 (922 A) In this year after autumn King Edward went with the army to Thelwall and ordered the borough to be built, occupied and manned; and while he stayed there he ordered another army, also from the people of Mercia, to occupy Manchester in Northumbria, and repair and man it. [In this year died Archbishop Plegmund.][5]

920 (923 A) In this year, before midsummer, King Edward went with the army to Nottingham, and ordered to be built the borough on the south side of the river, opposite the other, and the bridge over the Trent between the two boroughs.

Then he went from there into the Peak district to Bakewell, and ordered a borough to be built in the neighbourhood and manned. And then the king of the Scots and all the people of the Scots, and Ragnald, and the sons of Eadwulf and all who live in Northumbria,

Mercian Register

In this year also[4] the daughter of Ethelred, lord of the Mercians, was deprived of all authority in Mercia and taken into Wessex, three weeks before Christmas. She was called Ælfwyn.[6]

---

[1] Hywel and Clydog, sons of Cadell, son of Rhodri, ruled in South Wales, Idwal, son of Anarawd, in Gwynedd.
[2] 'D' adds: '12 June'.
[3] This annal is also in 'D', correctly dated.

[4] It is possible, as Dr Wainwright, *Eng. Hist. Rev.*, LX, p. 388, suggests, that this is really a continuation of the previous annal.
[5] The part in brackets is a late Canterbury addition.
[6] This annal is also in 'D', dated 919.

A	*Mercian Register*

both English and Danish, Norsemen and others, and also the king
of the Strathclyde Welsh and all
the Strathclyde Welsh, chose
him as father and lord.[1]

921   In this year King Edward built the borough at *Cledemutha*.[2]

E921[3] In this year King Sihtric killed his brother Niall.[4]
D, E923[3] In this year King Ragnald won York.

A (E, F)[5]	*Mercian Register*

924 (925 F) In this year King Edward   In this year King Edward died at Farndon in Mercia, and his son
died[6] and his son Athelstan suc-   Ælfweard died very soon after[7] at Oxford, and their bodies are
ceeded to the kingdom.   buried at Winchester. And Athelstan was chosen by the Mercians
                                         as king, and consecrated at Kingston,[8] and he gave his sister in
                                         marriage[9] [over the sea to the son of the king of the Old Saxons].

E925 In this year Bishop Wulfhelm was consecrated,[10] and in the same year King Edward died.

D

926   (925) In this year King Athelstan and Sihtric, king of the Northum-
                                   brians, met together at Tamworth on 30 January and Athelstan gave
                                   him his sister in marriage.

927   (926) In this year appeared fiery lights in the northern quarter of
                                   the sky, and Sihtric died, and King Athelstan succeeded to the
                                   kingdom of the Northumbrians; and he brought under his rule all
                                   the kings who were in this island: first Hywel, king of the West
                                   Welsh, and Constantine, king of the Scots, and Owain, king of the

---

[1] Here ends the long entry peculiar to 'A'.
[2] Wainwright, *Eng. Hist. Rev.*, LXV, pp. 203–212, suggests that this is the mouth of the Clwyd. 'D' has this annal. 'B' omits it.
[3] The true date of both these events is probably 919.
[4] This is an error, for Niall was not related to Sihtric.
[5] This annal could have been added into 'F' and the archetype of 'E' at Canterbury. 'B', 'C', 'D' have only the Mercian Register entry. 'B', 'C' have nothing more until 934.
[6] 17 July.
[7] 'D' adds: 'after 16 days'.

[8] This did not take place until 4 September 925.
[9] Here the copy used by 'B' and 'C' must have broken off. The conclusion is from 'D', but is probably only a guess. 'D''s reference is to the marriage of Edith to Otto the Great, but the Mercian Register may have gone on to tell of the marriage of another sister to Sihtric, king of York.
[10] As archbishop of Canterbury, as in 'F' (and addition to 'A'), which adds that Dunstan was born this year. This is erroneous. The true date is *c.* 909. See J. Armitage Robinson, *The Saxon Bishops of Wells*, pp. 28 ff.

D

people of Gwent, and Aldred, son of Eadwulf from Bamburgh. And they established peace with pledge and oaths in the place which is called Eamont, on 12 July, and renounced all idolatry and afterwards departed in peace.[1]

E927 In this year King Athelstan drove out King Guthfrith. And in this year Archbishop Wulfhelm went to Rome.

A931 [2] In this year Byrnstan was consecrated bishop of Winchester on 29 May, and he held his bishopric two and a half years.

A932 In this year Bishop Frithustan died.

E933 In this year the atheling Edwin was drowned at sea.

C (A, B, D, E, F)

934 (933 A) In this year King Athelstan went into Scotland with both a land force and a naval force, and ravaged much of it.[3]

A933 . . . and Bishop Byrnstan of Winchester died on All Saints' day.

A934 In this year Ælfheah succeeded to the bishopric.

C (A, B, D)

937[4] In this year King Athelstan, lord of nobles, dispenser of treasure to men, and his brother also, Edmund atheling, won by the sword's edge undying glory in battle round *Brunanburh*.[5] Edward's sons clove the shield-wall, hewed the linden-wood shields with hammered swords, for it was natural to men of their lineage to defend their land, their treasure, and their homes, in frequent battle against every foe. Their enemies perished; the people of the Scots and the pirates fell doomed. The field grew dark (?) with the blood of men, from the time when the sun, that glorious luminary, the bright candle of God, of the Lord Eternal, moved over the earth in the hours of morning, until that noble creation sank at its setting. There lay many a man destroyed by the spears, many a northern warrior shot over his shield; and likewise many a Scot lay weary, sated with battle.

The whole day long the West Saxons with mounted companies kept in pursuit of the hostile peoples, grievously they cut down the fugitives from behind with their whetted swords. The Mercians refused not hard conflict to any men who with Olaf had sought this land in the bosom of a ship over the

---

[1] If, as seems probable, the same meeting is meant by William of Malmesbury (*E.H.D.*, I, p. 280), Owain of Strathclyde should be added to those present.

[2] Mr R. Vaughan informs me that this and the three next annals in 'A' were originally dated 932–935.

[3] Florence adds that King Constantine was forced to give his son as a hostage.

[4] The annal is entirely in alliterative verse. Mr Vaughan says it was originally dated 938 in 'A'.

[5] *Sic* 'A', 'D'; *Brunnanburh*, 'B' and 'C' and a second *n* has been added later in 'A'. Æthelweard calls the place *Brunandun*, Simeon, *Wendun*; Florence says Olaf landed in the mouth of the Humber. For William of Malmesbury's account, see *E.H.D.*, I, pp. 282f.

C (A, B, D)

tumult of waters, coming doomed to the fight. Five young kings lay on that field of battle, slain by the swords, and also seven of Olaf's earls, and a countless host of seamen and Scots. There the prince of the Norsemen was put to flight, driven perforce to the prow of his ship with a small company; the vessel pressed on in the water, the king set out over the fallow flood and saved his life.

There also the aged Constantine, the hoary-haired warrior, came north to his own land by flight. He had no cause to exult in that crossing of swords.[1] He was shorn of his kinsmen and deprived of his friends at that meeting-place, bereaved[2] in the battle, and he left his young son on the field of slaughter, brought low by wounds in the battle. The grey-haired warrior, the old and wily one, had no cause to vaunt of that sword-clash; no more had Olaf. They had no need to gloat with the remnants of their armies, that they were superior in warlike deeds on the field of battle, in the clash of standards, the meeting of spears, the encounter of men, and the crossing of weapons, after they had contended on the field of slaughter with the sons of Edward.

Then the Norsemen, the sorry survivors from the spears, put out in their studded ships on to Ding's mere,[3] to make for Dublin across the deep water, back to Ireland humbled at heart. Also the two brothers, king and atheling, returned together to their own country, the land of the West Saxons, exulting in the battle. They left behind them the dusky-coated one, the black raven with its horned beak, to share the corpses, and the dun-coated, white-tailed eagle, the greedy war-hawk, to enjoy the carrion, and that grey beast, the wolf of the forest.

Never yet in this island before this, by what books tell us and our ancient sages, was a greater slaughter of a host made by the edge of the sword, since the Angles and Saxons came hither from the east, invading Britain over the broad seas, and the proud assailants, warriors eager for glory, overcame the Britons and won a country.

E937 In this year King Athelstan led an army to *Brunanburh*.

C (A, B, D)

940[4] (941 A) In this year King Athelstan died[5] on 27 October, 40 years except for one day after King Alfred died; and the atheling Edmund succeeded to the kingdom, and he was then 18 years old. And King Athelstan had reigned for 14 years and 10 weeks.[6]

D

(941) In this year the Northumbrians were false to their pledges, and chose Olaf from Ireland as their king.

---

[1] So in 'B', 'C'; 'A' is corrupt; 'D' reads, 'meeting of men'.
[2] So in all MSS. except 'B', 'worsted'.
[3] This allusion is quite obscure.
[4] Athelstan died in 939, reckoned 940 by writers who begin the year 24 September. Olaf's election followed soon after, in spite of 'D''s date. According to Mr Vaughan, 'A''s date was originally 940.

[5] In Gloucester, according to 'D'. Florence says that he was borne to Malmesbury and buried there with great honour.
[6] The regnal list (p. 4 above) says 14 years, seven weeks, and three days, which is correct. An addition to 'A' has: 'Then Wulfhelm was archbishop in Kent.'

E940 In this year King Athelstan died and his brother Edmund succeeded to the kingdom.

C (A, B, D)

942[1] In this year King Edmund, lord of the English, protector of men,[2] the beloved performer of mighty deeds, overran Mercia, as bounded by Dore, Whitwell gate, and the broad stream, the River Humber; and five boroughs, Leicester and Lincoln, Nottingham and likewise Stamford, and also Derby. The Danes were previously subjected by force under the Norsemen, for a long time in bonds of captivity to the heathens, until the defender of warriors, the son of Edward, King Edmund, redeemed them, to his glory.

E942 In this year King Olaf died.[3]

D

940–943[4]

(943) In this year Olaf took Tamworth by storm, and the losses were heavy on both sides, and the Danes were victorious and took away much booty with them. Wulfrun[5] was taken captive in that raid. In this year King Edmund besieged King Olaf and Archbishop Wulfstan in Leicester, and he could have subdued them if they had not escaped by night from the borough. And after that Olaf secured King Edmund's friendship.

C (A, B, D)

943[6] (No date in MSS.) In this year King Edmund stood sponsor to King Olaf at baptism,[7] and the same year, after a fairly big interval, he stood sponsor to King Ragnald at his confirmation.[8]

C (A, B, D, E, F)

944 In this year King Edmund reduced all Northumbria under his rule, and drove out two kings, Olaf, Sihtric's son, and Ragnald, Guthfrith's son.[9]

---

[1] This annal is in alliterative verse.

[2] 'A': 'kinsmen'.

[3] Olaf, Guthfrith's son, actually died before the end of 941. He was succeeded by his cousin Olaf, Sihtric's son.

[4] 'D' places under 943 events of 940 which precede the recapture of the Five Boroughs which it has already dealt with in the preceding annal. It then tacks on the annal for 943 of the main Chronicle.

[5] The mother of Ælfhelm, ealdorman of Northumbria, c. 993–1006, and of Wulfric Spott, on whom see E.H.D., I, No. 125.

[6] 'A' has run this on to the poem in its previous annal, which ended with 'Edmund king', by continuing after the first instead of the second occurrence of these words; 'B' and 'C' appear to start a new annal, but with no number, and 'C' puts a blank annal 943 after this one; 'D' reads straight on from its previous annal, omitting 'In this year' and supplying 'and'.

[7] 'D' adds: 'And he bestowed gifts on him royally.'

[8] 'F' and an addition to 'A' add: 'In this year King Edmund entrusted Glastonbury to St Dunstan, where he afterwards first became abbot.'

[9] 'E', 'F': 'two men of royal race, Olaf and Ragnald'. Æthelweard seems to be referring to this event under too late a date, when, along with events of 946 (which he dates 948, as he is two years out in this portion of his work) he says: 'Bishop Wulfstan and the ealdorman of the Mercians expelled certain "deserters", namely Ragnald and Olaf, from the city of York, and brought them into the power of the aforesaid king.' He continues: 'In the same year died Queen Ælfgifu, King Edmund's wife, and she was afterwards canonized and at her tomb in the nunnery which is commonly called Shaftesbury innumerable miracles have been performed with God's help until the present day.'

C (A, B, D, E, F)

945 In this year King Edmund ravaged all Cumberland,[1] and granted it all to Malcolm, king of the Scots, on condition that he should be his ally both on sea and on land.

C (A, B, D)

946 In this year King Edmund died on St. Augustine's day.[2]

D

It was widely known how he ended his life, that Leofa stabbed him at Pucklechurch.[3] And Æthelflæd of Damerham, Ealdorman Ælfgar's daughter, was then his queen.

C (A, B, D)

And he had held the kingdom six years and a half.[4] And then the atheling Eadred, his brother, succeeded to the kingdom and reduced all Northumbria under his rule. And the Scots gave oaths to him that they would agree to all that he wanted.

E948 In this year King Edmund was stabbed to death, and his brother Eadred succeeded to the kingdom, and immediately reduced all Northumbria under his rule; and the Scots swore oaths to him that they would agree to all that he wanted.

D

947   In this year King Eadred came to Tanshelf, and there Archbishop Wulfstan and all the councillors of the Northumbrians pledged themselves to the king, and within a short space they were false to it all, both pledge and oaths as well.

948   In this year King Eadred ravaged all Northumbria, because they had accepted Eric[5] as their king; and in that ravaging the glorious minister at Ripon, which St. Wilfrid had built, was burnt down. And when the king was on his way home, the army [which] was in York overtook the king's army at Castleford, and they made a

---

[1] At this date Cumberland means the kingdom of Strathclyde, not merely the modern county. 'E', 'F' omit the rest of this annal.

[2] 26 May.

[3] Florence is fuller; he says that Edmund was killed when trying to rescue his seneschal from being killed by a base robber, Leofa, and that Pucklechurch was a royal residence; that he reigned five years and seven months, and was buried at Glastonbury by the blessed abbot Dunstan; that Eadred was consecrated on 16 August at Kingston by Oda, archbishop of Canterbury.

[4] 'all but two days', regnal list, p. 4. This is probably reckoned from the coronation, while Florence reckons from the date of Athelstan's death, taken as 940.

[5] Eric Blood-axe, son of Harold Fairhair of Norway, who came to England as an exile. See E.H.D., I, No. 11.

D

great slaughter there. Then the king became so angry that he wished to march back into the land and destroy it utterly. When the councillors of the Northumbrians understood that, they deserted Eric and paid to King Eadred compensation for their act.

E

49

In this year Olaf Cwiran[1] came into Northumbria.

A951 In this year Ælfheah, bishop of Winchester, died on St. Gregory's day.[2]

52

D	E
In this year King Eadred ordered Archbishop Wulfstan to be taken into the fortress of *Iudan-byrig*, because accusations had often been made to the king against him. And in this year also the king ordered a great slaughter to be made in the borough of Thetford in vengeance for the abbot Eadhelm, whom they had slain.	In this year the Northumbrians drove out King Olaf, and received Eric, Harold's son.

D (E)

54

In this year the Northumbrians drove out Eric,[3] and Eadred succeeded to the kingdom of the Northumbrians.

D

In this year Archbishop Wulf-stan received a bishopric again, in Dorchester.[4]

C (B, E)	D
55 (956 B, C) In this year King Eadred died and Eadwig,	In this year King Eadred died, and he rests in the Old Minster,

---

[1] i.e. Sihtric's son.
[2] 12 March.
[3] Roger of Wendover, using a northern source, gives an account of his death. See *E.H.D.*, I, p. 257.

[4] This could read: 'received back his bishopric (York) at Dorchester'.

C (B, E)	D
[Edmund's son],[1] succeeded to the kingdom.	and Eadwig succeeded to the kingdom of the West Saxons, and his brother Edgar to the kingdom of the Mercians.[2] They were sons of King Edmund and St. Ælfgifu.

A955 In this year King Eadred died on St. Clement's day[3] at Frome and he had ruled nine and a half years; and then Eadwig, the son of King Edmund, succeeded to the kingdom [and exiled St. Dunstan from the land].[4]

C (B)	D (E)
956	(957 D) In this year Archbishop Wulfstan died

D

on 16 December,[5] and he was buried in Oundle. And in the same year Abbot Dunstan was driven across the sea.

C (B)	D (E)
957 In this year the atheling Edgar succeeded to the kingdom of the Mercians.[7]	(958)[6] In this year Archbishop Oda separated King Eadwig and Ælfgifu, because they were too closely related.

C (A, B, D, E, F)

959 (958 A, F) In this year King Eadwig died[8] and his brother Edgar succeeded to the kingdom;[9]

C (B)	D (E, F)[10]
both in Wessex and in Mercia and in Northumbria, and he was then 16 years old.	in his days things improved greatly, and God granted him that he lived in peace as long as he lived; and, as was necessary for him, he laboured zealously for this; he exalted God's praise far and wide,

---

[1] 'E' only.

[2] This clause is in 'F' also, so it may have been in the archetype of 'E'; but it is wrong, for the division of the kingdom did not take place until 957.

[3] 23 November.

[4] Canterbury addition.

[5] Florence, and York tradition, give 26 December.

[6] If we accept a story in the life of St Dunstan, this event belongs to 956. In any case 958 is too late.

[7] Florence adds: 'and the kingdom of the two kings was divided so that the River Thames should form the boundary between the two kingdoms'.

[8] 'A': on 1 October.

[9] 'A' ends the annal here; 'F' has: 'became king over all Britain'.

[10] This passage is written in alliterative prose, and is in the style of Archbishop Wulfstan II of York. It is influenced by Ælfric's 'Judges'. See E.H.D., I, p. 854.

D (E, F)

and loved God's law; and he improved the peace of the people more than the kings who were before him in the memory of man. And God also supported him so that kings and earls willingly submitted to him and were subjected to whatever he wished. And without battle he brought under his sway all that he wished. He came to be honoured widely throughout the countries, because he zealously honoured God's name, and time and again meditated on God's law, and exalted God's praise far and wide, and continually and frequently directed all his people wisely in matters of Church and State. Yet he did one ill-deed too greatly: he loved evil foreign customs and brought too firmly heathen manners within this land, and attracted hither foreigners and enticed harmful people to this country. But may God grant him that his good deeds may prove greater than his ill-deeds, for the protection of his soul on its everlasting journey.

F (and addition to A) 959 In this year Edgar sent for St. Dunstan, and gave him the bishopric of Worcester, and afterwards the bishopric of London.

F961 In this year the good Archbishop Oda died and Dunstan was elected archbishop.

A[1]

62 In this year Ælfgar, the king's kinsman in Devon, died, and his body rests in Wilton. And King Sigeferth[2] killed himself, and his body is buried at Wimborne. And then during the year there was a very great mortality, and the great and fatal fire occurred in London, and St. Paul's minster was burnt, and was rebuilt in the same year. And in this same year the priest Æthelmod went to Rome, and died there on 15 August.

63 In this year Wulfstan the deacon died on Holy Innocents' day,[3] and after that Gyric the priest died. In that same year Abbot Æthelwold succeeded to the bishopric of Winchester, and he was consecrated on the eve of St. Andrew's day. That day was a Sunday.

E

In this year St. Æthelwold was chosen for the bishopric of Winchester by King Edgar;[4] and the archbishop of Canterbury, St. Dunstan, consecrated him as bishop on the first Sunday of Advent, which was on 29 November.[5]

---

[1] For the next three years 'A' has fuller and less local annals than in the years preceding.

[2] A man of this name attests a charter (Birch, No. 909) of 955 along with a sub-king Morgen and two men with Welsh names. His name is Scandinavian, and he should perhaps be placed in the isles.

[3] 28 December.

[4] It is remarkable that 'E' and 'F' should be the only MSS. other than the Winchester 'A' to record Æthelwold's accession. 'F' has only a brief entry.

[5] 'E' has a long Peterborough addition, on the refoundation of the abbey.

A

964 In this year King Edgar drove the priests in the city[1] from the Old Minster and from the New Minster; and from Chertsey and from Milton (Abbas); and replaced them with monks. And he appointed Abbot Æthelgar as abbot of the New Minster, and Ordberht for Chertsey, and Cyneweard for Milton.

E

[In this year the canons were expelled from the Old Minster.][2]

D (F)[3]

965 In this year King Edgar took Ælfthryth as his queen. She was the daughter of Ealdorman Ordgar.

D (E, F)

966 In this year Thored, Gunnar's son, ravaged Westmorland, and that same year Oslac succeeded to the aldormanry.[4]

969 In this year King Edgar ordered all Thanet to be ravaged.[5]

C (B)

971 In this year died Archbishop Oscetel, who was first consecrated as a diocesan bishop, of Dorchester, and afterwards consecrated archbishop of York by the consent of King Eadred and of all his councillors;[6] and he was bishop for 22 years, and he died on All Saints' eve, ten days before Martinmas, at Thame. And his kinsman, Abbot Thurcetel, took the bishop's body to Bedford, because he was abbot there at that time.[7]

C (B, D, E, G)

972 (?) (970 D, E; 971 G)[8] In this year the atheling Edmund[9] died.

C (A, B)

973[10] (974 C) in this year Edgar, ruler of the English, with a great company, was consecrated king in the ancient borough, *Acemannesceaster* – the men who dwell in this island also call it by another name, Bath.

D (E)

(972) In this year the atheling Edgar was consecrated king at Bath on the day of Pentecost, on

---

[1] Winchester.

[2] This annal is in Latin. 'F' has an annal derived from 'A'.

[3] Agreement between 'D' and 'F' implies that the archetype of 'E', used by 'F', had this annal. It must have been omitted when 'E' was copied.

[4] Of Northumbria.

[5] To avenge the ill-treatment of York merchants. See Roger of Wendover (*E.H.D.*, I, p. 257).

[6] This is the reading in 'B'. 'C' reads: 'who was first consecrated as a diocesan bishop for Dorchester, and afterwards for York, by the consent of King Edward [*sic*] and of all his councillors, so that he was consecrated as archbishop'.

[7] Thurcetel was afterwards abbot of Crowland.

[8] 'A' originally had this annal, and in 'G' (a copy of 'A'), it ends: 'and his body is buried at Romsey'. It has been erased from 'A'.

[9] Infant son of Edgar and Ælfthryth.

[10] The entry in 'A', 'B', 'C' is in alliterative verse.

C (A, B)

There great joy had come to all on that blessed day which the children of men call and name the day of Pentecost. There was assembled a crowd of priests, a great throng of learned monks, as I have heard tell. And then had passed from the birth of the glorious King, the Guardian of Light, ten hundred years reckoned in numbers, except that there yet remained, by what documents say, seven and twenty of the number of years, so nearly had passed away a thousand years of the Lord of Victories, when this took place. And Edmund's son, bold in battle, had spent 29 years in the world when this came about, and then in the thirtieth was consecrated king.

975[2] In this year Edgar, king of the English, reached the end of earthly joys, chose for him the other light, beautiful and happy, and left this wretched and fleeting life. The sons of nations, men on the earth, everywhere in this country – those who have been rightly trained in computation – call the month in which the young man Edgar, dispenser of treasure to warriors, departed from life on the eighth day, the month of July. His son then succeeded to the kingdom, a child ungrown, a prince of nobles, whose name was Edward. And ten days before, there departed from Britain a famous man, the bishop, good from his innate virtue, whose name was Cyneweard.[4]

D (E)

11 May, in the thirteenth year after he succeeded to the kingdom, and he was but one year off thirty. And immediately after that the king took his whole naval force to Chester, and six[1] kings came to meet him, and all gave him pledges that they would be his allies on sea and on land.

In this year died Edgar,[3] ruler of the Angles, friend of the West Saxons and protector of the Mercians. It was widely known throughout many nations across the gannet's bath, that kings honoured Edmund's son far and wide, and paid homage to this king as was his due by birth. Nor was there fleet so proud nor host so strong that it got itself prey in England as long as the noble king held the throne.[5]

In this year Edgar's son Edward succeeded to the kingdom. And soon in the same year in harvest time there appeared the

---

[1] Florence says: 'and his eight sub-kings, namely Kenneth, king of the Scots, Malcolm, king of the Cumbrians, Maccus, king of many islands, and five others, Dufnal (i.e. Dunmail), Siferth, Hywel, Jacob (i.e. Iago), and Juchil, met him, as he commanded, and swore that they would be faithful to him and be his allies by land and sea. And on a certain day he went on board a boat with them, and, with them at the oars and himself seizing the helm, he steered it skilfully on the course of the River Dee, proceeding from the palace to the monastery of St John the Baptist, attended by all the crowd of ealdormen and nobles also by boat. And when he had completed his prayers he returned with the same pomp to the palace. As he entered he is reported to have said to his nobles that any of his successors might indeed pride himself on being king of the English, when he might have the glory of such honours, with so many kings subservient to him.'

The same incident is referred to in Ælfric's *Life of St Swithin*. See *E.H.D.*, No. 239 (G).

[2] The entry in 'A', 'B', 'C' is in alliterative metre, of a quality to make one glad that the chroniclers mainly used prose. The passage in 'D' and 'E' is not in this metre, but is strongly rhythmical with some assonance and rhyme.

[3] 'D' adds: '8 July'.

[4] Bishop of Wells.

[5] Here the annal reverts to prose.

D (E)

star 'comet', and in the next year there came a very great famine and very manifold disturbances throughout England.

C (A, B)

Then in Mercia, as I have heard tell, widely, almost everywhere, the praise of the Ruler was cast down to the ground; many of the wise servants of God were dispersed.[3] That was a great cause of mourning for any who bore in his breast and mind an ardent love for the Creator. There the Author of glories, the Ruler of victories, the Governor of the heavens, was too greatly scorned, when his rights were violated. And then also the valiant man Oslac was driven from the country, over the tossing waves, the gannet's bath, the tumult of waters, the homeland of the whale; a grey-haired man, wise and skilled in speech, he was bereft of his lands.

Then was also revealed up in the skies a star in the firmament, which men firm of spirit, wise in mind, skilled in science, wise orators,[4] far and wide call 'comet' by name. The vengeance of the Ruler was manifested widely throughout the

D[1]

In his days because of his youth, the adversaries of God, Ealdorman Ælfhere[2] and many others, broke God's law and hindered the monastic life,[3] and destroyed monasteries and dispersed the monks and put to flight the servants of God, whom King Edgar had ordered the holy Bishop Æthelwold to institute; and they plundered widows time and again. And many wrongs and evil lawless acts rose up afterwards, and ever after that it grew much worse.

E (F)

And Ealdorman Ælfhere[2] caused to be destroyed many monastic foundations which King Edgar had ordered the holy Bishop Æthelwold to institute.

D (E)

And at this time also the famous Earl Oslac was exiled from England.

---

[1] The passage peculiar to 'D' is in the style of Archbishop Wulfstan II.
[2] Of Mercia.
[3] cf. E.H.D., I, No. 236.
[4] 'A' has instead a unique word, literally 'truth-bearers'.

C (A, B)

people, a famine over the earth, which the Guardian of the heavens, the Prince of the angels, afterwards amended. He gave back bliss to each of the islanders through the fruits of the earth.[1]

C only

976 In this year the great famine occurred in England.

C (B)

977 In this year was the great assembly at Kirtlington, after Easter,[2] and Bishop Sideman died there by a sudden death on 30 April. He was bishop of Devonshire, and he had wished his burial to be at Crediton at his episcopal see. Then King Edward and Archbishop Dunstan ordered that he should be conveyed to St. Mary's monastery which is at Abingdon, and this was done, and he is honourably buried at the north side in St. Paul's chapel.[3]

D (E)

(978) In this year all the chief councillors of the English people fell from an upper storey at Calne, except that Archbishop Dunstan alone remained standing upon a beam; and some were very severely injured there, and some did not survive it.

C

978 In this year King Edward was martyred, and his brother Ethelred succeeded to the kingdom and was consecrated king in the same year. In that year Ælfwold, who was bishop of Dorset, died, and his body is buried in the minster at Sherborne.

D (E)

(979) In this year King Edward was killed at the gap of Corfe[4] on 18 March in the evening, and he was buried at Wareham without any royal honours. And no worse deed than this for the English people was committed since first they came to Britain. Men murdered him, but God honoured him. In life he was an earthly king; he is now after death a heavenly saint. His earthly kinsmen would not avenge him, but his heavenly Father has greatly avenged him. The earthly slayers wished to blot out his memory on earth, but the heavenly Avenger has spread abroad his memory in heaven and in earth. Those who would not bow to his living body, now bend humbly on their knees to his dead bones. Now we can perceive that the wisdom and contrivance of men and their plans are worthless against God's purpose.

---

[1] Here ends any agreement between 'A' and the other MSS. Its few later entries are peculiar to it.

[2] 8 April.

[3] 'B' ends at this point.

[4] The burial at Wareham is in favour of this, the traditional, identification, not of Coryates, which has been suggested. On this murder, see the *Life of St Oswald* (E.H.D., I, No. 236, pp. 841 f.).

C

(979) In this year Ethelred was consecrated king on Sunday, a fortnight after Easter,[1] at Kingston, and at his consecration were two archbishops and ten diocesan bishops. That same year a bloody cloud was often seen in the likeness of fire, and especially it was revealed at midnight, and it was formed in various shafts of light. When day was about to dawn, it disappeared.

D (E)

In this year Ethelred succeeded to the kingdom, and very quickly after that he was consecrated king at Kingston with much rejoicing by the councillors of the English people.

A978 In this year King Edward was killed. And in this same year the atheling Ethelred his brother succeeded to the kingdom.

C

979

D (E)

(980) In this year Ealdorman Ælfhere fetched the holy king's body from Wareham and bore it with great honour to Shaftesbury.

980 In this year Abbot Æthelgar was consecrated bishop for the see of Selsey on 2 May. And in the same year Southampton was sacked by a naval force, and most of the citizens killed or taken captive; and that same year Thanet was ravaged; and the same year Cheshire was ravaged by a northern naval force.

(981) In this year there first came seven ships and ravaged Southampton.

981 In this year St. Petroc's monastery[2] was sacked, and that same year great damage was done everywhere by the coast both in Devon and also in Cornwall. And in the same year Ælfstan, bishop of Wiltshire, died, and his body is buried in the monastery of Abingdon, and Wulfgar then succeeded to the bishopric. And in the same year Womer, abbot of Ghent, died.

982 In this year three ships of vikings arrived in Dorset and ravaged in Portland. That same year London was burnt down. And in the same year two ealdormen died, Æthelmær of Hampshire and Edwin of Sussex, and Æthelmær's body is buried in the New Minster at Winchester and Edwin's in the monastery of Abingdon. That same

[1] i.e. 14 April, if 'D' and 'E' are right in placing the coronation soon after the election. If, however, 'C''s date, 979, is correct, the coronation was on 4 May.

[2] Padstow. See W. G. Hoskins and H. P. R. Finberg, *Devonshire Studies* (London, 1952), p. 29, n. 2.

C

year two abbesses in Dorset died, Herelufu of Shaftesbury and Wulfwyn of Wareham. And that same year Odda,[1] emperor of the Romans, went to the land of the Greeks,[2] and he then encountered a great army of the Saracens coming up from the sea, wishing to make a raid on the Christian people; and then the emperor fought against them and a great slaughter was made on both sides, and the emperor had control of the field, and yet he was much harassed there before he left. And when he was on his way home, his brother's son died. He was called Odda and was the son of the prince Leodulf, and this Leodulf was the son of the old Odda and of King Edward's daughter.[3]

C (D, E)

83 In this year Ealdorman Ælfhere died,[4] and Ælfric succeeded to the same aldormanry, and Pope Benedict died.[5]

A

84 In this year the benevolent Bishop Æthelwold died, and the consecration of the succeeding bishop, Ælfheah, who was called by a second name, Godwine, was on 19 October, and he occupied the bishop's throne in Winchester on the festival of the two apostles, Simon and Jude.[8]

C (D, E)

In this year [the holy][6] Bishop Æthelwold, [father of the monks],[6] died on 1 August,[7] [and in this year Edwin was consecrated as Abbot of Abingdon].[9]

C (D, E)

85 In this year Ealdorman Ælfric was driven out of the land. And in the same year Edwin was consecrated abbot of the monastery of Abingdon.[10]

86 In this year the king laid waste the diocese of Rochester. In this year the great murrain first occurred in England.

88 (987 E, F) In this year Watchet was ravaged; (988, all MSS.) and Goda, the Devonshire thegn, was killed,[11] and many fell with him. In this year Archbishop Dunstan died,[12] and Bishop Æthelgar succeeded to the archiepiscopal see, and lived but a short while – one year and three months – after that.

---

[1] Otto II.

[2] This expression covered all the lands of the eastern emperor, and this expedition was to southern Italy.

[3] Otto the Great married Edith, daughter of Edward the Elder, and they had a son Liodulf.

[4] 'A' has this also, but not the rest of the annal.

[5] 'D', 'E' omit the last clause.

[6] Only in 'D' and 'E'.

[7] The date in 'C' only.

[8] 28 October. 'A' has no further entry until 991; 'F' combines 'A' and 'E' in this annal.

[9] Only in 'E'. cf. 985, 'C'.

[10] This sentence is only in 'C'. cf. 984, 'E'.

[11] Florence adds information that may come from the account of this engagement in the *Life of St Oswald*. See *E.H.D.*, 1, No. 236, p. 843.

[12] 'E': 'The holy Archbishop Dunstan left this life and attained the heavenly life.'

C (D, E)

990 (989 E, F) In this year Sigeric was consecrated archbishop,[1] and Abbot Edwin died and Abbot Wulfgar succeeded to the office.[2]

A

991[3] In this year Olaf came with 93 ships to Folkestone, and ravaged round about it, and then from there went to Sandwich, and so from there to Ipswich, and overran it all, and so to Maldon. And Ealdorman Brihtnoth came against him there with his army and fought against him; and they killed the ealdorman there and had control of the field.[4] And afterwards peace was made with them and the king stood sponsor to him afterwards at his confirmation.[5]

C (D, E)

In this year Ipswich was ravaged, and very soon afterwards Ealdorman Brihtnoth was killed at Maldon. And in that year it was determined that tribute should first be paid to the Danish men because of the great terror they were causing along the coast. The first payment was 10,000 pounds. Archbishop Sigeric first advised that course.

C (D, E)

992 In this year the holy Archbishop Oswald[6] left this life and attained the heavenly life, and Ealdorman Æthelwine[7] died in the same year. Then the king and all his councillors decreed that all the ships that were any use should be assembled at London. And the king then entrusted the expedition to the leadership of Ealdorman Ælfric[8] and Earl Thored[9] and Bishop Ælfstan[10] and Bishop Æscwig,[11] and they were to try if they could entrap the Danish army anywhere at sea. Then Ealdorman Ælfric[12] sent someone to warn the enemy, and then in the night before the day on which they were to have joined battle, he absconded by night from the army, to his own great disgrace, and then the enemy escaped, except that the crew of one ship was slain. And then the Danish army encountered the ships from East Anglia and from London, and they made a great slaughter there and captured the ship, all armed and equipped, on which the ealdorman was.[13]

---

[1] 'F' adds: 'and afterwards went to Rome for his *pallium*'.

[2] 'D' and 'F' omit the reference to the Abingdon abbots. 'E' puts it at the beginning instead of the end of the annal.

[3] It looks as if 'A' put this at 993, but Mr Alistair Campbell has called my attention to a caret mark over 991, showing that the scribe, who added this annal after the numbers from 989 to 992 had been written in a horizontal line, with 993 as the next marginal number, meant the entry to belong to 991. The annal can therefore be used as evidence for the presence of Olaf, i.e. Tryggvason, later king of Norway, at the battle of Maldon.

[4] A fragmentary Old English poem on this battle survives. See *E.H.D.*, I, No. 10. The rest of this annal appears to have been added as an afterthought, after the entry for 994 had been made, for most of it is entered in the margin. It should be noted

that the writer does not say that these events took place in 991, but merely *after* an event which did.

[5] A later Canterbury addition here reads: 'through the advice of Sigeric, bishop of the people of Kent, and of Ælfheah, bishop of Winchester'.

[6] Of York.

[7] Of East Anglia. He was a close friend of Archbishop Oswald and co-founder of the abbey of Ramsey.

[8] Of Hampshire.

[9] Of Northumbria.

[10] Of London or Rochester.

[11] Of Dorchester.

[12] 'F' adds: 'one of those in whom the king trusted most'.

[13] Florence adds: 'and he himself escaped with difficulty by flight'.

C (D, E)

And then after Archbishop Oswald's death, Abbot Ealdwulf[1] succeeded to the see of York and to Worcester, and Cenwulf to the abbacy of Peterborough.

993 In this year Bamburgh was sacked and much booty was captured there, and after that the army came to the mouth of the Humber and did great damage there, both in Lindsey and in Northumbria. Then a very large English army was collected, and when they should have joined battle, the leaders, namely Fræna, Godwine, and Frythegyst, first started the flight.[2] In this year the king had Ælfgar, son of Ealdorman Ælfric, blinded.

A	C (D, E)

994 In this year Archbishop Sigeric died, and Ælfric, bishop of Wiltshire, succeeded to the archbishopric.

In this year Olaf[3] and Swein[4] came to London on the Nativity of St. Mary[5] with 94 ships, and they proceeded to attack the city stoutly and wished also to set it on fire; but there they suffered more harm and injury than they ever thought any citizens would do to them. But the holy Mother of God showed her mercy to the citizens on that day and saved them from their enemies. And these went away from there, and did the greatest damage that ever any army could do, by burning, ravaging, and slaying, everywhere along the coast, and in Essex, Kent, Sussex, and Hampshire; and finally they seized horses and rode as widely as they wished, and continued to do indescribable damage. Then the king and his councillors determined to send to them and promise them tribute and provisions, on condition that they should cease that harrying. And they then accepted that, and the whole army came then to Southampton and took winter quarters there; and they were provisioned throughout all the West Saxon kingdom, and they were paid 16,000 pounds in money.

Then the king sent Bishop Ælfheah[6] and Ealdorman Æthelweard[7] for King Olaf, and hostages were given to the ships meanwhile. And they then brought Olaf to the king at Andover with much ceremony, and King Ethelred stood sponsor to him at confirmation, and bestowed gifts on him royally. And then Olaf promised – as also he performed – that he would never come back to England in hostility.

---

[1] 'E' adds: 'of Peterborough'.
[2] Florence adds: 'because they were Danes on the father's side'.
[3] Olaf Tryggvason.
[4] Swein Forkbeard, king of Denmark.
[5] 8 September.
[6] Of Winchester.
[7] Of the Western Provinces.

C (D, E)

995 In this year the star 'comet' appeared, and Archbishop Sigeric died.[1]

996 In this year Ælfric was consecrated archbishop at Christ Church.[2]

F996 In this year Wulfstan was consecrated bishop of London.[3]

C (D, E)

997 In this year the Danish army went round Devon into the mouth of the Severn and ravaged there, both in Cornwall, in Wales, and in Devon. And they landed at Watchet and did much damage there, burning and slaying; and after that they turned back round Land's End to the southern side, and then turned into the mouth of the Tamar, and went inland until they reached Lydford, burning and slaying everything they came across, and burnt down Ordwulf's monastery at Tavistock and took with them to their ships indescribable booty.

F997 In this year Archbishop Ælfric went to Rome for his *pallium*.

C (D, E)

998 In this year the army turned back east into the mouth of the Frome, and there they went inland everywhere into Dorset as widely as they pleased; and the English army was often assembled against them, but as soon as they were to have joined battle, a flight was always instigated by some means, and always the enemy had the victory in the end. And then for another period they stayed in the Isle of Wight, and meanwhile got their food from Hampshire and Sussex.

999 In this year the army came again round into the Thames and turned then up the Medway and to Rochester.[4] And the Kentish levy came against them there, and they then joined battle stoutly; but, alas! they too soon turned and fled [because they had not the support which they should have had],[5] and the Danes had control of the field. And they then seized horses and rode wherever[6] they pleased, and destroyed and ravaged almost all West Kent.[7] Then the king with his councillors determined that they should be opposed by a naval force and also by a land force. But when the ships were ready, one delayed[8] from day to day, and oppressed the wretched people who were on the ships. And ever, as things should have been moving, they were the more delayed from one hour to the next, and ever they

---

[1] 28 October 994 is the most probable date. The chronicler may have used an episcopal list which commenced the year on 24 September.

[2] 'F' dates his election 995, adding that it was done on Easter Day at Amesbury. A long spurious passage follows on his replacing canons by monks.

[3] This is the homilist, who became archbishop of York in 1002.

[4] Florence adds: 'and surrounded it with a siege for a few days'.

[5] In 'E' only.

[6] 'D', 'E': 'as widely as'.

[7] Literally 'the West Kentings', which implies that it was a separate administrative area.

[8] 'C''s 'the judges delayed' is a misreading, as the following singular verb bears out.

C (D, E)

let their enemies' force increase, and ever the English retreated inland and the Danes continually followed; and then in the end it effected nothing – the naval expedition or the land expedition – except the oppression of the people and the waste of money and the encouragement of their enemies.

1000 In this year the king went into Cumberland[1] and ravaged very nearly all of it; and his ships went out round Chester and should have come to meet him, but they could not. Then they ravaged the Isle of Man. And the enemy fleet had gone to Richard's kingdom[2] that summer.

A	C (D, E)
1001 In this year there was much fighting in England because of a naval force; and they ravaged and burnt almost everywhere, so that they betook themselves inland in one journey till they reached Dean;[3] and the people of Hampshire came against them there and fought against them, and there Æthelweard the king's high-reeve was killed, and Leofric of Whitchurch and Leofwine the king's high-reeve, and Wulfhere the bishop's thegn, and Godwine of Worthy, Bishop Ælfsige's[5] son, and 81 men in all; and there were far more of the Danes killed, although they had control of the field. And then they went west from there until they reached Devon; and Pallig[6] came to meet them there with the ships which he could collect, because he had deserted King Ethelred in spite of all the pledges which he had given him. And the king had also made great gifts to him, in estates and gold and silver. And they burnt Teignton and also many other good residences which we cannot name, and afterwards peace was made with them.	In this year the army came to the mouth of the Exe and then went inland to the borough, and proceeded to fight resolutely there, but they were very[4] stoutly resisted. Then they went through the land and did exactly as they were accustomed, slew and burnt. Then an immense army was gathered there of the people of Devon and of Somerset, and they met at Pinhoe; and as soon as they joined battle the people[7] gave way, and the Danes made a great slaughter there, and then rode over the land – and ever their next raid was worse than the one before it. And they brought much booty with them to their ships, and turned from there to the Isle of Wight. And there they went about as they pleased and nothing withstood
Then they went from there to the mouth of the Exe, so that they transported themselves in one journey until they reached Pinhoe; and opposing them there were Kola, the king's high-reeve, and Eadsige, the king's reeve, with what army they could gather, but they were put to flight there, and many were killed, and the Danes had control of the field. And the next morning they burnt the residence at Pinhoe and at Clyst[8] and also many good residences which	

---

[1] See p. 72, n. 1.

[2] Normandy.

[3] The *Æthelinga dene* of the text is shown to be in East or West Dean, Sussex, in *The Place-Names of Sussex*, 1, p. xlv; it is near enough to the border of Hampshire to account for the presence of the militia of this shire.

[4] 'E' adds: 'resolutely and'.

[5] Bishop of Winchester, 951–958.

[6] Brother-in-law of King Swein. According to William of Malmesbury, he and his wife Gunhild and their child were victims of the massacre of St Brice's day, 1002.

[7] 'D', 'E': 'the English army'.

[8] Probably Broad Clyst, Devon.

<table>
<tr><td>A</td><td>C (D, E)</td></tr>
</table>

A

C (D, E)

we cannot name, and then went back east till they reached the Isle of Wight. And the next morning they burnt the residence at Waltham and many other villages. And soon afterwards terms were made with them and they accepted peace.[1]

them, and no naval force on sea, nor land force, dared go against them, no matter how far inland they went. It was in every way grievous, for they never ceased from their evil-doing.

C (D, E)

1002 In this year the king and his councillors determined that tribute should be paid to the fleet and peace made with them on condition that they should cease their evil-doing. Then the king sent Ealdorman Leofsige[2] to the fleet, and he then, by the command of the king and his councillors, arranged a truce with them and that they should receive provisions and tribute. And they then accepted that, and 24,000 pounds were paid to them. Then meanwhile Ealdorman Leofsige killed the king's high-reeve, Æfic, and the king then banished him from the country. And then in the spring the queen, Richard's daughter,[3] came to this land. And in the same summer Archbishop Ealdwulf[4] died.

And in that year the king ordered to be slain all the Danish men who were in England – this was done[5] on St. Brice's day[6] – because the king had been informed that they would treacherously deprive him, and then all his councillors, of life, and possess this kingdom afterwards.[7]

1003 In this year Exeter was stormed on account of the French *ceorl* Hugh, whom the queen had appointed as her reeve, and the Danish army then destroyed the borough completely and seized much booty there.[8] And in that same year the army went inland into Wiltshire.[9] Then a great English army was gathered from Wiltshire and from Hampshire, and they were going very resolutely towards the enemy. Then Ealdorman Ælfric was to lead the army, but he was up to his old tricks. As soon as they were so close that each army looked on the other, he feigned him sick, and began retching to vomit, and said that he was taken ill, and thus betrayed the people whom he should have led. As the saying goes: 'When the leader gives way, the whole army will be much hindered.' When Swein saw that they were irresolute, and that they all dispersed, he led his army into Wilton, and they ravaged and burnt the borough, and he betook him then to Salisbury, and from there went back to the sea to where he knew his wave-coursers were.

---

[1] At this point the eleventh-century copy of 'A' (Brit. Mus. Cott. Otho B. xi) came to an end. Subsequent annals in 'A' are Canterbury additions.

[2] Of Essex.

[3] 'F', which has part of this annal, adds: 'Ymma [Ælfgifu]'.

[4] Of York.

[5] 'D', 'E', omit 'this was done'.

[6] 13 November. A reference to this massacre is contained in a charter, *E.H.D.*, I, No. 217.

[7] 'F' adds: 'without any opposition'.

[8] Florence is more explicit, in a passage that seems more than mere surmise from the Chronicle: 'Swein, king of the Danes, through the evil counsel, negligence, or treachery of the Norman count Hugh, whom Queen Emma had put over Devon, stormed and despoiled the city of Exeter, and destroyed the wall from the east to the west gate.'

[9] 'E' omits this sentence.

C (D, E)

1004 In this year Swein came with his fleet to Norwich and completely ravaged and burnt the borough. Then Ulfcetel[1] with the councillors in East Anglia determined that it would be better to buy peace from the army before they did too much damage in the country, for they had come unexpectedly and he had not time to collect his army. Then, under cover of the truce which was supposed to be between them, the Danish army stole inland from the ships, and directed their course to Thetford. When Ulfcetel perceived that, he sent orders that the ships were to be hewn to bits, but those whom he intended for this failed him; he then collected his army secretly, as quickly as he could. And the Danish army then came to Thetford within three weeks after their ravaging of Norwich, and remained inside there one night, and ravaged and burnt the borough. Then in the morning, when they wished to go to their ships, Ulfcetel arrived with his troops to offer battle there.[2] And they resolutely joined battle, and many fell slain on both sides. There the flower of the East Anglian people was killed. But if their full strength had been there, the Danes would never have got back to their ships; as they themselves said[3] that they never met worse fighting in England than Ulfcetel dealt to them.

1005 In this year occurred the great famine throughout England, such that no man ever remembered one so cruel, and the fleet returned from this country to Denmark this year, and let little time elapse before it came back.

A1005 In this year Archbishop Ælfric died.

C (D, E)

1006 In this year Archbishop Ælfric died and Bishop Ælfheah succeeded him to the archiepiscopal see [and Bishop Brihtwold succeeded to the bishopric of Wiltshire].[4] In the same year Wulfgeat was deprived of all his property,[5] and Wulfheah and Ufegeat were blinded and Ealdorman Ælfhelm killed.[6] And Bishop Cenwulf[7] died.

Then after midsummer[8] the great fleet[9] came to Sandwich, and did just as they were accustomed, ravaged, burnt, and slew as they went.[10] Then the king ordered the whole nation from Wessex and Mercia to be called out, and they were out on military service against the Danish army the whole autumn, yet it availed no whit more than it had often done before; for in spite of it all, the Danish army went about as it pleased, and the English levy caused the people of the country every sort

---

[1] Florence, 'ealdorman of the East Angles', but contemporary sources do not call him 'ealdorman'.

[2] 'D' and 'E' omit the last phrase.

[3] 'E' ends the annal here.

[4] In 'E' and 'F' only. 16 November 1005 is probably correct for Ælfric's death.

[5] Florence calls him Leofeca's son, whom Ethelred 'had loved almost more than anyone'. He attributes the forfeiture to 'unjust judgments and arrogant deeds which he had committed'.

[6] Florence has details perhaps drawn from a lost saga about Eadric Streona, whom he makes responsible for the crime. He says also that the blinding was at the king's command and took place at Cookham, where he was staying. Ælfhelm was ealdorman of southern Northumbria, and Wulfheah and Ufegeat were his sons.

[7] Of Winchester.

[8] Florence: 'in the month of July'.

[9] 'E': 'the Danish fleet'.

[10] Florence adds: 'now in Kent, now in Sussex'.

C (D, E)

of harm, so that they profited neither from the native army nor the foreign army. When winter approached, the English army went home, and the Danish army then came after Martinmas to its sanctuary, the Isle of Wight, and procured for themselves everywhere whatever they needed; and then towards Christmas they betook themselves to the entertainment waiting them, out through Hampshire into Berkshire to Reading; and always they observed their ancient custom, lighting their beacons as they went. They then turned to Wallingford and burnt it all, and were one night at Cholsey,[1] and then turned along Ashdown to Cuckamsley Barrow,[2] and waited there for what had been proudly threatened, for it had often been said that if they went to Cuckamsley,[3] they would never get to the sea. They then went home another way. The English army was then gathered at the Kennet, and they joined battle there, and at once they put that troop to flight, and afterwards carried their booty to the sea. There the people of Winchester could see that army, proud and undaunted, when they went past their gate to the sea, and fetched themselves food and treasures from more than 50 miles from the sea.

Then the king had gone across the Thames, into Shropshire, and received there his food-rents in the Christmas season. Then so great terror of the Danish army arose that no one could think or conceive how to drive them from the country, or to defend this country from them, for they had cruelly left their mark on every shire of Wessex with their burning and their harrying. The king then with his councillors began eagerly to consider what might seem to them all most advisable, that this country could be saved before it was completely destroyed. Then the king and his councillors, for the benefit of the whole nation, determined – hateful though it was to all of them – that tribute must needs be paid to the army. Then the king sent to the army to inform them that he desired that there should be a truce between them, and that tribute should be paid them and provisions given; and then they all accepted that, and they were supplied with food throughout England.

A1006 In this year Ælfheah was consecrated as archbishop.

C (D, E)

1007 In this year the tribute was paid to the army, namely 36,000[4] pounds. In this year also Eadric was appointed ealdorman over the kingdom of the Mercians.[5]

1008 In this year the king ordered that ships should be built unremittingly over all England, namely a warship from 310 hides,[6] and a helmet and corselet from eight hides.

---

[1] 'E' omits this clause.

[2] Cuckamsley or Scutchamfly Knob, on the edge of the Downs, near East Hendred.

[3] 'E' omits this section, from the first Cuckamsley.

[4] 'E', 'F': '30,000'.

[5] 'D' adds: 'In this year Bishop Ælfheah went to Rome for the *pallium*.'

[6] 'D' has 'ships' in error for 'hides'. 'E' repeats hides after 'ten'. The order in 'C' 'from three hundred hides and from ten' may have puzzled them; 310 is an unusual unit. It is sometimes assumed that something is omitted. Mr Garmonsway would read: 'one large warship from every three hundred hides and a cutter from every ten hides'.

C (D, E)

1009 In this year the ships which we mentioned above were ready, and there were more of them than ever before, from what books tell us, had been in England in any king's time; and they were all brought together at Sandwich and were to stay there and protect this country from every invading army. But yet we had not the good fortune or honour that the naval force was of use to this country, any more than it had been on many previous occasions.

Then it happened at this same time, or a little earlier, that Brihtric, Ealdorman Eadric's brother, accused Wulfnoth *Cild* [the South Saxon][1] to the king, and he went away and enticed ships to him until he had 20, and then he ravaged everywhere along the south coast, doing all manner of damage. Then the naval force was informed that they (Wulfnoth's party) could easily be surrounded if people were to set about it. Then the aforesaid Brihtric took with him 80 ships, intending to make a big reputation for himself[2] and to capture Wulfnoth alive or dead. But when they were on their way thither, such a wind blew against them that no man remembered its like, and it beat and dashed to pieces all the ships, and cast them ashore, and at once Wulfnoth came and burnt up the ships. When it became known to the other ships, where the king was, how the others had fared, it was as if everything was in confusion, and the king betook himself home, as did the ealdormen and chief councillors, and deserted the ships thus lightly. And the people who were on the ships took [the ships][3] back to London, and let the toil of all the nation thus lightly come to naught; and no better than this was the victory which all the English people had expected.

When this ship-levy had ended thus, there came at once after Lammas[4] the immense raiding army, which we called Thorkel's army,[5] to Sandwich,[6] and immediately turned their course to Canterbury and would quickly have captured the borough if the citizens had not still more quickly asked them for peace. And all the people of East Kent made peace with that army and gave them 3,000 pounds. And then immediately after that the army turned about till it reached the Isle of Wight, and from there they ravaged and burnt, as is their custom, everywhere in Sussex and Hampshire, and also in Berkshire. Then the king ordered all the nation to be called out,[7] so that the enemy should be resisted on every side; but nevertheless they journeyed just as they pleased.

Then on one occasion the king had intercepted them with all his army, when they wished to go to their ships, and the whole people was ready to attack them,[8] but it was hindered by Ealdorman Eadric, then as it always was. Then after Martinmas[9] they went back again to Kent, and took up winter quarters on the Thames, and lived off Essex and off the shires which were nearest, on both sides of the Thames,

---

[1] From 'D', 'E', 'F'.

[2] 'F' reads: 'Then Brihtric wished to earn praise for himself.'

[3] From 'D', 'E'.

[4] 1 August.

[5] Only 'C' has this clause. The Danish leader Thorkel the Tall is meant.

[6] Florence has an important addition: 'The Danish earl Thorkel came with his fleet to England; then, in the month of August, another immense fleet of Danes, which the earls Heming and Eilaf were leading, came to land at the island of Thanet and without delay joined the aforesaid fleet. They then both proceeded to the port of Sandwich.'

[7] Florence adds: 'and he placed it through the maritime provinces against their attacks'.

[8] *Id.*: 'prepared to die or to conquer'.

[9] 11 November.

C (D, E)

and often they attacked the borough of London. But, praise be to God, it still stands untouched, and they always suffered loss there.

Then after Christmas they chose a passage out through the Chilterns, and so to Oxford, and burnt the borough, and made their way then on both sides of the Thames towards their ships. Then they were warned that an army was collected against them at London; they then crossed at Staines. Thus they behaved the whole winter, and during the spring they were in Kent repairing their ships.

1010   In this year the afore-mentioned army came to East Anglia after Easter[1] and landed at Ipswich, and went straightway to where they had heard that Ulfcetel was with his army.[2] That was on Ascension day,[3] and at once the East Angles fled. The men of Cambridgeshire stood firm against them. The king's son-in-law[4] Athelstan was killed there, and Oswig and his son, and Wulfric, Leofwine's son, and Eadwig, Ælfic's brother, and many other good thegns and a countless number of the people. It was Thurcetel Mare's Head who first started that flight. The Danes had control of the field [and there they were provided with horses, and afterwards had control of East Anglia],[5] and ravaged and burnt that country for three months and even went into the wild fens, slaying the men and cattle, and burning throughout the fens; and they burnt down Thetford and Cambridge.

And afterwards they turned back southwards into the Thames Valley, and the mounted men rode towards the ships; and quickly afterwards they turned west again into Oxfordshire, and from there into Buckinghamshire, and so along the Ouse until they reached Bedford, and so on as far as Tempsford, and ever they burnt as they went. Then they turned back to the ships with their booty. And when they were journeying[6] to their ships, the English army should have come out again in case they wished to go inland. Then the English army went home. And when they were in the east, the English army was kept in the west, and when they were in the south, our army was in the north. Then all the councillors were summoned to the king, and it was then to be decided how this country should be defended. But even if anything was then decided, it did not last even a month. Finally there was no leader who would collect an army, but each fled as best he could, and in the end no shire would even help the next.

Then before St. Andrew's day[7] the Danish army came to Northampton and at once burnt that town and[8] as much round about it as they pleased, and from there went across the Thames into Wessex, and so towards Cannings marsh,[9] and burnt it all. When they had thus gone as far as they pleased, they came at Christmas to their ships.

---

[1] 9 April.

[2] Florence says it was at 'the place which is called *Ringmere*'. Old Norse poems also give this name to the battle. See *E.H.D.*, I, Nos. 12, 13.

[3] 18 May; but Florence puts the battle on 5 May, and this is shown to be correct by the entry of Oswig's death on that date in the Ely calendar discussed by B. Dickins in *Leeds Studies in English*, VI, pp. 14–24.

[4] Or brother-in-law, i.e. brother of Ethelred's first wife.

Ethelred's eldest son was called Athelstan, but this was too common a name in the West Saxon house for this fact to be significant in this connexion.

[5] From 'D', 'E'.

[6] 'E': 'were dispersing'.

[7] 30 November.

[8] 'E' adds: 'they seized'.

[9] Near All and Bishop's Cannings, Wilts.

C (D, E)

1011 In this year the king and his councillors sent to the army and asked for peace, and promised them tribute and provisions on condition that they should cease their ravaging. They had then overrun: (i) East Anglia, (ii) Essex, (iii) Middlesex, (iv) Oxfordshire, (v) Cambridgeshire, (vi) Hertfordshire, (vii) Buckinghamshire, (viii) Bedfordshire, (ix) half Huntingdonshire, (x) much of Northamptonshire;[1] and south of the Thames all Kent, Sussex, Hastings,[2] Surrey, Berkshire, Hampshire, and much of Wiltshire. All those disasters befell us through bad policy, in that they were never offered tribute in time nor fought against;[3] but when they had done most to our injury, peace and truce were made with them; and for all this truce and tribute they journeyed none the less in bands everywhere, and harried our wretched people, and plundered and killed them.

And then in this year, between the Nativity of St. Mary[4] and Michaelmas,[5] they besieged Canterbury,[6] and they got inside by treachery, for Ælfmær,[7] whose life Archbishop Ælfheah had saved, betrayed it. Then they captured there Archbishop Ælfheah, and the king's reeve Ælfweard, and Abbess Leofrun,[8] and Bishop Godwine;[9] and they let Abbot Ælfmær[10] escape. And they took captive there all the ecclesiastics, and men and women – it was impossible for any man to tell how much of that people that was[11] – and they stayed afterwards in that borough as long as they pleased. And when they had then ransacked the whole borough, they went to their ships and took the archbishop with them.

He was then a captive who had been head of the English people and of Christendom. There could misery be seen where happiness was often seen before, in that wretched city from which first came [to us][12] Christianity and happiness in divine and secular things. And they kept the archbishop with them till the time when they martyred him.

1012 In this year Ealdorman Eadric and all the chief councillors of England, ecclesiastical and lay, came to London before Easter – Easter Sunday was on 13 April – and they stayed there until the tribute, namely 48,000 pounds,[13] was all paid after Easter. Then on the Saturday the army became greatly incensed against the bishop because he would not promise them any money,[14] but forbade that anything should be paid for him. They were also very drunk, for wine from the south had been brought there. They seized the bishop, and brought him to their assembly on the eve of the Sunday of the octave of Easter, which was 19 April, and shamefully put him to death there:[15] they pelted him with bones and with

---

[1] Omitted in 'E'.

[2] Not merely the town. Hastings was the name of a district, long regarded as distinct from Sussex.

[3] Only 'C' has these last three words.

[4] 8 September.

[5] 29 September.

[6] Florence adds: 'on the twentieth day of the siege part of the city was burnt'.

[7] Id. adds: 'the archdeacon'.

[8] Of St Mildred's, Thanet. 'E', 'F' have (wrongly) 'Leofwine'.

[9] Of Rochester.

[10] Of St Augustine's, Canterbury.

[11] Florence adds: 'Then Christ Church was plundered and burnt.' He gives an account of further atrocities and of a sickness sent by God on the Danes in vengeance.

[12] From 'D', 'E'.

[13] 'E', 'F': '8,000'.

[14] According to Florence, 3,000 pounds was asked for him.

[15] This last clause is in 'C' only.

C (D, E)

ox-heads, and one of them[1] struck him on the head with the back[2] of an axe, that he sank down with the blow, and his holy blood fell on the ground, and so he sent his holy soul to God's kingdom. And in the morning his body was carried to London,[3] and the bishops Eadnoth and Ælfhun[4] and the citizens received it with all reverence and buried it in St. Paul's minster. And God now reveals there the powers of the holy martyr.[5]

When that tribute was paid and the oaths of peace were sworn, the Danish army then dispersed as widely as it had been collected. Then 45 ships from that army came over to the king,[6] and they promised him to defend this country, and he was to feed and clothe them.

1013 In the year after the archbishop was martyred, the king appointed Bishop Lifing to the archbishopric of Canterbury. And in this same year, before the month of August, King Swein came with his fleet to Sandwich, and then went very quickly round East Anglia into the mouth of the Humber, and so up along the Trent until he reached Gainsborough. And then at once Earl Uhtred and all the Northumbrians submitted to him, as did all the people of Lindsey, and then all the people belonging to the district of the Five Boroughs,[7] and quickly afterwards all the Danish settlers[8] north of Watling Street, and hostages were given to him from every shire. When he perceived that all the people had submitted to him, he gave orders that his army should be provisioned and provided with horses, and then he afterwards turned southward[9] with his full forces and left the ships and the hostages in charge of his son Cnut. When he had crossed the Watling Street, they did the greatest damage that any army could do. He then turned to Oxford, and the citizens at once submitted and gave hostages; and from there to Winchester, where they did the same. He then turned eastward to London, and many of his host were drowned in the Thames because they did not trouble to find a bridge. When he came to the borough the citizens would not yield, but resisted with full battle, because King Ethelred was inside and Thorkel with him.

Then King Swein turned from there to Wallingford, and so west across the Thames to Bath, where he stayed with his army. Then Ealdorman Æthelmær[10] came there, and with him the western thegns, and all submitted to Swein, and they gave him hostages. When he had fared thus,[11] he then turned northward to his ships, and all the nation regarded him as full king. And after that the citizens of

---

[1] Florence adds: 'Thrum by name, whom he had confirmed the day before, moved by impious pity.'

[2] The interpretation of *yr* as the blunt end of an axe-head is supported by *Leechdoms* (ed. Cockagne, III, p. 14), where an *yr* is used to crush bones.

[3] 'E', by changing the order, makes the bishops bring the body to London.

[4] Of Dorchester and London respectively.

[5] This annal was written before the translation of Ælfheah's body to Canterbury in 1023. A contemporary account of this martyrdom is given by the German chronicler, Thietmar of Merseburg. See *E.H.D.*, I, No. 27.

[6] They were commanded by Earl Thorkel.

[7] This presumably is the force of 'C''s expression *Fifburhingum*, as opposed to 'D', 'E''s *Fifburgum*, which could mean the boroughs without necessarily including the areas of which they were the centre.

[8] Literally 'the army', used in the sense of the organized inhabitants of an area of Danish settlement in England.

[9] Florence adds: 'against the South Mercians'.

[10] *Id.* adds: 'of Devon'.

[11] 'D', 'E': 'When he had won everything thus.'

C (D, E)

London submitted and gave hostages, for they were afraid that he would destroy them. Then Swein demanded full payment and provisions for his army that winter, and Thorkel demanded the same for the army which lay at Greenwich, and in spite of it all they ravaged as often as they pleased. Nothing therefore was of benefit to this nation, neither from the south nor from the north.

Then King Ethelred was for a time with the fleet which lay in the Thames, and the queen went across the sea to her brother Richard,[1] and with her Abbot Ælfsige of Peterborough, and the king sent Bishop Ælfhun across the sea with the athelings Edward and Alfred, that he should take care of them. And the king then went from the fleet to the Isle of Wight at Christmas and spent that festival there; and after the festival went across the sea to Richard and was there with him until the happy event of Swein's death.[2]

1014 In this year Swein ended his days at Candlemas, on 3 February,[3] and then all the fleet elected Cnut king. Then all the councillors who were in England,[4] ecclesiastical and lay, determined to send for King Ethelred, and they said that no lord was dearer to them than their natural lord if he would govern them more justly than he did before. Then the king sent his son Edward hither with his messengers, and bade them greet all his people, and said that he would be a gracious lord to them, and reform all the things which they all hated; and all the things that had been said and done against him should be forgiven, on condition that they all unanimously turned to him without treachery. And complete friendship was then established with oath and pledge on both sides, and they pronounced every Danish king an outlaw from England for ever. Then during the spring King Ethelred came home to his own people and he was gladly received by them all.

Then after Swein was dead, Cnut stayed in Gainsborough with his army until Easter,[5] and he and the people in Lindsey came to an agreement that they would provide him with horses and then go out and ravage all together. Then King Ethelred came there to Lindsey with his full force before they were ready, and it was ravaged and burnt, and all the men who could be got at were killed; and Cnut put out to sea with his fleet, and thus the wretched people were betrayed by him. And he then turned south till he reached Sandwich, and he caused to be put ashore the hostages who had been given to his father, and he cut off their hands, ears, and noses.[6] And on top of all these evils, the king ordered 21,000[7] pounds to be paid to the army which lay at Greenwich; and in this year on Michaelmas eve[8] the great tide of the sea flooded widely over this country, coming up higher than it had ever done before, and submerging many villages and a countless number of people.

---

[1] Richard II, duke of Normandy.

[2] 'E' adds a Peterborough insertion on the collection of relics by Abbot Ælfsige when he was abroad.

[3] 'D' adds: 'and in the same year Ælfwig was consecrated bishop of London at York, on St Juliana's day (16 February)'. According to Gaimar and Simeon of Durham, Swein was first buried at York. See also Thietmar's story of the removal of his remains to Denmark (*E.H.D.*, I, No. 27).

[4] This clause is in 'C' only.

[5] 25 April.

[6] Florence adds: 'and then he set out for Denmark, to return the next year'.

[7] *Id.*: 30,000.

[8] 28 September.

C (D, E)

1015 In this year the great assembly at Oxford took place, and there Ealdorman Eadric betrayed Sigeferth and Morcar,[1] the chief thegns belonging to the Seven Boroughs:[2] he enticed them into his chamber, and they were basely killed inside it. And the king then seized all their property and ordered Sigeferth's widow[3] to be seized and brought to Malmesbury. Then after a short interval, the atheling Edmund went and took the woman against the king's will and married her. Then before the Nativity of St. Mary[4] the atheling went from the west, north to the Five Boroughs, and at once took possession of all Sigeferth's estates and Morcar's, and the people all submitted to him.

Then at that same time King Cnut came to Sandwich, and then turned at once round Kent into Wessex, until he reached the mouth of the Frome, and ravaged then in Dorset, in Wiltshire, and in Somerset. The king then lay sick at Cosham. Then Ealdorman Eadric collected an army, and so did the atheling Edmund in the North. When they united, the ealdorman wished to betray the atheling, and on that account they separated without fighting, and retreated from their enemies. And then Ealdorman Eadric seduced 40 ships[5] from the king, and then went over to Cnut; and the West Saxons submitted and gave hostages and supplied the Danish army with horses, and it then stayed there until Christmas.

1016 In this year Cnut came with his army,[6] and Ealdorman Eadric with him, across the Thames into Mercia at Cricklade, and they turned then into Warwickshire within the Christmas season, and ravaged and burnt, and killed all they came across. Then the atheling Edmund began to gather the English army. When the army was assembled,[7] nothing would satisfy them except that the king should be there with them and they should have the assistance of the citizens of London. They then desisted from that expedition and each man took himself home. Then after that festival, the army was ordered out again on pain of the full penalty, every man to go forth who was capable of service. And word was sent to the king in London, begging him to come to join the army with the forces which he could muster. When they all came together, it availed nothing, no more than it had done often before. The king was then informed that those who should support him wished to betray him; he then left the army and returned to London.

Then the atheling Edmund rode to Northumbria to Earl Uhtred, and every one thought that they would collect an army against King Cnut. Then they led an army into Staffordshire and into Shropshire and to Chester, and they ravaged on their side[8] and Cnut on his side. He then went out through Buckinghamshire into Bedfordshire, from there to Huntingdonshire, and so into Northamptonshire,[9]

---

[1] Florence adds: 'the sons of Earngrim'. Wulfric Spott bequeathed estates in Derbyshire and Yorkshire to Morcar (see *E.H.D.*, I, No. 125), and both Morcar and Sigeferth are mentioned in the will of Ethelred's son Athelstan (*ibid.*, No. 130).

[2] The Five Boroughs probably with the addition of York and Torksey.

[3] Florence names her Aldgyth.

[4] Florence: 'between the Assumption (15 August) and the Nativity (8 September) of St Mary'.

[5] Florence adds: 'manned by Danish soldiers'.

[6] 'E', 'F' add: 'of 160 ships'. This must be erroneous, for no naval force is in question.

[7] Florence says: 'The Mercians would not engage with the West Saxons and Danes.'

[8] *Id.* explains: 'because they would not go out to fight the army of the Danes'.

[9] This phrase is omitted in 'E'.

C (D, E)

along the fen to Stamford, and then into Lincolnshire; then from there to Nottinghamshire and so into Northumbria towards York. When Uhtred learned this, he left his ravaging and hastened northwards, and submitted then out of necessity, and with him all the Northumbrians, and he gave hostages. And nevertheless he was killed by the advice of Ealdorman Eadric,[1] and with him Thurcetel, Nafena's son. And then after that the king[2] appointed Eric[3] for the Northumbrians, as their earl, just as Uhtred had been, and then turned him[4] southward by another route, keeping to the west, and the whole army then reached the ships before Easter.[5] And the atheling Edmund went to London to his father. And then after Easter, King Cnut turned with all his ships towards London.

Then it happened that King Ethelred died before the ships arrived. He ended his days on St. George's day,[6] and he had held his kingdom with great toil and difficulties as long as his life lasted.[7] And then after his death, all the councillors who were in London and the citizens chose Edmund as king, and he stoutly defended his kingdom while his life lasted. Then the ships came to Greenwich at the Rogation days,[8] and within a short space of time they turned to London. And the Danes then dug a large ditch on the south side and dragged their ships on to the west side of the bridge, and then afterwards surrounded the borough with a ditch, so that no man could go in or out, and repeatedly attacked the borough, but they withstood them stoutly.[9]

King Edmund had previously gone out and he took possession of Wessex, and all the people submitted to him.[10] And soon after that he fought against the Danish army at Penselwood near Gillingham, and he fought a second battle after midsummer at Sherston;[11] and a great number on both sides fell there, and the armies separated of their own accord. In that battle Ealdorman Eadric and Ælfmær Darling[12] were supporting the Danish army against King Edmund. Then he collected the army for the third time, and went to London, keeping north of the Thames, and so out through *Clayhanger*,[13] and relieved the citizens and sent the enemy in flight to their ships. And then two days after that, the king crossed over at Brentford, and then fought against the army and put it to flight; and a great number of

---

[1] Only 'C' mentions Eadric. Florence adds: 'by Thurbrand'. The latter was a Yorkshire magnate who had a personal feud against Earl Uhtred.

[2] 'E': Cnut.

[3] Eric of Hlathir, Norway, a most famous Scandinavian leader.

[4] 'E': 'they turned them'.

[5] 1 April.

[6] 23 April.

[7] 'D' and 'E' say only: 'on St George's day, after great toil and difficulties of his life'. Florence has important additional information: 'His body was buried with great honour in the church of St Paul the Apostle. And after his death, the bishops, abbots, ealdormen, and all the more important men of England assembled together and unanimously elected Cnut as their lord and king; and coming to him at Southampton and repudiating and renouncing in his presence all the race of King Ethelred, they concluded a peace with him, and swore loyalty to him;

and he also swore to them that he would be a loyal lord to them, in affairs both of Church and State.'

[8] 7-9 May.

[9] Florence: 'Therefore, raising the siege for the time, and leaving part of the army to guard the ships, they went away, hastening to Wessex, and gave no time for King Edmund Ironside to raise his army. However, he met them bravely in Dorset with the army which he had been able to collect in so short a time, supported by God's help, and engaging them at a place called Penselwood near Gillingham, he conquered and put them to flight.'

[10] *Id.* adds: 'with great joy'.

[11] *Id.* adds: 'in Hwiccia.'

[12] *Id.* adds: 'and Ælfgar, son of Meaw'.

[13] Clayhill Farm in Tottenham, Middlesex. See *The Place-Names of Middlesex*, p. 79. This account of the route taken is only in 'C'.

C (D, E)

the English people who went ahead of the main force, wishing to get booty, were drowned there through their own carelessness. And the king turned to Wessex after that and collected his army.

Then the Danish army returned at once to London, and besieged the borough, attacking it strongly both by water and by land, but the Almighty God delivered it. The army then turned after that with their ships from London into the Orwell, and went inland there, and went into Mercia, slaying and burning whatever was in their path, as is their custom, and procured provisions for themselves; and they drove both their ships and their herds into the Medway. Then King Edmund collected all his army[1] for the fourth time, and crossed the Thames at Brentford, and went into Kent.[2] And the Danish army fled before him with their horses into Sheppey. The king killed as many of them as he could overtake, and Ealdorman Eadric came to meet the king at Aylesford. No greater folly was ever agreed to than that was. The army went again inland into Essex, and proceeded into Mercia and destroyed everything in its path.

When the king learnt that the army had gone inland, for the fifth time he collected all the English nation; and pursued them and overtook them in Essex at the hill which is called Ashingdon, and they stoutly joined battle there.[3] Then Ealdorman Eadric did as he had often done before: he was the first to start the flight with the *Magonsæte*,[4] and thus betrayed his liege lord and all the people of England. There Cnut had the victory and won for himself all the English people. There was Bishop Eadnoth[5] killed, and Abbot Wulfsige,[6] and Ealdorman Ælfric,[7] and Godwine, the ealdorman of Lindsey,[8] and Ulfcetel of East Anglia, and Æthelweard, son of Ealdorman Æthelwine,[9] and all the nobility of England was there destroyed.

Then after this battle King Cnut went inland with his army to Gloucestershire, where he had learnt that King Edmund was. Then Ealdorman Eadric and the councillors who were there advised that the kings should be reconciled, and they exchanged hostages.[10] And the kings met at Alney[11] and established their friendship there both with pledge and with oath,[12] and fixed the payment for the Danish army.[13] And with this reconciliation they separated, and Edmund succeeded to Wessex and Cnut to Mercia.[14] And the army then went to the ships with the things that they had captured, and the Londoners came to terms with the army and bought peace for themselves; and the army brought their ships into London and took up winter quarters inside.

---

[1] 'D', 'E': 'all the English nation'.

[2] Florence adds: 'and fought a battle against the Danes by Otford'.

[3] On 18 October.

[4] The people of Herefordshire; the name survives in Maund Bryan and Rose Maund.

[5] Of Dorchester.

[6] Of Ramsey.

[7] Of Hampshire.

[8] 'D', 'E' omit 'of Lindsey'.

[9] 'D': Ælfwine; 'E', 'F': Æthelsige. Æthelwine of East Anglia is meant.

[10] 'D' omits this last clause.

[11] 'D' adds: 'by Deerhurst'.

[12] 'D' has instead: 'and became partners and sworn brothers and established that both with pledge and also with oaths'.

[13] Florence adds that Edmund was dissuaded from continuing fighting by Eadric and others, and that the kings met at Deerhurst before going to Alney.

[14] Instead of 'Mercia', 'D' reads: 'to the north part'; Florence's text is corrupt at this point. He then adds that the sovereignty remained with Edmund.

C (D, E)

Then on St. Andrew's day King Edmund died[1] and his body is buried in Glastonbury along with his grandfather Edgar. And in the same year Wulfgar, abbot of Abingdon, died, and Æthelsige succeeded to the abbacy.[2]

1017 In this year King Cnut succeeded to all the kingdom of England[3] and divided it into four, Wessex for himself, East Anglia for Thorkel, Mercia for Eadric, and Northumbria for Eric. And in this year Ealdorman Eadric was killed,[4] and Northman,[5] son of Ealdorman Leofwine, and Æthelweard, son of Æthelmær the Stout,[6] and Brihtric, son of Ælfheah[7] of Devonshire. And King Cnut exiled the atheling Eadwig[8] and afterwards had him killed.[9] And then before 1 August the king ordered the widow of[10] King Ethelred, Richard's daughter, to be fetched as his wife.[11]

A1017 In this year Cnut was chosen as king.

C (D, E)

1018 In this year the tribute was paid over all England, namely 72,000 pounds in all, apart from what the citizens of London paid, namely ten and a half[12] thousand pounds. Then some of the army went to Denmark, and 40 ships remained with King Cnut, and the Danes and the English reached an agreement at Oxford.[13]

1019 In this year King Cnut returned to Denmark[14] and stayed there all the winter.

[1] Florence adds: 'in London'.

[2] Only 'C' and 'E' have this Abingdon entry.

[3] The Chronicle is a scanty record for the reigns of the Danish kings. Florence becomes fuller, but it is uncertain how much of his information is drawn from the versions of the Chronicle which he used. He gives an account of a discussion in which the English nobles falsely told Cnut that Edmund had wished Cnut to succeed him and be guardian to his sons, which reads more like saga.

[4] 'F' says he was 'very rightly' killed, at London, and Florence says his corpse was thrown over the city wall and left unburied.

[5] Called 'ealdorman' by Florence, who adds that his brother Leofric was made ealdorman in his place. His father Leofwine had been ealdorman of part of Mercia.

[6] i.e. Æthelmær, ealdorman of the Western Provinces.

[7] 'E': 'Ælfgeat'.

[8] Son of King Ethelred. 'D', 'E' add: 'and Eadwig, king of the ceorls' (see annal 1020 'C'); they then omit the next clause. Florence attributes his exile to Eadric's counsel, and says that Eadwig, king of the ceorls, was afterwards reconciled with the king.

[9] By the treachery of his friends, according to Florence, though Cnut's attempt to persuade a certain Æthelweard to

murder him failed. Florence gives here the story (referred to in annal 1057 'D') of how Cnut, advised by Eadric to kill Edmund's young sons, Edmund and Edward, sent them to the king of the Swedes to be killed; but he sent them to Solomon, king of the Hungarians, and later Edward married Agatha, called a niece of the Emperor Henry, by whom he had three children: Margaret, Christina, and Edgar.

[10] 'D', 'E' add: 'the other'.

[11] 'F' adds: 'namely Ælfgifu in English, Emma in French'.

[12] 'E', 'F' have 'eleven', misunderstanding the idiom 'the eleventh half'=10½.

[13] 'D' and Florence add: 'according to Edgar's law'. What was probably the agreement on this occasion is preserved in Corpus Christi College, Cambridge, MS. 201, with a preface saying that it 'took place as soon as King Cnut with the advice of his councillors completely established peace and friendship between the Danes and the English'. See E.H.D., I, No. 47.

'E' adds: 'And in this year Abbot Æthelsige died at Abingdon and Æthelwine succeeded.' As Abingdon sources know only one abbot, Æthelwine, between Wulfgar and Siward, Plummer suggests that 'E' has made two abbots out of one called Æthelsige and Æthelwine in different sources.

[14] 'D' adds: 'with nine ships'.

D

And in this year[1] died Archbishop Ælfstan, who was called Lifing, and he was a very prudent man, both in matters of Church and State.

C

1020[2] In this year Archbishop Lifing died, and King Cnut came back to England. And then at Easter[3] there was a great assembly at Cirencester. Then Ealdorman Æthelweard and Eadwig, king of the *ceorls*, were outlawed. And in this year the king went to Ashingdon, and Archbishop Wulfstan and Earl Thorkel, and with them many bishops; and they consecrated the minster at Ashingdon.

D

In this year King Cnut came back to England, and then at Easter there was a great assembly at Cirencester. Then Ealdorman Æthelweard was outlawed. And in this year the king and Earl Thorkel went to Ashingdon, and Archbishop Wulfstan and other bishops and also abbots and many monks; and they consecrated the minster at Ashingdon. And the monk Æthelnoth,[5] who was dean at Christ Church, was consecrated bishop for Christ Church on 13 November in that same year.

E (F)

In this year King Cnut came to England, and then at Easter there was a great assembly at Cirencester. Then Ealdorman Æthelweard was outlawed. And in this year the king went to Ashingdon,[4] and Archbishop Lifing died. And Æthelnoth,[5] monk and dean of Christ Church, was in that same year consecrated to it as bishop.

C (D, E)

1021 In this year, at Martinmas,[6] King Cnut outlawed Earl Thorkel.[7]

D

And Ælfgar the charitable bishop[8] died in the early morning of Christmas Day.[9]

C (D, E)

1022 In this year King Cnut went out with his ships to the Isle of Wight, and Archbishop Æthelnoth went to Rome,

---

[1] Only 'D' puts Lifing's death in 1019. He died on 12 June, so the discrepancy cannot be due to a different method of beginning the year. Florence has 1020.

[2] This annal has the same base in all MSS., but each has its own additions or omissions.

[3] 17 April.

[4] 'F' adds: 'and had a minster built there of stone and mortar, for the souls of the men who had been slain there, and gave it to a priest of his who was called Stigand'.

[5] Florence adds: 'son of the nobleman Æthelmær'.

[6] 11 November.

[7] Florence: 'and his wife Edith'.

[8] Of Elmham.

[9] Florence adds that Ælfwine succeeded him.

D (E, F)

and was received there with much honour by the venerable Pope Benedict,[1] who placed the *pallium* on him with his own hands, and consecrated and blessed him as archbishop with great solemnity on 7 October,[2] and the archbishop immediately on that same day celebrated Mass wearing the *pallium* [as the pope directed him][3] and then afterwards dined in state with the pope himself;

C	D	E (F)
	and also he himself took the *pallium* from St. Peter's altar. And then he afterwards journeyed happily home to his country.	and afterwards returned home with his full blessing. And Abbot Leofwine, who was wrongfully driven from Ely, was his companion, and cleared himself there from everything that had been said against him, as the pope directed him, in the witness of the archbishop and of all the company which was with him.
In this year King Cnut came back to England, and Thorkel and he were reconciled, and he entrusted Denmark and his son for Thorkel to maintain and the king took Thorkel's son with him to England. And afterwards he had St. Ælfheah's relics moved from London to Canterbury.	In this year in St. Paul's minster in London, King Cnut gave full permission to Archbishop Æthelnoth and Bishop Brihtwine[5] and to all the servants of God who were with them to take up the archbishop St. Ælfheah from the tomb, and they did so on 8 June. And the illustrious king, and the archbishop and the diocesan bishops, and the earls, and very many ecclesiastics and also lay-folk, conveyed his holy body on a ship across the Thames to	In this year Archbishop Wulfstan died,[4] and Ælfric succeeded. And in the same year Archbishop Æthelnoth moved the relics of St. Ælfheah, the archbishop, from London to Canterbury.[6]

1023 (marginal)

---

[1] Benedict VIII.

[2] 'E' and 'F', which have a few unimportant variations from the wording in 'D', omit this date.

[3] 'E' only.

[4] Florence says he died at York and was buried at Ely, and was succeeded by Ælfric Puttoc.

[5] Of Wells.

[6] 'E' then adds a Latin entry relating to Norman history.

D

Southwark, and there entrusted the holy martyr to the archbishop and his companions. And they then bore him with a distinguished company and happy jubilation to Rochester. Then on the third day Queen Emma came with her royal child Hardacnut, and they then all conveyed the holy archbishop with much glory and joy and songs of praise into Canterbury, and thus brought him with due ceremony into Christ Church on 11 June. Afterwards on the eighth day, on 15 June, Archbishop Æthelnoth and Bishop Ælfsige[1] and Bishop Brihtwine and all who were with them placed St. Ælfheah's holy body on the north side of Christ's altar, to the praise of God and the honour of the holy archbishop, and to the eternal salvation of all those who daily visit his holy body there with devout hearts and with all humility. May Almighty God have mercy on all Christian men, through the holy merits of St. Ælfheah.

1026   In this year Bishop Ælfric[2] went to Rome and received the *pallium* from Pope John[3] on 12 November.

E (F)

(1025) In this year King Cnut went with ships to Denmark to the Holme at the Holy River,[4] and there came against him Ulf and Eilaf and a very great army, both a land force and a naval force, from Sweden. And there very many men on King Cnut's side were destroyed, both Danish and English men, and the Swedes had control of the field.[5]

C (D, E, F)

1028   In this year King Cnut went [from England][6] to Norway with 50 ships,[7]

---

[1] Of Winchester.
[2] Of York.
[3] John XIX.
[4] In Skåne, Sweden. On this battle, see poems by the scalds Ottar the Black and Sighvat (*E.H.D.*, I, Nos. 15, 16) and Snorri Sturlason's *Heimskringla: Saga of St. Olaf*, chap. 149f. The latter says that Earl Ulf had been scheming to replace Cnut in Denmark by his son Hardacnut, and that Cnut lost many ships at the Holy River when his enemies Olaf of Norway and Önund of Sweden burst a dam which they had built; and that

Ulf claimed that he had come to Cnut's assistance. Saxo (*History of the Danes*, Book XI, chap. 16) depicts Ulf as engineering the alliance against Cnut, and ascribes the losses at the Holy River to the collapse of a bridge laden with Danish troops, instead of a burst dam. Both sources make Cnut responsible for Ulf's death.
[5] Florence has an annal dated 1027 describing how Cnut bribed the Norwegians to desert King Olaf.
[6] From 'D', 'E', 'F'.
[7] 'F' adds: 'of English thegns'.

D (E, F)

and drove King Olaf from the land, and made good his claim to all that land.[1]

029

In this year King Cnut came back home to England.[2]

C	D (E)

030 In this year King Olaf was killed in Norway by his own people,[3] and was afterwards holy. And previously in this year the brave Earl Hákon died at sea.[4]

In this year King Olaf came back into Norway and the people gathered against him and fought with him, and he was killed there.[3]

D (E, F)

027   (1031)[5] In this year King Cnut went to Rome, and as soon as he came home[6] he went to Scotland, and the king of the Scots surrendered to him,

D	E (F)

and became his man, but he observed it but little time.

Malcolm, and two other kings, Mælbæth and Iehmarc.[7]

A1031 Here Cnut came back to England.[8]

---

[1] For Old Norse poems concerning this expedition, see *E.H.D.*, I, Nos. 18, 19.

[2] Florence's additional matter makes the next annal in 'C' intelligible. He says that Cnut sent Hákon and his wife Gunnhild, daughter of Cnut's sister and Wyrtgeorn, king of the Wends, into exile under pretence of an embassy, because he was afraid he might be killed or deposed by him.

[3] This is the famous battle of Stiklestad.

[4] Florence adds that some say that he was killed in Orkney; Theodric, the Norwegian author of a late-twelfth-century Latin history of the kings of Norway, says he perished in the Pentland Firth when returning from fetching his bride from England.

[5] The simplest explanation of this misdating of Cnut's journey is that the chronicler knew that it followed a great battle in Scandinavia, and placed it after Stiklestad, 1030,

instead of the Holy River, 1026. Continental evidence fixes the date as 1027. Florence dates 1031 and inserts the letter sent by Cnut to England, which is also in William of Malmesbury. See *E.H.D.*, I, No. 49. Sighvat the Scald also mentions this visit to Rome. See *ibid.*, No. 16. The date of the Scottish expedition is uncertain.

[6] 'E', 'F' add: 'in the same year'.

[7] With this statement compare Sighvat the Scald: 'The most famous princes in the North from the midst of Fife have brought their heads to Cnut; that was to buy peace.' See *E.H.D.*, I, No. 18.

At this point 'E' and 'F' have a note on Norman history, 'E' in Latin, 'F' in English.

[8] 'A' adds here a charter concerning harbour rights at Sandwich.

	D	E (F)
1032		In this year there appeared the wild-fire, such as no man ever remembered before, and also it did damage all over in many places. And in the same year Ælfsige, bishop of Winchester, died, and was succeeded by the king's priest, Ælfwine.[1]
1033	In this year Bishop Leofsige died[2] and his body is buried in Worcester, and Brihtheah was chosen to his see.	In this year Merehwit, bishop of Somerset,[3] died, and he is buried in Glastonbury.

C (D, E)

1034 In this year Bishop Æthelric[4] died,[5] and he is buried in Ramsey.

D

And that same year King Malcolm of Scotland died.

C (D)

1035 In this year King Cnut died[6] on 12 November at Shaftesbury, and he was brought from there to Winchester and buried there; and Ælfgifu, the queen, then stayed there. And Harold, who

E (F)

(1036) In this year King Cnut died at Shaftesbury and he is buried in Winchester in the Old Minster; and he was king over all England for very nearly 20 years. And immediately after his death there was an assembly of all the councillors at Oxford. And Earl Leofric and almost all the thegns north of the Thames and the shipmen in London chose Harold to the regency[7] of all England, for himself

---

[1] The only event of 1032 in Florence is the dedication of the church of St Edmund at Bury.

[2] Florence adds that he died at Kempsey on 19 August and that his successor was a sister's son of Archbishop Wulfstan of York, and was abbot of Pershore.

[3] i.e. of Wells.

[4] Of Dorchester. 'D': Ælfric (wrongly). Florence adds that Eadnoth succeeded him.

[5] 'E' ends the annal here.

[6] 'D' inserts: 'and Harold his son succeeded to the kingdom'. Florence says that Cnut, before his death, established Swein, reputed to be his son by Ælfgifu of Northampton, daughter of Ealdorman Ælfhelm and Wulfrun, as king of the Norwegians.

He tells a story of a fraud by which Ælfgifu made Cnut believe Swein to be his son. He says also that Cnut appointed his son Hardacnut as king of the Danes.

[7] The chronicler uses a rare word meaning vaguely 'protection', 'support', and thus avoids an implication of kingly authority. Hermann's *De miraculis sancti Eadmundi* shows that Harold was regent for a year before he became king. Florence says: 'He began to reign as if the legitimate heir, not, however, as powerfully as Cnut, because the more rightful heir, Hardacnut, was expected. Hence, after a short time, the kingdom of England was divided by lot, and the north part fell to Harold, the south to Hardacnut.'

C (D)

said that he was the son of Cnut and the other Ælfgifu[1] – though it was not true – sent there and had all the best treasures taken from her, which she could not keep back,[2] which King Cnut had possessed. Yet she continued to stay there as long as she was allowed.

1036 In this year the innocent atheling Alfred, the son of King Ethelred, came into this country, wishing to go to his mother who was in Winchester, but Earl Godwine did not allow him, nor did the other men who had great power,[4] because feeling was veering much towards Harold,[5] although this was not right.[6]

But Godwine[7] then stopped him and put him in captivity, and he dispersed his companions and killed some in various ways; some were sold for money,

E (F)

and for his brother Hardacnut, who was then in Denmark. And Earl Godwine and all the chief men in Wessex opposed it as long as they could, but they could not contrive anything against it. And it was then determined that Ælfgifu, Hardacnut's mother, should stay in Winchester with the housecarls of her son the king, and they should keep all Wessex in his possession; and Earl Godwine was their most loyal man. Some men said about Harold that he was the son of King Cnut and of Ælfgifu, the daughter of Ealdorman Ælfhelm, but it seemed incredible to many men; and yet he was full king over all England.[3]

---

[1] 'D': 'and Ælfgifu of Northampton'. Florence says he was the son of a shoemaker and that Ælfgifu used a similar fraud as in the case of Swein.

[2] This clause is only in 'C'. I am unsure of its implications. Does it mean, 'which she was in no position to refuse' or that they took such treasures as she did not manage to secrete?

[3] cf. Hermann, *De miraculis sancti Eadmundi* (ed. Arnold), pp. 47 f.: 'England . . after being bereft of a king for the space of a year, at length received the rule of the two sons of the afore-mentioned king, namely Harold for two and a half years, and after him Hardacnut for three half years' (probably for two and a half, an error due to a misunderstanding of an Old English idiom).

[4] 'D' has a significant variant; it omits reference to Godwine, reading simply: 'but those who had much power in the land did not permit it'. Yet Florence, though usually close to 'D', says 'especially, it is said, Earl Godwine', and the *Encomium Emmae* (ed. A. Campbell, p. 43; *E.H.D.*, I, No. 28) says Godwine met Alfred, swore an oath to him, and took him under his protection, though it attributes the atrocities merely to 'men in league with the most abominable tyrant, Harold'.

[5] Or perhaps better 'the popular cry was greatly in favour of Harold' (Garmonsway).

[6] The rest of this annal is in rhymed verse. In both MSS., but more in 'D', the regularity of the metre is upset here and there.

[7] 'D' again omits to mention Godwine, having 'he' instead, which presumably refers back to Harold.

C (D)   E (F)

some were cruelly killed, some were put in fetters, some were
blinded, some were mutilated,[1] some were scalped.[2] No more
horrible deed was done in this land since the Danes came
and peace was made here. Now we must trust to the beloved
God that they rejoice happily with Christ who were without
guilt so miserably slain. The atheling still lived. He was threatened with every evil, until it was decided to take him thus in bonds
to Ely. As soon as he arrived, he was blinded on the ship, and thus
blind was brought to the monks, and he dwelt there as long as he
lived. Then he was buried as well befitted him, very honourably, as
he deserved, in the south chapel at the west end, full close to the
steeple. His soul is with Christ.[3]

1037 In this year Harold[4] was chosen as king everywhere, and Hardacnut   In this year Ælfgifu, King Cnut's
was deserted because he was too long in Denmark; and then his   widow, who was King Harda-
mother, Queen Ælfgifu, was driven out without any mercy to face   cnut's mother,[5] was driven out.
the raging winter. And she then went across the sea[6] to Bruges, and And she then sought Baldwin's[7]
Earl Baldwin[7] received her well there and maintained her there as   protection south of the sea, and
long as she had need. And previously in this year, Æfic, the noble   he gave her a residence in Bruges
dean of Evesham, died.   and protected and maintained
                                                                       her as long as she was there.

1038 In this year the good Archbishop Æthelnoth died, and Æthelric,   In this year Archbishop Æthel-
bishop of Sussex [who desired of God that he should not let him live   noth died on 1 November,[8] and
any while after his dear father Æthelnoth, and he also departed   a little while afterwards Æthel-
within seven days after him],[9] and Ælfric, bishop of East Anglia,[10] ric, bishop of Sussex, and then
and Brihtheah bishop of Worcester, on 20 December.   Brihtheah, bishop of Worcester,

---

[1] 'D' omits this clause.

[2] 'D' adds: 'shamefully'.

[3] Florence tells us that the massacre took place at Guildford
and 600 men were killed. He says Edward came to England
also, but was sent back by his mother when she heard of
Alfred's fate. The *Encomium Emmae*, along with much rhetorical
and legendary expansion, such as the luring of the princes by
a letter forged in the queen's name, supplies some probably
authentic information: that Alfred came from Flanders, where
he refused Baldwin's offer of troops, and that his first attempt
at landing was opposed. It, too, places the massacre at Guildford.

[4] Florence: 'king of the Mercians and Northumbrians'.

[5] 'F' adds: 'and King Edward's'.

[6] 'D' omits 'across the sea'.

[7] Baldwin V, count of Flanders.

[8] Florence: '29 October'.

[9] In 'D' only.

[10] 'D' does not mention him. Florence says he was succeeded
by Stigand, the king's chaplain, who was afterwards deposed,
and Grimcetel, bishop of Sussex, appointed instead, only to be
ejected later in favour of Stigand. Two Suffolk writs (Harmer,
Anglo-Saxon Writs, Nos. 9, 10) include Grimcetel in their
address. 'C' in annal 1043 records Stigand's appointment as
bishop of East Anglia and his ejection in the same year. 'E'
records his reinstatement in 1044. On this matter, see R. R.
Darlington, in *Eng. Hist. Rev.*, LI, p. 400n. Florence has probably confused Bishop Ælfric with his successor of the same
name, and thus wrongly dated Stigand's appointment.

E (F)

before Christmas, and quickly after that Ælfric, bishop of East Anglia. And then Eadsige¹ succeeded to the archbishopric, and Grimcetel to the bishopric of Sussex, and Bishop Lifing to Worcestershire and to Gloucestershire.

C *only*

039 In this year occurred the great wind, and Brihtmær, bishop of Lichfield, died.² And the Welsh killed Edwin, Earl Leofric's brother, and Thorkil and Ælfgeat³ and very many good men with them. And in this year also Hardacnut came to Bruges, where his mother was.

C (D)

040 In this year King Harold died. Then they sent to Bruges for Hardacnut, thinking that they were acting wisely, and he then came here with 60 ships⁶ before midsummer, and then imposed a very severe tax, which was endured with difficulty, namely eight marks to the rowlock.⁸ And all who had wanted him before were then ill-disposed towards him. And also he did nothing worthy of a king as long as he ruled. He had the dead Harold dug up and thrown into the fen.⁹

(1039)⁴ In this year King Harold died in Oxford⁵ on 17 March, and he was buried at Westminster. And he ruled England four years and sixteen weeks.⁷ And in his time 16 ships were paid for at eight marks to each rowlock, just as had been done in King Cnut's time. And in this same year King Hardacnut came to Sandwich seven days before midsummer, and he was immediately received both by the English and the Danes, though his advisers afterwards requited it very sternly, when they decreed that 62 ships should be paid for at eight marks to each rowlock.⁸ And in this same year the sester of wheat rose to 55 pence, and even higher.

---

¹ 'F': 'the king's priest'; Florence: 'the king's chaplain'.
² Florence: 'and Wulfsige succeeded him'.
³ *Id*.: 'son of Eadsige'.
⁴ 'E' is a year behind the true date from here until 1044, when, by repeating the number 1043, it becomes two years behind.
⁵ Florence has instead 'London'.
⁶ Florence: 'and manned them with Danish troops'.
⁷ If this is accurately calculated, it is reckoning Harold's succession from about a fortnight after Cnut's death on 12 November 1035.
⁸ Florence: 'and twelve to each steersman'.
⁹ Florence gives a fuller account, stating that the king sent Ælfric, archbishop of York, Earl Godwine, Stir, the master of his household, Eadric his steward, Thrond his executioner, and

others to London with orders that Harold's body be thrown into a fen and then into the Thames; and that it was recovered by a fisherman and buried by the Danes in their cemetery in London.
Florence adds also that Ælfric, archbishop of York, and others accused Earl Godwine and Lifing, bishop of Worcester, of complicity in the murder of the atheling Alfred, so that the king deprived Lifing of his see and gave it to Archbishop Ælfric, though he held it only till Lifing made his peace with the king the next year. He says that Godwine gave to the king a splendid galley, manned with 80 picked soldiers, each equipped with valuable weapons and with gold armlets, and swore an oath, supported by the ealdormen and more important thegns, that it was not with his consent that Alfred was blinded, and that all he had done was by order of King Harold.

A1040 In this year Archbishop Eadsige went to Rome, and King Harold died.

C (D)

1041 In this year Hardacnut had all Worcestershire ravaged for the sake of his two housecarls,[2] who had exacted that severe tax. The people had then killed them within the town in the minster. And soon in that year there came from beyond the sea Edward, his brother on the mother's side, the son of King Ethelred, who had been driven from his country many years before – and yet he was sworn in as king;[4] and he thus stayed at his brother's court as long as he lived. And in this year also Hardacnut betrayed Earl Eadwulf[5] under his safe-conduct and he was then a pledge-breaker. [And in this year Æthelric was consecrated bishop[6] in York on 11 January.][7]

1042 In this year Hardacnut died in this way: he was standing at his drink and he suddenly fell to the ground with fearful convulsions, and those who were near caught him, and he spoke no word afterwards. He died on 8 June. And all the people then received Edward as king,[10] as was his natural right.

E (F)

(1040)[1] In this year the army-tax was paid, namely 21,099 pounds, and later 11,048 pounds were paid for 32 ships. And in the same year Edward, son of King Ethelred, came to this land from France. He was brother of King Hardacnut. They were both sons of Ælfgifu, who was count Richard's daughter.[3]

(1041)[1] In this year Hardacnut died at Lambeth on 8 June,[8] and he was king over all England two years all but ten days, and he is buried in the Old Minster with King Cnut his father.[9] And before he was buried, all the people chose Edward as king, in London. May he hold it as long as God will grant him. And all that year was very distressing in many ways. Storms did much damage to

---

[1] See p. 105, n. 4.

[2] Florence adds their names, Feader and Thurstan, and that they were killed on 4 May when hiding in an upper room of a tower of the monastery of Worcester. He gives a detailed account of the king's vengeance, which was carried out while Archbishop Ælfric was in charge of the see of Worcester, by the earls Thuri of the Midlanders, Leofric of the Mercians, Godwine of the West Saxons, Siward of the Northumbrians, and Hrani of the *Magonsæte* (the people of Herefordshire), and by the king's housecarls. The people had warning and fled, and a number of the citizens successfully defended themselves on Bevere Island in the Severn. The ravaging began on 12 November and lasted four days.

[3] Ælfgifu, or Emma, was daughter of Richard I, duke of Normandy.

[4] These remarks could apply to Ethelred or Edward, but more naturally to the latter. The *Encomium Emmae* says Hardacnut asked Edward to come and hold the kingdom with him.

[5] Of Northumbria.

[6] Of Durham. The expression *to Eoferwic*, presumably meaning 'in York', may have been the origin of the later belief that Æthelric was consecrated bishop of York. See annal 1072, and p. 155, n. 2.

[7] This sentence is in 'D' only.

[8] According to Florence, he was taken ill at the wedding of Gytha, daughter of Osgod Clapa, to Tofi the Proud.

[9] 'F' adds: 'and his mother gave to the New Minster for his soul the head of St Valentine the martyr'.

[10] 'D' reads: 'chose Edward and received him as king'. Florence adds: 'chiefly by the exertions of Earl Godwine and Lifing, bishop of Worcester'.

E (F)

the crops; and more cattle were destroyed during this year than anyone remembered before, both through various diseases and through storms. And in this year Ælfsige, abbot of Peterborough, died, and the monk Arnwig was chosen as abbot because he was a very good and very gentle man.[1]

A1042 In this year King Hardacnut died.

C (E)

043 (1042 E)[2] In this year Edward was consecrated king at Winchester on Easter Day with great ceremony; and Easter was on 3 April. Archbishop Eadsige[4] consecrated him and gave him good instruction before all the people, and admonished him well for his own sake and for the sake of all the people. Stigand the priest[5] was consecrated bishop of the East Angles.[7] And soon after this the king brought all the lands his mother owned forcibly into his own control and took from her all that she owned in gold and silver and things beyond description, because she had withheld it too firmly from him.[8]

C only

And soon after this Stigand was deprived of his bishopric, and all that he owned was placed in the king's control because he was closest in his mother's counsel, and because it was suspected that she did as he advised.

D

In this year Edward was consecrated king at Winchester on the first day of Easter. And this year, a fortnight before St. Andrew's Day,[3] the king was advised to ride from Gloucester, together with Earl Leofric and Earl Godwine and Earl Siward and their retinue, to Winchester. And they came unexpectedly upon the lady,[6] and deprived her of all the treasures which she owned, and which were beyond counting, because she had formerly been very hard to the king, her son, in that she did less for him than he wished both before he became king and afterwards as well. And they allowed her to stay there afterwards.[8]

---

[1] This last sentence, which is not in 'F', is clearly a Peterborough addition.

[2] See p. 105, n. 4.

[3] i.e. 16 November, St Andrew's Day being 30 November.

[4] Florence adds: 'and Ælfric, archbishop of York'.

[5] i.e. a royal chaplain, a common meaning of the term in the later part of the Chronicle.

[6] Ælfgifu Emma, widow of Ethelred and Cnut. See annals 1002, 1017.

[7] i.e of Elmham. See note to annal 1038.

[8] The *Translation of St. Mildred* adds some important information on this matter:

'So according to the dispensation of God who governs all things, England received the native-born Edward for king. He was the offspring of King Ethelred and Emma. While he was reigning in peace like unto Solomon, his own mother was accused of inciting Magnus, king of Norway, to invade England, and it was said that she had given countless treasures to Magnus. Wherefore this traitor to the kingdom, this enemy of the country, this betrayer of her own son, was judged, and everything she possessed was forfeited to the king.' (T. D. Hardy, *Catalogue of Materials*, vol. I, p. 381.)

A1043 In this year Edward was consecrated king.

C (E)

1044 (1043 E)[1] In this year Archbishop Eadsige resigned the bishopric because of his infirmity, and consecrated to it as bishop[2] Siward, abbot of Abingdon. He did this with the permission and by the advice of the king and of Earl Godwine. Otherwise it was known to few people before it was done, because the archbishop suspected that somebody else would ask for it, or purchase it, whom he less trusted and favoured, if more people knew about it. In this year there was a very great famine over all England, and corn dearer than anyone remembered, so that a sester of wheat went up to 60 pence and even more. And this same year the king went out to Sandwich with 35 ships. And Athelstan the sacristan succeeded to the abbacy of Abingdon.

D

(1045)[1] In this year Bishop Ælfweard of London died on 25 July. He had first been abbot of Evesham, and he greatly promoted the good of that monastery while he was there; then he went to Ramsey,[3] and there he passed away. And Manni[4] was chosen abbot and consecrated on 10 August. And in the course of the year, Gunnild, that noble lady, King Cnut's kinswoman,[5] was banished, and she then stayed at Bruges for a long time, and then went to Denmark.

C

And in the same year King Edward married Edith, daughter of Earl Godwine, ten nights before Candlemas.[7]

E

And Stigand obtained his bishopric.[6]

C

1045 In this year Bishop Brihtwold died on 22 April, and King Edward gave the bishopric to Hereman his priest. And in the same summer King Edward

D

(1046)[8] This year Brihtwold, the bishop of Wiltshire, died, and Hereman[9] was appointed to his see. In this year King Edward collected a great naval force at

E

(1043)[8] This year King Edward took as his queen the daughter of Earl Godwine. And in the same year Bishop Brihtwold died. He held the bishopric[10]

---

[1] 'E' remains one year behind the true date, but 'D', having omitted the number 1044, is now a year in advance and remains so until 1052.

[2] Siward was never archbishop of Canterbury, but assistant or suffragan to Eadsige.

[3] Florence says that the reason why Ælfweard, who had retained the abbacy while bishop of London, went to Ramsey was because he was refused admission at Evesham, and the Chronicle of Ramsey Abbey says he was suffering from leprosy. The entry in 'D', with its emphasis on what Evesham owed to an abbot whom they turned away as a sick old man, is an argument against the assigning of 'D' to Evesham. On the interest of 'D' in the diocese of Worcester, see p. xv.

[4] Florence says his other name was Wulfmær and he was elected at a general council in London.

[5] See note to annal 1030. According to Florence, she married earls Hákon and Harold, and her sons Hemming and Thurkil were exiled with her.

[6] Of East Anglia; see annal 1043 'C'.

[7] i.e. 1045. 'C' commences the year at Lady Day (25 March).

[8] 'D' remains one year in advance of the true date; 'E' by repeating 1043 here becomes two years behind.

[9] Florence: 'born in Lotharingia.'

[10] Of Ramsbury. Hereman became bishop of Sherborne also, and later removed the two sees to Sarum.

C

went out with his ships to Sandwich, and there was so large a force collected there that no one had ever seen a larger naval force in this country. And in the same year Bishop Lifing died on 20 March,[2] and the king gave the bishopric to his priest Leofric.

1046 In this year Earl Swein went into Wales, and Griffith the northern king[5] with him, and hostages were given him. When he was on his way home, he ordered the abbess of Leominster to be brought to him and kept her as long as it suited him, and then he let her go home.[9] In this same year Osgod Clapa[7] was outlawed before Christmas. In this same year after Candlemas the hard winter came with frost and snow and every sort of bad weather, so that there was no one alive who could remember so hard a winter as that was, both for pestilence and murrain, and birds and fish perished through the great cold and through hunger.

D

Sandwich because of the threat of Magnus of Norway, but the fighting between him and Swein of Denmark prevented him from coming here.[1]

(1047)[3] This year Lifing, the eloquent bishop, died on 23 March, and he had three bishoprics, one in Devon and one in Cornwall and one in Worcester. Then Leofric[4] succeeded to Devon and Cornwall[6] and Bishop Aldred[8] to Worcester. And this year Osgod, the staller, was outlawed.[7] And Magnus conquered Denmark.[10]

E

thirty-eight years, and Hereman, the king's priest, succeeded to it. And this same year Wulfric was consecrated abbot of St. Augustine's at Christmas-time on St. Stephen's Day by permission of the king and of Abbot Ælfstan, because of the abbot's great infirmity.

(1044)[3] This year Lifing, bishop of Devonshire, died, and Leofric,[4] the king's priest, succeeded to it. And in this same year Ælfstan, abbot of St. Augustine's, died on 5 July, and in this same year Osgod Clapa[7] was expelled.

---

[1] 'D' alone gives these details relating to Scandinavia.

[2] i.e. 1046, since 'C' is beginning the year on 25 March.

[3] 'D' remains one year in advance of the true date; 'E' is still two years behind.

[4] The donor of many books, including the Exeter Book of English poetry, to Exeter. Florence says he was 'the king's chancellor' and calls him *Brytonicus*; William of Malmesbury says he was reared and educated in Lotharingia.

[5] i.e. Griffith ap Llewelyn, king of Gwynedd and Powys. See J. E. Lloyd, *A History of Wales from the Earliest Times*

to the Edwardian Conquest (London, 3rd edit.), II, pp. 359-371.

[6] This is the see of Crediton, which Leofric transferred to Exeter in 1050.

[7] On this Danish notable, see annals 1049 and 1054.

[8] Florence says he was first a monk at Winchester, then abbot of Tavistock.

[9] 'C' alone gives this information damaging to the family of Godwine.

[10] From Swein Estrithson.

C

1047 In this year Bishop Grimcetel, the bishop of Sussex, died, and he lies in Christ Church at Canterbury. And King Edward gave the bishopric to Heca[2] his priest. And in this same year Bishop Ælfwine died on 29 August, and King Edward gave the bishopric to Bishop Stigand. And Abbot Athelstan of Abingdon died in the same year on 29 March – Easter Day was this year on 3 April[6] – and there was a very great pestilence throughout all England in this year.

1048 In this year there was a great earthquake far and wide in England, and in the same year Sandwich and the Isle of Wight were ravaged, and the best men who were there were killed.

D

(1048)[1] This year was the severe winter, and in the course of this year Ælfwine, bishop of Winchester, died, and Bishop Stigand was raised to his see. Before that in the same year Grimcetel, bishop of Sussex, died, and Heca,[2] the priest, succeeded to the bishopric. And Swein[3] also sent here asking for help against Magnus, king of Norway, that fifty ships should be sent to his support, but it seemed a foolish plan to everybody and it was hindered because Magnus had a great naval force.[7] And Magnus then drove out Swein and seized the country with great slaughter, and the Danes paid him a large amount of money and accepted him as king. And the same year Magnus died.[8]

(1049)[9] This year Swein[10] came back to Denmark, and Harold[12] the paternal uncle of Magnus went to Norway after Magnus was dead and the Norwegians accepted him.[13] And he sent to

E

(1045)[1] In this year Grimcetel, bishop of Sussex, died, and Heca,[2] the king's priest, succeeded to it. And in this year Ælfwine, bishop of Winchester, died on 29 August, and Stigand, bishop in the north, succeeded to it. And in the same year Earl Swein[4] went out to Baldwin's country,[5] to Bruges, and stayed there all winter, and went away in the summer.

(1046)[9] Battle at Val-ès-Dunes.[11] In this year Athelstan, abbot of Abingdon, died, and Sparrowhawk, a monk from Bury St. Edmunds, succeeded. And in this same year Bishop Siward[14] died

---

[1] 'D' remains one year in advance of the true date, 'E' two years behind it.

[2] Florence: 'The king's chaplain.'

[3] Swein Estrithson, son of Earl Ulf and Estrith, sister of Cnut.

[4] Swein, son of Godwine.

[5] i.e. Flanders, where Baldwin V was count at this time.

[6] 1048. 'C' appears to have entered this accession a year too early.

[7] Florence says that Earl Godwine advised sending 50 ships, but that Earl Leofric and all the people opposed sending help.

[8] Magnus died 25 October 1047.

[9] 'D' remains a year in advance; 'E' is two years behind the true date.

[10] Swein Estrithson.

[11] This is an interpolation in Latin, wrongly dated. The battle of Val-ès-Dunes between Duke William and his rebellious vassals from Lower Normandy took place in 1047.

[12] i.e. Harold Hardrada. Florence wrongly calls him 'Fairhair', but gives his parents correctly, as the mother of St Olaf and Siward, whom he calls king of the Norwegians, though he actually ruled only a small district.

[13] Note that again it is only 'D' that gives details of Scandinavian history.

[14] Suffragan of Canterbury.

C

And after that King Edward and the earls went out with their ships. And in the same year Bishop Siward[1] resigned the bishopric because of his infirmity and went to Abingdon, and Archbishop Eadsige succeeded to the bishopric again, and he [Siward] died within eight weeks on 23 October.

D

this country to treat about peace. And Swein also sent from Denmark and asked King Edward for naval assistance, which was to be fifty ships at least, but all the people refused.[3] And this year also there was an earthquake on 1 May in many places – at Worcester and Droitwich and Derby and elsewhere. Also there was a very great pestilence among men and beasts; also wild-fire did much harm in Derbyshire and elsewhere.

E

and Archbishop Eadsige succeeded again to all the bishopric. And in this same year Lothen and Yrling came to Sandwich with twenty-five ships and[2] captured an indescribable amount of plunder in men and gold and silver, so that nobody knew how much it was altogether; and then they went round Thanet and meant to do the same there, but the local people firmly resisted them, and prevented them both from coming ashore and from obtaining water, and drove them out completely from those parts. So they went off to Essex, which they ravaged, and there they captured people and whatever they could find, and then they went east to Baldwin's country,[4] and sold whatever they had got from their raid, and thence they went east to the country from which they had come.

1049 In this year the emperor[5] collected an immense force against Baldwin of Bruges[7] because he had stormed the palace of Nymegen, and because of many

(1050)[6] In this year the emperor[5] collected an immense force against Baldwin of Bruges[7] because he had stormed the palace of Nymegen, and because of

(1046)[6] In this year was the great synod held at Rheims. Pope Leo[8] was there and the archbishop of Burgundy, and the archbishop of Besançon,

---

[1] Suffragan of Canterbury.

[2] 'E', being for this period a transcript of a chronicle kept at St Augustine's, Canterbury, gives greater details of this south-eastern raid.

[3] This may be a repetition of the account in the previous annal, and Florence repeats what he added to 1047; but there may have been a second request.

[4] Flanders.

[5] Henry III.

[6] 'D' remains one year in advance of the true date; 'E' by repeating the number 1046 becomes three years in arrears.

[7] Baldwin V of Flanders.

[8] Leo IX.

C

other injuries done by Baldwin. This force which the emperor had collected was beyond counting. Pope Leo[1] was there from Rome and many famous men from many peoples.[3] He[4] also sent to King Edward and asked him for naval support – that he would not let Baldwin escape by sea. The king therefore went to Sandwich and stayed there with a large naval force until the emperor obtained from Baldwin all he wanted. Then[6] Earl Swein came back again to King Edward and asked him for land to support himself upon. But Harold,[9] his brother, opposed it together with Earl Beorn.[10] They declared they would give up to him nothing that the king had given them. Swein came hypocritically and said he would be the king's liegeman, and he asked Earl Beorn for support. But the king refused him in everything. Then Swein went to his ships at Bosham, and Earl Godwine came from Sandwich to Pevensey with forty-two ships, and

D

many other injuries done by Baldwin. This force which the emperor had collected was beyond counting. The pope[1] was in it and the patriarch, and many other famous men from every people.[3] He[4] also sent to King Edward and asked him for naval support – that he would not let Baldwin escape by sea. The king therefore went to Sandwich and stayed there with a large naval force until the emperor obtained from Baldwin all he wanted. Then[6] Earl Swein came back also who had gone from this country to Denmark,[8] and there ruined himself with the Danes. He came here hypocritically and said he wished again to submit to the king, and Earl Beorn[10] promised to help him. Then after the agreement between the emperor and Baldwin many of the ships went home, but the king stayed at Sandwich with a few ships. And Earl Godwine also went with forty-two ships from Sandwich to Pevensey, and Earl Beorn went with him.

E

and the archbishop of Trèves, and the archbishop of Rheims, and many others, both clerks and lay. And King Edward sent there Bishop Dudoc[2] and Wulfric, abbot of St. Augustine's, and Abbot Ælfwine[5] so that they might inform the king of whatever was there decided in the interests of Christendom. And in this same year King Edward went out to Sandwich with a large naval force, and Earl Swein[7] came in with seven ships to Bosham and made peace with the king,[6] and he was promised that he should be restored to every honour that he had previously held. Then Earl Harold,[9] his brother, and Earl Beorn[10] withstood it, contending that Swein was not entitled to any of those things that the king had granted him. He was however given four days' safe-conduct to enable him to get back to his ships. Now it happened meanwhile that word had come to the king that hostile ships lay to the west

---

[1] Leo IX. The name in 'C' is interlined.

[2] Of Wells.

[3] Florence adds: 'Moreover Swein, king of the Danes, was there at the Emperor's bidding, with his fleet, and he swore fealty for that occasion to the Emperor.'

[4] Henry III

[5] Of Ramsey.

[6] The three accounts that follow differ as to details, and they cannot wholly be reconciled. For an analysis of the versions, see J. Earle and C. Plummer, *op. cit.*, II, pp. 229–231.

[7] Swein, son of Godwine.

[8] Florence gives as the cause of his outlawry his abduction of the abbess of Leominster (see annal 1046 'C'), adding her name, Eadgifu. He says Swein returned with eight ships.

[9] This is the first mention in the chronicle of Harold, son of Godwine, later to be king of England.

[10] Florence adds: 'son of his uncle the Danish earl Ulf, who was the son of Spracling, the son of Urse (i.e. Beorn), and the brother of Swein, king of the Danes'. Beorn Ulf's son had been given an English earldom which included Hertfordshire.

C

Earl Beorn along with him. And then the king allowed all the Mercians to go home, and they did so. When the king was informed that Osgod[1] lay at Wulpe[2] with twenty-nine ships the king sent for all the ships he could summon which were within the 'Northmouth'.[6] But Osgod placed his wife in Bruges and turned back again with six ships, and the others went to Essex to *Eadulfesness*,[8] and there they did damage, and then turned back to the ships. Then Earl Godwine and Earl Beorn were lying at Pevensey with their ships. Then Earl Swein came and treacherously asked Earl Beorn to accompany him to the king at Sandwich, saying that he would swear oaths to him and be faithful to him. Then Beorn thought that because of their kinship he would not be betrayed. He took with him three companions and, exactly as if they were going to Sandwich, they rode to Bosham where Swein's ships were lying. But he was bound at once and carried on board, and then they

D

Then the king was informed that Osgod[1] was at Wulpe[2] with thirty-nine[3] ships, and the king sent for all the ships he could summon from among those which had gone home. And Osgod placed his wife at Bruges,[4] and they went back again with six ships, and the others went to Sussex[7] to *Eadulfesness*,[8] and they did damage there and then returned to the ships, and then a strong wind overtook them so that they were all lost except for four[9] that were killed overseas. While Earl Godwine and Earl Beorn were staying at Pevensey, Earl Swein came and treacherously asked Earl Beorn, who was his uncle's son, to accompany him to the king at Sandwich in order to improve his relations with the king. Beorn went then with three companions because of their kinship, but he was taken to Bosham where Swein's ships were lying, and there he was bound and carried on board. Then he was taken to Dartmouth and there Swein ordered him to be killed and buried deep. He was found

E

and were ravaging there. Then Earl Godwine turned west with two of the king's ships, one of which was captained by Earl Harold and the other by Tosti his brother, and also with forty-two ships belonging to the local people. Then Earl Beorn[5] was appointed to the king's ship that Earl Harold had captained, and they went west to Pevensey and lay there weather-bound. Then within two days Earl Swein came there and spoke with his father and with Earl Beorn and asked him to go with him to the king at Sandwich in order that he might help him regain the king's friendship. Beorn agreed to do this and they departed as if they were meaning to go to the king. Then as they were riding Swein asked him to go with him to his ships, telling him that his sailors would desert him unless he got there quickly. So they both went to where his ships were lying. When they got there Earl Swein asked him to go aboard with him. Beorn refused firmly and so long that the sailors took him and threw

---

[1] Osgod Clapa.
[2] In Flanders.
[3] Florence has '29'.
[4] Florence's version may be a misunderstanding of the Old English. He has: 'Osgod, taking with him his wife whom he had left at Bruges, returned with six ships to Denmark.'

[5] MS. gives 'Harold', an obvious error.
[6] Of the Kentish Stour.
[7] A mistake for Essex.
[8] The Naze, Essex.
[9] Florence has 'two'.

C	D	E

went to Dartmouth and there he was put to death, and buried deep. Harold, however, his kinsman, fetched him and took him to Winchester and buried him there near Cnut his uncle. And the king and all the host declared Swein a scoundrel.[1] He had eight ships before he murdered Beorn, but afterwards all but two deserted him, and he then went to Bruges and stayed there with Baldwin. And in this year Eadnoth the good bishop of Oxfordshire[4] died, and Oswig, abbot of Thorney, and Wulfnoth, abbot of Westminster. And King Edward gave the bishopric to Ulf his priest – which was a bad appointment. And in this same year, King Edward paid off nine ships, and they went away, ships and all, and five ships were left behind and the king promised the sailors twelve months' pay. In the same year Bishop Hereman

again, however, and taken to Winchester and buried with Cnut his uncle. A little before this the men of Hastings and its neighbourhood captured two of his ships with their ships, and they killed all the men and brought the ships to the king at Sandwich. Swein had eight ships before he betrayed Beorn, but afterwards all but two deserted him.[2] In the same year[3] thirty-six ships came up the Usk from Ireland and did damage in those parts with the help of Griffith, the Welsh king.[5] The people gathered together against him, and Bishop Aldred was there with them, but they had too little support, and the enemy came on them by surprise quite early in the morning, and killed many good men there; and the others escaped with the bishop. This was done on 29 July. This year [Eadnoth, bishop] of Oxfordshire, died, and Oswig,

him into the boat and bound him and rowed to a ship and put him on board. Then they hoisted sail and ran west to Axmouth. And they kept Beorn with them until they killed him, and they took the body and buried it in a church. But his friends and his sailors came from London and disinterred him and took him to the Old Minster at Winchester, where they buried him with King Cnut his uncle. And Swein went east to Baldwin's country and stayed there all winter at Bruges under Baldwin's full protection. And in the same year Eadnoth, bishop to the north,[6] died and Ulf was appointed bishop.

---

[1] *Nithing*.

[2] Though Florence's account is close to 'D', he differs here. He places the capture of the two ships by the men of Hastings *after* Beorn's murder, stating them to be two of the six ships which deserted Swein. He then adds that Swein fled to Flanders with two ships (see 'C', 'E') and stayed there until Aldred, bishop of Worcester, brought him back and made his peace with the king.

[3] Florence: 'In the month of August.'

[4] i.e. of Dorchester-on-Thames.

[5] Florence: 'King of the South Britons.' He is Griffith ap Rhydderch, on whom see Lloyd, *op. cit.*, II, pp. 361–364. Florence has a fuller account: 'Then joining forces, the king

and they crossed the Wye and burnt *Dymedham* [Tidenham?] and slew all whom they found there. Aldred, bishop of Worcester, and a few of the men of Gloucestershire and Herefordshire hastily rose against them; but the Welsh whom they had with them, and who had promised fealty to them, secretly sent a messenger to King Griffith, asking him to attack the English as quickly as he could. He at once rushed both with his own men and with the Irish pirates, and, attacking the English at daybreak, killed many of them and the rest escaped by flight.'

[6] This indicates the southern provenance of 'E', for the see of Dorchester-on-Thames is meant, which extended to the Humber.

C | D | E

C

and Bishop Aldred went to Rome to the pope on the king's business.[1]

D

abbot of Thorney, and Wulf-noth, abbot of Westminster. And the priest[2] Ulf was appointed as pastor of that bishopric which Eadnoth had held, but he was expelled from it afterwards because he did nothing like a bishop in it, so much so that we are ashamed to say anything more about it. And Bishop Siward[3] died, who lies at Abingdon. And this year the great minster at Rheims was consecrated; Pope Leo was there and the emperor and they had a great synod there about the service of God. St. Leo, the pope, presided over that synod.[4] It is difficult to know what bishops came to it and in particular what abbots, but two were sent from this country – from St. Augustine's and from Ramsey.

C

1050 In this year the bishops came home from Rome, and Earl Swein was reinstated. And in this same year Archbishop Eadsige died on 29 October. Also in this same year Ælfric, archbishop of Yorkshire, died on

D

(1051)[5] In this year Eadsige, archbishop of Canterbury, died and the king gave the archbishopric to Robert the Frenchman,[6] who had been bishop of London; and Sparrowhawk, abbot of Abingdon, succeeded to

E

(1047)[5] In this year there was a big council at London in the middle of Lent, and nine ships of the sailors were dismissed and five remained. And in this same year Earl Swein came into England. And in this same year was

---

[1] Later Lives of Edward the Confessor say that the mission was to ask the pope to release the king from a vow to go on pilgrimage. The entry of their journey by 'C' here instead of in annal 1050 (as in 'D' and 'E') suggests that they left before 25 March, the date at which 'C' commences the year.

[2] Florence: 'the king's chaplain, a Norman'.

[3] He had been assistant bishop to Eadsige, archbishop of Canterbury.

[4] Florence says it lasted six days.

[5] 'D' remains a year in advance;' E' is three years behind the true date.

[6] Abbot of Jumièges.

C	D	E

C

22 January,[1] and his body lies at Peterborough. Then King Edward held a council at London in mid-Lent and appointed Robert[3] as archbishop of Canterbury, and he appointed Abbot Sparrowhawk to London, and gave Bishop Rothulf his kinsman the abbacy of Abingdon.[4] In the same year he laid off all the sailors.

D

the bishopric of London, but it was taken from him[2] before he was consecrated. And Bishop Hereman and Bishop Aldred went to Rome.

E

the great synod at Rome, and King Edward sent Bishop Hereman and Bishop Aldred to it, and they got there on Easter eve. And the pope held another synod at Vercelli, and Bishop Ulf went there, and they are said to have nearly broken his staff if he had not given more treasure, because he could not perform his duties as he ought. And in this year Archbishop Eadsige died on 29 October.

A1050 In this year Archbishop Eadsige died, and Robert succeeded to the archbishopric.

C

1051 In this year Archbishop Robert came here from overseas with his *pallium*, and in this same year Earl Godwine and all his sons were driven out of England. He went to Bruges with his wife and with his three sons, Swein, Tosti, and Gyrth. And Harold and Leofwine went to Ireland and stayed there that winter. And in this same year on 14 March,[8] there died the queen-mother, the mother of King Edward and Hardacnut, whose name was Emma,[9] and her body

D

(1052)[5] This year Ælfric, archbishop of York,[6] died, a man who was very venerable and wise. And in the same year King Edward abolished the army-tax which King Ethelred had imposed, that is in the thirty-ninth[7] year after it had been instituted. That tax oppressed all the English people for as long a space of time as we have written above. That tax always came before other taxes, which were variously paid, and it oppressed people in many ways. In the

E

(1048)[5] In this year in Lent King Edward appointed Robert of London to be archbishop of Canterbury, and in the course of the same Lent Robert went to Rome for his *pallium*. And the king gave the bishopric of London to Sparrowhawk, abbot of Abingdon, and he gave the abbacy to Bishop Rothulf his kinsman. Then the archbishop came from Rome one day before the eve of the Feast of St. Peter, and occupied his archiepiscopal throne at Christ Church on St.

---

[1] 1051—evidence of the Lady Day reckoning in 'C'.
[2] Florence: 'by King Edward'.
[3] Abbot of Jumièges.
[4] He had apparently been bishop of Nidaros, Norway.
[5] 'D' remains a year in advance; 'E' is three years behind the true date.

[6] Florence adds that he died at Southwell and was buried at Peterborough, and that Kynsige succeeded him.
[7] Florence: '38th'.
[8] 1052. A Winchester calendar dates her death 6 March. 'C' seems to have read 'ides' in error for 'nones'.
[9] This name is written over an erasure.

C

lies in the Old Minster near King Cnut.

D

same year Eustace,[1] who had married King Edward's sister, landed at Dover.[3] Then his men went foolishly looking for billets and killed a certain man of the town, and another of the towns-men [killed] their comrades,[4] so that seven of his comrades were struck down. And great damage was done on either side with horses and with weapons until the people assembled, and then Eustace's men fled to the king at Gloucester, who granted them protection. Then Earl Godwine was indignant that such things should happen in his earldom, and he began to gather his people from all over his earl-dom,[5] and Earl Swein his son did the same over all his,[6] and Harold his other son over all his.[8] And they all assembled in Gloucestershire at Langtree,[9] a great and innumerable force all ready to do battle against the king unless Eustace were sur-rendered and his men handed over to them, as well as the Frenchmen who were in the

E

Peter's Day,[2] and soon after he went to the king. Then Abbot Sparrowhawk met him on the way with the king's writ and seal to the effect that he was to be consecrated bishop of London by the archbishop. But the arch-bishop refused and said the pope had forbidden it him. Then the abbot went to the archbishop again about it and asked for ordination as bishop, and the archbishop refused him reso-lutely and said that the pope had forbidden it him. Then the abbot went back to London and occupied the bishopric that the king had given him; he did this with the king's full permission all that summer and autumn. Then Eustace came from over-seas[7] soon after the bishop, and went to the king and told him what he wished, and then went homewards. When he came east to Canterbury, he and his men took refreshment there, and went to Dover. When he was some miles[10] or more on this side of Dover he put on his corselet

---

[1] Eustace 'aux Grenons', count of Boulogne, married Gode, sister of Edward the Confessor and widow of Dreux, count of the French Vexin.

[2] 29 June.

[3] Florence: 'in September'.

[4] *geferan* can be singular or plural. Florence takes it as singular, and puts later on the reference to seven men. He greatly exaggerates the evil behaviour of Eustace's party, making them kill men and women and trample on children with their horses.

[5] Florence: 'Kent, Sussex, and Wessex'.

[6] *Id.*: 'Oxfordshire, Gloucestershire, Herefordshire, Somerset, and Berkshire'.

[7] William of Malmesbury: 'from Wissant'.

[8] Florence: 'Essex, East Anglia, Huntingdonshire, and Cambridgeshire'.

[9] The hundred in which Beverstone is situated; cf. 'E'.

[10] A numeral may have been omitted.

C

D

E

D

castle.[1] This was done a week before the second Feast of St. Mary.[3] King Edward was then residing at Gloucester. He sent for Earl Leofric,[4] and to the north for Earl Siward,[5] and asked for their troops. And they came to him at first with a small force, but after they had understood how things were in the south, they sent north throughout all their earldoms and had a great army called out for the help of their liege lord, and Ralph[6] did the same throughout his earldom; and they all came to Gloucester to the help of the king, though it was late. They were all so much in agreement with the king that they were willing to attack the army of Godwine if the king had wished them to do so. Then some of them thought it would be a great piece of folly if they joined battle, for in the two hosts there was most of what was noblest in England, and they considered that they would be opening a way for our enemies to enter the country and to cause great ruin among ourselves. They

E

and all his companions did likewise.[2] So they went to Dover. When they got there, they wished to lodge where it suited their own convenience. Then one of Eustace's men came and wished to stay at the home of a householder against his will, and he wounded the householder, and the householder killed him. Then Eustace got upon his horse and his companions upon theirs, and went to the householder and killed him upon his own hearth, and afterwards they went up towards the town and killed, within and without, more than twenty men. And the townsmen killed nineteen men on the other side and wounded they did not know how many. And Eustace escaped with a few men and went back to the king and gave him a prejudiced account of how they had fared, and the king grew very angry with the townsmen. And the king sent for Earl Godwine and ordered him to carry war into Kent to Dover because Eustace had informed the king that it was more the townsmen's fault than

---

[1] Florence says this message was sent to the king at Gloucester, and that it demanded also the surrender of the men of Boulogne who were holding the castle of Dover. The king was alarmed, but refused when he knew that the forces of Leofric, Siward, and Ralph were approaching.

[2] These details suggest local knowledge. The archetype of 'E' was being written at Canterbury.

[3] The Nativity, 8 September; but Florence dates the event after the Nativity, not before it.

[4] Earl of Mercia.

[5] Earl of Northumbria.

[6] Florence: 'Son of Gode, King Edward's sister.' He was her son by her first husband, Drew, count of the French Vexin, and was nicknamed 'the Timid'.

C

D

E

advised the exchange of hostages, and they issued summonses for a meeting at London; the folk throughout all this northern province,[1] in Siward's earldom and Leofric's and elsewhere, were ordered to go there. And Earl Godwine and his sons were to come there to defend themselves.[4] Then they came to Southwark, and a great number with them from Wessex, but his force dwindled more and more as time passed. And all the thegns of Harold his son were transferred to the king's allegiance, and Earl Swein his other son was outlawed. Then it did not suit him to come to defend himself against the king and against the force that was with the king. Then Godwine went away by night, and next morning the king held a meeting of his council and he and all the army declared him an outlaw, and all his sons with him. And he went south to Thorney[6] and so did his wife and his sons Swein and Tosti, with his wife who was a kinswoman of Baldwin of Bruges, and his son Gyrth. And

his. But it was not so. And the earl would not consent to this expedition because he was reluctant to injure his own province. Then the king sent for all his council and ordered them to come to Gloucester near the later Feast of St. Mary. The foreigners[2] then had built a castle[3] in Herefordshire in Earl Swein's province, and had inflicted every possible injury and insult upon the king's men in those parts. Then Earl Godwine and Earl Swein and Earl Harold came together at Beverstone,[5] and many men with them, intending to go to their royal lord and to all the councillors who were assembled with him, so that they should have the advice and support of the king and of all the councillors as to how they should avenge the insult to the king and to all the people. Then the foreigners went beforehand to the king and accused the earls, so that they were not allowed to come into his sight, because, they said, they meant to come to betray the king. Earl Siward and Earl Leofric had

---

[1] This shows that the version in 'D' was written in the north.

[2] The Norman colony established in Herefordshire under Earl Ralph 'the Timid'.

[3] On this and other castles built about this time in this neighbourhood, see E. S. Armitage, *The Early Norman Castles of the British Isles*, pp. 23 f., 192.

[4] According to Florence, hostages were given and Godwine went to Wessex while the king assembled a greater army from all Mercia and Northumbria, and led it to London.

[5] In the hundred of Langtree, Gloucestershire.

[6] An island off the coast of Sussex and Hampshire. Florence adds: 'where a ship was ready for them, into which they put as much gold and silver and other treasures as it could carry'.

C

D

E

Earl Harold and Leofwine went to Bristol to the ship which Earl Swein had equipped and provisioned for himself. And the king sent Bishop Aldred from London with a force, and they were to intercept him before he got on board, but they could not – or would not. And he went out from the estuary of the Avon, and had such stiff weather that he escaped with difficulty, and he suffered great losses there. He continued his course to Ireland when sailing weather came. And Godwine and those who were with him went from Thorney to Bruges, to Baldwin's country, in one ship with as much treasure for each person as they could stow away. It would have seemed remarkable to everyone in England if anybody had told them that it could happen, because he had been exalted so high, even to the point of ruling the king and all England, and his sons were earls and the king's favourites, and his daughter was married to the king.[1] She was brought to Wherwell[2] and they entrusted her to the abbess. Then forthwith Count William[3] came

come there to the king and a large company with them from the north, and Earl Godwine and his sons were informed that the king and the men who were with them meant to take measures against them. And they strengthened themselves firmly in reply, though they were reluctant to have to stand against their royal lord. Then the councillors gave advice that evil doing should cease on both sides, and the king gave the peace of God, and his complete friendship to both sides. Then the king and his councillors decided that there should be a meeting of all the councillors a second time at London at the autumnal equinox, and the king ordered the force to be called out both south of the Thames and in the north, all the best of them. Then Earl Swein was declared an outlaw and Earl Godwine and Earl Harold were ordered to come to the meeting as quickly as ever they could make the journey. When they got there they were summoned to the meeting. Then Godwine asked for safe-conduct and hostages, so that he could

---

[1] The details given above in 'D' are irreconcilable with those in 'E'. 'D' is on the whole less favourable to the family of Godwine. For a criticism of these variations, see B. Wilkinson in *Bulletin of the John Rylands Library*, XXII, (1938), pp. 368–387.

[2] Florence: 'without honour, with one female attendant'.

[3] 'William eorl.' This is generally considered to be a reference to Duke William of Normandy, later William I of England. The visit is asserted only in 'D'. Whether Duke William of Normandy in fact visited England in 1051 is discussed by D. C. Douglas in *Eng. Hist. Rev.*, LXVIII (1953), pp. 526–545, and by T. J. Oleson, *ibid.*, LXXII (1957), pp. 221–228.

C

D

E

from overseas with a great force of Frenchmen, and the king received him and as many of his companions as suited him, and let him go again. This same year William the priest[1] was given the bishopric of London which had been given to Sparrow-hawk.

come to the meeting, and leave it, without being betrayed. Then the king asked for all those thegns that the earls had had, and they were all handed over to him. Then the king sent to them again and ordered them to come with twelve men into the king's council. Then the earl again asked for a safe-conduct and hostages so that he might be allowed to exculpate himself of all the charges that were brought against him. But he was refused hostages and granted five days' safe-conduct to leave the country. Then Earl Godwine and Earl Swein went to Bosham and there launched their ships and went overseas and sought Bald-win's protection, and stayed there all the winter. Earl Harold went west to Ireland, and was there all the winter under that king's protection.[2] And as soon as this had happened the king put away the lady who was consecrated his queen,[3] and deprived her of all that she owned, land and gold and silver and everything; and entrusted her to his sister at Wherwell. And Abbot Sparrowhawk was expelled from the bishopric of

[1] He was a Norman.
[2] The oldest *Life of St Edward* calls him Dermod, i.e. Diarmaid, king of Leinster.

[3] Edith, Godwine's daughter.

C

D

E

London, and William the king's priest was consecrated to it; and Odda[1] was appointed earl over Devon and Somerset and Dorset and Cornwall; and Ælfgar, son of Earl Leofric, was granted the earldom which Harold had possessed.[2]

1052[3]

This year on 6 March the Lady Ælfgifu,[4] the widow of King Ethelred and of King Cnut, died. In the same year Griffith the Welsh king[5] was ravaging in Herefordshire so that he came quite close to Leominster, and people gathered against him, both natives and the Frenchmen from the castle. And very many good Englishmen were killed and Frenchmen too. It was the same day that Edwin and his comrades had been killed thir-

In this year Ælfgifu Emma, mother of King Edward and of King Hardacnut, died. And in the same year the king and his council decided that ships should be sent to Sandwich, and they appointed Earl Ralph[6] and Earl Odda[1] as their captains. Then Earl Godwine went out from Bruges with his ships to the Isere, and put out to sea a day before the eve of the mid-summer festival,[7] so that he came to Dungeness, which is south of Romney. Then it came to the knowledge of the earls

(1052)[8] In this year Earl Harold[9] came from Ireland with his ships to the mouth of the Severn near the boundary of Somerset and Devon, and there did much damage, and the local people gathered together against him out of Somerset and Devon, and he put them to flight and killed more than thirty good thegns, apart from other people, and imme-diately after that he went round Land's End.[10] Then King Edward

teen years before. And forthwith

out at Sandwich, and they then went out in pursuit of the other ships, and a land force was called out against the ships. Then meanwhile Earl Godwine was

---

[1] Odda, whom William of Malmesbury calls the king's kinsman, built a chapel at Deerhurst which still stands. He was a benefactor of Pershore (see A. J. Robertson, *Anglo-Saxon Charters*, pp. 456–458). See also annal 1056 'C', 'D'.

[2] East Anglia.

[3] 'E' omits the numbers 1049, 1050, and 1051, while 'D' repeats number 1052. All the versions thus at last become chronologically in harmony.

[4] Florence adds that she died at Winchester and was buried there. See also p. 116, n. 8.

[5] Griffith ap Llewelyn, king of Gwynedd and Powys.

[6] Earl Ralph 'the Timid'.

[7] 24 June.

[8] See n. 3 above.

[9] Florence: 'and his brother Leofwine'.

[10] *Penwithsteort.*

C   D   E

had forty small boats manned which lay at Sandwich[1] in order that they might keep watch for Earl Godwine, who was in Bruges that winter. But despite this, he got into this country[2] without their knowing anything about it. And while he was here in this country he enticed all the men of Kent and all the sailors from the district of Hastings and from the region round about there by the sea-coast, and all Essex[3] and Surrey and much else beside. Then they all said that they would live and die with him. When the fleet that was lying at Sandwich found out about Godwine's expedition, they set out after him; and he escaped them,[4] and the fleet turned back to Sandwich, and so homeward to London. When Godwine found out that the fleet that had been lying at Sandwich was on its way home, he went back again to the Isle of Wight, and lay off the coast there long enough for Earl Harold his son[5] to join him. And they would not do any great harm afterwards[6] except that they lived off the countryside. But they enticed all the local people to their side, both along the sea-coast and inland also. And they went towards Sandwich and kept on collecting all the sailors that they met, and so they came to Sandwich with an overwhelming force. When Edward found out about this, he sent inland for more help, but it came very slowly, and Godwine kept on advancing towards London with his fleet, until he came to Southwark, where he waited some time until the tide came up. In that interval he treated with the citizens so that they nearly all wanted what he wanted.[7] When Godwine had arranged all his expedition, the tide came in, and they forthwith weighed anchor and proceeded through the bridge[8] always keeping to the southern bank, and the land force came from above and drew themselves up along the shore, and they formed a wing with their ships[9] as if they meant to encircle the king's ships. The king had also a large land force on his side in addition to the sailors. But it was hateful to almost all of them to fight against men of their own race, for there was little else that was worth anything apart from Englishmen

warned; and he went to Pevensey, and the storm became so violent that the earls could not find out what had happened to Earl Godwine. And then Earl Godwine put out again so that he got back to Bruges, and the other ships went back again to Sandwich. Then it was decided that the ships should go back again to London, and that other earls and other oarsmen should be appointed to them. But there was so long a delay that the naval expedition was quite abandoned and all the men went home. Earl Godwine found out about this and hoisted his sail – and so did his fleet – and they went westward direct to the Isle of Wight and there landed, and ravaged there so long that the people paid them as much as they imposed upon them, and then they went westward until they came to Portland and landed there, and did whatever damage they could. Then Harold had come from Ireland with nine ships, and he landed at Porlock, and there was a great force gathered there to oppose

---

[1] 'C' adds: 'for many weeks'.

[2] Florence: 'with a few ships'.

[3] 'C' reads: 'and all the east province' and then adds 'and Sussex'.

[4] 'C' adds: 'and protected himself wherever he could' Florence's text had this reading also.

[5] Florence adds: 'and Leofwine'.

[6] 'C' adds: 'after they came together'.

[7] Florence says that he had previously made them many promises.

[8] Florence: 'meeting no opposition at the bridge'.

[9] C' adds: 'towards the north shore', and Florence agrees.

C	D	E

on either side; and also they did not wish the country to be laid the more open to foreigners through their destroying each other. Then it was decided that wise men should go between the parties, and they made a truce on both sides.[1] And Godwine and his son Harold went ashore and as many of their sailors as suited them, and then there was a meeting of the council, and Godwine was given his earldom unconditionally and as fully and completely as he had ever held it, and all his sons all that they had held before,[2] and his wife and his daughter as fully and completely as they had held it before. And they confirmed full friendship with them, and promised the full benefits of the laws[3] to all the people. And they outlawed all the Frenchmen who had promoted injustices and passed unjust judgments and given bad counsel in this country, with the exception, as they decided, of as many as the king should wish to have with him, who were loyal to him and to all the people.[4] And Archbishop Robert and Bishop William and Bishop Ulf escaped with difficulty with the Frenchmen who were with them and so got away overseas.[5]

C only

And Earl Godwine and Harold and the queen stayed on their estates. Swein had gone to Jerusalem from Bruges, and died on the way home at Constantinople, at Michaelmas. It was on the Monday after St. Mary's Day[7] that Godwine came to Southwark with his ships, and

him, but he did not hesitate to obtain provisions for himself, and he landed and killed a great part of the force that opposed him, and seized for himself what came his way in cattle, men, and property; and then he went east to his father, and they both went eastward until they came to the Isle of Wight, and there took what they had left behind them. Then they went on to Pevensey and took with them as many ships as were serviceable and so proceeded to Dungeness. And he took all the ships that were at Romney and Hythe and Folkestone, and then they went east to Dover and landed and seized ships for themselves and as many hostages as they wished. So they came to Sandwich and there they did exactly the same, and everywhere they were given hostages and provisions wherever they asked for them. They went on to the 'Northmouth',[6] and so towards London, and some of the ships went within Sheppey

---

[1] Florence: 'They ordered the army to lay down their arms.'

[2] Florence says 'except Swein', and puts here the information given by 'C' below about his pilgrimage and death, adding that he went barefoot, in penance for his murder of Beorn, and died in Lycia from the extreme cold.

[3] 'C': 'good laws'.

[4] Florence lists these: 'Robert the deacon and his son-in-law Richard, son of Scrob, Alfred the king's equerry, and Anfrid, nicknamed *Ceocesfot*.'

[5] 'D' ends the annal at this point, but Florence continues:

'William, however, being a man of good-will, was recalled after a short time and received in his bishopric. Osbern, nicknamed Pentecost, and his companion Hugh, surrendered their castles, and with the permission of Earl Leofric they passed through his earldom and went into Scotland, where they were received by Macbeth, king of the Scots.'

[6] The northern mouth of the Kentish Stour.

[7] The Monday after the Nativity of St Mary was 14 September, and Florence gives the same date, the Exaltation of the Holy Cross.

C

the morning after, on the Tuesday, that they came to the agreement which has been stated
above. Then Godwine fell ill
soon after he landed, and recovered again, but he did all too
little reparation about the property of God which he had from
many holy places. In the same
year came the strong wind on
the night of the Feast of St.
Thomas,[3] and did great damage
everywhere.[4] Also Rhys the
Welsh king's brother was killed.[5]

D

E

and did much damage there, and
they went to King's Milton and
burnt it[1] down to the ground.
Thus they proceeded on their
way to London in pursuit of the
earls. When they came to London the king and earls were all
lying there with fifty ships ready
to meet them. Then the earls[2]
sent to the king and asked him
legally to return to them all
those things of which they had
been unjustly deprived. But the
king refused for some time – for
so long that the men who were
with the earl were so incensed
against the king and against his
men that the earl himself had
difficulty in calming those men.
Then Bishop Stigand with the
help of God went there and the
wise men both inside the city
and without, and they decided
that hostages should be arranged
for on both sides. And so it was
done. Then Archbishop Robert
found out about this, and the
Frenchmen, so that they took
horses and departed, some west
to Pentecost's castle, and some
north to Robert's castle.[6] And
Archbishop Robert and Bishop
Ulf and their companions went

---

[1] 'E', although favourable to Godwine, gives from local
knowledge most details of his ravages in the south-east.
[2] Godwine and Harold.
[3] 21 December.

[4] Florence says: 'It blew down many churches and houses
and broke or uprooted innumerable trees.'
[5] He was brother of Griffith ap Rhydderch, and was killed
early in 1053.
[6] On these Herefordshire castles, see E. S. Armitage, *loc. cit.*

C	D	E

E

out at the east gate and killed or otherwise injured many young men, and went right on to *Eadulfesness*,[1] and he[2] there got on board a broken-down ship, and went right on overseas, and left behind him his *pallium* and all the Church in this country.[3] This was God's will, in that he had obtained the dignity when it was not God's will. Then a big council was summoned outside London, and all the earls and the chief men who were in the country were at the council. Then Earl Godwine expounded his case, and cleared himself before King Edward, his liege lord, and before all his countrymen, declaring that he was guiltless of the charges brought against him, and against Harold his son and all his children. Then the king granted the earl and his children his full friendship and full status as an earl, and all that he had had. And all the men who were with him were treated likewise. And the king gave the lady[4] all that she had had. And Archbishop Robert was declared utterly an outlaw, and all the Frenchmen too, because they were most responsible for the

---

[1] The Naze, Essex.
[2] Archbishop Robert.

[3] William of Malmesbury adds that he took his case to Rome, and died at Jumièges on his return.
[4] Edith, Godwine's daughter, King Edward's wife.

C

D

E

disagreement between Earl Godwine and the king. And Bishop
Stigand succeeded to the archbishopric of Canterbury. And[1]
at this time Arnwig, abbot of
Peterborough, relinquished his
abbacy while well and strong,
and gave it to the monk Leofric
with the permission of the king
and the monks. And this Abbot
Arnwig survived eight years;
and the Abbot Leofric so en-
riched the monastery that it was
called the Golden Borough.
Then it grew greatly in land and
gold and silver.

1053 In this year the king was at
Winchester at Easter, and Earl
Godwine with him, and Earl
Harold his son and Tosti. Then
on Easter Monday as he was
sitting with the king at a meal,
he suddenly sank towards the
foot-stool, bereft of speech and
of all his strength. Then he was
carried[6] to the king's private
room and they thought it was
about to pass off. But it was not
so. On the contrary, he continued like this without speech
or strength right on to the
Thursday[2] and then lost his life.
And he lies there in the Old

This year was the big wind on
the night of the Feast of St.
Thomas;[3] all through Christmas also there was a big wind.
And it was decided that Rhys,
the Welsh king's brother, should
be killed,[4] because he was causing injuries; and his head was
brought to Gloucester on the
eve of the Epiphany.[7] In the
same year before All Saints'
Day, Wulfsige, bishop of Lichfield, and Godwine, abbot of
Winchcombe, and Æthelweard,
abbot of Glastonbury, all died
within one month; and Leofwine succeeded to the bishopric

In this year Earl Godwine died
on 15 April[2] and he is buried at
Winchester in the Old Minster,
and Earl Harold his son succeeded to the earldom and to all
that his father had had, and Earl
Ælfgar succeeded to the earldom that Harold had had.[5]

---

[1] What follows is clearly a Peterborough addition.
[2] The Thursday after Easter was in fact 15 April in 1053.
[3] 21 December 1052.
[4] See p. 125, n. 5. Florence adds that he was killed in *Bulendun*,
by order of King Edward.

[5] East Anglia.
[6] Florence: 'by his sons Harold, Tosti, and Gyrth'.
[7] 5 January.

C

Minster; and his son Harold succeeded to his earldom and resigned the one he had previously held,[3] and to this Ælfgar succeeded. In the course of this year Wulfsige, bishop of Lichfield, died, and Leofwine, abbot of Coventry, succeeded to the bishopric; and Æthelweard, abbot of Glastonbury, died, and Godwine, abbot of Winchcombe. Also Welshmen killed a great number of Englishmen of the patrols near Westbury. In this year there was no archbishop in the land,[5] but Bishop Stigand held the bishopric in Canterbury at Christ Church and Kynsige at York. And Leofwine and Wulfwig went overseas and had themselves consecrated there. This Wulfwig succeeded to the bishopric that Ulf had had[6] while Ulf was still alive and expelled.

D

of Lichfield, and Bishop Aldred succeeded to the abbacy of Winchcombe,[1] and Æthelnoth[2] to the abbacy at Glastonbury. And in the course of the same year Ælfric, Odda's brother, died at Deerhurst,[4] and his body rests at Pershore. And in the course of the same year Earl Godwine died, and he was taken ill while he was sitting with the king at Winchester. And Harold his son succeeded to the earldom his father had had, and Ælfgar succeeded to the earldom that Harold had had.[3]

E

A1053 In this year Earl Godwine died.

C

1054 In this year Earl Siward went with a large force into Scotland

D

In this year Earl Siward proceeded[9] with a large force to

E

(1053)[7] Battle at Mortemer.[8] In this year Leo the holy pope of

---

[1] Florence: 'until Godric, son of the king's chaplain, Godman, was appointed abbot'.

[2] *Id.*: 'a monk of that same monastery'.

[3] East Anglia.

[4] Florence gives 22 December as the date of his death. On Odda, see p. 122, n. 1.

[5] Because Stigand had failed to receive canonical recognition as archbishop of Canterbury and Kynsige of York had not yet received his *pallium*. This explains why Leofwine and Wulfwig went overseas to be consecrated.

[6] Dorchester-on-Thames.

[7] 'E' repeats the number 1053.

[8] An addition in Latin. At the battle of Mortemer, vassals of Duke William of Normandy defeated troops of the French king, Henry I.

[9] Florence: 'by the king's command'. Gaimar, ll. 5043–5046, says that Siward had been to Scotland, apparently in the previous year, and had made an agreement with the Scots king, but Macbeth broke the peace.

C

and inflicted heavy losses on the Scots and routed them, and the king escaped. Also many fell on his side both among Danes and English, his own son also. In the course of this same year the church of Evesham was consecrated on 10 October. In the same year Bishop Aldred went south overseas into Saxony, and was received there with great honour.[5] In the same year Osgod Clapa died suddenly as he was lying in bed.

D

Scotland, both with a naval force and with a land force, and fought there with the Scots and routed the king Macbeth,[2] and killed all the best in the land,[3] and carried off a large amount of plunder such as had never been captured before. But his son Osbeorn and his sister's son Siward and some of his housecarls, and also some of the king's, were killed there on the Day of the Seven Sleepers.[6] In the course of this same year Bishop Aldred went overseas to Cologne on the king's business,[5] and there was received with great honour by the emperor,[7] and he stayed there for nearly a year, and the bishop of Cologne and the emperor both gave him entertainment. And he permitted Bishop Leofwine to consecrate the monastic church of Evesham on 10 October. And this year Osgod died suddenly in his bed. And St. Leo, the pope,[1] died, and Victor[4] was elected pope in his stead.

E

Rome died.[1] And in this year there was so great a pestilence among cattle that no one remembered anything as bad for many years. And Victor[4] was elected pope.

---

[1] Leo IX.

[2] On Macbeth, see W. F. Skene, *Celtic Scotland*, I, pp. 395 ff., and R. L. G. Ritchie, *The Normans in Scotland*, pp. 4, 7 f., 17, 92.

[3] Florence adds that all the Normans whom he had mentioned above (see p. 124, no. 5) were killed; and that Siward by the king's orders made Malcolm, son of the king of the Cumbrians, king. For other accounts of this campaign, see A. O. Anderson, *Scottish Annals from English Chroniclers*, p. 85.

[4] Victor II.

[5] Florence explains that the purpose of this mission was to suggest to the emperor that messengers should be sent to Hungary to bring back Edward's brother's son, Edward, and cause him to come to England.

[6] 27 July.

[7] Henry III. Florence adds: 'and by Heriman, archbishop of Cologne'.

C

1055[1]In this year Earl Siward died at York and his body lies in the minster at Galmanho which he himself had built to the glory of God and all his saints.[2] Then after that within a short space there was a council at London, and Earl Ælfgar, son of Earl Leofric, was outlawed without any guilt;[4] and he then went to Ireland and there got himself a fleet – it was eighteen ships apart from his own – and then they went to Wales to King Griffith[5] with that force, and he took him into his protection. And then they gathered a large force with the Irishmen and with the Welsh, and Earl Ralph gathered a large force against them at Hereford town, and there battle was joined.[6] But before any spear had been thrown the English army fled because they were on horseback,[7] and many were killed there – about four or five hundred men – and they killed none in return. And then they went back to the town and burnt it with the glorious min-

D

In this year Earl Siward died at York, and he lies at Galmanho in the minster which he himself had built and consecrated in the name of God and Olaf.[2] And Tosti succeeded to the earldom he had had.[3] And Archbishop Kynsige fetched his *pallium* from Pope Victor. And soon after that Earl Ælfgar, Earl Leofric's son, was outlawed, having committed hardly any crime.[4] But he went to Ireland and Wales and got himself a large force and so came to Hereford. But Earl Ralph came against him with a large force, but after a little struggle this was put to flight and many people were killed in the flight. The invaders then went to Hereford town and ravaged it, and burnt the glorious minster which Bishop Athelstan had built, and killed the priests[8] inside the minster and many others as well, and captured all the treasures and took them away. And when they had done the greatest damage, it was decided to reinstate Earl

E

In this year Earl Siward died, and a meeting of all the councillors was ordered a week before mid-Lent, and Earl Ælfgar was outlawed because he was charged with being a traitor to the king and to all the people of the country.[4] And he admitted this before all the people who were assembled there, though the words escaped him against his will. And the king gave Tosti, son of Earl Godwine, the earldom that Siward had had, and Earl Ælfgar sought the protection of Griffith[5] in Wales; and in this year Griffith and Ælfgar burned down St. Ethelbert's minster and all the city of Hereford.

---

[1] 'C' omits the number of this annal.

[2] Bootham Bar in York was formerly called Galmanhithe. The dedication to St Olaf illustrates Earl Siward's Scandinavian sentiments. The monastery of Galmanho was subsequently given to St Mary's, York.

[3] Northumbria.

[4] The several explanations given in 'C', 'D', and 'E' aptly illustrate their attitude to the politics of the king. Florence agrees with 'C'.

[5] Griffith ap Llewelyn.

[6] Florence: 'two miles from Hereford'.

[7] Earl Ralph was making them fight on horseback after the manner of Norman mounted knights. But Florence says that the earl with his Frenchmen and Normans set the example of flight, and only then did the English flee. He omits the statement that none of the enemy was killed.

[8] Florence: 'seven canons who guarded the doors of the cathedral'.

C

ster which Athelstan the venerable bishop had had built. They stripped and robbed it of relics[1] and vestments and everything, and killed the people and some they carried off. Then a force was collected from very nearly all over England, and they came to Gloucester, and went a little way out into Wales, and stayed there for some time.[2] And Earl Harold had a ditch made about the town during that time. Then meanwhile peace was discussed, and Earl Harold and those who were with him came to Billingsley and there confirmed peace and friendship between them. And Ælfgar was reinstated and given all that had been taken from him, and the fleet went to Chester and there waited for their pay which Earl Ælfgar promised them.[3] This slaughter was on 24 October. In the same year Tremerig, the Welsh bishop, died soon after the devastation – he was Bishop Athelstan's deputy after he became infirm.[4]

D

Ælfgar and give him his earldom, and all that had been taken from him. This devastation happened on 24 October. In the same year Tremerig, the Welsh bishop, died soon after the devastation. He was Bishop Athelstan's deputy after he became infirm.

E

---

[1] *Id.*: 'of St Ethelbert, king and martyr, and other saints'.

[2] Florence adds: 'beyond Straddle (the Golden Valley); but they, knowing him (Harold) to be a brave and warlike man, dared not risk a battle with him, but fled into South Wales. When he learnt of this, he left there the greater part of his army with orders to resist the enemy manfully, if necessary, and himself returned with the rest of his host to Hereford and surrounded it with a broad and deep ditch and fortified it with gates and bars.'

[3] *Id.* adds: 'He himself came to the king and received back his earldom from him.'

[4] *Id.* explains 'for he had been blind for thirteen years'. He then adds that Herman, bishop of Wiltshire, was offended because the king would not allow him to transfer his see from Ramsbury to the abbey of Malmesbury, and left England and became a monk at St Bertin's, where he stayed three years.

C

1056[1] In this year Athelstan the venerable bishop died on 10 February,[2] and his body lies in Hereford town, and Leofgar was appointed bishop. He was Earl Harold's priest, and he wore his moustaches during his priesthood until he became a bishop. He gave up his chrism and his cross, his spiritual weapons, and took his spear and his sword after his consecration as bishop, and so went campaigning against Griffith the Welsh king,[5] and they killed him there[6] and his priests with him, and Ælfnoth the sheriff and many good men with them; and the others fled. This was eight days before midsummer.[7] It is hard to describe the oppression and all the expeditions and the campaigning and the labours and the loss of men and horses that all the army of the English suffered, until Earl Leofric came there, and Earl Harold and Bishop Aldred, and made an agreement between them according to which Griffith swore oaths that he would be a

D

In this year Bishop Æthelric relinquished his bishopric at Durham and went to Peterborough to St. Peter's monastery,[4] and his brother Æthelwine succeeded him. Also Bishop Athelstan died on 10 February, and his body lies at Hereford, and Leofgar who was Harold's priest was appointed bishop, and in his priesthood he had his moustaches until he was a bishop. He gave up his chrism and his cross and his spiritual weapons, and took his spear and his sword, and so went campaigning against Griffith the Welsh king,[5] and they killed him there and his priests with him, and Ælfnoth the sheriff and many other good men. This was eight days before midsummer. And Bishop Aldred succeeded to the bishopric that Leofgar had held for eleven weeks and four days. In the course of this year Earl Odda[8] died, and he lies at Pershore, and he was consecrated monk before his end. He was a good man and pure and very

E

In this year Henry, emperor of the Romans, died and his son, Henry, succeeded him.[3]

---

[1] 'C' omits the number of this annal.
[2] Florence: 'in the episcopal estate called Bosbury'.
[3] An addition in Latin. The emperor is Henry III.
[4] Florence: 'where he stayed 12 years'.
[5] Griffith ap Llewelyn.
[6] Florence: 'at *Clafibyrig*'. An identification with Glasbury, Herefordshire, has been suggested.

[7] 16 June.
[8] On him, see annal 1051 and p. 122, n. 1. Florence, who says he died at Pershore, calls him 'a lover of churches, a restorer of the poor, a defender of widows and orphans, a helper of the oppressed, a preserver of chastity'. His other name was Æthelwine.

C	D	E
loyal and faithful underking to King Edward. And Bishop Aldred succeeded to the bishopric[1] which Leofgar had held for eleven weeks and four days. In the same year the emperor Cona[2] died. In the course of this year Earl Odda[3] died, and his body lies at Pershore, and he was consecrated monk[4] before his end. He died on 31 August.[5]	noble, and he went hence on 31 August. And the emperor Cona[2] died.	

D

57 This year the atheling Edward came to England[6] who was the son of King Edward's brother, King Edmund who was called Ironside because of his valour. This prince King Cnut had banished to Hungary in order to betray him. But there he became a distinguished man, as God granted it to him and as was his proper destiny, so that he won a kinswoman of the emperor for his wife, and by her begot a noble family. She was called Agatha. We do not know for what reason it was brought about that he was not allowed to see[11] [the face?] of his kinsman King Edward. Alas, that was a miserable fate and grievous to all this people that he so speedily ended his life after he came to England, to the misfortune of this poor people. In

E

In this year the atheling Edward, son of King Edmund, came to this country and soon after died, and his body is buried in St. Paul's minster in London. And Pope Victor[7] died, and Stephen[8] was elected pope who was abbot of Monte Cassino. And Earl Leofric died,[9] and Ælfgar, his son, succeeded to the earldom which his father had held.[10]

---

[1] Hereford. Aldred, bishop of Worcester, administered the see of Hereford until he became archbishop of York in 1060.

[2] The emperor, Henry III, has here been confused with his predecessor, Conrad II.

[3] See p. 132, n. 8.

[4] Florence: 'by Aldred, bishop of Worcester'.

[5] 'C' has no further entry until 1065.

[6] Florence adds: 'for the king had determined to make him heir to the kingdom after him'. He omits the account of his family in 'D', having put it in earlier (see p. 97, n. 9). The

atheling's death is one of the unsolved mysteries of the period.

On the significance of this interest shown by 'D' in the family of this atheling, the father of Margaret of Scotland, see p. xvi.

[7] Victor II.

[8] Stephen IX.

[9] Florence: 'in his own vill, called Bromley.'

[10] Mercia.

[11] Something must have been omitted here, for *geseon* 'see, visit' should not govern the genitive case.

D   E

the same year on 30 September[1] Earl Leofric died.
He was very wise in divine and temporal matters;
that was a benefit to all this people. He lies at
Coventry, and his son, Ælfgar, succeeded to his
authority. And in the same year Earl Ralph[2] died
on 21 December, and he lies at Peterborough.
Also Heca, bishop of Sussex,[3] died and Æthelric[4]
was elevated to his see. And this year Pope Victor
died and Stephen[5] was elected pope.

1058 In this year Earl Ælfgar was banished but he came   In this year Pope Stephen[5] died and Benedict[6] was
back forthwith by violence through Griffith's   consecrated pope. This same sent the *pallium* into
help. And a naval force came from Norway.[7] It is   this country for Archbishop Stigand. And in this
tedious to relate fully how things went. In the   year Heca, bishop of Sussex, died and Archbishop
same year Bishop Aldred consecrated the monastic   Stigand consecrated Æthelric, a monk of Christ
church at Gloucester that he himself brought to   Church, as bishop of Sussex, and Abbot Siward[8]
completion to the glory of God and of St. Peter,[9]   as bishop of Rochester.
and so he went to Jerusalem in such state as none
had done before him, and there he committed
himself to God, and also offered a worthy gift for
our Lord's tomb. It was a golden chalice worth
5 marks, of very wonderful workmanship. In the
same year Pope Stephen[5] died, and Benedict[6] was
appointed pope, who sent the *pallium* to Bishop
Stigand. And Æthelric was consecrated bishop of
Sussex, and Abbot Siward[8] was consecrated bishop
of Rochester.

---

[1] Florence has 'ii kal. Sept.' (31 August). He adds a long   [7] According to Florence, this force, which came unexpectedly,
passage on the foundation and enrichment of monasteries by   supported Earl Ælfgar. Celtic sources show it to have been a
Leofric and his wife Godgifu, at Coventry, Leominster,   large expedition, attempting to conquer England. It was led by
Wenlock, St John the Baptist's and St Werburg's at Chester,   Magnus, son of Harold Hardrada, king of Norway. See F. M.
St Mary's at Stow, and on their gift of lands to Worcester, and   Stenton, *Anglo-Saxon England*, pp. 566f.
of lands, buildings, and ornaments to Evesham.   [8] Abbot of Chertsey.
[2] Earl Ralph 'the Timid'.   [9] Florence adds that he made Wulfstan, whom he ordained
[3] Selsey, later to be removed to Chichester.   as a monk at Worcester, abbot of Gloucester. Aldred then gave
[4] Florence: 'a monk of Christ Church, Canterbury'.   up the episcopate of Wiltshire, which he had been in charge of
[5] Stephen IX. Florence says he died on 30 March, 1058.   during Herman's absence (see p. 131, n. 4), on the latter's return,
[6] Benedict X.   and went to Jerusalem via Hungary.

D *and* E

59 In this year Nicholas,[1] who had previously been bishop of the city of Florence, was elected pope and Benedict, who was pope there before, was expelled.

D *only*

And this year the tower of Peterborough was consecrated on 17 October.[2]

<table>
<tr><td>

D

60 In this year there was a great earthquake on the Translation of St. Martin.[4] And King Henry[3] died in France. And Archbishop Kynsige of York died on 22 December, and he lies at Peterborough. And Bishop Aldred succeeded to the office.[7] And Walter[6] succeeded to the bishopric of Hereford-shire,[8] and Bishop Dudoc, who was bishop of Somerset,[9] also died, and the priest Gisa was appointed in his place.[10]

61 In this year Bishop Aldred went to Rome for his *pallium* and received it from Pope Nicholas.[11] And the Earl Tosti and his wife[12] also went to Rome. And the bishop and the earl experienced much hardship when they were coming home.[13] And in this year Godwine, bishop at St. Martin's, died; and Wulfric, abbot of St. Augustine's, on 19

</td><td>

E

In this year Henry, king of the French,[3] died, and his son Philip[5] succeeded him. In this year Kynsige, archbishop of York, died on 22 December, and Bishop Aldred succeeded him. And Walter[6] succeeded to the bishopric of Hereford.

In this year Dudoc, bishop of Somerset,[9] died and Gisa succeeded him. And in the same year God-wine, bishop of St. Martin's, died on 9 March. And in the same year Wulfric, abbot at St. Augustine's, died in Easter week on 18 April.[14] When word came to the king that Abbot Wulfric was dead, he chose the monk Æthelsige of the

</td></tr>
</table>

---

[1] Nicholas II.

[2] Simeon of Durham adds to Florence's annal for this year the important information that Kynsige, archbishop of York, Æthelwine, bishop of Durham, and Earl Tosti escorted Malcolm, king of the Scots, to King Edward. This is also in Gaimar, ll. 5085–5097.

[3] Henry I.

[4] 4 July.

[5] Philip I. This sentence is in Latin.

[6] Florence: 'Queen Edith's chaplain'.

[7] *Id.*: 'on the Lord's Nativity'.

[8] *Id.*: 'which had been committed to Aldred on account of his diligence'.

[9] i.e. of Wells.

[10] Walter, Dudoc, and Gisa were Lotharingians.

[11] Florence adds that Gisa of Wells and Walter of Hereford were consecrated by the pope; but neither he nor any version of the Anglo-Saxon Chronicle mentions the pope's refusal to grant the *pallium* to Aldred until he had surrendered the see of Worcester. For this, see William of Malmesbury's *Life of Wulfstan*, chap. 10.

[12] Judith, sister of Baldwin V of Flanders and of Maud, wife of William the Conqueror.

[13] This refers to their being attacked and stripped of their possessions by robbers, and thus obliged to return to Rome. See *Life of Wulfstan*, *loc. cit.* Simeon of Durham (*History of the Kings*, ed. Arnold, II, p. 174) and Gaimar (ll. 5101–5104) both record an invasion by Malcolm of Scotland during Tosti's absence, in which Lindisfarne was ravaged.

[14] 'E', a copy of a St Augustine's chronicle, is more likely to be correct than 'D'.

D

March.[1] And Pope Nicholas[2] died and Alexander,[3] who was bishop of Lucca, was elected pope.

1062[5]

1063 In this year after Christmas Earl Harold went from Gloucester[6] to Rhuddlan, which belonged to Griffith,[7] and there he burnt the residence and the ships and all the equipment which belonged to them; and he put him to flight. And then at Rogationtide[8] Harold went with ships from Bristol round Wales, and that people made peace and gave hostages. And Tosti went against them with a land force and they subdued the country.[9] But in the same year[10] in autumn King Griffith was killed on 5 August by his own men because of the fight he fought against Earl Harold. He was king over all the Welsh, and his head was brought to Earl Harold, and Harold brought it to the king, and the figurehead of his ship and the ornaments with it. And King Edward entrusted the country to the two brothers of Griffith, Bleddyn and Rhiwallon,[11] and they swore oaths and gave

E

Old Minster for the office; he then followed Archbishop Stigand and was consecrated abbot at Windsor on St. Augustine's Day.[4]

In this year Maine was subjected to William, count of Normandy.

In this year Earl Harold and his brother Earl Tosti went into Wales with both a land force and a naval force and subdued the country. And that people gave hostages and surrendered, and then went out and killed their king, Griffith,[7] and brought his head to Harold, who appointed another king for them.

---

[1] See p. 135, n. 14.

[2] Nicholas II.

[3] Alexander II.

[4] Either 26 May (St Augustine of Canterbury) or 28 August (St Augustine of Hippo), probably the former.

[5] 'C' and 'D' have no entry for this year, and 'E' only one in Latin. In contrast to the Chronicle, Florence has a long account of St Wulfstan and his election to the see of Worcester. On the significance of the lack of interest in this prelate in 'D', see p. xv.

[6] Florence: 'where the king was staying'. Gaimar (l. 5076) says Harold came from Oxford.

[7] Griffith ap Llewelyn. Florence says that Harold intended to kill him because of his frequent raids into England and insults to King Edward, but Griffith was warned and escaped by ship with difficulty. For this Welsh campaign, see Lloyd, *op. cit.*, II, pp. 366–371.

[8] 25–28 May.

[9] According to Florence, the Welsh gave hostages, promised tribute, and renounced and exiled Griffith.

[10] 5 August 1064, according to Florence.

[11] They were only half-brothers of Griffith ap Llewelyn, whose mother, Angharad, married their father Cynfyn after the death of Llewelyn.

D

hostages to the king and the earl, promising that they would be faithful to him in everything, and be everywhere ready on water and on land, and likewise would pay such dues from that country as had been given before to any other king.

E

1064[1]

C

1065 In this year before Lammas Earl Harold ordered some building to be done in Wales – at Portskewet – when he had subdued it, and there he got together many goods and thought of having King Edward there for hunting. And when it was nearly all got together, Caradoc, son of Griffith,[3] went there with all those he could get, and killed nearly all the people who were building there, and took the goods that were collected there. This slaughter was on St. Bartholomew's Day.[4] And then after Michaelmas all the thegns of Yorkshire went to York and killed there all Tosti's housecarls that they could find and took

D[2]

In this year before Lammas Earl Harold ordered some building to be done in Wales – at Portskewet – when he had subdued it, and there he got together many goods and thought of having King Edward there for hunting. And when it was all ready, Caradoc, son of Griffith,[3] went there with all the following he could get and killed nearly all the people who were building there, and they took the goods that were got ready there. We do not know who first suggested this conspiracy. This was done on St. Bartholomew's Day.[4] And soon after this all the thegns in Yorkshire and in Northumberland

E

(1064)[5] In this year the men of Northumbria

---

[1] All the versions are blank for this year.

[2] In this annal and the next, 'D' is a combination of 'C' and 'E'.

[3] Florence correctly calls him king of the South Welsh, killed a few years before by Griffith, king of the North Welsh. Griffith ap Llewelyn brought about the death of Griffith ap Rhydderch in 1055.

[4] 24 August.

[5] 'E', having nothing for 1064, places this entry opposite that figure, and thus falls a year behind the true date. The bulk of its entry is shared with 'D'.

C

his treasure.[1] And Tosti was then at Britford with the king. And very soon after this there was a big council meeting at Northampton, and likewise one at Oxford on the Feast of St. Simon and St. Jude.[3] And Earl Harold was there and wanted to bring about an agreement between them if he could. But he could not. But all Tosti's earldom unanimously deserted him, and outlawed him,[4] and all those with him who had committed lawless deeds; because first he robbed God, and all those who were less powerful than himself he deprived of life and land. And they adopted Morcar as their earl, and Tosti went overseas and his wife with him, to Baldwin's country, and took up winter quarters at St. Omer.

D   **E**

came together and outlawed their Earl Tosti and killed his body-guard, and all they could get at, both English and Danish, and took all his weapons in York, and gold and silver and all his treasure they could hear about anywhere. And they sent for Morcar, son of Earl Ælfgar,[2] and chose him as their earl, and he went south with all the people of the shire, and of Nottinghamshire, Derbyshire, and Lincolnshire until he came to Northampton. And his brother Edwin came to meet him with the men that were in his earldom, and also many Welsh came with him. Thereupon Earl Harold came to meet them, and they entrusted him with a message to King Edward, and also sent messengers with him, and asked that they might be allowed to have Morcar as their earl. And the king granted this and sent Harold back to them at Northampton on the eve of St. Simon and St. Jude.[3] And he proclaimed this to them and gave them surety for it, and he renewed there the law of King Cnut. And the northern men did much damage round Northampton while he was gone on their errand, in that they killed people and burned houses and corn and took all the cattle that they could get at – which was many thousands – and captured many hundreds of people and took them north with them, so that that shire and other neighbouring shires were the worse for it for many years. And Earl Tosti and his wife and all those who wanted what he wanted went south overseas to Count Baldwin, and he received them all and there they remained all the winter.[5]

C (D)

And King Edward came to Westminster at Christmas[6] and had the minster consecrated which he had himself built to the glory of God

---

[1] Florence adds important information. He says that on Monday, 3 October, the Northumbrian thegns, Gamelbearn, Dunstan, son of Æthelnoth, and Glonieorn, son of Heardwulf, came with 200 men at arms to York, where they seized Tosti's housecarls Amund and Ravenswart and killed them outside the walls, and killed next day more than 200 of his followers on the north of the Humber. They broke open his treasury and withdrew, carrying off his effects. This was done in revenge for the slaughter of noble Northumbrian thegns, Gospatric, slain by Queen Edith's orders for her brother's sake at the king's court on 28 December, and Gamel, son of Orm, and Ulf, son of Dolfin, both of whom Tosti had treacherously killed in his own

chamber at York the previous year, though under pledge of peace; and also because of an immense tax which he had wrongly taken from all Northumbria. The oldest *Life of St Edward*, on the other hand, attributes Tosti's unpopularity to his attempts to restore order in an unruly province.

[2] Of Mercia.

[3] 28 October.

[4] Florence: 'after the Feast of All Saints (1 November), with the help of Earl Edwin'.

[5] 'E' ends its annal here.

[6] Florence says he held his court in London, 'as well as he could'.

C (D)

and of St. Peter and of all God's saints.[1] The consecration of the church was on Holy Innocents' Day.[2] And he died on the eve of the Epiphany,[3] and was buried on the Feast of the Epiphany,[4] in the same minster – as it says below:

Now royal Edward, England's ruler
To the Saviour resigns his righteous soul,
His sacred spirit to God's safe keeping.
In the life of this world he lived awhile
In kingly splendour strong in counsel.
Four and twenty was his tale of winters,
That ruler of heroes lavish of riches,
And half a year.[5] He governed the Welshmen,
Ethelred's son, ruled Britons and Scots,
Angles and Saxons, his eager soldiers.
All that the cold sea waves encompass
Young and loyal yielded allegiance,
With all their heart to King Edward the noble.
Ever gay was the courage of the guiltless king
Though long ago, of his land bereft,
He wandered in exile, over earth's far ways,
After Cnut overcame Ethelred's kin
And Danes had rule of the noble realm
Of England for eight and twenty years,
In succession distributing riches.
At length he came forth in lordly array,
Noble in goodness, pure and upright,
Edward the glorious, guarding his homeland,
Country and subjects – till on a sudden came
Death in his bitterness, bearing so dear
A lord from the earth. And angels led
His righteous soul to heaven's radiance.
Yet the wise ruler entrusted the realm
To a man of high rank, to Harold himself,

---

[1] Westminster Abbey.
[2] 28 December 1065.
[3] 5 January 1066.
[4] 6 January 1066.

[5] This is the reading in 'C', where 'D' has 'in fortunate time', but over an erasure. Florence gives the length of the reign correctly as 23 years, 6 months, and 27 days.

C (D)

A noble earl who all the time
Had loyally followed his lord's commands
With words and deeds, and neglected nothing
That met the need of the people's king.

And Earl Harold was now consecrated king[1] and he met little quiet in it as long as he ruled the realm.[2]

C	D	E
1066[3] In this year Harold came from York to Westminster at the Easter following the Christmas that the king died, and Easter was then on 16 April. Then over all England there was seen a sign in the skies such as had never been seen before.[7] Some said it was the star 'comet' which some call the long-haired star, and it first appeared on the eve of the Greater Litany, that is 24 April, and so shone all the week. And soon after this Earl Tosti came from overseas[8] into the Isle of Wight with as large a fleet as he could muster, and both money and provisions were given him. And then he went away from	In this year King Harold came from York to Westminster at the Easter following the Christmas that the king died, and Easter was then on 16 April. Then over all England there was seen a sign in the skies such as had never been seen before.[7] Some said it was the star 'comet' which some call the long-haired star; and it first appeared on the eve of the Greater Litany, that is 24 April, and so shone all the week. And soon after this Earl Tosti came from overseas into the Isle of Wight with as large a fleet as he could muster and both money and provisions were given him. And King	In this year the minster of Westminster was consecrated on Holy Innocents' Day,[4] and King Edward died on the eve of the Epiphany,[5] and was buried on the Feast of the Epiphany[6] in the newly consecrated church at Westminster. And Earl Harold succeeded to the realm of England, just as the king had granted it to him, and as he had been chosen to the position. And he was consecrated king on the Feast of the Epiphany.[6] And the same year that he became king he went out with a naval force against William,[9] and meanwhile Earl Tosti came into the Humber with sixty ships; and

---

[1] Harold was crowned on the day of Edward's funeral.

[2] Florence adds an eulogy on Harold's just rule.

[3] 'C' omits the number of this annal. 'E', having omitted the number 1065, returns to the true date. As in the previous annal, 'D' combines 'C' and 'E'.

[4] 28 December 1065.

[5] 5 January 1066.

[6] 6 January 1066.

[7] Halley's comet.

[8] Florence: 'from Flanders'. Gaimar says that most of Tosti's men were Flemings, and that they landed at *Wardstane* and

harried there, and then went to Thanet, where they were joined by Copsi (Tosti's subordinate when he was earl of Northumbria) with 17 ships from Orkney. Having caused great damage in *Brunemue* and elsewhere, they went to the Humber. After their defeat by Edwin and Morcar, the Flemings deserted Tosti (ll. 5159–5188). On the course of Tosti's raid, see F. M. Stenton, *Anglo-Saxon England*, pp. 578 f., where *Brunemue* is taken to refer to the mouth of the Burnham river in Norfolk.

[9] This, in 'E' only, perhaps refers to a skirmish off the southeast coast.

C

there and did damage everywhere along the sea-coast wherever he could reach, until he came to Sandwich. When King Harold, who was in London, was informed that Tosti his brother was come to Sandwich, he assembled a naval force and a land force larger than any king had assembled before in this country, because he had been told as a fact that Count William from Normandy, King Edward's kinsman,[2] meant to come here and subdue this country. This was exactly what happened afterwards. When Tosti found that King Harold was on his way to Sandwich, he went from Sandwich and took some of the sailors with him, some willingly and some unwillingly, and then went north to [   ][7] and ravaged in Lindsey[9] and killed many good men there. When Earl Edwin and Earl Morcar[10] understood about this, they came there and drove him out of the country; and then he went to Scotland, and the king of Scots[12]

D

Harold his brother assembled a naval force and a land force larger than any king had assembled before in this country, because he had been told that William the Bastard[2] meant to come here and conquer this country. This was exactly what happened afterwards. Meanwhile Earl Tosti came into the Humber with sixty ships and Earl Edwin came with a land force and drove him out, and the sailors deserted him. And he went to Scotland with twelve small vessels, and there Harold, king of Norway,[3] met him with three hundred[5] ships, and Tosti submitted to him and became his vassal; and they both went up the Humber until they reached York. And there Earl Edwin and Morcar his brother fought against them; but the Norwegians had the victory. Harold, king of the English, was informed that things had gone thus; and the fight was on the Vigil of St. Matthew.[11] Then Harold our king[13] came upon

E

Earl Edwin[1] came with a land force and drove him out and the sailors deserted him, and he went to Scotland with twelve small vessels, and Harold, the Norse king,[3] met him with three hundred ships, and Tosti submitted to him; and they both went up the Humber until they reached York. And Earl Morcar and Earl Edwin fought against them, and the Norse king had the victory.[4] And King Harold was informed as to what had been done, and what had happened, and he came with a very great force of Englishmen and met him at Stamford Bridge,[6] and killed him and Earl Tosti and valiantly overcame all the invaders. Meanwhile Count William landed at Hastings on Michaelmas Day,[8] and Harold came from the north and fought with him before all the army had come, and there he fell and his two brothers Gyrth and Leofwine; and William conquered this country, and came to Westminster,

---

[1] He had succeeded his father, Ælfgar, as earl of Mercia.

[2] Note the difference of emphasis. 'C' may imply that William had some claim to the throne.

[3] Harold Hardrada.

[4] The battle of Fulford took place on Wednesday, 20 September 1066.

[5] Florence: 'more than 500'.

[6] The battle of Stamford Bridge took place on Monday, 25 September.

[7] Florence, who is following the 'C' version, omits the reference to this unnamed place.

[8] 29 September.

[9] Florence: 'where he burnt many villages'.

[10] Earls respectively of Mercia and Northumbria.

[11] i.e. 20 September.

[12] Malcolm Canmore.

[13] The note of enthusiasm in 'D' should be remarked.

C

gave him protection, and helped him with provisions, and he stayed there all the summer. Then King Harold came to Sandwich and waited for his fleet there, because it was long before it could be assembled; and when his fleet was assembled, he went into the Isle of Wight and lay there all that summer and autumn; and a land force was kept everywhere along by the sea, though in the end it was no use. When it was the Feast of the Nativity of St. Mary,[3] the provisions of the people were gone, and nobody could keep them there any longer. Then the men were allowed to go home, and the king rode inland, and the ships were brought up to London, and many perished before they reached there. When the ships came home, Harold, king of Norway, came by surprise north into the Tyne with a very large naval force – no small one: it could be [   ] or more.[7] And Earl Tosti came to him with all those he had mustered, just as they had agreed beforehand, and

D

the Norwegians by surprise and met them beyond York at Stamford Bridge with a large force of the English people; and that day there was a very fierce fight on both sides. There was killed Harold Fairhair[2] and Earl Tosti, and the Norwegians who survived took to flight; and the English attacked them fiercely as they pursued them until some got to the ships. Some were drowned, and some burned, and some destroyed in various ways so that few survived and the English remained in command of the field. The king gave quarter to Olaf, son of the Norse king, and their bishop and the earl of Orkney[4] and all those who survived on the ships, and they went up to our king and swore oaths[5] that they would always keep peace and friendship with this country; and the king let them go home with twenty-four[6] ships. These two pitched battles were fought within five nights. Then Count William came from Normandy to Pevensey on Michaelmas Eve,[9] and as soon as they were

E

and Archbishop Aldred consecrated him king, and people paid taxes to him, and gave him hostages and afterwards bought their lands. And[1] Leofric, abbot of Peterborough, was at that campaign and fell ill there, and came home and died soon after, on the eve of All Saints. God have mercy on his soul. In his day there was every happiness and every good at Peterborough, and he was beloved by everyone, so that the king gave to St. Peter and him the abbacy of Burton and that of Coventry which Earl Leofric, who was his uncle, had built, and that of Crowland and that of Thorney. And he did much for the benefit of the monastery of Peterborough with gold and silver and vestments and land, more indeed than any before or after him. Then the Golden City became a wretched city. Then the monks elected Brand, the provost, as abbot, because he was a very good man and very wise, and sent him to the atheling Edgar[8] because the local people expected that he would be king,

---

[1] What follows in 'E' is a Peterborough addition.
[2] An error for Hardrada.
[3] 8 September.
[4] Florence: 'Paul, who had been sent off with part of the army to guard the ships'.
[5] Id.: 'and gave hostages'.

[6] Id.: '20'.
[7] The text is corrupt. Florence, who is close to 'C', reads: 'with a powerful fleet, more than 500 large ships'.
[8] Son of the atheling Edward who died in 1057.
[9] 28 September, but 'E' has 29 September.

C

they both went with all the fleet up the Ouse towards York.[1] Then King Harold in the south was informed when he disembarked that Harold, king of Norway, and Earl Tosti were come ashore near York. Then he went northwards day and night as quickly as he could assemble his force. Then before Harold could get there Earl Edwin and Earl Morcar assembled from their earldom as large a force as they could muster, and fought against the invaders[5] and caused them heavy casualties, and many of the English host were killed and drowned and put to flight, and the Norwegians remained masters of the field. And this fight was on the eve of St. Matthew the Apostle, and that was a Wednesday. And then after the fight Harold, king of Norway, and Earl Tosti went into York[6] with as large a force as suited them, and they were given hostages[7] from the city and also helped with provisions,

D

able to move on they built a castle at Hastings.[2] King Harold was informed of this[3] and he assembled a large army and came against him at the hoary apple-tree.[4] And William came against him by surprise before his army was drawn up in battle array. But the king nevertheless fought hard against him, with the men who were willing to support him, and there were heavy casualties on both sides. There King Harold was killed and Earl Leofwine his brother, and Earl Gyrth his brother, and many good men, and the French remained masters of the field, even as God granted it to them because of the sins of the people. Archbishop Aldred and the citizens of London wanted to have Edgar *Cild* as king, as was his proper due; and Edwin and Morcar promised him that they would fight on his side; but always the more it ought to have been forward the more it got behind, and the worse it

E

and the atheling gladly gave assent to it. When King William heard about this he grew very angry, and said the abbot had slighted him. Then distinguished men acted as intermediaries and brought them into agreement, because the abbot was of good family. Then he gave the king 40 marks of gold as settlement. And he lived a little while after this – only three years. Then all confusions and evils came upon the monastery. May God take pity on it!

---

[1] Florence says they landed at Riccall. Gaimar says they left their ships at 'St Wilfrid's'.

[2] Florence, who has mainly followed 'C' until this ends, and who then for the battle of Stamford Bridge is close to 'D', seems independent of the Chronicle for his account of the battle of Hastings.

[3] According to Gaimar (ll. 5252–5255), he entrusted his booty to Archbishop Aldred and left Mærleswein in charge when he went south. On Harold's actions, see F. M. Stenton, *Anglo-Saxon England*, pp. 583 f.

[4] The only narrative contemporary description of the battle;

cf. the Norman accounts, *E.H.D.*, II, Nos. 3 and 4, and see also the chapter by Sir Frank Stenton on 'The Historical Background' in *The Bayeux Tapestry: A Comprehensive Survey* (London, 1957).

[5] Florence: 'on the northern bank of the R. Ouse, near York'. Simeon of Durham inserts the name Fulford into Florence's account, and Gaimar gives this name also.

[6] On Sunday, 24 September.

[7] According to Florence, they were given 150 hostages, and left 150 of their men as hostages in York when they went to their ships.

C

and so went from there on board ship and settled a complete peace, arranging that they should all go with him southwards and subdue this country. Then in the middle of these proceedings Harold, king of the English, came on the Sunday[2] with all his force to Tadcaster, and there marshalled his troops, and then on Monday[3] went right on through York. And Harold, king of Norway, and Earl Tosti and their divisions were gone inland beyond York to Stamford Bridge, because they had been promised for certain that hostages would be brought to them there out of all the shire. Then Harold, king of the English, came against them by surprise beyond the bridge, and there they joined battle, and went on fighting strenuously till late in the day. And there Harold, king of Norway, was killed and Earl Tosti, and numberless men with them both Norwegians and English, and the Norwegians[5] fled from the English. There was one of the Norwegians there who with-

D

grew from day to day, exactly as everything came to be at the end. The battle took place on the festival of Calixtus the pope.[1] And Count William went back to Hastings, and waited there to see whether submission would be made to him. But when he understood that no one meant to come to him, he went inland with all his army that was left to him, and that came to him afterwards from overseas, and ravaged all the region that he overran until he reached Berkhamstead.[4] There he was met by Archbishop Aldred and Edgar *Cild*, and Earl Edwin and Earl Morcar, and all the chief men from London. And they submitted out of necessity after most damage had been done – and it was a great piece of folly that they had not done it earlier, since God would not make things better, because of our sins. And they gave hostages and swore oaths to him, and he promised them that he would be a gracious liege lord, and yet in the meantime they ravaged all that they overran. Then on

E

---

[1] Saturday, 14 October.
[2] 24 September.
[3] 25 September.
[4] In what follows, Florence again has points of agreement with 'D', though he is fuller. He adds to the list of those who submitted at Berkhamstead Wulfstan, bishop of Worcester, and

Walter, bishop of Hereford, and explains that it was Stigand's uncanonical position that led to Aldred's crowning of William.

[5] Here the original part of 'C' ends at the foot of a folio, and what follows is on an added page in much later handwriting and language. On this, see B. Dickins, 'The Late Addition to ASC 1066 C', *Proc. Leeds Phil. and Lit. Soc.*, v (1940), pp. 148 f.

C

D

E

stood the English host so that they could not cross the bridge nor win victory. Then an Englishman shot an arrow, but it was no use, and then another came under the bridge and stabbed him under the corselet. Then Harold, king of the English, came over the bridge and his host with him, and there killed large numbers of both Norwegians and Flemings, and Harold let the king's son Hetmundus[1] go home to Norway with all the ships.[2]

Christmas Day, Archbishop Aldred consecrated him king at Westminster. And he promised Aldred on Christ's book and swore moreover (before Aldred would place the crown on his head) that he would rule all this people as well as the best of the kings before him, if they would be loyal to him. All the same he laid taxes on people very severely, and then went in spring overseas to Normandy, and took with him Archbishop Stigand, and Æthelnoth, abbot of Glastonbury, and Edgar *Cild* and Earl Edwin and Earl Morcar, and Earl Waltheof,[3] and many other good men from England. And Bishop Odo[4] and Earl William[5] stayed behind and built castles far and wide throughout this country, and distressed the wretched folk, and always after that it grew much worse. May the end be good when God wills!

1066 In this year King Edward died and Earl Harold succeeded to the kingdom, and held it 40 weeks and one day; and in this year William came and conquered England. And in this year Christ Church was burnt and a comet appeared on 18 April.

[1] Or 'who was called "Mundus" (the Elegant?)', see B. Dickins, *op. cit.*

[2] Here 'C' ends.

[3] Florence adds: 'the son of Earl Siward, and the noble leader Æthelnoth the Kentishman'. He puts William's journey in 1067, whereas 'D', using Lady Day reckoning, puts it in 1066.

[4] Odo, half-brother of the Conqueror, being the son of Herluin and Herleva, was bishop of Bayeux from 1049 to 1097. He became earl of Kent shortly after 1066.

[5] William fitz Osbern, son of Osbern the steward, was given the Isle of Wight and the earldom of Hereford shortly after 1066.

D

1067[1]This year the king came back to England on St. Nicholas's Day.[2] And that day Christ Church at Canterbury was burnt down. And Bishop Wulfwig died and is buried in his cathedral town of Dorchester. And Eadric Cild[3] and the Welsh became hostile, and fought against the garrison of the castle at Hereford, and inflicted many injuries upon them. And the king imposed a heavy tax on the wretched people, and nevertheless caused all that they overran to be ravaged. And then he went to Devon and besieged the city of Exeter for eighteen days, and there a large part of his army perished.[5] But he made fair promises to them, and fulfilled them badly; and they gave up the city to him because the thegns had betrayed them. And in the course of the summer, Edgar Cild went abroad with his mother Agatha and his two sisters, Margaret and Christina, and Mærleswein[4] and many good men with them, and came to Scotland under the protection of King Malcolm, and he received them all.[6] Then the aforesaid King Malcolm began to desire his sister Margaret for his wife, but he and his men all opposed it for a long time; and she also refused, saying that she would have neither him nor any other if the heavenly mercy would graciously grant it to her to please in virginity with human heart the mighty

E

In this year the king went overseas and took with him hostages and money and came back the next year on St. Nicholas's Day.[2] And that day Christ Church at Canterbury was burnt down. And he gave away every man's land when he came back. And that summer Edgar Cild went abroad, and Mærleswein,[4] and many people with them, and went into Scotland. And King Malcolm received them all and married the atheling's sister, Margaret.

---

[1] The events of 1067–1069 are not all correctly assigned; 1067 'E' has the correct order, but the journey of the atheling Edgar belongs to the summer of 1068. 'D', probably combining two sources, enters the rebellion of Eadric the Wild after the king's return, whereas Florence places it before this. After the mention of the atheling's journey, 'D' has a long interpolation, probably from some Life of St Margaret, and then goes back to the spring of 1068 to record events not entered in 'E', continuing with events of the summer of 1068. Thus in both MSS. events from 6 December 1067 to the summer of 1068 are placed under 1067.

[2] 6 December 1067.

[3] An error for Eadric 'the Wild'. Florence calls him 'silvaticus, a powerful thegn, son of Ælfric, the brother of Eadric Streona'. He adds that Eadric refused to surrender his land, and that the castle-guards of Hereford and Richard son of Scrob lost many knights and squires when they raided it; Eadric then raided Herefordshire with the help of Bleddyn and Rhiwallon (cf. annal 1063) as far as the bridge over the Lugg, taking much booty. Florence records his reconciliation with William in 1070.

[4] The sheriff of Lincoln, who held lands in Lincolnshire, Yorkshire, Devon, and Somerset.

[5] This campaign took place in the spring of 1068.

[6] Florence, who puts this correctly in annal 1068, after Whitsuntide, adds the flight of Gospatric and certain Northumbrian nobles, which 'D' mentions later as an event unconnected with the atheling's flight. The marriage between Margaret and Malcolm probably took place in 1070. Part of the following account in 'D' is in loose alliterative verse.

D

Lord in pure continence through this short life. The king pressed her brother until he said 'yes', and indeed he dared not do anything else, because they had come into his control. It then turned out as God had foreseen (otherwise it could not have happened) even as he himself says in his Gospel that not even a sparrow can fall into a trap without his providence. The Creator in his foreknowledge knew beforehand what he wished to do through her, because she was destined to increase the glory of God in the land, and set the king right from the path of error, and turn him to the better way, and his people as well, and put down the evil customs that this nation had practised, just as she afterwards did. Then the king received her, though it was against her will, and her behaviour pleased him, and he thanked God who by his power had given him such a consort; and he meditated wisely, like the very sensible man he was, and turned to God and despised every impurity. About this the apostle Paul, the teacher of all nations, said, 'Salvabitur vir infidelis per mulierem fidelem sic et mulier infidelis per virum fidelem', etc. – that is, in our language, 'Very often the unbelieving husband is made holy and saved through the righteous[1] wife, and likewise the wife through a believing husband.'[2] The aforesaid queen afterwards performed many useful acts in that country to the glory of God, and she also prospered in the State even as was natural to her. She was descended from a believing and a noble family: her father was the atheling Edward, son of King Edmund, son of Ethelred, son of Edgar, son of Eadred[3] and so on in that royal race.[4] Her

E

[1] The original scribe has added 'believing' over this word.
[2] I Corinthians vii. 14.
[3] Edgar was son of Edmund, Eadred's brother.

[4] The insistence on Margaret's descent from the West Saxon royal line may suggest that the interpolation was made after Henry I's marriage to her daughter Maud in 1100. But see p. xvi.

D

E

mother's family goes back to the emperor Henry who ruled over Rome. And Gytha, Harold's mother, and many distinguished men's wives with her, went out to Flatholme and stayed there for some time and so went from there overseas to St. Omer.[1] This Easter the king came to Winchester, and Easter was then on 23 March.[2] And soon after that the Lady Maud came to this country and Archbishop Aldred consecrated her as queen at Westminster on Whit-Sunday.[3] Then the king was informed that the people in the north were gathered together and meant to make a stand against him if he came.[4] He then went to Nottingham and built a castle there, and so went to York and there built two castles,[5] and in Lincoln and everywhere in that district. And Earl Gospatric and the best men went to Scotland.[6] And in the meanwhile Harold's sons[7] came unexpectedly from Ireland with a naval force into the mouth of the Avon, and ravaged all over that district. Then they went to Bristol and meant to take the city by storm but the citizens fought against them fiercely. And when they could not get anything out of the city, they went to their ships with what they had won by plunder, and so went to Somerset and landed there. And Eadnoth, the staller, fought against them and was killed there, and many good men on both sides. And those who survived went away.[8]

---

[1] These events probably belong to 1068.

[2] The correct date for Easter, 1068.

[3] She was crowned on 11 May, which was Whit Sunday in 1068.

[4] Gaimar (ll. 5380–5401) has a story that William sent a message to York by Archbishop Aldred, that all the thegns who came to him should have safe conduct and receive their inheritance, but when they came he imprisoned them and gave their lands to the French.

[5] Florence: 'and placed 500 knights in them'.

[6] These events belong to the summer of 1068.

[7] Godwine, Edmund, and Magnus, according to Florence, but Gaimar mentions only two sons, Godwine and Edmund, and with them Tosti, son of Swein.

[8] These events also belong to the summer of 1068. Florence adds that the raiders seized no little booty in Devon and Cornwall, and returned to Ireland.

D

1068[1] In this year King William gave Earl Robert the aldormanry of Northumberland; but the local people surrounded him in the city of Durham and killed him and nine hundred men with him.[2] And soon after that the atheling Edgar came to York with all the Northumbrians, and the citizens made peace with him. And King William came on them by surprise from the south with an overwhelming army and routed them, and killed those who could not escape, which was many hundreds of men, and ravaged the city, and made St. Peter's minster an object of scorn, and ravaged and humiliated all the others. And the atheling went back to Scotland.[3]

1069[4] After[5] this Harold's sons came from Ireland at midsummer with sixty-four ships into the mouth of the Taw, and landed incautiously. And Count Brian[6] came against them by surprise with no little force, and fought against them and killed all the best men who were in that fleet; and the others escaped with a small force to the ships. And Harold's sons went back to Ireland again. In this year Archbishop Aldred of York died, and he is buried there in his cathedral city. He died on the day of SS. Protus and Hyacinthus.[8] He occupied the archiepiscopal see with great honour for ten years all but fifteen weeks. Soon after that three

E

In this year King William gave Earl Robert the earldom of Northumberland. Then the local people came against him and killed him and nine hundred men with him.[2] And the atheling Edgar came then with all the Northumbrians to York, and the citizens made peace with him. And King William came from the south with all his army and ravaged the city, and killed many hundreds of men. And the atheling went back to Scotland.[3]

In this year Bishop Æthelric in Peterborough had an accusation brought against him, and was sent to Westminster, and his brother Bishop Æthelwine was outlawed. Then between the two feasts of St. Mary[7] they – that is the sons of King Swein and his brother Earl Osbeorn – came from the east from Denmark with three hundred ships. And then Earl Waltheof went out, and he and the atheling Edgar and many hundreds of men with them came and met the fleet in the Humber, and went to York and landed and won the castles, and killed many hundreds of men and took a large amount of treasure on board ship, and kept the

---

[1] The events in 'E' are correctly placed in 1068 if 'E' is using the Lady Day reckoning. But 'D' begins with an event of the end of 1068 and then continues without a break right through the events of 1069 and on until William's return to Winchester in time for Easter, 1070. Thorpe assumed a break where the entry of Archbishop Aldred's death begins with a capital, but a better break comes (as given here) at the point where 'E' ends its annal 1068.

[2] On 28 January 1069.

[3] Early spring of 1069.

[4] The precise date of Bishop Æthelric's downfall is uncertain. Otherwise the events in this annal are in the proper order, except

that 'D' is wrong in placing Aldred's death before the arrival of the Danish fleet (see n. 8 below). By mentioning the length of William's stay in the North, 'D' continues to Easter, 1070.

[5] 'D' has no sign of a break at this point. See n. 1 above.

[6] Brian, a count of Brittany. For the family, see C. T. Clay, *Early Yorkshire Charters*, iv (1935), pp. 84 ff.

[7] The Assumption and the Nativity, 15 August and 8 September.

[8] 11 September. Whereas 'D' says that the Danes came soon after, 'E' dates their arrival before Aldred's death, as does Florence, who attributes his sickness and death to his grief at their arrival.

D

sons[1] of King Swein came from Denmark with two hundred and forty ships into the Humber, together with Earl Osbeorn and Earl Thorkil. And there came to meet them the atheling Edgar and Earl Waltheof and Mærleswein and Earl Gospatric with the Northumbrians and all the people, riding and marching with an immense army rejoicing exceedingly;[2] and so they all went resolutely to York, and stormed and razed the castle and captured an incalculable treasure in it, and killed many hundreds of Frenchmen and took many with them to the ships. And before the shipmen got there the Frenchmen had burned the city,[3] and had also thoroughly ravaged and burnt the holy minster of St. Peter. When the king found out about this, he went northwards with all his army that he could collect, and utterly ravaged and laid waste that shire. And the fleet lay all the winter in the Humber where the king could not get at them.[4] And the king was in York on Christmas Day, and so was in the country all the winter. And he came to Winchester that same Easter.[5] And Bishop Æthelric, who was at Peterborough, had an accusation brought against him, and was taken to Westminster, and his brother Bishop Æthelwine was outlawed.

1070 (1071)[6] In this year Earl Waltheof[7] made peace with the king. And in the following spring the

E

chief men in bonds, and lay between the Ouse and the Trent all that winter. And King William went into the shire and ruined it completely. And in the same year Brand, abbot of Peterborough, died on 27 November.

In this year Earl Waltheof made peace with the king. And in the following spring the king had all

---

[1] Florence mentions only two sons, Harold and Cnut. He agrees with 'D' against 'E' on the number of ships. Gaimar (l. 5434) names three sons, Harold, Cnut, and Beorn *Leriz*.

[2] Florence does not mention Gospatric and the Northumbrians, but Simeon adds to Florence's account: 'There was present Earl Gospatric with all the force of the Northumbrians, unanimously assembled against the Normans.'

[3] According to Florence, the Normans in charge of the castle set fire to the houses near it on 19 September, to prevent the Danes from using them as material for filling the ditch; the fire spread and burnt the city and the minster. He regards the capture of the castle by the Danes on the Monday, when more

than 3000 Frenchmen were killed and many prisoners, including William Malet, his wife, and sons, taken, as divine vengeance.

[4] But, according to Florence, William offered money to Earl Osbeorn, and gave him permission to seize provisions for his army, on condition that he promised to return home without fighting when winter was over. Florence then describes the famine that followed the king's ravages.

[5] 4 April 1070.

[6] 'D', having left a blank annal 1070, becomes a year in advance of the true date.

[7] Son of Siward, earl of Northumbria. He held an earldom in the Midlands.

D

E

king had all the monasteries that were in England plundered.[1] And this year there was great famine. And the monastery at Peterborough was plundered, namely by the men that Bishop Æthelric had excommunicated because they had taken there all that he had. And in the same summer that fleet came into the Thames and lay there two nights, and then went on to Denmark.[3] And Count Baldwin[4] died, and Arnulf, his son, succeeded him. And the king of the French[5] and Earl William[6] were to be his protectors. But Robert[7] came there and killed Arnulf, his kinsman, and Earl William and routed the king, and killed many thousands of his men.[9]

the monasteries that were in England plundered.[1] Then in the same year King Swein came from Denmark into the Humber, and the local people came to meet him and made a truce with him – they expected that he was going to conquer the country. Then there came to Ely, Christian, the Danish bishop,[2] and Earl Osbeorn and the Danish housecarls with them, and the English people from all the Fenlands came to them and expected that they were going to conquer all the country. Then the monks of Peterborough heard it said that their own men meant to plunder the monastery – that was Hereward[8] and his following. That was because they heard it said that the king had given the abbacy to a French abbot called Turold,[10] and he was a very stern man, and had then come to Stamford with all his Frenchmen. There was then a sacristan called Yware; he took by night all he could, the Gospels, and chasubles, and copes and robes, and some such small things – whatever he could – and went at once before dawn to the abbot Turold, and told him he was seeking his protection, and informed him how the outlaws were alleged to be coming to Peterborough. He did all that according to the monks' advice. Then forthwith in the morning all the outlaws came with many ships, and wanted to enter the monastery, and the monks withstood them so that they could not get in. Then they set fire to it and burnt down all the monks' houses and all the town except one house. Then they got in by means of fire at

---

[1] Florence: 'by the counsel of William, earl of Hereford and certain others'. What follows in 'E' is a Peterborough addition.

[2] Bishop of Aarhus.

[3] Florence says King Swein exiled his brother Osbeorn for accepting William's bribes.

[4] Baldwin VI, count of Flanders.

[5] Philip I.

[6] William Fitz Osbern.

[7] Brother of Baldwin VI and uncle of Arnulf.

[8] Hereward 'the Wake', on whom see E. A. Freeman, *Norman Conquest*, IV, pp. 454 ff.

[9] Battle of Cassel, 20 February 1071.

[10] He had been a monk of Fécamp, but he came to Peterborough from Malmesbury, where he had been abbot.

D

E

Bolhithe Gate, and the monks came towards them
and asked them for a truce, but they paid no
attention, and went into the church, climbed up
to the Holy Rood and took the crown off our
Lord's head – all of pure gold – and then took the
foot-rest that was underneath his feet, which was
all of red gold. They climbed up to the steeple,
brought down the altar-frontal that was hidden
there – it was all of gold and silver – and took
there two golden shrines and nine of silver, and
they took fifteen great crucifixes, of both gold and
silver. They took there so much gold and silver,
and so many treasures in money and vestments
and books, that no man can reckon it up to
another. They said they did it out of loyalty to
the monastery. Then they went on board ship and
proceeded to Ely, where they deposited all the
treasure. The Danes expected that they were going
to overcome the Frenchmen. Then all the monks
were scattered and none remained there but one
monk who was called Leofwine the Tall; he was
lying ill in the infirmary. Then came Abbot
Turold and one hundred and sixty Frenchmen
with him, and all fully armed. When he arrived,
he found everything burnt inside and out except
the church. The outlaws were then all afloat – they
knew he would be bound to come there. This was
done on 2 June. The two kings, William and
Swein, came to an agreement. Then the Danes
proceeded out of Ely with all the above-mentioned treasures, and took them with them. When
they were in the middle of the sea there came a
great storm, and scattered all the ships carrying the
treasures – some went to Norway, some to
Ireland, some to Denmark and all that reached
there was the altar-frontal and some shrines and
some crosses and much of the other treasure, and

D

E

they brought it to a royal town called   ,[1] and then put it all in the church. Then afterwards through their carelessness and drunkenness the church was burnt one night with everything that was in it. Thus was the monastery of Peterborough burnt down and plundered. Almighty God have pity on it through his great mercy! And thus Abbot Turold came to Peterborough, and the monks came back, and performed the service of Christ in the church, which had stood a whole week without any kind of service. When Bishop Æthelric heard tell about it, he excommunicated all the men who had done this wicked deed. There was a great famine in the course of the year. And the following summer the fleet came from the north from the Humber into the Thames, and lay there two nights, and then held on their course to Denmark. And Count Baldwin died, and his son Arnulf succeeded him, and Earl William was to be his protector, and the king of the French also. And then came Count Robert and killed his kinsman Arnulf and the earl, and routed the king, and killed many thousands of his men.

A1070 In this year Lanfranc, who was abbot of Caen, came to England and after a few days he became archbishop of Canterbury.[2] He was consecrated on 29 August at his own see by eight of his suffragan bishops; the others who were not present explained through messengers and letters why they could not be there. In that year[3] Thomas, who was bishop-elect of York, came to Canterbury to be consecrated there according to the ancient custom. When Lanfranc demanded the confirmation of his obedience by oath, he refused and said that he ought not to do it. Then Archbishop Lanfranc got angry, and ordered the bishops, who had come there at Archbishop Lanfranc's orders to perform the service, and all the monks to unrobe, and at his orders they did so. So Thomas went back that time without consecration. Then immediately after this it happened that Archbishop Lanfranc went to Rome, and Thomas along with him. When they arrived there, and had spoken about other things

[1] A gap in the MS.
[2] Florence says he was made archbishop on 15 August and consecrated on 29 August.
[3] On this controversy and the forged documents adduced to

support the Canterbury claim, see A. J. Macdonald, *Lanfranc* (1944), pp. 271–296; Z. N. Brooke, *The English Church and the Papacy* (1931), pp. 118–131; R. W. Southern, 'The Canterbury Forgeries', *Eng. Hist. Rev.*, LXXIII (1958), pp. 193–226.

which they wished to discuss, Thomas brought forward his case, how he had gone to Canterbury and how the archbishop had asked for his obedience on oath, and he had refused it. Then Archbishop Lanfranc began to explain with clear reasoning that what he had demanded he had demanded legitimately, and he established the same with firm argument before Pope Alexander[1] and all the council that was assembled there. And so they went home. After this Thomas came to Canterbury and humbly fulfilled all that the archbishop demanded of him, and then received the consecration.[2]

D	E
1071 (1072)[3] In this year Earl Edwin and Earl Morcar fled away and travelled aimlessly in woods and moors until Edwin was killed by his own men and Morcar went to Ely by ship. And Bishop Æthelwine and Siward Bearn came there, and many hundred men with them.[4] But when King William found out about this, he called out a naval force and a land force, and invested that part of the country from outside, and made a bridge and placed a naval force on the seaward side. And they then all surrendered to the king, that is to say Bishop Æthelwine and Earl Morcar and all who were with them except Hereward alone and those who could escape with him, and he led them out valiantly. And the king took their ships and weapons and plenty of money, and he took all the men prisoner and did as he pleased with them: Bishop Æthelwine he sent to Abingdon, and there he died.[5]	In this year Earl Edwin and Earl Morcar fled away and travelled aimlessly in woods and moors. Then Earl Morcar went to Ely in a ship, and Earl Edwin was killed treacherously by his own men. And Bishop Æthelwine and Siward Bearn came to Ely and many hundred men with them.[4] And when King William found out about this, he called out a naval force and a land force, and invested that part of the country from outside, and made a bridge and went in, and placed the naval force on the seaward side. And the outlaws then all surrendered to the king, that is to say Bishop Æthelwine and Earl Morcar and all who were with them except Hereward alone and those who wished to go with him, and he led them out valiantly. And the king took their ships and weapons and plenty of money, and did as he pleased with the men: Bishop Æthelwine he sent to Abingdon, and there he died soon after in the course of the winter.
1072 (1073)[3] In this year King William led a naval force and a land force to Scotland,[6] and blockaded that country from the sea with ships. And he went himself with his land force in over the Forth, and there he found nothing that they were any the	In this year King William led a naval force and a land force to Scotland and blockaded that country from the sea with ships. And he led his land force in at the Forth, and there he found nothing that he was any the better for. And King Malcolm

---

[1] Alexander II.

[2] This is the last entry of 'A'. It is immediately followed in the MS. by the Latin *Acta* of Lanfranc.

[3] 'D' remains a year in advance of the true date.

[4] Gaimar (ll. 5457–5463) says they came from Scotland into the Humber, and Earl Morcar took ship and joined them; they met the English at *Welle*.

[5] Florence uses this annal, but adds that Edwin and Morcar fled because William wished to imprison them, and that Edwin was killed when on his way to join Malcolm of Scotland. He says the bridge built by William's orders was two miles long.

[6] Florence gives the date 'after the Assumption of St Mary (15 August)', and says Eadric *silvaticus* (see p. 146, n. 3) accompanied him.

D

better for. And King Malcolm came and made peace with King William[1] and was his vassal and gave him hostages, and afterwards went home with all his force. And Bishop Æthelric died; he was consecrated bishop of York, but it was taken from him unjustly,[2] and he was given the bishopric of Durham, and he held it as long as he wished, and he relinquished it later, and went to St. Peter's monastery at Peterborough and lived there for twelve years. Then after William conquered England, he had him taken from Peterborough and sent him to Westminster. He died there on 15 October, and is buried there in St. Nicholas's chapel.[3]

E

came and made peace with King William[1] and gave hostages and was his vassal, and the king went home with all his force. And Bishop Æthelric died; he was consecrated bishop of York, but it was taken from him unjustly,[2] and he was given the bishopric of Durham, and he held it as long as he wished, and he relinquished it later, and went to St. Peter's monastery at Peterborough and lived there for twelve years. Then after King William conquered England, he took him from Peterborough and sent him to Westminster. He died on 15 October and is buried in that church in St. Nicholas's chapel.

D and E

1073 (1074 D)[4] In this year King William led an English and French force overseas and conquered the country of Maine; and the English damaged it severely: they destroyed vineyards and burned down cities, and damaged the country severely, and made all the country surrender to the king. And afterwards they went home to England.[5]

D

1074 (1075)[4] In this year King William went overseas to Normandy. And Edgar *Cild* came from Flanders into Scotland on St. Grimbald's Day.[6] And[7] King Malcolm and Edgar's sister, Margaret, received him with great honour. At the same time the king of France, Philip, sent a letter to him and ordered him to come to him, saying he would give him the castle of Montreuil so that he could do daily harm to those who were not his friends. So now King Malcolm and Edgar's sister,

E

In this year King William went overseas to Normandy. And Edgar *Cild* came from Scotland to Normandy, and the king reversed his outlawry and that of all his men. And he was in the king's court and received such dues as the king granted him.[8]

---

[1] Florence: 'at Abernethy'; so also Gaimar (l. 5717). On the pact made on this occasion, see R. L. G. Ritchie, *op. cit.*, pp. 29–38.

[2] This statement may be a misunderstanding of annal 1041 (see p. 106, n. 6). The same story is told by the Peterborough chronicler, Hugh Candidus (ed. W. T. Mellows, pp. 73 f.).

[3] Florence: 'Walcher, a Lotharingian, succeeded him to the bishopric of Durham.'

[4] 'D' remains a year in advance of the true date.

[5] 'D' omits the last two words.

[6] 8 July.

[7] What follows is another indication of the interest taken by 'D' in Scottish affairs. Florence, who has only a very brief reference to the incident, dates it 1073, but from here to 1079 he is a year behind the true dating.

[8] Edgar survived until about 1125.

D

Margaret, gave him and all his men great gifts and many treasures consisting of skins covered with purple cloth, and robes of marten's skin and of grey fur and ermine, and costly robes and golden vessels and silver, and led him and all his naval force out of his jurisdiction with great honour. But on the journey it turned out badly for them when they were out at sea, in that they met very rough weather, and the raging sea and the strong wind cast them ashore so that all their ships foundered and they themselves got to land with difficulty and their treasure was nearly all lost. And some of his men were captured by the French, but he and his fittest men went back to Scotland, some walking miserably on foot, and some riding wretchedly. Then King Malcolm advised him to send overseas to King William and ask for his protection, and he did so; and the king granted it to him and sent for him. And again King Malcolm and Edgar's sister gave him and all his men immense treasure, and again very honourably sent him out of their jurisdiction. And the sheriff of York came to meet them at Durham and went all the way with them and had them provided with food and fodder at every castle they came to, until they got overseas to the king. And King William received him with great honour and he stayed there at court and received such dues as were appointed him.

1075 (1076)[1] In this year King William gave to Earl Ralph[2] the daughter of William fitz Osbern.[3]

E

In this year King William gave to Earl Ralph[2] the daughter of William fitz Osbern.[3] This same

---

[1] 'D' remains a year in advance of the true date, Florence is a year behind. Though he shares parts of the Chronicle account, he has some important differences. He says that Roger gave his sister to Ralph against the king's will, and that the marriage was at Exning in Cambridgeshire (now in Suffolk); that Waltheof joined the plot under compulsion, then confessed to Lanfranc, and on his advice went to the king in Normandy; that Roger was prevented from crossing the Severn by Wulfstan, bishop

of Worcester, Æthelwig, abbot of Evesham, Urse the sheriff, and Walter de Lacy; and that Ralph was met near Cambridge by Odo, bishop of Bayeux, and Geoffrey, bishop of Coutances, and fled to Brittany.

[2] Ralph 'Guader', earl of Norfolk, lord of Gael in Brittany. For the family, see *Complete Peerage*, IX, pp. 568 ff.

[3] Emma.

D

This same Ralph was Breton on his mother's side, and Ralph his father was English, and was born in Norfolk, and the king therefore gave the earldom there and Suffolk as well to his son. He then took the lady to Norwich.[1]

> There was that bride-ale
> That was many men's bale.

Earl Roger[2] was there and Earl Waltheof[3] and bishops and abbots, and there they plotted to drive their royal lord out of his kingdom. And the king in Normandy was soon informed about this. Earl Ralph and Earl Roger were the ringleaders in this conspiracy; and they lured the Bretons to their side; and they also sent to Denmark for a naval force. And Roger went west to his earldom[4] and assembled his people for the king's undoing, as he thought, but it turned out to his own great harm. Ralph also wanted to go forward with the men of his earldom, but the castle garrisons which were in England and also the local people came against them and prevented them all from doing anything; but he was glad to escape to the ships. And his wife remained behind in the castle, and held it until she was given safe-conduct; and then she went out of England, and all her men who wished to go with her. And the king afterwards came to England, and captured Earl Roger, his kinsman, and put him in prison. And Earl Waltheof went overseas and accused himself and asked for pardon and offered treasure. But the king made light of it until he came to England and then had him captured. And soon after this two hundred ships came from Denmark,[5] and the commanders aboard

E

Ralph was Breton on his mother's side, and his father named Ralph was English and was born in Norfolk. Then the king gave his son the earldom of Norfolk and Suffolk. Then he took the lady to Norwich.[1]

> There was that bride-ale
> – [Many] men's bale.

Earl Roger[2] was there and Earl Waltheof[3] and bishops and abbots, and there they plotted to expel the king from the realm of England. And soon the king in Normandy was informed about this, how it was planned. It was Earl Roger and Earl Ralph who were the principals in this conspiracy; and they lured the Bretons to their side; and also sent east to Denmark for a naval force to help them. And Roger went west to his earldom[4] and assembled his people for the king's undoing, but he was prevented. And Ralph also in his earldom wanted to go forward with his people, but the castle garrisons which were in England and also the local people came against him, and brought it about that he did nothing, but went on board ship at Norwich. And his wife was in the castle, and held it until she was given safe-conduct; and then she went out of England and all her men who wished to go with her. And the king afterwards came to England, and seized Earl Roger, his kinsman, and imprisoned him, and he seized Earl Waltheof as well. And soon after that two hundred ships came from the east from Denmark,[5] and there were two commanders on board, Cnut, son of Swein, and Earl Hákon. And they dared not fight with King William but proceeded over-

---

[1] See p. 156, n. 1.
[2] Roger of Breteuil, second son of William fitz Osbern by his first wife and thus brother of the bride. He succeeded his father as Earl of Hereford in 1071.

[3] Son of Siward, earl of Northumbria.
[4] Hereford.
[5] Florence does not mention this Danish raid. Note the interest in York shown by 'D'.

D

were Cnut, son of King Swein, and Earl Hákon. And they dared not fight with King William but went to York and broke into St. Peter's Minster and captured a large amount of property there and so departed. But all who took part in this scheme died – that is to say the son of Earl Hákon and many others with him. And the Lady Edith, who was King Edward's widow, died at Winchester a week before Christmas, and the king had her brought to Westminster with great honour, and laid her near King Edward her husband. The king was that Christmas at Westminster; there all the Bretons who were at the marriage feast at Norwich were sentenced.

> Some of them were blinded
> And some banished from the land
> And some were put to shame.
> Thus were the traitors to the king
> Brought low.

1076 (1077)[1] In this year Swein, king of Denmark, died, and Harold, his son, succeeded to his realm. King William gave the abbacy at Westminster to Abbot Vitalis who had been a monk[2] at Bernay. And in this year Earl Waltheof was beheaded at Winchester on St. Petronella's Day;[3] and his body was taken to Crowland, and he is buried there. And King William went overseas and led a force to Brittany and besieged the castle at Dol; but the Bretons held it until the king came from France, and then King William went away and lost there both men and horses and incalculable treasure.

E

seas to Flanders. And the Lady Edith died at Winchester a week before Christmas, and the king had her brought to Westminster with great honour, and laid her near King Edward her husband. And the king was at Westminster that Christmas, and all the Bretons who were at the wedding feast at Norwich were destroyed.

> Some of them were blinded
> And some driven from the land.
> So were the traitors to William
> Brought low.

In this year Swein, king of Denmark, died, and Harold, his son, succeeded to the realm. And the king gave Westminster to Abbot Vitalis who had been abbot of Bernay. And Earl Waltheof was beheaded at Winchester; and his body was taken to Crowland. And the king went overseas and led his force to Brittany and besieged the castle at Dol; and the Bretons held it until the king came from France, and William went away and lost there both men and horses and much of his treasure.

---

[1] 'D' remains a year in advance, Florence a year behind, the true date. Florence does not mention Swein, but greatly expands the account of Waltheof's execution.

[2] 'abbot' is written above this word in the MS.
[3] 31 May.

D

77[1] (1078) This year the moon was eclipsed three nights before Candlemas. And Æthelwig, the abbot of Evesham, who was skilled in secular affairs, died on St. Juliana's Day,[2] and Walter was appointed abbot in his place. And Bishop Hereman died who was bishop of Berkshire and Wiltshire and Dorset. And King Malcolm captured the mother of Mælsnechtan[4] . . .[5] and all his best men and all his treasure and his cattle; and he himself escaped with difficulty. . . .[7] And this year there was the dry summer; and wildfire came upon many shires and burned down many villages; and also many towns were burned down.

79[8] In this year Robert, son of King William, deserted from his father to his uncle Robert, in Flanders,[9] because his father would not let him rule his county in Normandy, which he himself and also King Philip with his consent had given him; and the chief men in that county had sworn oaths to him and accepted him as liege lord. Robert fought against his father and wounded him in the hand; and his horse was shot under him; and the man who brought him another horse was at once shot from a cross-bow; his name was Toki, son of Wigod;[13] and many were killed there and

E

In this year the king of the French and William, king of England, came to an agreement, but it held good for only a little while. And in the course of the year London was burned down one night before the Assumption of St. Mary,[3] worse than ever it had been since it was founded. And in this year Æthelwig, abbot of Evesham, died on 16 February. And Bishop Hereman also died, on 20 February.[6]

In this year King Malcolm came from Scotland into England between the two feasts of St. Mary[10] with a great army, and ravaged Northumberland as far as the Tyne, and killed many hundreds of people, and took home much money and treasure and people in captivity. And in the same year King William fought against his son, Robert, outside Normandy near a castle called Gerberoi,[11] and King William was wounded there,[12] and the horse he rode was killed, and also William, his son, was wounded there, and many men were killed.

---

[1] Apart from the entry of Abbot Æthelwig's death (on 16 February), the events in this annal all are correctly placed in 1077 in a chronicle beginning the year on 25 March. The agreement between William and the French king, and the fire of London, belong to 1077, and there was an eclipse of the moon on 30 January 1078, which would be 1077 on this reckoning. 'D' is a year in advance as in the last seven annals.

[2] 16 February 1077.

[3] 14 August.

[4] Mormaer of Moray, whose death is recorded in 1085 in the *Annals of Ulster*. He was the son of Macbeth's stepson, Lulach, who contested the throne with Malcolm III and was killed in 1058.

[5] One line is left blank.

[6] 1078.

[7] Six lines are left blank.

[8] Neither version had anything to record under 1078, as the events before 25 March in this year were entered under 1077. The chronological dislocation in 'D' now ends. Florence is now closer to 'E' than to 'D'.

[9] Robert of Flanders was brother of Maud, wife of William the Conqueror.

[10] 15 August and 8 September.

[11] MS. *Gerborneð*. Florence adds: 'which King Philip had given him'.

[12] In the arm, according to Florence, who adds that the prince recognized his father's voice and let him go away.

[13] Probably the son of Wigod of Wallingford, who is frequently mentioned in Domesday Book.

D   E

captured; and Robert came back to Flanders; nor will we here write more of the harm he inflicted on his father. . . .[1]

E

1080   In this year Bishop Walcher of Durham was killed at a meeting, and a hundred men with him, French and Flemish. And he himself was born a Lotharingian.[2] The Northumbrians did this in the month of May.[3]

1081   In this year the king led an army into Wales and there liberated many hundreds of men.

1082   In this year the king seized Bishop Odo.[4] And in this year there was a great famine.

1083   In this year the discord arose at Glastonbury between the abbot Thurstan[5] and his monks. In the first instance, it came of the abbot's lack of wisdom in misgoverning the monks in many matters,[6] and the monks complained of it to him in a kindly way and asked him to rule them justly and to love them, and they would be loyal and obedient to him. But the abbot would do nothing of the sort, but gave them bad treatment and threatened them with worse. One day the abbot went into the chapter and spoke against them and wanted to ill-treat them, and sent for some laymen,[7] and they came into the chapter, and fell upon the monks fully armed. And then the monks were very much afraid of them, and did not know what they had better do. But they scattered: some ran into the church and locked the doors on themselves – and they went after them into the monastery and meant to drag them out when they dared not go out. But a grievous thing happened that day – the Frenchmen[7] broke into the choir and threw missiles towards the altar where the monks were, and some of the retainers went up to the upper story and shot arrows down towards the sanctuary, so that many arrows stuck in the cross that stood above the altar; and the wretched monks were lying round about the altar, and some crept under it, and cried to God zealously, asking for his mercy when they could get no mercy from men. What can we say, except that they shot fiercely, and the others broke down the doors there, and went in and killed some of the monks and wounded many there in the church, so that the blood came from the altar on to the steps, and from the steps on to the floor. Three were killed there and eighteen wounded.[8] And in the same year Maud, William's queen, died the day after All Saints' Day.[9] And in

---

[1] This is the end of 'D' except for one much later entry (see p. 196). Henceforth, apart from the fragment 'H' in 1113–1114, 'E' is the sole remaining chronicle.

[2] He came from Liège. For a full account of this murder, see Simeon of Durham, *History of the Church of Durham*, Book III, chapter 24, and Florence, *s.a.* 1080.

[3] Simeon and Florence: 14 May.

[4] On the king's quarrel with his brother, see F. M. Stenton, *Anglo-Saxon England*, p. 608.

[5] Florence adds that he was from the monastery of Caen.

[6] Including, according to Florence, an attempt to replace the Gregorian chant by that of William of Fècamp.

[7] Household knights.

[8] William of Malmesbury, whose fullest account is in his work *On the Antiquity of Glastonbury* (ed. T. Hearne, *Adami de Domerham Historia*, I, pp. 113–116), and Florence give the figure as two killed and fourteen wounded, and give further details of the fight. An inquiry was made and the abbot was removed and several of the monks placed under the charge of various bishops and abbots. Later, Thurstan bought back the abbacy from William II for £500.

[9] 2 November.

E

this same year, after Christmas, the king had a great and heavy tax ordered all over England – it was 72*d*. for every hide.[1]

1084 In this year Wulfwold, abbot of Chertsey died, on 19 April.

1085 In this year[2] people said and declared for a fact, that Cnut, king of Denmark, son of King Swein, was setting out in this direction and meant to conquer this country with the help of Robert, count of Flanders, because Cnut was married to Robert's daughter. When William, king of England, who was then in Normandy – for he was in possession of both England and Normandy – found out about this, he went to England[3] with a larger force of mounted men and infantry from France and Brittany than had ever come to this country, so that people wondered how this country could maintain all that army. And the king had all the army dispersed all over the country among his vassals,[4] and they provisioned the army each in proportion to his land. And people had much oppression that year, and the king had the land near the sea laid waste, so that if his enemies landed, they should have nothing to seize on so quickly. But when the king found out for a fact that his enemies had been hindered and could not carry out their expedition – then he let some of the army go to their own country, and some he kept in this country over winter.

Then at Christmas,[5] the king was at Gloucester with his council, and held his court there for five days, and then the archbishop and clerics had a synod for three days. There Maurice was elected bishop of London, and William for Norfolk, and Robert for Cheshire – they were all clerics of the king.

After this, the king had much thought and very deep discussion with his council about this country – how it was occupied or with what sort of people. Then he sent his men[6] over all England into every shire and had them find out how many hundred hides there were in the shire, or what land and cattle the king himself had in the country, or what dues he ought to have in twelve months from the shire. Also he had a record made of how much land his archbishops had, and his bishops and his abbots and his earls – and though I relate it at too great length – what or how much everybody had who was occupying land in England, in land or cattle, and how much money it was worth. So very narrowly did he have it investigated, that there was no single hide nor virgate of land, nor indeed (it is a shame to

[1] The *Inquisitio Geldi* (see R. W. Eyton, *Domesday Studies: an analysis and digest of the Somerset Survey*, 2 vols., 1880) was an account of this levy. The inquisition was made in the early months of 1084, but is placed under 1083 because 'E' is using Lady Day reckoning.

[2] A very important annal. On the mutual relationship of the events described in it and in the next annal, see D. C. Douglas, *The Domesday Monachorum of Christ Church, Canterbury* (1944), pp. 26f.

[3] Florence: 'in the autumn'.

[4] *Id.*: 'bishops, abbots, earls, barons, sheriffs, and king's reeves'.

[5] 1085.

[6] The inquisition which resulted in Domesday Book. For a collection of other descriptions of its making, see *E.H.D.*, II, Nos. 198–204, 215, 217. No. 202, from a compilation made *c.* 1125–1140, probably at Worcester, is of special interest, for it is in the main a literal translation of this passage in the Chronicle. But it adds that inquiry was made into what the lands could render in the time of Edward the Confessor, and it concludes: 'And the king ordered that all should be written in one volume, and that that volume should be placed in his Treasury at Winchester and kept there.'

E

relate but it seemed no shame to him to do) one ox nor one cow nor one pig which was there left out, and not put down in his record; and all these records were brought to him afterwards.

1086 (1085)[1] In this year the king wore his crown and held his court at Winchester for Easter, and travelled so as to be at Westminster for Whitsuntide, and there dubbed his son, Henry, a knight. Then he travelled about so as to come to Salisbury at Lammas;[2] and there his councillors came to him, and all the people occupying land who were of any account over all England,[3] no matter whose vassals they might be; and they all submitted to him and became his vassals, and swore oaths of allegiance to him, that they would be loyal to him against all other men.[4] From there he went into the Isle of Wight, because he meant to go to Normandy, and so he did later. But all the same he first acted according to his custom, that is to say he obtained a very great amount of money from his men where he had any pretext for it either just or otherwise. He afterwards went into Normandy. And the atheling Edgar, King Edward's kinsman, left him because he did not have much honour from him,[5] but may Almighty God grant him honour in the future. And Christina, the atheling's sister, sought refuge in the convent at Romsey and took the veil.

And in the course of the same year, it was a very severe year, and a very laborious and sorrowful year in England, in cattle plague; and corn and crops were checked, and there was such great misfortune with the weather as cannot easily be conceived – there were such big thunderstorms and such lightning that many people were killed and it kept on getting worse and worse among the people. May God Almighty make things better when it is his will.

1087 (1086)[6] A thousand and eighty-seven years after the birth of our Lord Jesus Christ, in the twenty-first year since William ruled and governed England as God had granted him, it became a very severe and pestilential year in this country. Such a disease came on people that very nearly every other person was ill with the worst of diseases – high fever – and that so severely that many people died of the disease. Afterwards because of the great storms that came as we described them above, there came so great a famine over all England that many hundreds of people died a miserable death because of the famine. Alas, how miserable and pitiable a time it was then. Then the wretched people lay driven very nearly to death, and afterwards there came the sharp famine and destroyed them utterly. Who cannot pity such a time? Or who is so hard-hearted that he cannot weep for such misfortune? But such things happen because of the people's sins, in that they will not love God and righteousness. So it was in those days, there was little righteousness in this country in anyone, except in monks alone where they behaved

---

[1] 'E' by repeating the figure 1085 falls a year behind the true date and remains so until 1089.

[2] 1 August.

[3] Florence: 'archbishops, bishops, abbots, earls, barons, sheriffs, with their knights'.

[4] The 'Oath of Salisbury' about which there has been much

discussion. See especially F. M. Stenton, *The First Century of English Feudalism, 1066–1166* (1932), pp. 111–113.

[5] Florence merely says he went with the king's permission with 200 knights to Apulia.

[6] 'E' remains a year behind the true date, but has this in the text.

E

well. The king and the chief men loved gain much and over-much – gold and silver – and did not care how sinfully it was obtained provided it came to them. The king sold his land on very hard terms – as hard as he could. Then came somebody else, and offered more than the other had given, and the king let it go to the man who had offered him more. Then came the third, and offered still more, and the king gave it into the hands of the man who offered him most of all, and did not care how sinfully the reeves had got it from poor men, nor how many unlawful things they did. But the more just laws were talked about, the more unlawful things were done. They imposed unjust tolls and did many other injustices which are hard to reckon up.

Also, in the same year before autumn, the holy minster of St. Paul, the cathedral church of London, was burnt down, and many other churches, and the largest and noblest part of all the city. Similarly also, at the same time nearly every chief town in all England was burnt down. Alas, a miserable and lamentable time was this year that brought so many misfortunes into being.

Also, in the same year before the Assumption of St. Mary,[1] King William went from Normandy, into France with an army and made war on his own liege lord King Philip, and killed a large part of his men and burnt down the city of Mantes, and all the holy churches that were in the city; and two holy men, who served God living in an anchorite's cell, were burnt to death there.

This having been thus done, King William turned back to Normandy. A miserable thing he did, and more miserable was his fate. How more miserable? He fell ill, and he was severely afflicted by it. What account can I give? That fierce death, which spares neither powerful men nor mean, seized him. He died in Normandy on the day after the Nativity of St. Mary,[2] and he was buried at Caen in St. Stephen's monastery: he had built it, and afterwards had endowed it richly.

Alas, how deceitful and untrustworthy is this world's prosperity. He who had been a powerful king and lord of many a land, had then of all the land only a seven-foot measure; and he who was once clad in gold and gems, lay then covered with earth. He left behind him three sons. The oldest was called Robert, who was count of Normandy after him, the second was called William, who wore the crown after him in England. The third was called Henry, and his father bequeathed to him incalculable treasures.

If anyone wishes to know what sort of a man he was, or what dignity he had or of how many lands he was lord – then we will write of him even as we, who have looked upon him, and once lived at his court, have perceived him to be.

This King William of whom we speak was a very wise man,[3] and very powerful and more worshipful and stronger than any predecessor of his had been. He was gentle to the good men who loved God, and stern beyond all measure to those people who resisted his will. In the same place where God permitted him to conquer England, he set up a famous monastery and appointed monks for it,[4] and

---

[1] 15 August.
[2] 9 September.
[3] The remarkable account which follows was clearly written

by a man who had attended William's court. For two other accounts of William, see *E.H.D.*, II, Nos. 6 and 7.
[4] Battle Abbey.

E

endowed it well. In his days the famous church at Canterbury was built,[1] and also many another over all England. Also, this country was very full of monks, and they lived their life under the rule of St. Benedict, and Christianity was such in his day that each man who wished followed out whatever concerned his order. Also, he was very dignified: three times every year he wore his crown, as often as he was in England. At Easter he wore it at Winchester, at Whitsuntide at Westminster, and at Christmas at Gloucester, and then there were with him all the powerful men over all England, archbishops and bishops, abbots and earls, thegns and knights. Also, he was a very stern and violent man, so that no one dared do anything contrary to his will. He had earls in his fetters, who acted against his will. He expelled bishops from their sees, and abbots from their abbacies, and put thegns in prison, and finally he did not spare his own brother, who was called Odo; he was a very powerful bishop in Normandy (his cathedral church was at Bayeux) and was the foremost man next the king, and had an earldom in England. And when the king was in Normandy, then he was master in this country;[2] and he [the king] put *him* in prison. Amongst other things the good security he made in this country is not to be forgotten – so that any honest man could travel over his kingdom without injury with his bosom full of gold; and no one dared strike[3] another, however much wrong he had done him. And if any man had intercourse with a woman against her will, he was forthwith castrated.

He ruled over England, and by his cunning it was so investigated that there was not one hide of land in England that he did not know who owned it, and what it was worth, and then set it down in his record.[4] Wales was in his power, and he built castles there, and he entirely controlled that race. In the same way, he also subdued Scotland to himself, because of his great strength. The land of Normandy was his by natural inheritance, and he ruled over the county called Maine; and if he could have lived two years more, he would have conquered Ireland by his prudence and without any weapons. Certainly in his time people had much oppression and very many injuries:

> He had castles built
> And poor men hard oppressed.
> The king was so very stark
> And deprived his underlings of many a mark
> Of gold and more hundreds of pounds of silver,
> That he took by weight and with great injustice
> From his people with little need for such a deed.
> Into avarice did he fall
> And loved greediness above all.

---

[1] Lanfranc's rebuilding of Christ Church, Canterbury.
[2] See above, p. 145.
[3] Or 'kill'.
[4] Domesday Book.

E

He made great protection for the game
And imposed laws for the same,
That who so slew hart or hind
Should be made blind.

He preserved the harts and boars
And loved the stags as much
As if he were their father.
Moreover, for the hares did he decree that they should go free.
Powerful men complained of it and poor men lamented it,
But so fierce was he that he cared not for the rancour of them all,
But they had to follow out the king's will entirely
If they wished to live or hold their land,
Property or estate, or his favour great.
Alas! woe, that any man so proud should go,
And exalt himself and reckon himself above all men!
May Almighty God show mercy to his soul
And grant unto him forgiveness for his sins.

These things we have written about him, both good and bad, that good men may imitate their good points, and entirely avoid the bad, and travel on the road that leads us to the kingdom of heaven.

We can write many things that happened in the same year. The state of affairs in Denmark was such that the Danes who had been reckoned the most trustworthy of nations became perverted to the greatest disloyalty and the greatest treachery that could ever happen. They chose King Cnut and submitted to him and swore oaths to him, and then basely killed him in a church.[1] Also it happened in Spain that the heathens went and made war upon the Christians and forced much into their power. But the Christian king, who was called Alfonso,[2] sent everywhere into every country and asked for help, and help came to him from every country that was Christian, and they marched and killed and drove off all the heathen people, and conquered their land again through the help of God.

Also in this country in the same year there died many powerful men: Stigand, bishop of Chichester,[3] and the abbot of St. Augustine's,[4] and the abbot of Bath,[5] and that of Pershore:[6] and the liege lord of them all, William, king of England, of whom we spoke before. After his death, his son, called William like his father, succeeded to the kingdom[7] and was consecrated king by Archbishop Lanfranc at

---

[1] Florence gives the date, correctly, as 10 July.

[2] Alfonso VI of Castile was a great opponent of the Moors in Spain, but the chronicler's knowledge of his activities seems to be very limited.

[3] He transferred the see of Selsey to Chichester. He should not be confused with the archbishop of this name.

[4] Scotland.

[5] Ælfsige.

[6] Thurstan.

[7] Florence adds that he brought to England Wulfnoth and Morcar, but imprisoned them in Winchester.

E

Westminster, three days before Michaelmas day, and all the men in England submitted and swore oaths to him. This having been thus done, the king went to Winchester and scrutinized the Treasury and the treasure that his father had accumulated. It was impossible for anyone to describe how much was accumulated there in gold and silver and vessels and costly robes and jewels, and many other precious things that are hard to recount. The king did as his father told him before he died – gave a part of the treasure for his father's soul to each minster that there was in England; to some minsters 10 marks of gold, to some 6, and to each country church[1] 60d.; and into every shire were sent 100 pounds of money to be distributed among poor men for his soul;[2] and before he died, he ordered that all the people under his jurisdiction who were in captivity should be set free.[3] And the king was in London at Christmas.

1088 (1087)[4] In this year this country was very much disturbed, and filled with great treachery, so that the most powerful Frenchmen who were in this country intended to betray their lord the king and to have as king his brother, Robert, who was count of Normandy. At the head of this plot was Bishop Odo,[5] with Bishop Geoffrey[6] and William,[7] bishop of Durham. The king treated the bishop[8] so well that all England went by his counsel and did exactly as he wished; and he thought to treat him just as Judas Iscariot did our Lord; and Earl Roger[9] was also in this conspiracy, and a very great number of people with them, all Frenchmen, and this conspiracy was plotted during Lent. As soon as Easter was reached, they marched and ravaged and burned and laid waste the king's demesnes, and they ruined the lands of all those men who were in allegiance to the king. And each of them went to his castle and manned it and provisioned it as best they could. Bishop Geoffrey and Robert of Montbrai[10] went to Bristol and ravaged it and carried the plunder to the castle, and then went out of the castle and ravaged Bath and all the surrounding area,[11] and laid waste all the district of Berkeley. Those who were the chief men of Hereford, and all that shire with them, and the men of Shropshire, with a large force from Wales,[12] came and ravaged and burned in Worcestershire until they came to Worcester itself, and intended to burn the town and plunder the monastery and get the king's castle by force into their hands. Seeing these things, the reverend bishop, Wulfstan, was much distressed in mind because the castle had been committed to him to hold; nevertheless, the members of his household marched out with a few men

---

[1] Florence: 'churches in the cities and villages'.

[2] While William of Malmesbury's passage on this almsgiving is almost identical with that in the Chronicle, Florence says nothing about gifts to the poor; but he refers to a generous distribution by Robert to the monasteries, churches, and poor in Normandy for his father's soul.

[3] Florence specifies Odo, bishop of Bayeux, Earls Morcar and Roger, Siward Bearn, Wulfnoth, brother of King Harold; and he says that Robert released Ulf, son of King Harold, and Duncan, son of King Malcolm.

[4] 'E' remains a year behind the true date.

[5] Bishop of Bayeux.

[6] Bishop of Coutances, a very large landowner in England.

See J. H. Le Patourel, in *Eng. Hist. Rev.*, LIX (1944), pp. 129–161.

[7] William of St Calais.

[8] Odo.

[9] Roger of Montgomery, earl of Shrewsbury.

[10] The English form of the name is Mowbray.

[11] Florence, who attributes these ravages to William of Eu, says they reached Ilchester.

[12] Florence says it was a large army of English, Normans, and Welshmen, led by Bernard of Newmarch, Roger de Lacy, who had seized Hereford from the king, and Ralph Mortimer, with the men of Roger of Shrewsbury.

E

from the castle, and through God's mercy and the bishop's merits killed and captured five hundred men and routed all the rest. The bishop of Durham did whatever damage he could everywhere to the north. One of them was called Roger,[1] who threw himself into the castle of Norwich and did always the worst of all throughout all the country. There was also one Hugh[2] who did not mend matters at all, neither in Leicestershire nor Northampton. Bishop Odo, with whom all these affairs originated, went to Kent to his earldom, and injured it severely and they utterly laid waste the king's land and the archbishop's and he carried all the goods into his castle at Rochester.

When the king understood all these matters, and what treachery they were committing against him, he grew much disturbed in mind. Then he sent for Englishmen and explained his need to them and asked for their help, and promised them the best law that there had ever been in this country, and forbade every unjust tax and granted people their woods and hunting rights – but it did not last any time. But, nevertheless, the Englishmen came to the help of their liege lord the king. They marched towards Rochester,[3] and intended to capture Bishop Odo – they thought that if they had the one who had been the head of the plot they could the better get hold of all the rest. Then they came to the castle at Tonbridge.[4] Odo's soldiers were then in the castle, and many others who meant to support him against the king. But the Englishmen proceeded and stormed the castle, and the men who were in it made truce with the king. The king with his army marched towards Rochester, and they thought the bishop was there, but it became known to the king that the bishop had gone to the castle at Pevensey.[5] And the king went in pursuit with his army, and besieged the castle with a very large army for a full six weeks. Meanwhile, the count of Normandy, Robert, the king's brother, collected a very large force and thought to conquer England with the help of the men who were opposed to the king in this country. And he sent some of his men to this country and meant to follow himself. But the English, who guarded the sea, captured some of the men, and killed and drowned more than anyone could count. Afterwards, their food failed in the castle; then they asked for a truce and rendered it up to the king, and the bishop swore he would go out of England and never more come into this country unless the king sent for him, and that he would render up the castle at Rochester. Just as the bishop went and was to render up the castle, and as the king sent his men with him, the men who were in the castle rose up and seized the bishop and the king's men and put them in prison. In the castle were very good knights – Eustace the Young,[6] and Earl Roger's three sons,[7] and all the highest-born men in this country or in Normandy.

When the king understood these matters, he followed with the army that he had there, and sent over all England and ordered that everyone who was not a scoundrel[8] should come to him, French and

---

[1] Roger Bigot, a large landowner in Norfolk at the time of Domesday Book.

[2] Hugh of Grantmesnil, an important landowner in Domesday Book, lord of Leicester.

[3] Florence says Odo had put it into the charge of Eustace, count of Boulogne, and Robert of Bellême.

[4] Florence: 'which was commanded by Gilbert, son of Richard'.

[5] Id.: 'belonging to his brother, Robert, earl of Mortain'.

[6] Eustace III, count of Boulogne, son of the Eustace who opposed Godwine in 1051.

[7] Robert of Bellême, Hugh and Roger, sons of Roger of Montgomery.

[8] William of Malmesbury (ed. Stubbs, II, p. 362), who is using the Chronicle for this annal, retains the Old English word, *nithing*, and interprets it *nequam*.

E

English, from town and country. Then a great company came to him and went to Rochester and besieged the castle until those inside made a truce and rendered up the castle. Bishop Odo, with the men who were in the castle, went overseas, and the bishop thus relinquished the dignity that he had in this country.[1]

Then the king sent an army to Durham and had siege laid to the castle; and the bishop made a truce and rendered up the castle, and relinquished his bishopric and went to Normandy. Also, many Frenchmen relinquished their lands and went overseas, and the king gave their lands to the men who were loyal to him.

1089[2] In this year, the reverend father and consoler of monks, Archbishop Lanfranc, departed this life;[3] but we are confident that he went to the heavenly kingdom. Also, there was a great earthquake over all England on 11 August,[4] and it was a very late year for corn and every kind of crop, so that many people were reaping their corn round about Martinmas[5] and still later.

1090 *Thirteenth Indiction.* (1090) Things having proceeded, even as we have described above, concerning the king and his brother and his vassals, the king was considering how he could take vengeance on his brother Robert and do most injury to him, and wrest Normandy from him by force. However, by his prudence, or by treasure, he got hold of the castle at St. Valery,[6] and the harbour, and in the same way he got the one[7] at Aumale, and put his retainers into it, and they did injuries to the country in ravaging and burning. After this, he got hold of more castles in the country, and placed his knights in them. After the count of Normandy had perceived that his sworn vassals had betrayed him, and rendered up their castles to his detriment, he sent to his liege lord Philip, king of the French, and he came to Normandy with a large army, and the king and the count with an immense force besieged the castle in which the king of England's men were. King William of England sent to Philip, king of the French, and he, either for love of him, or for his great treasure, left his vassal Count Robert[8] and his country, and went back to France and so let them be: and in the course of these proceedings, this country was severely injured by unjust taxes and many other misfortunes.

1091[9] In this year King William held his court at Christmas[10] at Westminster, and afterwards, at Candlemas,[11] he went for his brother's undoing out of England into Normandy. While he was there, an agreement was reached between them, on the condition that the count handed over Fécamp and the county of Eu,[12]

---

[1] The earldom of Kent.
[2] 'E' by omitting the figure 1088 comes back to the true dating.
[3] 24 May.
[4] Florence: 'about the third hour of the day'.
[5] 11 November.
[6] Florence: 'belonging to Walter of St Valery'.

[7] *Id.*: 'belonging to Odo of Aumale'.
[8] Duke of Normandy, son of William I.
[9] Here starts the practice of beginning the annal with the Christmas court of the preceding year.
[10] 1090.
[11] 2 February 1091.
[12] Florence: 'and the abbey situated on Mont S. Michel'.

E

and Cherbourg. And in addition to this, the king's men were to be unmolested in the castles which they had taken against the count's will. And the king promised him in return to reduce to obedience Maine, which his father had conquered, which had then revolted from the count, and all that his father had over there except what he had granted to the king, and that all those in England who had lost their land for the count's sake were to have it by this agreement, and the count was to have all as much in England as was in their agreement. And if the count died without a son born in lawful wedlock, the king was to be heir to all Normandy. By this same agreement, if the king died, the count was to be heir to all England. Twelve of the best men on the king's side and twelve on the count's swore to this agreement, though it lasted only a little while after.[1]

During the course of this reconciliation, the atheling Edgar was deprived of his lands – of those that the count had handed over to him – and went from Normandy to Scotland to the king his brother-in-law, and to his sister. While King William was out of England, King Malcolm came from Scotland into England[2] and ravaged a great part of it until the good men who guarded this country sent an army against him and turned him back. When King William heard of this in Normandy, he prepared for his journey and came to England,[3] and his brother, Count Robert, with him, and forthwith ordered an army to be called out, both a naval force and a land force; but nearly all the naval force perished miserably before he could reach Scotland, a few days before Michaelmas. And the king and his brother went with the land force, but when King Malcolm heard that he was going to be attacked by an army, he went with his army out of Scotland into Lothian in England and stayed there. When King William approached with his army, Count Robert and the atheling Edgar acted as intermediaries and so made an agreement between the kings, that King Malcolm came to our king and became his vassal to the extent of such allegiance as he had done to his father,[4] and confirmed it with an oath; and King William promised him in land and in everything what he had had under his father.[5]

In this reconciliation, the atheling Edgar also was brought into agreement with the king; and the kings separated in great accord, but it lasted only a little while. And Count Robert stayed here with the king till nearly Christmas, and found little to rely on in their agreement; and two days before that festival he took ship in the Isle of Wight and went to Normandy and the atheling Edgar with him.

1092 In this year King William with a great army went north to Carlisle, and restored the city and erected the castle, and drove out Dolfin,[6] who had ruled the country, and garrisoned the castle with his men, and then came here to the south, and sent many peasant people there with their wives and cattle to live there to cultivate the land.[7]

---

[1] Florence adds an account of the seizure of Mont S. Michel by the king's brother, Henry.

[2] Florence: 'in May'.

[3] Id.: 'in August'.

[4] i.e. in 1072.

[5] According to Florence, 12 estates; and William was to give Malcolm 12 marks of gold every year.

[6] Son of Gospatric, formerly earl of Northumbria.

[7] On these events, see R. L. G. Ritchie, op. cit., pp. 52–66. Florence omits the mention of Dolfin and of the resettlement of the district, but adds that Carlisle had been destroyed by the Danes 200 years before and remained deserted ever since.

E

1093 In this year King William was taken so seriously ill in Gloucester[1] in the spring that everywhere he was declared to be dead; and in his affliction he made many vows to God to lead his own life justly, and to protect and secure God's churches, and never more again to sell them for money, and to have all just laws among his people. And the archbishopric of Canterbury, which had remained in his own control, he committed to Anselm,[2] who had been abbot at Le Bec; and to Robert,[3] his chancellor, the bishopric of Lincoln, and he granted land to many monasteries, but he soon took it away when he had recovered, and dispensed with all the good laws he had promised us.[4]

Then, after this,[5] the king of Scotland sent and asked for the fulfilment of the terms that had been promised him, and King William summoned him to Gloucester and sent him hostages to Scotland, and the atheling Edgar afterwards; and then later he sent men to meet him, who brought him to the king with great honour. But when he came to the king, he could not be granted speech with our king nor the fulfilment of the terms that had been promised him,[6] and so they separated with great dissension, and King Malcolm turned back to Scotland. But soon after he came home, he assembled his army and harried England, thus engaging on a foolish and improper project. And Robert, earl of Northumbria,[7] with his men entrapped him by surprise and killed him. He was killed by Moræl of Bamburgh,[8] who was the earl's steward and in spiritual affinity with King Malcolm.[9] With him also Edward his son was killed, who should have been king after him if he had lived. When the good queen Margaret heard of this – that her dearest husband and son were thus betrayed – she was distressed in mind to the point of death, and went to church with her priests and received her rites and, in answer to her prayer, God granted that she gave up her spirit. And then the Scots chose Malcolm's brother Dufenal[10] as king and drove out all the English who had been with King Malcolm. When Duncan, King Malcolm's son, heard all this had happened in this way (he was at King William's court as his father had given him as a hostage to our king's father and so he had remained here), he came to the king, and did such homage as the king wished to have from him, and so with his consent went to Scotland with such support as he could get from Englishmen and Frenchmen, and deprived his kinsman Dufenal of the kingdom, and was accepted as king. But some of the Scots assembled again and killed nearly all his force, and he himself escaped with a few men. Afterwards they came to an agreement, to the effect that he would never again bring Englishmen nor Frenchmen into the country.

---

[1] Florence: 'He was taken ill in the royal vill of Alveston, and hastened to Gloucester.'

[2] 4 December 1093.

[3] Robert Bloet was apparently consecrated on 12 February 1094.

[4] Florence records a raid on Brecknock by Rhys, whom he calls the last Welsh king, and his death there.

[5] Florence: 'on St Bartholemew's Day' (24 August).

[6] Florence explains that this was because of William's pride and power, and because he wished to force Malcolm to render obedience to him in his court, but Malcolm would do this only on the borders of their kingdoms, as had been done in the past, and by the judgment of the leading men of both kingdoms.

[7] Robert of Mowbray.

[8] Florence, who does not mention Moræl, dates the killing St Brice's Day (13 November). Gaimar (ll. 6111–6123) attributes it to Geoffrey 'de Gulevent' along with Moræl, and places it at Alnwick.

[9] King Malcolm's 'gossip', i.e. one of them had acted as sponsor to the other's child, or they had both stood sponsor to the same child.

[10] Donald Bane, whose reign marked a short-lived Celtic reaction against St Margaret's reforms.

E

094 In this year King William held his court at Christmas[1] at Gloucester, and messengers came to him from his brother, Robert of Normandy, who informed him that his brother utterly repudiated the truce and terms, unless the king would carry out all that they had arranged by way of agreement, and upon that called him forsworn and faithless, unless he kept to those agreements or went to where the agreement had been made and sworn, and cleared himself there.

Then the king went to Hastings at Candlemas,[2] and while he was there waiting for good weather, he had the monastery at Battle consecrated, and deprived Herbert Losinga,[3] the bishop of Thetford, of his pastoral staff; and after that in mid-Lent went overseas to Normandy. After he arrived there he and his brother, Count Robert, agreed to come together peaceably, and they did so – and could not be reconciled. Then again they came together with the same men who had made that settlement, and also had sworn the oaths, and they blamed all the breach upon the king, but he would not assent to it, nor further keep to the agreement, and therefore they separated with much dissension.

And the king then conquered the castle at Bures, and captured the count's men inside, and sent some of them to this country. On the other hand, the count conquered the castle at Argentan with the help of the king of France and seized Roger of Poitou[4] in it, and seven hundred of the king's soldiers with him, and then the castle at Le Houlme,[5] and often each of them burned the other party's villages and took people prisoner.

Then the king sent into this country and ordered twenty thousand Englishmen to be called out to his aid in Normandy; but when they reached the sea, they were ordered to turn back and give for the king's profit the money that they had received: that was half a pound for each man, and they did so.

And the count of Normandy[6] with the king of France and all those that they could assemble went after this towards Eu, in which place King William was; and intended to besiege him inside it and so proceeded until they came to Longueville. There the king of France was turned from his purpose by intrigue, and so afterwards all the expedition dispersed. Meanwhile, King William sent for his brother Henry, who was in the castle at Domfront; but because he could not go through Normandy in peace he sent ships after him, and Hugh, earl of Chester.[7] But when they were to go towards Eu where the king was, they went to England and landed at Southampton, on the eve of All Saints', and stayed here afterwards and were in London at Christmas.

Also in this year the Welshmen[8] gathered together and started a fight with the French who were in Wales or in the neighbourhood and had deprived them of land, and they stormed many fortresses and castles,[9] and killed the men. And after their forces grew they divided themselves into more divisions.

---

[1] 1093.

[2] 2 February 1094.

[3] On him, see Freeman, *The Reign of William Rufus*, I, pp. 354-356.

[4] A son of Roger of Montgomery.

[5] Florence: 'until William Peverel and 800 men surrendered'.

[6] Robert.

[7] Hugh, son of Richard, *vicomte* of Avranches, became earl of Chester about 1071, and died 27 July 1101.

[8] Florence: 'First the North Welsh, then the West Welsh and the South Welsh.'

[9] *Id.*: 'which were established in West Wales, and burnt villages and seized booty in Cheshire, Shropshire, and Herefordshire; they also took by storm the castle on Anglesey'.

E

Hugh, earl of Shropshire,[1] fought with one of these parties and routed them. But nevertheless all that year the others did not desist from doing all the damage they could.

In the course of this year also, the Scots trapped their king, Duncan, and killed him, and afterwards once more chose his paternal uncle, Dufenal,[2] as king, through whose instruction and instigation he had been betrayed to death.

1095 In this year[3] King William was at Wissant at Christmas[4] for the first four days of the festival, and after the fourth day came into this country[5] and landed at Dover. And Henry, the king's brother, stayed in this country till spring,[6] and then went overseas to Normandy with great treasures, in fealty to the king against their brother, Count Robert; and fought frequently against the count and did him much damage both in land and men.

And then at Easter the king held his court at Winchester, and Earl Robert of Northumbria would not come to court, and therefore the king was very much incensed against him and sent to him and ordered him firmly to come to court at Whitsuntide if he wanted to be entitled to protection.

In this year Easter was on 25 March, and then after Easter on the eve of St. Ambrose's Day, which is 4 April,[7] there were seen nearly all over this country nearly all night very many stars falling from the sky, not by ones or twos but so thickly that nobody could count them. After this, at Whitsuntide, the king was at Windsor and all his council with him except the earl of Northumbria;[8] because the king would neither give him hostages nor grant him on pledges to come and go with a safe-conduct.[9] And the king therefore summoned his army and went to Northumbria against the earl; and soon after he got there he overcame many of the earl's household – nearly all the best of them – in a fortress,[10] and placed them in custody, and besieged the castle at Tynemouth until he conquered it, and the earl's brother inside it, and all who were with him, and afterwards proceeded to Bamburgh and besieged the earl inside it. But when the king saw that he could not take it by force of arms, he ordered a castle to be built in front of Bamburgh, and in his language called it 'Malveisin', i.e. in English 'Bad Neighbour', and garrisoned it strongly with his men, and then went southwards. Then, soon after the king was gone away south, one night the earl went out of Bamburgh towards Tynemouth but those who were in the new castle became aware of this and went after him and fought against him and wounded him and then captured him and killed some who were with him, and took some alive.

---

[1] The second son of Roger of Montgomery. He succeeded to the earldom of Shrewsbury on the death of Roger on 27 July of this year.

[2] Donald Bane.

[3] In contrast to the Chronicle, which does not even mention the death of Wulfstan, bishop of Worcester, Florence devotes a long passage to it.

[4] 1094.

[5] Florence, at the end of his annal 1094, says that the king returned on the 29 December in order to fight the Welsh, and at once led an army into Wales.

[6] 1095.

[7] This is the date of St Ambrose's Day, not of the eve.

[8] Robert of Mowbray.

[9] Florence says Robert was conspiring with William of Eu and others to kill William II and make Stephen of Aumale king. He adds to the Chronicle account that William besieged Tynemouth for two months, that the guards of Newcastle had promised to admit Robert if he came secretly, and that he escaped from Bamburgh with 30 knights to the monastery of Tynemouth, where he was wounded and captured.

[10] Plummer says this is Newcastle, but Gaimar (ll. 6149–6154) mentions the capture of William de Morley's castle of Morpeth, after William had built Newcastle.

E

Meanwhile it became known to the king that in Wales the Welsh had stormed a certain castle called Montgomery, and killed Earl Hugh's men whose duty it was to hold it, and therefore he ordered another army to be instantly called out, and marched into Wales after Michaelmas and dispersed his army and traversed all the country so that all the army came together at All Saints' at Snowdon. But the Welsh always went ahead into mountains and moors so that they could not be reached; and the king then turned homewards because he saw that he could do nothing more there that winter.

When the king came back he ordered Earl Robert of Northumbria to be seized and taken to Bamburgh, and both his eyes to be put out, unless those who were within would give up the castle. His wife and Moræl, who was his steward and his kinsman too, were holding it. Through this scheme the castle was then given up, and Moræl entered the king's court; and through him were discovered many people, both clerics and lay, who had been instigators of rebellion against the king, some of whom the king had ordered to be reduced to captivity before that time. And, afterwards, he ordered it to be announced very peremptorily all over this country that all those who held land of the king must be at court in season if they wished to be entitled to the king's protection. And the king ordered Earl Robert to be brought to Windsor and to be kept in the castle there.

Also in this same year towards Easter, the pope's legate came to this country – that was Bishop Walter, a man very good in the conduct of his life, of the city of Albano, and he gave the *pallium* to Archbishop Anselm at Whitsuntide on behalf of Pope Urban,[1] and he received him at his archiepiscopal see of Canterbury, and Bishop Walter stayed here in this country a long time after during the year, and the Romescot[2] was afterwards sent by him, which had not been done for many years.

This same year also there was much unseasonable weather, so that all over this country the crops ripened very slightly.

096   In this year King William held his court at Christmas[3] at Windsor, and William, bishop of Durham, died there on New Year's Day.[4] And on the Octave of the Epiphany[5] the king and all his councillors were at Salisbury. There Geoffrey Bainard[6] accused William of Eu,[7] the king's kinsman, of having been a party to the treason against the king; and fought it out with him, and overcame him in trial by battle, and when he was overcome, the king ordered his eyes to be put out and that afterwards he should be castrated. And his steward, called William,[8] who was son to his mother's sister, the king ordered to be hanged on a gallows. Also, Odo, count of Champagne, the king's uncle,[9] and many others were deprived of their lands there, and some men taken to London and there destroyed.

In this year also at Easter there was a very great commotion over all this nation, and many other

---

[1] Urban II.

[2] Peter's Pence.

[3] 1095.

[4] 1 January 1096.

[5] 13 January 1096.

[6] Possibly sheriff of York in the time of the Conqueror. On the family, which gave its name to 'Baynard's Castle' in London, see J. Armitage Robinson, *Gilbert Crispin* (1911), p. 38.

[7] Not to be confused with William, count of Eu.

[8] Florence: 'William de Alderi'. William of Malmesbury calls him the king's *compater*, i.e. his connexion by spiritual affinity (see p. 179, n. 9).

[9] *aðum* usually means 'son-in-law' or 'brother-in-law', but here must be 'uncle by marriage', for he was the husband of the Conqueror's sister, Adelaide. He was father of Stephen of Aumale, whom the plotters wished to make king.

E

nations, because of Urban who was called pope though he had no seat at Rome,[1] and an immense host, with women and children, went out because they wanted to fight against heathen nations. By means of this expedition, the king and his brother Count Robert came to an agreement, so that the king went overseas and redeemed all Normandy from him for money[2] according as they had come to an agreement; and then the count departed, and with him the count of Flanders[3] and the count of Boulogne,[4] and also many other chief men. And Count Robert and those who went with him stayed the winter in Apulia. But of the people who went by way of Hungary many thousands perished there, and on the way, miserably, and many dragged themselves home towards winter, wretched and hunger-bitten.

This was a very severe year among all the people of England, both because of all sorts of taxes and because of the very severe famine which very much oppressed this country this year.

Also, in this year, the chief men who ruled this country frequently sent armies into Wales, and oppressed many a man very much thereby, but there was no success in it, only destruction of men and waste of money.

1097 In this year King William was in Normandy at Christmas,[5] and came to this country towards Easter, because he thought he would hold his court at Winchester, but he was prevented by bad weather, until Easter Eve,[6] so that he first landed at Arundel, and therefore held his court at Windsor.

And after that he went to Wales with a large army and traversed the country widely, by means of some of the Welsh who had come to him and were his guides; and he stayed there from midsummer nearly to August, and had great losses there in men and horses and many other things too. Then the Welshmen revolted from the king, and chose many chiefs from among themselves. One of them, who was the most honourable of them, was called Cadwgan – he was the son of King Griffith's brother.[7] But when the king saw that he could accomplish nothing of his purpose, he came back into this country and soon after that he had castles built along the Marches.

Then after Michaelmas, on 4 October, there appeared a marvellous star shining in the evening and soon setting. It was seen in the south-west, and the ray that shone from it appeared very long shining south-east, and it appeared nearly all the week in this fashion. Many people said it was a comet.[8]

Soon after this, Anselm, archbishop of Canterbury, got permission from the king – though the king was unwilling, so people said – and went overseas,[9] because it seemed to him that in this people little

---

[1] A reference to the earlier struggle between Urban II and the anti-pope Clement III. Florence adds a fuller account of the Council of Clermont where the Crusade was preached, with a list of those who went.

[2] 10,000 marks of silver, according to Florence, who adds that to obtain it bishops, abbots, and abbesses broke up the ornaments of the Church, while earls, barons, and sheriffs despoiled their knights and villeins. In September the king went to Normandy and received this from his brother in pledge for 6,666 pounds.

[3] Robert 'of Jerusalem'.

[4] Eustace III.

[5] 1096.

[6] 1097.

[7] Bleddyn, half-brother of Griffith ap Llewelyn; see p. 136, and n. 11.

[8] Florence says it appeared for 15 days, from 29 September, and that some people saw a burning cross in the sky.

[9] The breach between the king and Anselm was caused partly by the king's complaint that the military contingent provided by the archbishop was inadequately equipped. See F. M. Stenton, *The First Century of English Feudalism, 1066–1166*, pp. 147f.

E

was done according to justice and according to his orders. And the king, after that, at Martinmas,[1] went overseas into Normandy, but while he was waiting for good weather, his court did the greatest damage in the districts where they stayed that ever court or army was reported to have done in a land at peace. This was in every respect a very severe year, and over-oppressive with bad weather, when cultivation was due to be done or crops to be got in, and with excessive taxes that never ceased. Also, many shires whose labour was due at London were hard pressed because of the wall that they built about the Tower, and because of the bridge that was nearly all carried away by a flood, and because of the work on the king's hall, that was being built at Westminster, and many a man was oppressed thereby.

Also in this same year, soon after Michaelmas, the atheling Edgar went with an army, with the king's support, into Scotland, and conquered the country in a severe battle, and drove out King Dufenal;[2] and his kinsman, Edgar, who was son of King Malcolm and Margaret, the queen, he established as king in allegiance to King William, and then came back into England.

1098 In this year at Christmas,[3] King William was in Normandy. And Walkelin, bishop of Winchester, and Baldwin, abbot of St. Edmunds, both died during that time.[4] And in this year also Turold, abbot of Peterborough, died.

In the course of this year also in the summer, in Berkshire, at Finchampstead, a pool bubbled up with blood, as many trustworthy men said who were alleged to have seen it.

And Earl Hugh[5] was killed in Anglesey by sea-rovers,[6] and his brother Robert[7] became his heir, even as he obtained it from the king.

Before Michaelmas the sky looked as if it were burning nearly all night. This was a very oppressive year because of all sorts of excessive taxes, and great rains that did not cease throughout the year; nearly all the cultivation perished on marshland.

1099 This year King William was in Normandy at Christmas[8] and came to this country at Easter,[9] and at Whitsuntide held his court for the first time in his new building at Westminster, and there gave the bishopric of Durham to his chaplain, Rannulf,[10] who had managed his councils over all England, and superintended them. And soon after that he went overseas and drove Count Elias[11] out of Maine, and then established it under his control, and so came back to this country at Michaelmas.

---

[1] 11 November, but Florence says he went about the feast of St Andrew (30 November).

[2] Donald Bane.

[3] 1097.

[4] Walkelin on 3 January 1098 and Baldwin on 29 December 1097.

[5] Son of Roger of Montgomery and, like his father, earl of Shrewsbury.

[6] Florence has a fuller account of this incident. It followed a raid on Anglesey by the Earls Hugh of Chester and Hugh of Shrewsbury. The viking leader was Magnus 'Bareleg', king of Norway, son of King Olaf 'the Peaceful', who had come to visit Orkney and *Mevania* (Man and Anglesey), which belonged to him. William of Malmesbury (ed. Stubbs, II, pp. 318, 376) says he had with him a son of Harold Godwineson.

[7] Robert of Bellême, elder brother of Hugh. Up till now he had held only the Norman lands of the family.

[8] 1098.

[9] 1099.

[10] Rannulf Flambard. He held the see until 1128.

[11] Elias 'de la Flèche'.

E

This year also on St. Martin's Day,[1] the tide rose so much and did so much damage that it could not be remembered to have done so much before, and there was on the same day a new moon.

And Osmund, bishop of Salisbury, died in Advent.[2]

1100 In this year King William held his court at Christmas[3] at Gloucester, and at Easter[4] at Winchester, and at Whitsuntide at Westminster.

And at Whitsuntide at a village in Berkshire there was seen blood bubbling out of the earth, as many said who were alleged to have seen it. And after that, in the morning after Lammas,[5] King William when hunting[6] was shot with an arrow by one of his own men,[7] and then brought to Winchester and buried in that bishopric[8] – that was in the thirteenth year after his succession to the throne.

He was very strong and fierce to his country and his men and to all his neighbours, and very terrible. And because of the counsels of wicked men, which were always agreeable to him, and because of his avarice, he was always harassing this nation with military service and excessive taxes, for in his days all justice was in abeyance, and all injustice arose both in ecclesiastical and secular matters. He kept down God's Church, and all the bishoprics and abbacies whose incumbents died in his days he sold for money or kept in his own hands and let out for rent, because he intended to be the heir of everyone, cleric and lay; and so on the day he died he had in his own hands the archbishopric of Canterbury, and the bishopric of Winchester and that of Salisbury, and eleven abbacies all let out for rent. And though I prolong it further – all that was hateful to God and just men was customary in this country in his time; and therefore he was hateful to nearly all his people, and odious to God, just as his end showed, because he departed in the midst of his injustice without repentance and any reparation.

On the Thursday he was killed, and buried next morning; and when he was buried the councillors who were near at hand chose his brother Henry as king, and he forthwith gave the bishopric of Winchester to William Giffard,[9] and then went to London, and on the Sunday after that, before the altar at Westminster, he vowed to God and all the people to put down all the injustices that there were in his brother's time,[10] and to maintain the best laws that had stood in any king's day before him. And after that Maurice, the bishop of London, consecrated him king,[11] and all in this country submitted to him and swore oaths and became his men.

And soon after this, the king, by the advice of those who were around him, had Bishop Rannulf of Durham seized and brought into the Tower of London and kept there.[12] Then before Michaelmas,[13]

---

[1] 11 November, but Florence dates it 3 November.

[2] On 3 December.

[3] 1099.

[4] 1100.

[5] 2 August.

[6] Florence: 'in the New Forest, which is called in the English language (the forest) of the Jutes'.

[7] Id.: 'Walter, surnamed Tirell'.

[8] The usual meaning of biscopric is 'diocese'. Its use here, instead of minster, may be compared with in episcopatum in

William of Malmesbury. On the doubts whether William II was buried with full rites, see Freeman, op. cit., II, pp. 338–341, 676–680.

[9] He was not consecrated until 1107.

[10] A reference to the so-called 'coronation charter' of Henry I. See E.H.D., II, No. 19.

[11] On 5 August.

[12] He was arrested on 15 August.

[13] He arrived on 23 September.

E

Archbishop Anselm of Canterbury came into this country, as King Henry sent for him on the advice of his council, because he had gone out of this country as a result of the great injustice that King William did him.

And then soon after this the king married Maud, daughter of Malcolm, king of Scotland, and of Margaret, the good queen, the kinswoman of King Edward, of the true royal family of England, and on St. Martin's Day[1] she was given to him at Westminster with great ceremony, and Archbishop Anselm married her to him and then consecrated her queen.

And Archbishop Thomas of York died soon after this.[2]

In the course of this same year also, in autumn, Count Robert came home to Normandy,[3] and Count Robert of Flanders and Eustace, count of Boulogne, from Jerusalem, and as soon as Count Robert came into Normandy he was joyfully received by all the people, apart from the castles that were garrisoned with King Henry's men, against which he had many struggles and battles.

101 In this year at Christmas[4] King Henry held his court at Westminster, and at Easter at Winchester; and then soon after, the chief men in the country grew hostile to the king, both because of their great disloyalty and because of Count Robert of Normandy, who set out to carry war into this country. And the king then sent ships out to sea for the injury and hindrance of his brother, but some of them failed again at this crisis, and deserted from the king and went over to Count Robert. Then at midsummer the king marched out to Pevensey with all his army against his brother and waited for him there; but meanwhile Count Robert landed at Portsmouth twelve nights before Lammas,[5] and the king with all his army came against him. The chief men, however, went between them and reconciled the brothers[6] on the condition that the king gave up all he was forcibly holding against the count in Normandy, and that all in England who had lost their land because of the count should have it again. And Count Eustace[7] also should have his father's land in this country, and every year Count Robert should have 3,000 marks of silver from England, and whichever of the brothers should survive the other should be heir of all England and of Normandy as well, unless the deceased should have an heir in lawful wedlock. And this twelve of the men of highest rank on both sides confirmed with an oath. And the count afterwards stayed in this country until after Michaelmas; and his men always did much damage wherever they went while the count was staying in this country.

In the course of this year also, Bishop Rannulf escaped by night at Candlemas[8] from the Tower of London, where he was in captivity, and went to Normandy. It was chiefly through his contrivance and instigation that Count Robert had come to this country this year with warlike intent.

---

[1] 11 November.
[2] 18 November.
[3] Florence: 'with the wife whom he had married in Sicily'.
[4] 1100.

[5] i.e. on 20 July.
[6] The so-called 'Treaty of Alton'.
[7] Eustace of Boulogne.
[8] 2 February 1101.

E

1102 In this year at the Nativity,[1] King Henry was at Westminster, and at Easter[2] at Winchester. And soon after that there was a disagreement between the king and Earl Robert of Bellême, who had here in this country the earldom of Shrewsbury, that his father, Earl Roger,[3] had had, and authority over a wide area as well, both on this side of the sea and beyond it. And the king went and besieged the castle at Arundel.[4] When, however, he could not take it by force so quickly, he had castles made before it and garrisoned them with his men, and then with all his army marched to Bridgnorth and stayed there until he had the castle and deprived Earl Robert of his lands and took from him all he had in England; and the earl went overseas, and the army then turned back home.

Then after that, at Michaelmas, the king was at Westminster, and all the chief men in this country, cleric and lay; and Archbishop Anselm held a synod of clerics and there they prepared many decrees pertaining to Christianity, and many, both French and English, lost their pastoral staffs and their authority, which they had obtained unjustly or lived in wrongfully.[5]

And in this same year in Whitsun week, there came thieves, some from Auvergne, some from France, and some from Flanders, and broke into the monastery of Peterborough and took in it much of value in gold and silver – crosses and chalices and candlesticks.

1103 In this year at Christmas[2] King Henry was at Westminster, and soon after that Bishop William Giffard[6] went out of this country, because he did not wish to receive his consecration uncanonically from Archbishop Gerard of York;[7] and then at Easter the king held his court at Winchester, and after that Archbishop Anselm went from Canterbury to Rome,[8] as he and the king agreed.

In the course of this year also, Count Robert of Normandy came to speak with the king in this country, and before he went away he remitted the 3,000 marks that King Henry had to give him every year by compact.[9]

In this year also, at Finchampstead in Berkshire, blood was seen coming from the earth. This was a very grievous year in this country through all sorts of taxes, and cattle plague and ruin of crops – both corn and all the produce of trees. Also, on the morning of St. Laurence's Day,[10] the wind did so much damage to all crops in this country that no one remembered it ever doing so much before.

In this same year Matthias, abbot of Peterborough, died – he lived no longer than a year after he was abbot. After Michaelmas, on 21 October, he was received as abbot with a procession and on the same day next year he died at Gloucester, and was buried there.

---

[1] 1101.

[2] 1102.

[3] Roger of Montgomery.

[4] Belonging to Robert of Bellême: it had been given by William the Conqueror to Roger of Montgomery.

[5] Though Florence is much fuller both on Robert's rebellion and Anselm's council, there is enough identity of wording to show that he and 'E' are based on the same source.

[6] See above, p. 176.

[7] Gerard had a bad character, but the real dispute was that between the king and Anselm on the matter of investiture. See Z. N. Brooke, op. cit., p. 163.

[8] Florence, who is closely connected to 'E' in this annal, adds: 'on 27 April, having with him William, bishop-elect of Winchester, and the abbots deposed from their abbeys, Richard of Ely and Ealdwine of Ramsey'.

[9] See above, p. 177.

[10] 10 August.

E

104 In this year at Christmas,[1] King Henry held his court at Westminster, and at Easter[2] at Winchester, and at Whitsuntide again at Westminster. This year Whit-Sunday was on 5 June, and on the Tuesday after there appeared at midday four circles all round the sun, of white colour, each intertwined under the other as if they were painted. All who saw them were astonished for they did not remember anything like it before.

After this, an agreement was reached between Count Robert of Normandy and Robert of Bellême whom King Henry had deprived of his lands and expelled from England, and through their agreement the king of England and the count of Normandy were set at emnity, and the king sent his people overseas into Normandy, and the chief men in that country received them and, to the betrayal of their liege lord the count, introduced them into their castles, from which they did many injuries to the count, in ravaging and burning. Also in the course of this year William, count of Mortain,[3] went away from this country into Normandy, but after he had gone he worked against the king, for which reason the king deprived him of everything and confiscated what land he had in this country.

It is not easy to describe the miseries this country was suffering at this time, because of various and different injustices and taxes that never ceased or diminished, and always wherever the king went there was complete ravaging of his wretched people caused by his court, and in the course of it often [there were] burnings and killings:

> All this was to anger God
> And these wretched folk to vex.

105 In this year at the Nativity,[2] King Henry held his court at Windsor, and after that in spring[4] he went overseas into Normandy against his brother Count Robert, and in the course of his stay there he won Caen and Bayeux[5] from his brother, and nearly all the castles and the chief men in that country were subjected to him, and then he came back to this country again in the autumn. And what he had won in Normandy remained afterwards in peace, and obedient to him, except those who lived anywhere near William, count of Mortain, who frequently oppressed them as hard as he could because of his loss of lands in this country. And then before Christmas Robert of Bellême came into this country to the king. This was a very grievous year in this country because of the ruin of crops and the various taxes that never ceased, before the king crossed over, and while he was there, and after he came back again.

106 In this year King Henry was at Westminster at the Nativity[6] and there held his court. At that festival Robert of Bellême left the king in hostile fashion and went out of this country into Normandy. Then, after this, before spring, the king was at Northampton; and Count Robert of Normandy, his brother,

---

[1] 1103.
[2] 1104.
[3] Son of Robert, count of Mortain, uterine half-brother of the Conqueror.

[4] 2–8 April 1105.
[5] Bayeux was burnt on 13 April; the surrender of Caen followed.
[6] 1105.

E

came there to him, and because the king would not give up to him what he had won from him in Normandy, they separated without coming to an agreement, and the count went back overseas again forthwith.

In the first week of Lent, on the Friday, 16 February, in the evening, there appeared an unusual star, and for a long time[1] after that it was seen shining a while every evening. This star appeared in the south-west; it seemed small and dark. The ray that shone from it, however, was very bright, and seemed to be like an immense beam shining north-east; and one evening it appeared as if this beam were forking into many rays towards the star from an opposite direction. Some said that at this time they saw more strange stars. However, we do not write of it more plainly because we did not see it ourselves. On the eve of *Cena Domini*,[2] that is the Thursday before Easter, two moons were seen in the sky before day, one to the east and one to the west, both full, and the moon on that day was a fortnight old.

At Easter the king was at Bath, and at Whitsuntide at Salisbury, because he did not wish to hold court on his departure overseas. After that, before August, the king went overseas into Normandy and nearly all who were in that country submitted to his will, apart from Robert of Bellême and the count of Mortain and a few other of the chief men who still held with the count of Normandy; and therefore the king afterwards went with an army and besieged a castle of the count of Mortain called Tinchebrai. While the king was besieging the castle, Count Robert of Normandy came upon the king with his army, on the eve of Michaelmas, and with him Robert of Bellême and William, count of Mortain, and all who agreed with them. But the superiority and the victory were the king's.[3] There the count of Normandy was captured and the count of Mortain and Robert of Estouteville, and they were sent to England and reduced to captivity. Robert of Bellême was put to flight, and William Crispin[4] captured and many together with him. The atheling Edgar, who had shortly before gone over from the king to the count, was also captured there. The king afterwards let him go unmolested. Afterwards the king overran everything in Normandy and arranged it according to his pleasure and power.

This year also there were serious and sinful[5] struggles between the emperor of Saxony and his son, and in the course of the struggle the father died and the son succeeded to the throne.[6]

1107 In this year at Christmas,[7] King Henry was in Normandy and brought it under his control and organized it, and after that in spring[8] came to this country and held his court at Easter at Windsor, and at Whitsuntide at Westminster, and afterwards again at the beginning of August was at Westminster, and there he gave and disposed of the bishoprics and abbacies that there were in England or Normandy without ruler or pastor.[9] These were so many that nobody could remember that so many had ever been given

---

[1] Florence: 'for 25 days'.

[2] i.e. on 21 March.

[3] For further details, see C. W. David, *Robert Curthose*, pp. 171–176.

[4] William Crispin II, brother of Gilbert Crispin, abbot of Westminster.

[5] Or perhaps 'constant'; cf. *gesinlice* 'continually'.

[6] Henry IV was deposed on 31 December 1105 and died 7 August 1106.

[7] 1106.

[8] 1107.

[9] Florence adds a long account of this council, important in relation to the Investiture Contest.

E

together before; and at this same time, among the others who received abbacies, Ernulf, who had been prior at Canterbury,[1] succeeded to the abbacy of Peterborough. This was just seven years after King Henry had received the kingship, and it was the forty-first year after the French had been in control of this country. Many said that they saw various signs in the moon during this year, and its beams waxing and waning contrary to nature.

In the course of this year died Maurice, bishop of London,[2] and Robert, abbot of Bury St. Edmunds,[3] and Richard, abbot of Ely.[4] In the course of this year also, King Edgar of Scotland died on 13 January,[5] and Alexander, his brother,[6] succeeded to the throne with King Henry's consent.

108 In this year at the Nativity,[7] King Henry was at Westminster, and at Easter[8] at Winchester, and at Whitsuntide again at Westminster, and after that, before August, he went into Normandy; and the king of France, Philip, died on 5 August,[9] and his son, Louis,[10] succeeded to the throne; and there were many struggles between the king of France and the king of England while he stayed in Normandy.

In this year also Archbishop Gerard of York died[11] before Whitsuntide, and afterwards Thomas[12] was appointed to the see.

109 In this year King Henry was in Normandy at Christmas[8] and Easter,[13] and before Whitsuntide[14] came here to this country, and held court at Westminster. There the agreements were completed and the oaths sworn to give his daughter to the emperor[15] in marriage.

In the course of this year there were very many thunderstorms and very terrible they were. And Archbishop Anselm of Canterbury died on 22 March,[16] and Easter Sunday was on the Feast of the Greater Litany.[17]

110 In this year King Henry held his court at Christmas[13] at Westminster, and at Easter[18] he was at Marlborough, and at Whitsuntide he held his court for the first time at the New Windsor.

In this year before spring, the king sent his daughter overseas with many and various treasures and gave her in marriage to the emperor. On the fifth night in the month of May, the moon appeared in the evening shining bright, and then little by little its light faded until early in the night it was quenched entirely, so much so that neither light nor circle nor anything of it at all was seen; and so it continued

---

[1] In 1114 he became bishop of Rochester. He is reputed to have been the compiler of *Textus Roffensis*.

[2] 26 September.

[3] 17 October.

[4] 16 June. After his death Ely was transformed into a bishopric.

[5] 6 January 1107, according to Florence, 8 January according to Simeon of Durham and some other authorities.

[6] Alexander I.

[7] 1107.

[8] 1108.

[9] The correct date is 29 July.

[10] Louis VI, 'le Gros'.

[11] 21 May.

[12] He was the son of Samson, bishop of Worcester.

[13] 1109.

[14] Florence: 'about Rogation time'.

[15] Henry V.

[16] A mistake for 21 April. The chronicler wrote '11th kalends of April' instead of '11th kalends of May'.

[17] 25 April.

[18] 1110.

E

until nearly day, and then it appeared full and brightly shining – it was a fortnight old that same day. All that night the sky was very clear, and the stars all over the heaven shining very bright, and fruits were badly damaged by frost that night. After that, in the month of June,[1] a star appeared from the north-east and its beam went out in front of it in the south-west, and it was seen like this for many nights, and later on in the night, after it had risen higher, it was seen going backwards to the north-west.

In the course of this year, Philip of Briouze,[2] William Malet, and William Bainard were deprived of their lands.

Also in the course of this year Count Elias died, who held Maine from King Henry, and did acknowledgment for it, and after his decease the count of Anjou[3] succeeded and held it against the king.

This was a very severe year in this country because of taxes that the king took for the marriage of his daughter, and because of storms by which the products of the soil were badly damaged and the fruits of trees over all this country nearly all perished.

In the course of this year work was begun on the new monastery at Chertsey.

1111   In this year King Henry did not wear his crown at Christmas[4] nor Easter[5] nor Whitsuntide, and in August he went overseas into Normandy because of the disagreement that some people had with him on the boundaries of France, and mostly because of the count of Anjou who held Maine against him; and when he got over there, between them they perpetrated many cruel raids and burnings and ravagings. In this year Robert, count of Flanders, died[6] and his son, Baldwin,[7] succeeded. In the course of this year there was a very long and troublesome and severe winter, and as a result all the produce of the soil was very badly damaged, and there was the greatest cattle plague that anyone could remember.

1112   All this year King Henry stayed in Normandy because of the disagreement he had with France, and with the count of Anjou who held Maine against him. And while he was there he deprived the count of Evreux[8] and William Crispin of their land and drove them out of Normandy, and gave back his land to Philip of Briouze who had formerly been deprived of his estates. And he caused Robert of Bellême to be captured and put into prison.[9] This was a very good year and very productive in woods and fields, but it was very troublesome and sorrowful because of excessive plague.

<table>
<tr><td align="center">E</td><td align="center">H[10]</td></tr>
<tr><td>1113   In this year King Henry was in Normandy at the Nativity,[11] at Easter[12] and at Whitsuntide; and after</td><td>. . . so that they could speak with difficulty. After that Abbot Peter of Gloucester died on 17 July;</td></tr>
</table>

---

[1] Florence says it appeared on 8 June and was visible for 3 weeks.

[2] Son of William of Briouze, an important tenant-in-chief in Domesday Book.

[3] Fulk V.

[4] 1110.

[5] 1111.

[6] On 4 or 5 October.

[7] Baldwin VII.

[8] William, count of Evreux.

[9] Florence: 'In Cherbourg.'

[10] This fragment is Brit. Mus. Cott. Domit. ix, on which see p. xvii.

[11] 1112.

[12] 1113.

E

that in summer he sent Robert of Bellême into this country to the castle at Wareham, and came himself into the country soon after.

1114 In this year King Henry held his court at the Nativity[1] at Windsor, and he did not hold court again in the course of this year. And at midsummer he went with an army into Wales, and the Welsh came and made a truce with the king, and he had castles built among them. And after that, in September, he went overseas into Normandy. In this year late in May there was seen a strange star with long rays shining for many nights. Also in this same year there was one day so great an ebb everywhere as nobody could remember before, and so that the Thames,[4] east of the bridge at London, was crossed by people riding and on foot. In the course of this year there were many strong winds in the month of October, but it was extremely strong on the night which was the Octave of St. Martin,[6] and it was evident everywhere in woods and villages. Also in this year the king gave the archbishopric of Canterbury to Ralph, who had been bishop of Rochester. And the archbishop of York, Thomas, died, and Thurstan, who had been the king's chaplain, succeeded him.[8] In this same year the king went towards the sea and meant to cross over but the weather prevented him. Meanwhile he sent his writ to Abbot Ernulf of Peterborough, and ordered him to come to him quickly because he

H

and on 5 October the king appointed to the office William, who was a monk of the same monastery.

In this year King Henry was at Windsor at Christmas,[1] and wore his crown there; and there he gave the bishopric of Worcester to Theobald,[2] his chaplain. Also he gave the abbacy of Ramsey to Rainold who was a monk of Caen. Also he gave the abbacy of York to Richard who was a monk of the same monastery. Also he gave the abbacy of Thorney to Robert who was a monk of St. Evroul. Also he gave the earldom of Northamptonshire to David who was the queen's brother.[3] After that Thomas, archbishop of York, died on 17 February.[5] After that the king gave the abbacy of Cerne Abbas to William who was a monk of Caen. Then at Easter he was at Thorpe near Northampton. After that he gave the archbishopric of Canterbury to Ralph who was bishop of Rochester; and he succeeded to it on 24 February.[7] After that Abbot Nigel of Burton died on 3 May. After that Chichester was burnt down, and the minster there as well, on 5 May. Then at Whitsuntide the king was at St. Albans. Afterwards he went with his army into Wales at midsummer and built castles there, and the Welsh kings came to him and became his vassals and swore oaths of allegiance to him. After that he went to Winchester and there gave the archbishopric of York to his chaplain, Thurstan,[8] and the abbacy of Bury

---

[1] 1113.

[2] An error for Theowulf, who received the see on 28 December 1113.

[3] King of Scotland.

[4] Florence: 'On 10 October.'

[5] 19 February according to Hugh the Chanter, who presumably gives the York tradition; 24 February according to Florence.

[6] 18 November.

[7] He was elected at Windsor on Sunday, 26 April; 'H' reads '6th kalends of March' in error for '6th kalends of May'.

[8] He was elected at Winchester on August 15. Owing to the quarrel with Canterbury he was not consecrated until 1119.

E

wished to have a secret conversation with him. When he came to him, he forced the bishopric of Rochester on him, and so did the archbishops and bishops and the nobility that was in England together with the king; and he resisted a long time but it was of no avail. And the king then ordered the archbishop to conduct him to Canterbury and consecrate him bishop whether he would or no. This took place at the town called *Burne*:[3] it was on 15 September. When the monks of Peterborough heard tell of this, they were more grieved than they had ever been, because he was a very good and gentle man, and did much conducive to good within and without while he was there. God Almighty be with him always!

Then soon after that, the king gave the abbacy[4] to a monk of Séez, called John, at the desire of the archbishop of Canterbury, and soon after, the king and the archbishop of Canterbury sent him to Rome for the archbishop's *pallium*, and a monk, who is[5] called Warner, with him, and the archbishop's nephew, the archdeacon, John; and they got on well there. This took place on 21 September at the town called Rowner;[6] and the same day the king went on board ship at Portsmouth.

H

St. Edmunds he gave to Albold who was a monk at Le Bec. This was on 16 August. After that he gave the abbacy of Muchelney to Ealdwulf, who was a monk in that same monastery, on the Feast of the Exaltation of the Cross.[1] Also he gave the abbacy of Burton to Geoffrey who was a monk at the Old Minster.[2] At the same time Archbishop Ralph gave the bishopric of Rochester. . . .

E

1115   In this year King Henry was in Normandy at the Nativity,[7] and while he was there he brought it about that all the chief men in Normandy did homage and swore oaths of allegiance to his son, William, whom he had by his queen, and after that, in the month of July, he came to this country.

In the course of this year there was a winter so severe, what with snow and frost, that nobody then living remembered any more severe, and because of that there was an excessive plague among cattle.

In this year Pope Paschal sent the *pallium* to this country for Ralph, archbishop of Canterbury, and

---

[1] 14 September.
[2] Winchester.
[3] Probably Westbourne, Sussex.
[4] Of Peterborough.

[5] This has been altered to 'was', obviously after Warner's death.
[6] Near Gosport, Hampshire.
[7] 1114.

E

he received it[1] with great honour at his archiepiscopal see in Canterbury. Abbot Anselm,[2] who was a nephew of Archbishop Anselm (and Abbot John of Peterborough),[3] brought it from Rome.

1116 In this year King Henry was at St. Albans at the Nativity,[4] and had the minster there consecrated; and at Easter[5] he was at Odiham. And in the course of this year there was a very bad and severe and long winter for cattle and everything. And the king went overseas into Normandy soon after Easter, and there were many cruel raids and robberies and castles taken between France and Normandy. This disagreement was mostly because King Henry was supporting his nephew, Theobald, count of Blois,[6] who was carrying on a war against his liege lord, Louis,[7] king of France.

This was a very toilsome and disastrous year in the matter of the produce of the earth, because of the excessive rains that came shortly before August, and were causing much distress and toil when Candlemas[8] was reached. Also this year was so short of mast that none was heard of in all this country, nor even in Wales. This country and the people also this year were often severely oppressed by the taxes the king took both in boroughs and outside them.

In this same year all the monastery at Peterborough was burnt, and all the buildings except the chapter-house and the dormitory, and in addition most of the town was burnt. All this happened on a Friday – it was 4 August.

1117 All this year King Henry stayed in Normandy because of the quarrel with the king of France and his other neighbours; and then in the summer the king of France and the count of Flanders with him came with an army into Normandy and stayed there one night, and in the morning went back without a fight. And Normandy was very much distressed because of taxes and because of the army King Henry had assembled against them. Also this people was severely oppressed on the same account, because of many various taxes.

In the course of this year, on the night of 1 December, there were excessive storms with thunder and lightning and rain and hail. And on the night of 11 December the moon late in the night became as if it were all bloody, and then was eclipsed. Also on the night of 16 December the sky appeared very red as if it were on fire. And on the Octave of St. John the Evangelist[9] there was the great earthquake in Lombardy, because of which monasteries and towers and houses fell down and did much damage amongst people. This was a very disastrous year for corn, because of the rains that hardly ceased nearly all the year.

And Abbot Gilbert of Westminster died on 6 December and Faritius, abbot of Abingdon, on 23 February. And in this same year. . . .[10]

---

[1] Florence: 'On 27 June.'
[2] Abbot of St Saba in Rome. He became abbot of Bury St Edmunds in 1121.
[3] Added in the margin by a later hand.
[4] 1115.
[5] 1116.

[6] He was the son of Adela, sister of Henry I, by Stephen, count of Blois.
[7] Louis VI, 'le Gros'.
[8] 2 February.
[9] 3 January.
[10] More than a line in the MS. is here left blank.

E

1118   All this year King Henry stayed in Normandy because of the war with the king of France and the count of Anjou and the count of Flanders; and the count of Flanders was wounded in Normandy, and wounded as he was, he went to Flanders. Because of these hostilities the king was very much distressed and lost a great deal both in money and also in land, and the people who troubled him most were his own men, who frequently deserted him and betrayed him and went over to his enemies, and gave their castles up to them for the injury and betrayal of the king. England paid dear for all this, because of the various taxes that never ceased in the course of all this year.

In this year, in the week of the Epiphany, there was very much lightning one evening and excessive thunder after it.

And Queen Maud died at Westminster on 1 May and was buried there. And Robert, count of Meulan,[1] also died in the course of the year.

Also in this year, on St. Thomas's Day,[2] there was a wind so very excessively strong that nobody then alive remembered any worse, and its effect was obvious everywhere both on houses and trees.

In the course of this year also Pope Paschal died;[3] and John of Gaeta, whose other name was Gelasius,[4] succeeded to the papacy.

1119   All this year King Henry stayed in Normandy and was very often much troubled because of the war with the king of France and with his own men who had deserted him treacherously, until the two kings came together in Normandy with their forces. There the king of France was routed and all his best men captured,[5] and then many of King Henry's men came back to him, and those who had used their castles against him made agreement with him, and some of the castles he took by force.

In the course of this year William, son of King Henry and Queen Maud, went into Normandy to his father and there the count of Anjou's daughter[6] was given and betrothed to him.

On the eve of Michaelmas there was a great earthquake at some places in this country, though most severe in Gloucestershire and Worcestershire.

In this same year Pope Gelasius[7] died on this side of the Alps and was buried at Cluny, and after him the archbishop of Vienne was elected pope, who took the name Calixtus;[8] and afterwards, on the Feast of St. Luke the Evangelist,[9] he came into France to Rheims, and there held a council, and Archbishop Thurstan of York went to it; and because he had accepted his office from the pope against justice and against the archiepiscopal see of Canterbury and against the king's will, the king refused to let him return to England, and so he lost his archbishopric and went towards Rome with the pope.

Also in this year Count Baldwin[10] of Flanders died of the wounds that he received in Normandy;

---

[1] Robert of Beaumont, who fought at Hastings, was the son of Roger of Beaumont who appears in Norman history as early as the time of Duke Robert. He was earl of Leicester.

[2] 21 December.

[3] Paschal II. He died 21 January 1118.

[4] Gelasius II. He was elected pope on 24 January 1118 and was consecrated 10 March 1118.

[5] The battle of Brémule, 2 August 1119.

[6] Maud.

[7] Gelasius II.

[8] Calixtus II.

[9] 18 October, but the continuator of Florence has 20 October.

[10] Baldwin VII.

E

and after him Charles, son of his father's sister, succeeded to power. He was son of St. Cnut, king of Denmark.

1120 In the course of this year the king of England and the king of France were reconciled, and following their agreement King Henry's own men in Normandy all came into accord with him, and so did the counts of Flanders and of Ponthieu.[1] Then after this King Henry disposed of his castles and his land in Normandy according to his desire, and so came into this country before Advent.

And on that journey the king's two sons, William and Richard, were drowned,[2] and Richard,[3] earl of Chester, and Ottuel, his brother, and very many of the king's court, stewards and chamberlains and cupbearers and people of various offices, and a very immense number of excellent people with them. Their death was a double grief to their friends – one that they lost this life so suddenly, the other that the bodies of few of them were found anywhere afterwards.

In the course of this year the light came to the Sepulchre of the Lord in Jerusalem twice, once at Easter and the other time at the Assumption of St. Mary,[4] as trustworthy people reported who came from there.

And Archbishop Thurstan of York was reconciled with the king through the pope, and came into this country and received his bishopric, though it was very displeasing to the archbishop of Canterbury.

1121 In this year King Henry was at Brampton at Christmas;[5] and after that, before Candlemas,[6] at Windsor, Adela was given to him as wife and then consecrated as queen. She was the daughter of the duke of Louvain.[7]

And the moon was eclipsed on the eve of 5 April, and the moon was a fortnight old.

And the king was at Berkeley at Easter, and after that at Whitsuntide he held a great court at Westminster, and then in the summer went into Wales with an army; and the Welsh came to meet him, and they made an agreement with him according to the king's desire.

In the course of this year the count of Anjou came from Jerusalem into his country and then sent into this country and had his daughter fetched who had been given as wife to William, the king's son.

And on the night of Christmas Eve there was a great wind all over this country, and that was very obvious in many ways.[8]

1122 In this year King Henry was at Norwich at Christmas[9] and at Easter[10] he was at Northampton. And in spring, before that, the borough at Gloucester was burnt down. While the monks were

---

[1] Charles of Flanders and William I of Ponthieu.

[2] The White Ship was wrecked in the night between 25 and 26 November.

[3] Son of Hugh of Avranches. He became earl of Chester in 1101.

[4] 15 August.

[5] 1120.

[6] 2 February 1121. The continuator of Florence places the marriage on 29 January and the consecration the day following.

[7] Godfrey VII, duke of Lower Lorraine and count of Louvain.

[8] At this point the section of 'E' written all at one stretch comes to an end, and annals 1122–1131, though in the same hand, seem to have been added at intervals. Presumably they were written at Peterborough, but some points of contact with annal 1130 in the continuation of Florence suggests a shared source.

[9] 1121.

[10] 1122.

E

singing their mass, and the deacon had begun the gospel *Preteriens Jesus*,[1] the fire reached the upper part of the tower, and all the monastery was burnt and all the treasures that were there except a few books and three mass vestments: that was on 8 March.

And after that on the Tuesday after Palm Sunday there was a very big wind, on 22 March.[2] After that came many signs far and wide in England and many illusions were seen and heard. And on the night of 25 July there was a very big earthquake over all Somerset and in Gloucestershire. Then on 8 September – that was on St. Mary's Feast Day[3] – there was a very big wind from 9 a.m. till dark night.

This same year Ralph, the archbishop of Canterbury, died; that was on 20 October. After that there were many sailors, at sea and on inland waters, who said that they saw in the north-east a great and broad fire near the earth, and it increased in length continuously up to the sky, and the sky opened on four sides and fought against it, as if it was going to quench it, and the fire increased no more then up towards the heavens. They saw this fire at daybreak, and it lasted until it was light everywhere. That was 7 December.

1123 In this year King Henry was at Dunstable at Christmas,[4] and messengers of the count of Anjou came there to him,[5] and from there he went to Woodstock, and his bishops and all his court with him.

It happened on a Wednesday (it was 10 January) that the king was riding in his deer-park, and Bishop Roger of Salisbury on one side of him, and Bishop Robert Bloet of Lincoln on the other, and they were riding and talking there. Then the bishop of Lincoln sank down and said to the king, 'Lord King, I am dying', and the king dismounted from his horse and caught him in his arms and had him carried home to his lodging; and he forthwith died. He was taken to Lincoln with great honour and buried before St. Mary's altar, and the bishop of Chester, who was called Robert Pecceth, buried him.

Then, soon after, the king sent his writs over all England, and ordered his bishops and abbots and thegns all to come and meet him for his council meeting on Candlemas Day[6] at Gloucester, and they did so. When they were assembled there, the king ordered them to elect an archbishop of Canterbury for themselves, whomsoever they wished, and he would grant it to them. Then the bishops talked among themselves and said they wished never again to have a monk as archbishop over them, but they all went together to the king and desired that they might elect whomsoever they wished as archbishop from the secular clerks; and the king granted it to them. That had all been done through the bishop of Salisbury and the bishop of Lincoln before his death, because they never loved the monastic rule but were always against monks and their rule; and the prior and the monks of Canterbury and all the other monks who were there opposed it for a full two days, but it was of no avail, because the bishop of

---

[1] The gospel for the Wednesday after the fourth Sunday in Lent, which fell on 8 March in 1122.

[2] A day wrong. Tuesday after Palm Sunday was 21 March in 1122.

[3] The Nativity of the Blessed Virgin Mary.

[4] 1122.

[5] To negotiate about the dowry of Fulk's daughter, Maud, widowed by the drowning of Henry's son William on the White Ship.

[6] 2 February.

E

Salisbury was strong and controlled all England, and was against them with all his power and ability. Then they elected a clerk called William of Corbeil – he was canon of a monastery called *Cicc*[1] – and they brought him before the king, and the king gave him the archbishopric and all the bishops received him. The monks and earls and thegns, nearly all that were there, opposed him.

At the same time the count's[2] messengers left the king without reaching agreement, and thought nothing of his gifts.[3]

At the same time there came a legate from Rome called Henry;[4] he was abbot of the monastery of St. Jean d'Angely, and he came for the Romescot.[5] And he told the king it was uncanonical to set a clerk over monks, and especially so when they had previously elected their archbishop in their chapter canonically – but the king would not cancel it because of his love for the bishop of Salisbury. Then the archbishop soon after that went to Canterbury and was received there, though it was against their will, and was there forthwith consecrated bishop by the bishop of London and Bishop Ernulf of Rochester and Bishop William Giffard of Winchester and Bishop Bernard of Wales[6] and Bishop Roger of Salisbury. Then soon, in the spring, the archbishop went to Rome for his *pallium*, and with him went Bishop Bernard of Wales and Sefred,[7] abbot of Glastonbury, and Anselm, abbot of St. Edmunds,[8] and John, archdeacon of Canterbury, and Giffard, who was the king's court chaplain.

At this same time Archbishop Thurstan of York went to Rome at the pope's command and arrived there three days before the archbishop of Canterbury arrived,[9] and was there received with great honour. Then the archbishop of Canterbury came and was there a full week before he could have any conversation with the pope – that was because the pope was given to understand that he had received the archbishopric in opposition to the monks of the monastery and uncanonically. But the thing that overcomes all the world overcame Rome – that is, gold and silver; and the pope relented, and gave him his *pallium*, and the archbishop swore on the altar[10] of SS. Peter and Paul obedience to him in all the things that the pope imposed upon him, and [the pope] sent him home then with his blessing.

While the archbishop was out of the country, the king gave the bishopric of Bath to the queen's chancellor who was called Godfrey. He was born at Louvain. This took place at Woodstock on the day of the Annunciation to St. Mary.[11] Then soon after that the king went to Winchester and was there

---

[1] i.e. St Osyth's, Essex.

[2] The count of Anjou.

[3] *na of his gyfe ne rohton*. This is ambiguous. It could mean that they thought him niggardly, or that they refused to be bribed. I see no reason to assume that there has been confusion with another verb *reccan* as G. N. Garmonsway, *The Anglo-Saxon Chronicle*, p. 252, n. 1, suggests as an alternative. This verb usually means 'to narrate', but does occur rarely with the meaning 'to unravel a difficulty'. Garmonsway thinks the *gyfe* may be the dowry which Henry refused to return, and renders tentatively 'got no satisfaction about his (Fulk's) dowry'. But the normal meaning of *rohton* makes sense, i.e. they had no reason to respect his liberality.

[4] Henry of Poitou, whose further adventures are recorded under 1127, 1128, 1130–1132.

[5] Peter's Pence.

[6] i.e bishop of St David's.

[7] He was brother to Archbishop Ralph.

[8] Formerly abbot of St Saba in Rome.

[9] Reference has been made to the dispute between the two archbishops under 1119. See further Z. N. Brooke, *op. cit.*, pp. 168–173.

[10] Accepting Thorpe's emendation of *heuod* 'head' to *weuod* 'altar'.

[11] 25 March.

E

all Eastertide; and while he was there he gave the bishopric of Lincoln to a clerk called Alexander.[1] He was nephew to the bishop of Salisbury.[2] The king did all this out of love for the bishop.

Then the king went from there to Portsmouth and stayed there all over Whitsun week. Then as soon as he had a wind, he went over to Normandy and committed all England to the care and government of Bishop Roger of Salisbury.

Then the king was in Normandy all the year, and then great hostility arose between him and his thegns,[3] so that Waleran, count of Meulan,[4] and Amaury[5] and Hugh of Montfort[6] and William of Roumare and many others deserted from him and held their castles against him; and the king resisted them stoutly, and in the course of this same year he won his castle of Pont Aldemer from Waleran and Montfort from Hugh; and afterwards the longer he went on the better he prospered.

In the course of this same year, before the bishop of Lincoln came to his diocese, nearly all the city of Lincoln was burnt down, and an immense number of people, men and women, were burnt to death, and so much damage was done there that no one could describe it to another. That was on 19 May.

1124 All this year King Henry was in Normandy. That was because of the great hostilities he had with King Louis of France and with the count of Anjou and with his own men most of all.

Then it happened on the day of the Annunciation to St. Mary[7] that Waleran, count of Meulan, went from a castle of his called Beaumont[8] to another of his castles called Walterville; with him went Amaury, steward of the king of France, and Hugh, son of Gervase, and Hugh of Montfort and many other good knights.[9]

Then there came against them the king's knights[9] from all the castles that were thereabouts, and fought against them and routed them, and captured Count Waleran and Hugh, son of Gervase, and Hugh of Montfort and twenty-five other knights, and brought them to the king; and the king had Count Waleran and Hugh, son of Gervase, put in custody in the castle of Rouen, and Hugh of Montfort he sent to England and had him put into grievous bonds in the castle at Gloucester, and he sent as many of the others as he pleased north and south to his castles into custody. Then, afterwards, the king went and gained all Count Waleran's castles that there were in Normandy, and all the others that his opponents were holding against him.

All this hostility was because of the son of Robert, count of Normandy, called William.[10] This same William had married the younger daughter of Fulk, count of Anjou, and therefore the king of France and all the counts held with him, and all the powerful men, and said that the king was wrongfully

---

[1] Alexander was consecrated bishop of Lincoln, 22 July 1123. He died 20 February 1148.

[2] Roger, bishop of Salisbury, 1107–1139.

[3] The use of the Old English term in this connexion is curious.

[4] Twin brother of Robert, earl of Leicester, and son of Robert of Beaumont, count of Meulan and earl of Leicester.

[5] Of Montfort l'Amaury, father-in-law of Waleran.

[6] Of Montfort-sur-Risle, brother-in-law of Waleran.

[7] 25 March.

[8] Beaumont-le-Roger, on the Risle.

[9] 'Knight' is here used correctly. Contrast the use of 'thegn' in the previous annal.

[10] William 'Clito'.

E

holding his brother, Robert, in custody, and had unjustly caused his son, William, to flee from Normandy.

In the course of this same year the weather in England was very bad for corn and all crops, so that between Christmas and Candlemas seed wheat for an acre – i.e. 2 seedlips – was sold at 6 shillings, and barley – i.e. 3 seedlips – at 6 shillings, and seed oats for an acre – i.e. 4 seedlips – at 4 shillings. That was because the corn was scarce, and the penny so bad that if a man had a pound at a market he could not by any means get the value of 12 pence for it.

In the course of this same year the blessed Bishop Ernulf of Rochester, who had been abbot of Peterborough previously, died – that was on 15 March – and after that King Alexander of Scotland died on 23 April, and his brother, David,[1] who was then earl of Northampton, succeeded to the throne and had both together – the kingship in Scotland and the earldom in England. And on 14 December the pope of Rome, called Calixtus,[2] died and Honorius[3] succeeded to the papacy.

In the course of this same year after St. Andrew's Day, before Christmas, Ralph Basset[4] and the king's thegns[5] held a council at *Hundehoge*[6] in Leicestershire, and hanged there more thieves than ever had been hanged before; that was in all forty-four men in that little time; and six men were blinded and castrated. A large number of trustworthy men said that many were destroyed very unjustly there, but our Lord God Almighty that sees and knows all secrets – he sees the wretched people are treated with complete injustice: first they are robbed of their property and then they are killed. It was a very troublous year: the man who had any property was deprived of it by severe taxes and severe courts; the man who had none died of hunger.

1125   In this year King Henry sent to England from Normandy before Christmas,[7] and ordered that all the moneyers who were in England should be mutilated – i.e. that each should lose the right hand and be castrated. That was because the man who had a pound could not get a pennyworth at a market. And Bishop Roger of Salisbury sent over all England and ordered them all to come to Winchester at Christmas.[7] When they got there, they were taken one by one and each deprived of the right hand, and castrated. All this was done before Twelfth Night,[8] and it was done very justly because they had ruined all the country with their great false-dealing, which they all paid for.

In the course of this same year the pope of Rome sent to this country a cardinal called John of Crema.[9] He came first to the king in Normandy, and the king received him with great honour, and then commended him to William, archbishop of Canterbury; and he conducted him to Canterbury

---

[1] David I, 1124–1153.
[2] Calixtus II.
[3] Honorius II.
[4] A prominent member of the king's court acting as itinerant justice.
[5] Note the use of the Old English term.
[6] There seems no reason to identify this with Hundcot. See C. Clark, *The Peterborough Chronicle, 1070–1154*, p. 88.

[7] 1124.
[8] 6 January 1125.
[9] An important legatine commission involving jurisdictional controversies. Henry of Huntingdon is pleased to be able to tell a scandalous story respecting the legate's personal conduct while in England.

E

and he was there received with great honour and with a great procession, and he sang High Mass on Easter Day at Christ's altar, and then he went over all England to all the bishoprics and abbacies that there were in the country and he was received with honour everywhere, and they all gave him great and splendid gifts. And then he held his council at London[1] for a full three days at the Nativity of St. Mary, in September,[2] with archbishops and diocesan bishops and abbots and clerics and laity, and promulgated there the same laws that Archbishop Anselm had previously promulgated, and many more, though it was of little avail. And from there he went overseas soon after Michaelmas, and so to Rome, and with him went Archbishop William of Canterbury and Archbishop Thurstan of York and Bishop Alexander of Lincoln and John, bishop of Lothian,[3] and Geoffrey, abbot of St. Albans, and they were there received by Pope Honorius[4] with great honour, and stayed there all the winter.

In the course of the same year there was so great a flood on St. Laurence's Day[5] that many villages were flooded and many people drowned, and bridges broken down, and corn and meadows utterly ruined, and famine and disease among men and cattle; and there was more bad weather for all crops than there had been for many years before.

And in the course of the same year Abbot John of Peterborough died on 14 October.

1126   All this year King Henry was in Normandy right up to after harvest time. Then he came to this country between the Nativity of St. Mary[2] and Michaelmas,[6] and with him came the queen and his daughter[7] whom he had previously married to the emperor, Henry of Lorraine,[8] and he brought with him Count Waleran and Hugh, son of Gervase, and he sent the count to Bridgnorth in custody, and from there he sent him afterwards to Wallingford, and Hugh [he sent] to Windsor and had him put into strict confinement.

And then after Michaelmas, David, king of Scots, came from Scotland into this country and King Henry received him with great honour, and he stayed all the year in this country.

In the course of this same year, the king had his brother, Robert, taken from Bishop Roger of Salisbury and entrusted him to his son, Robert, earl of Gloucester,[9] and had him taken to Bristol and put in the castle there. This was all done on the advice of his daughter, and through the king of Scots, David, her uncle.[10]

1127   This year King Henry held his court at Christmas[11] at Windsor, and David, king of Scots, was there, and all the chief men, both clerics and laymen, that there were in England. And there he [King Henry] caused archbishops and bishops and abbots and earls and all the thegns that were there to swear to give

---

[1] For its acts, see the comments of Z. N. Brooke in *op. cit.,* p. 169.

[2] 8 September.

[3] Bishop of Glasgow, 1118–1147.

[4] Honorius II.

[5] 10 August.

[6] Henry arrived in this country on 11 September.

[7] Maud.

[8] Henry V.

[9] For his colourful career, see *Complete Peerage,* v, pp. 683–686.

[10] David I, son of Malcolm Canmore and Margaret, was brother-in-law to Henry I, who married his sister Maud.

[11] 1126.

E

England and Normandy after his death into the hand of his daughter Athelic,[1] who had been wife of the emperor of Saxony;[2] and then he sent her to Normandy (and with her went her brother, Robert, earl of Gloucester, and Brian, son of Count Alan Fergant), and had her married to the son of the count of Anjou, called Geoffrey Martel. All the same, it displeased all the French and English; but the king did it to have peace with the count of Anjou and to have help against his nephew, William.[3]

In the course of this same year, in spring, Charles, count of Flanders, was killed by his own men in a church where he lay prostrate and praying to God before the altar, during Mass; and the king of France brought William, son of the count of Normandy, and gave him the county, and the people of that land accepted him. This same William had earlier married the daughter of the count of Anjou,[4] and they were afterwards separated for being within the prohibited degrees of relationship; that was all owing to King Henry of England. Afterwards he married the king of France's sister,[5] and for this reason the king gave him the county of Flanders.

In the course of this same year King Henry gave the abbacy of Peterborough to an abbot called Henry of Poitou,[6] who had possession of his abbacy of St. Jean d'Angely, and all the archbishops and bishops said that it was uncanonical and that he could not have possession of two abbacies. But this same Henry gave the king to understand that he had left his abbacy because of the great disturbance that there was in the country, and that he did it by the advice and permission of the pope of Rome and of the abbot of Cluny, and because he was legate in respect of Rome-scot; but it was not so any the more for that, but he wished to have possession of both; and so he had, as long as it was God's will. While a secular clerk, he was bishop of Soissons; then he became a monk at Cluny, then prior in this same monastery, and then he became prior at Savigny; after that, because he was a relative of the king of England and the count of Poitou, the count gave him the abbacy of the monastery of St. Jean d'Angely.

Afterwards, by means of his great stratagems, he then obtained the archbishopric of Besançon and had possession of it for three days. Then he justly lost it because he had unjustly obtained it. Then he afterwards obtained the bishopric of Saintes which was five miles from where he was abbot; he had possession of that very nearly a week. Then the abbot of Cluny took him out of that as he had done earlier out of Besançon. Then he bethought himself that if he could get himself rooted in England, he could have everything he wished. He besought the king, and told him that he was an old and broken-down man, and he could not put up with the great injustices and the great disturbances that there were in their country. Then personally and through all his friends he especially desired the abbacy of Peterborough; and the king granted it to him because he was his relative and because he was a principal man in swearing the oath and bearing witness when the son of the count of Normandy and the daughter of the count of Anjou were separated for being within the prohibited degrees of relationship. Thus

[1] Better known by her other name of Maud.
[2] Henry V.
[3] William 'Clito'.
[4] Maud, daughter of Fulk V of Anjou. She later became a nun at Fontevrault, where subsequently she was abbess.

[5] Joan, daughter of Rainier of Montferrat. She was half-sister to Adelaide of Savoy, wife of Louis VI of France.
[6] See above, under 1123.

E

miserably was the abbacy given, between Christmas and Candlemas, at London, and so he went with the king to Winchester and from there he came to Peterborough, and there he stayed exactly as drones do in a hive. All that the bees carry in, the drones eat and carry out, and so did he: all that he could take inside and outside from clerics and laymen he thus sent overseas and did nothing good there and left nothing good there.

Let it not be thought remarkable, when we tell the truth, because it was fully known over all the country, that as soon as he came there (that was on the Sunday when *Exsurge quare obdormis Domine* is sung),[1] then soon afterwards many people saw and heard many hunters hunting. The hunters were black and big and loathsome, and their hounds all black and wide-eyed and loathsome, and they rode on black horses and black goats.[2] This was seen in the very deer-park in the town of Peterborough, and in all the woods that there were between this town and Stamford, and the monks heard the horns blow that they were blowing at night. Trustworthy people noticed them at night, and said that it seemed to them there might well be about twenty or thirty hornblowers. This was seen and heard from the time he came there all Lent up to Easter. This was his coming in – of his going out we can say nothing yet. May God provide!

1128 All this year King Henry was in Normandy because of the hostility that there was between him and his nephew, the count of Flanders.[3] But the count was wounded by a retainer in a fight and, wounded as he was, he went to St. Bertin's monastery and forthwith became a monk there, and lived five days after that, and then died, and was buried there. God have mercy on his soul! That was on 27 July.

In the course of this same year Bishop Rannulf Passeflambard[4] of Durham died, and was buried there on 5 September.

And in the course of this same year the aforesaid Abbot Henry went home, by leave of the king, to his own monastery in Poitou. He gave the king to understand that he would give up the monastery and that land completely, and stay with him in England and in the monastery of Peterborough, but it was not so any the more for that – he did it because he meant to stay there through his great trickery whether it were twelve months or more, and then to come back. God Almighty have mercy on that wretched place!

In the course of the same year Hugh of the Temple[5] came from Jerusalem to the king in Normandy, and the king received him with great honour and gave him great treasures, consisting of gold and silver; and then he sent him to England and there he was received by all good men and they all gave him treasures – and in Scotland also – and sent by him to Jerusalem great property entirely in gold and silver; and he summoned people out to Jerusalem, and then there went with him and after him so large a number of people as never had done since the first expedition in the days of Pope Urban[6] – though it

---

[1] This is the Introit at Mass for Sexagesima Sunday, which in 1127 fell on 6 February.

[2] Hugh Candidus has *edos* (i.e. *haedos*).

[3] William 'Clito'.

[4] Usually known as Rannulf Flambard.

[5] Hugh 'de Payen', one of the founders of the Templars.

[6] Urban II. The reference is to the First Crusade.

E

came to little. He said that a great war was afoot between the Christians and the heathens. Then when they arrived there it was nothing but lies – thus miserably were all the people afflicted.

129 In this year the king sent to England for Count Waleran[1] and for Hugh, son of Gervase, and there they gave hostages for themselves, and Hugh went home to his own land, to France, and Waleran remained with the king; and the king gave him all his land except his castle only.

Then the king came to England in autumn and the count came with him, and they became quite as good friends as before they had been enemies.

Then soon by the advice and permission of the king, Archbishop William of Canterbury sent over all England and ordered bishops and abbots and archdeacons and all the priors, monks, and canons that there were in all the cells in England, and all those that had to care for and look after Christianity, all to come to London at Michaelmas and there to discuss all God's dues. When they arrived there, the meeting began on Monday and continued right on to the Friday. When it all came out, it turned out to be all about archdeacons' wives and priests' wives, that they were to give them up by St. Andrew's Day, and anyone who would not do so, should forgo his church and his house and his home, and never more have a claim to them. This was ordered by William of Canterbury, the archbishop, and all the diocesan bishops that were in England, and the king gave them all permission to go home, and so they went home, and all the orders availed nothing – they all kept their wives by permission of the king as they had done before.

In the course of this year William Giffard, bishop of Winchester, died, and was buried there on 25 January, and King Henry gave the bishopric after Michaelmas to Henry, abbot of Glastonbury, his nephew,[2] and he was consecrated bishop by Archbishop William of Canterbury on 17 November.

In the course of this year Pope Honorius[3] died. Before he was well dead, two popes were elected there. One was called Peter[4] – he was a monk of Cluny and was descended from the most powerful men of Rome, and the people of Rome and the duke of Sicily[5] held with him. The other was called Gregory,[6] and he was a secular clerk and was chased out of Rome by the other pope and his relatives. With him held the emperor of Saxony[7] and the king of France[8] and King Henry of England and all those on this side of the Alps.

There now grew up such heresy as there had never been before. May Christ establish counsel for his wretched people!

In the course of this same year on St. Nicholas's eve,[9] a little before day, there was a great earthquake.

---

[1] Count of Meulan.

[2] Henry of Blois, brother of King Stephen, being the son of Stephen, count of Blois, by Adela, sister of Henry I. He administered the revenues of Glastonbury during a vacancy.

[3] Honorius II.

[4] Peter 'de Pier-leoni', who, as anti-pope, took the title of Anacletus.

[5] Roger II.

[6] He became Innocent II.

[7] Lothair II.

[8] Louis VI.

[9] 5 December.

D

1130 (1080)[1] In this year Angus[2] was killed by a Scottish army, and there were great casualties on his side. There God's right was avenged on him because he was altogether perjured.

E

In the course of this year the church of Canterbury was consecrated by Archbishop William on 4 May. These bishops were present: John of Rochester, Gilbert 'Universalis' of London, Henry of Winchester, Alexander of Lincoln, Roger of Salisbury, Simon of Worcester, Roger of Coventry, Godfrey of Bath, Everard of Norwich, Seffrid of Chichester, Bernard of St. David's, Audoen[3] of Evreux from Normandy, John of Séez.

On the fourth day after that, King Henry was at Rochester and the town was nearly burnt down; and Archbishop William consecrated St. Andrew's Cathedral,[4] and the aforesaid bishops with him. And King Henry went overseas into Normandy in autumn.[5]

In the course of this same year, Abbot Henry of Angely[6] came after Easter to Peterborough, and said he had entirely given up the monastery. After him the abbot of Cluny, Peter,[7] came to England by permission of the king and was received everywhere, wherever he came, with great honour. He came to Peterborough, and there Abbot Henry promised him that he would obtain the monastery of Peterborough for him so that it should be subjected to Cluny; but it is said as a proverb 'The hedge remains that divides the fields.' God Almighty destroy all wicked plans! And soon after that the abbot of Cluny went home to his own country.

---

[1] On this entry, wrongly dated 1080 to make it follow the preceding entry in 'D', 1079, see p. xvi.

[2] Angus, earl of Moray, was the son of the sister of the Mælsnechtan mentioned in annal 1078 'D'. He rebelled against King David in 1130. See A. O. Anderson, *op. cit.*, pp. 166f. It is interesting that even as late as this twelfth-century entry the 'D' MS. retains its interest in the kings of Scotland and their opponents.

[3] He was brother of Thurstan, archbishop of York. For him, see *Gallia Christiana*, XI, col. 573.

[4] 'On the following day, Ascension Day', continuator of Florence.

[5] So far, this annal and that in the continuation of Florence are closely connected. The list of bishops present at Canterbury is identical.

[6] See annal 1123.

[7] Peter 'the Venerable'.

E

1131 This year, after Christmas, on a Sunday night at first sleep, the sky in the north was all as if it was a burning fire, so that all who saw it were afraid as they had never been before – that was on 11 January. In the course of this same year, there was such a great cattle plague all over England as had never been before in the memory of man – that was among cattle and pigs, so that in a village that had ten or twelve ploughs in action, there was not one left, and the man who had two hundred or three hundred pigs had not one left. After that, the hens died, then the meat and cheese and butter ran short. May God amend it when it is his will!

And King Henry came home to England before autumn, after the earlier Feast of St. Peter.[1]

In the course of this same year, before Easter, Abbot Henry went from Peterborough overseas to Normandy and there spoke with the king and told him that the abbot of Cluny had ordered him to come to him and hand over to him the abbacy of Angely; and then with his permission he would come home – and so he went home to his own monastery, and stayed there right up to Midsummer Day. And the next day after St. John's Day,[2] the monks elected an abbot from among themselves and brought him into the church with a procession, sang *Te Deum Laudamus*, rang the bells, set him on the abbot's throne, and did all such obedience to him as they ought to do to their abbot. And the count and all the chief men and the monks of the monastery chased the other abbot, Henry, out of the monastery. They had to, of necessity – in five and twenty years they never experienced one good day. Now all his great trickery failed him; now he was forced to creep into his big wallet, into every corner of it, to see whether there were at least one poor trick left so that he could deceive Christ and all Christ's people yet once more. Then he went to Cluny and there was kept, so that he could go neither east nor west – the abbot of Cluny said that they had lost St. John's monastery through him and his great folly. Then he knew of no better remedy for himself than to promise them, and to swear oaths on the relics, that if he might visit England, he would get possession of the monastery of Peterborough for them so that he should appoint a prior from Cluny to it, and the sacristan and treasurer and keeper of the wardrobe, and all the things that were in the monastery, and outside it, he would commit to them. Thus he went into France, and stayed there all the year. Christ take counsel for the wretched monks of Peterborough and for the wretched place! Now they need Christ's help and that of all Christian people.[3]

1132 This year King Henry came to this country. Then Abbot Henry came and accused the monks of Peterborough to the king, because he wished to put the monastery under the rule of Cluny, with the result that the king was nearly deceived, and sent for the monks. And by the mercy of God and by means of the bishop of Salisbury, the bishop of Lincoln, and the other powerful men who were there, the king perceived that he was behaving treacherously. When he could do no more, he wished that his nephew should be abbot in Peterborough, but Christ did not wish it. It was not long after that, that the king sent for him, and made him give up the abbacy of Peterborough, and go out of the country.

---

[1] 29 June.
[2] i.e. 25 June.

[3] Here ends the first scribe of 'E'. The remaining entries were all written at a stretch, some time after 1154.

E

And the king gave the abbacy to a prior of St. Neot's called Martin. He came into the monastery on St. Peter's Day with great dignity.

1135 In this year King Henry went overseas at Lammas, and the next day, when he was lying asleep on board ship, the day grew dark over all lands, and the sun became as if it were a three-nights'-old moon, with stars about it at midday.[1]

People were very much astonished and terrified, and said that something important would be bound to come after this – so it did, for that same year the king died the second day after St. Andrew's Day,[2] in Normandy. Then forthwith these lands grew dark, for everyone who could forthwith robbed another. Then his son and his friends took his body and brought it to England and buried it at Reading. He was a good man, and people were in great awe of him. No one dared injure another in his time. He made peace for man and beast. Whoever carried his burden of gold and silver, nobody dared say anything but good to him.

Meanwhile his nephew, Stephen of Blois, had come to England and went to London. The Londoners received him, and sent for the archbishop, William of Corbeil, who consecrated him king on Christmas Day.[3]

In this king's time there was nothing but disturbance and wickedness and robbery, for forthwith the powerful men who were traitors rose against him. First of all Baldwin of Reviers,[4] and he held Exeter against him and the king besieged it, and then Baldwin came to an agreement. Then the others took and held their castles against him, and David, king of Scotland, began to make war on him. Then, in spite of that, their messengers went between them, and they came together and were brought to agreement, though it was of little use.

1137 This year King Stephen went overseas to Normandy, and was received there because they expected that he would be just as his uncle had been, and because he still had his treasure; but he distributed it and squandered it like a fool. King Henry had gathered a great amount – gold and silver – and no good to his soul was done with it.

When King Stephen came to England he held his council at Oxford,[5] and there he took Roger, bishop of Salisbury, and Alexander, bishop of Lincoln, and the chancellor Roger, his nephews,[6] and put them all in prison till they surrendered their castles. When the traitors understood that he was a mild

---

[1] The king's journey and the eclipse took place in 1133. The continuation of Florence of Worcester wrongly puts the eclipse in 1132. It is a sign of the late writing of this section of 'E' that the eclipse has been transferred, with dramatic effect, to just before the king's death.

[2] This makes the king die on 2 December, the date given by the continuators of Florence and of Simeon of Durham; William of Malmesbury has 1 December.

[3] Authorities vary on the date of this coronation, William of Malmesbury giving 22 December (which was a Sunday), the continuator of Florence 20 December (which he wrongly calls Sunday), Roger of Hoveden 26 December, Orderic Vitalis 15 December, and the continuator of Simeon of Durham 1 January 1136.

[4] He became earl of Devon before midsummer 1141.

[5] In the summer of 1139.

[6] i.e. nephews of Roger, bishop of Salisbury.

E

man, and gentle and good, and did not exact the full penalties of the law, they perpetrated every enormity. They had done him homage, and sworn oaths, but they kept no pledge; all of them were perjured and their pledges nullified, for every powerful man built his castles and held them against him and they filled the country full of castles. They oppressed the wretched people of the country severely with castle-building. When the castles were built, they filled them with devils and wicked men. Then, both by night and day they took those people that they thought had any goods – men and women – and put them in prison and tortured them with indescribable torture to extort gold and silver – for no martyrs were ever so tortured as they were. They were hung by the thumbs or by the head, and corselets were hung on their feet. Knotted ropes were put round their heads and twisted till they penetrated to the brains. They put them in prisons where there were adders and snakes and toads, and killed them like that. Some they put in a 'torture-chamber' – that is in a chest that was short, narrow and shallow, and they put sharp stones in it and pressed the man in it so that he had all his limbs broken. In many of the castles was a 'noose-and-trap' – consisting of chains of such a kind that two or three men had enough to do to carry one. It was so made that it was fastened to a beam, and they used to put a sharp iron around the man's throat and his neck, so that he could not in any direction either sit or lie or sleep, but had to carry all that iron. Many thousands they killed by starvation.

I have neither the ability nor the power to tell all the horrors nor all the torments they inflicted upon wretched people in this country; and that lasted the nineteen years while Stephen was king, and it was always going from bad to worse. They levied taxes on the villages every so often, and called it 'protection money'.[1] When the wretched people had no more to give, they robbed and burned the villages, so that you could easily go a whole day's journey and never find anyone occupying a village, nor land tilled. Then corn was dear, and meat and butter and cheese, because there was none in the country. Wretched people died of starvation; some lived by begging for alms, who had once been rich men; some fled the country.

There had never been till then greater misery in the country, nor had heathens ever done worse than they did. For contrary to custom, they respected neither church nor churchyard, but took all the property that was inside, and then burnt the church and everything together. Neither did they respect bishops' land nor abbots' nor priests', but robbed monks and clerics, and everyone robbed somebody else if he had the greater power. If two or three men came riding to a village, all the villagers fled from them; they expected they would be robbers. The bishops and learned men were always excommunicating them, but they thought nothing of it, because they were all utterly accursed and perjured and doomed to perdition.[2]

---

[1] *tenserie.*

[2] Similar passages describing the horrors of this reign occur elsewhere. Particularly interesting are those in the continuation of Simeon of Durham (ed. Arnold, I, pp. 153 f.) and in William of Malmesbury's *Historia Novella* (ed. Stubbs, II, pp. 560 ff.; K. R. Potter, pp. 40 f.). The former agrees with the Chronicle with regard to the hanging of men with weights (armour or large stones) tied on them, and the pressing of men into a narrow chest; the latter seems to have verbal parallels to the passage in 'E', e.g. 'sparing neither churches nor graveyards', 'they kidnapped under-tenants, peasants, any whom they thought wealthy, and compelled them to promise anything by the severity of their tortures'. It speaks, as does 'E', of the ineffective excommunication of the wrong-doers.

E

Wherever cultivation was done, the ground produced no corn, because the land was all ruined by such doings, and they said openly that Christ and his saints were asleep. Such things, too much for us to describe, we suffered nineteen years for our sins.

In all this evil time, Abbot Martin held his abbacy for twenty years and a half, and eight days, with great energy, and provided for the monks and the guests everything they needed, and held great commemoration feasts in the house, and nevertheless worked at the church and appointed lands and income for it, and endowed it richly and had it roofed, and brought them into the new monastery on St. Peter's Day[1] with great ceremony – that was A.D. 1140, twenty-three years since the fire. And he went to Rome and was there well received by Pope Eugenius,[2] and obtained there privileges, one in respect of all the lands of the abbacy, another in respect of all the lands pertaining to the office of sacristan, and if he could have lived longer, he meant to do the same in the case of the office of treasurer. And he got back lands that powerful men were holding by force: from William Maudit who held Rockingham Castle, he recovered Cottingham and Easton; from Hugh of Walterville he recovered Irthlingborough and Stanwick and 60 shillings each year from Aldwinkle. And he made many monks, and planted a vineyard, and did much building and made the village better than it had ever been before,[3] and was a good monk and a good man, and therefore God and good men loved him.

Now we wish to describe to some extent what happened in King Stephen's time. In his time, the Jews of Norwich bought a Christian child before Easter and tortured him with all the torture that our Lord was tortured with; and on Good Friday hanged him on a cross on account of our Lord, and then buried him. They expected it would be concealed, but our Lord made it plain that he was a holy martyr, and the monks took him and buried him with ceremony in the monastery, and through our Lord he works wonderful and varied miracles, and he is called St. William.[4]

1138   In this year David, king of Scotland, came to this country with an immense army: he meant to conquer this country. And Earl William of Aumale,[5] to whom the king had entrusted York, and the other reliable men with a few men, came to meet him and fought with them and routed the king at the Standard and killed very many of his followers.[6]

1140[7] In this year King Stephen meant to capture Robert, earl of Gloucester, King Henry's son, but he could not because he became aware of it.[8]

After that, in spring, the sun grew dark, and the day, about midday when people were eating, so

---

[1] 29 June.
[2] Eugenius III, who succeeded to the papacy in 1145.
[3] From the Peterborough historian Hugh Candidus (ed. W. T. Mellows, p. 122) we learn that he altered for the better the position of the entrance to the monastery, the market, the quay, and the village.
[4] On him, see A. Jessopp and M. R. James, St William of Norwich (1896).
[5] Lord of Holderness.

[6] On this battle, which was fought near Northallerton, 22 August 1138, see the collection of authorities by A. O. Anderson, op. cit., pp. 176–213, and cf. E.H.D., II, No. 11.
[7] This annal is made up of events in Stephen's reign, which the chronicler was probably incapable of assigning to their true date. On these events, see J. H. Round, Geoffrey de Mandeville (1892).
[8] April 1137.

E

that they lit candles to eat by. That was 20 March,[1] and people were very much astonished. After that William, archbishop of Canterbury, died,[2] and the king made Theobald archbishop,[3] who was abbot of Le Bec.

After that there arose a great war between the king and Rannulf, earl of Chester, not because he did not give him all that he could ask him (as he did everybody else) but always the more he gave them the worse they were to him. The earl held Lincoln against the king, and deprived him of all that he ought to have had, and the king went there and besieged him and his brother, William of Roumare,[4] in the castle; and the earl got out secretly, and went after Robert, earl of Gloucester, and brought him there with a large army, and they fought fiercely on Candlemas Day[5] against their liege lord, and captured him (for his men failed him and fled) and took him to Bristol and put him in prison and fetters there. Then all England was disturbed more than it had been before and there was every evil in the country.

After that came King Henry's daughter[6] who had been empress in Germany and was now countess of Anjou, and came to London; and the Londoners wanted to capture her, and she fled and lost a great deal there.

After that, the bishop of Winchester, Henry, King Stephen's brother, spoke with Earl Robert, and with the empress, and swore oaths to them that he would never again support the king his brother; and he excommunicated all the men who supported him, and told them he would give up Winchester to them, and had them come there. When they were in the town, the king's wife came with all her forces, and besieged them[7] so that there was a great famine in the town. When they could endure it no longer, they got out secretly and fled and those outside became aware of it and pursued them and captured Robert, earl of Gloucester, and took him to Rochester and put him in prison there; and the empress fled to a monastery. Then the wise men went between the king's friends and the earl's friends and agreement was reached, the terms being that the king should be let out of prison in exchange for the earl, and the earl for the king, and so they did.[8]

Then, after that,[9] the king and Earl Rannulf[10] came to an agreement at Stamford, and swore oaths and confirmed pledges that neither of them should betray the other; and it came to nothing, because afterwards[11] the king captured him at Northampton through bad counsel, and put him in prison; and soon he let him out through worse counsel, on condition that he swore on the relics and found hostages [to assure] that he would surrender his castles. Some he surrendered and some he did not, and did worse than he ought to have done here.

---

[1] There was an eclipse of the sun on 20 March 1140.
[2] 21 November 1136.
[3] He was consecrated on 8 January 1139.
[4] Earl of Lincoln.
[5] 2 February 1141.
[6] Maud arrived in England in September 1139. Her entry into and flight from London took place in June 1141.

[7] August–September 1141.
[8] Stephen was released 1 November 1141.
[9] In 1142.
[10] Earl of Chester.
[11] In 1146.

E

Then England was very much divided: some supported the king and some the empress, because when the king was in prison, the earls and the powerful men expected that he would never get out again, and made an agreement with the empress and brought her into Oxford and gave her the borough. When the king was out of prison, he heard this said and took his army and besieged her in the tower,[1] and she was let down at night from the tower with ropes, and she stole out and fled and went on foot to Wallingford.[2]

After that she went overseas,[3] and those of Normandy all deserted from the king to the count of Anjou, some of their own accord and some not of their own accord, because he besieged them till they gave up their castles, and they had no help from the king.[4]

Then Eustace, the king's son, went to France and married the king of France's sister,[5] by which he expected to obtain all Normandy, but he did not prosper much, and by good right for he was a bad man, for wherever he went he did more harm than good. He robbed the lands and levied heavy taxes. He brought his wife to England and put her in the castle in Canterbury. A good woman she was, but she had little happiness with him, and it was not Christ's will that he should rule long – and he died[6] and his mother as well.[7]

And the count of Anjou died,[8] and his son, Henry, succeeded to the dominions; and the queen of France[9] separated from the king and came to young Count Henry, and he took her as his wife, and all Poitou with her. Then he went with a big army into England,[10] and won castles, and the king went against him with a much bigger army, and all the same they did not fight, but the archbishop and the wise men went between them and made an agreement that the king should be liege lord and king as long as he lived and after his day Henry should be king; they should be as father and son; and there should be peace and concord between them, and in all England.[11] This, and all the other conditions that they made, the king and the count and the bishop and the earls and powerful men all swore to keep. Then the count was received in Winchester and in London with great honour, and all did him homage, and swore to keep the peace; and it soon became a very good peace, such as there never was before. Then the king was stronger than he had been till then, and the count went overseas,[12] and everybody loved him because he maintained strict justice and made peace.

1154 In this year King Stephen died,[13] and was buried where his wife and son were buried at Faversham, the monastery they had founded. When the king was dead, the count was overseas, and nobody dared do

---

[1] 26 September–December 1142.
[2] December 1142.
[3] February 1148; see A. Lane Poole, *From Domesday Book to Magna Carta*, p. 148, n. 4.
[4] Geoffrey of Anjou had won Normandy 1141–1144.
[5] February 1140.
[6] August 1153.
[7] May 1152.

[8] 7 September 1151.
[9] Eleanor, wife of Louis VII. Their formal separation took place in March 1152 and her marriage with Henry in May 1152.
[10] January 1153.
[11] The 'Treaty of Winchester' was made on 6 November 1153. See *E.H.D.*, II, No. 22.
[12] Before Easter 1154.
[13] 25 October 1154.

E

anything but good to another because they were in such great awe of him. When he came to England, he was received with great honour, and consecrated king in London on the Sunday before Christmas,[1] and there he held a great court.

That same day that Abbot Martin of Peterborough was to have gone there, he fell ill, and died on 2 January,[2] and the monks within the day chose another from among themselves, whose name is William of Walterville, a good cleric and a good man, and well loved by the king and by all good men. And they buried the abbot with ceremony in the morning,[3] and soon the abbot-elect went (and the monks with him) to Oxford to the king, and he gave him the abbacy; and he went shortly to Lincoln and was there consecrated abbot before he came home, and was then received with great ceremony at Peterborough with a great procession. And so he was also at Ramsey and Thorney and Crowland and Spalding and St. Albans and . . . ;[4] and now is abbot, and has made a fine beginning. Christ grant him to end thus.[5]

---

[1] 19 December 1154.

[2] 1155.

[3] Accepting the suggestion of C. Clark, *op. cit.*, p. 98.

[4] The MS. is illegible, but the first word seems to begin with E or F. It is tempting to read 'Ely', but the space is too long for any form of this name except the rare *Elibyrig*, and a scribe who was squeezing his material to get it all on to this last leaf of the gathering would hardly have chosen this. There is not enough room for any early form of Eynesbury (St Neots), another neighbouring house. It is possible that what is missing is not a place-name, but words such as 'went back'.

[5] The Chronicle ends in the bottom right-hand corner of the folio, but there is no reason to suppose that it is incomplete, for the scribe has been compressing and abbreviating in order to get in all he has to say.

Genealogies of the chief dynasties and noble houses mentioned in the Anglo-Saxon Chronicle

1. The West Saxon royal house (*a*)
2. The West Saxon royal house (*b*)
3. The West Saxon royal house (*c*)
4. The royal house of Deira
5. The royal house of Bernicia: (*a*) main branch
6. The royal house of Bernicia: (*b*) subordinate branches
7. The royal house of Mercia
8. The Norman ducal dynasty and some of its connexions
9. The connexions of Emma, and the Scandinavian interest in the succession to the English throne
10. The descendants of William I
11. The family of Godwine, earl of Wessex
12. The family of Leofric, earl of Mercia
13. The family of the earls of Northumbria
14. Some descendants of Siward, earl of Northumbria, and the descent of the earldom of Huntingdon
15. Some connexions of William fitz Osbern, steward and earl of Hereford, to illustrate the history of the Conqueror's reign, and in particular the Anglo-Saxon Chronicle for 1075
16. The family of Montgomery in connexion with its English lands before the rebellion of 1102, and with particular reference to the earldom of Shrewsbury
17. The vicomtes of the Avranchin and the Bessin in relation to the descent of the earldom of Chester
18. The descendants of Malcolm I, king of Scotland

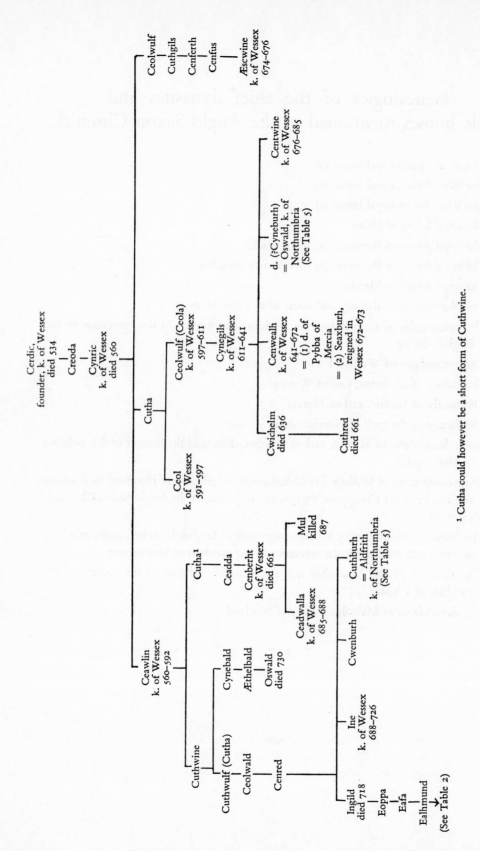

Table 1. *The West Saxon royal house* (a).

¹ Cutha could however be a short form of Cuthwine.

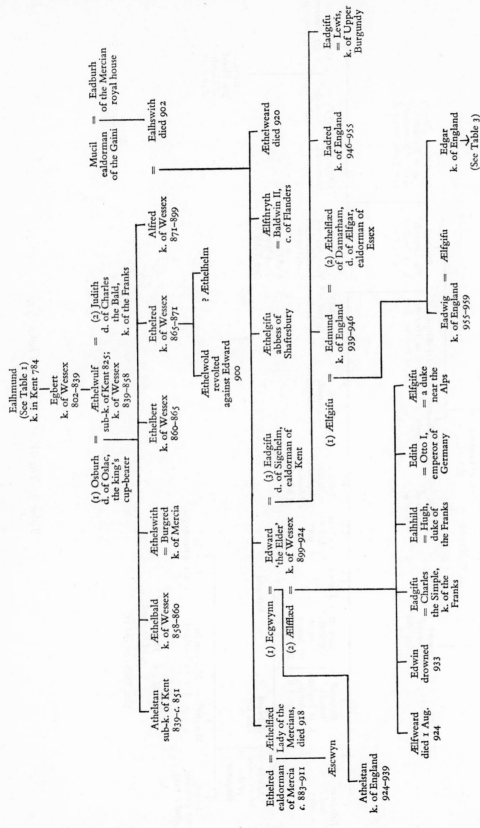

Table 2. The West Saxon royal house (b).

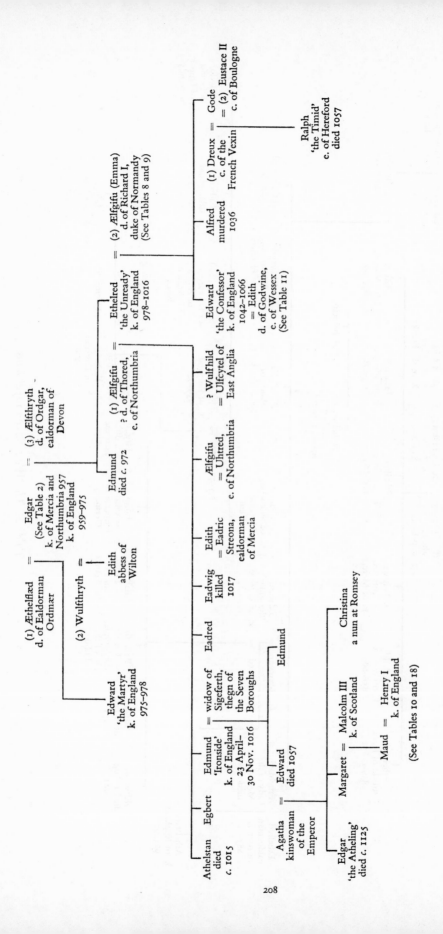

Table 3. The West Saxon royal house (c).

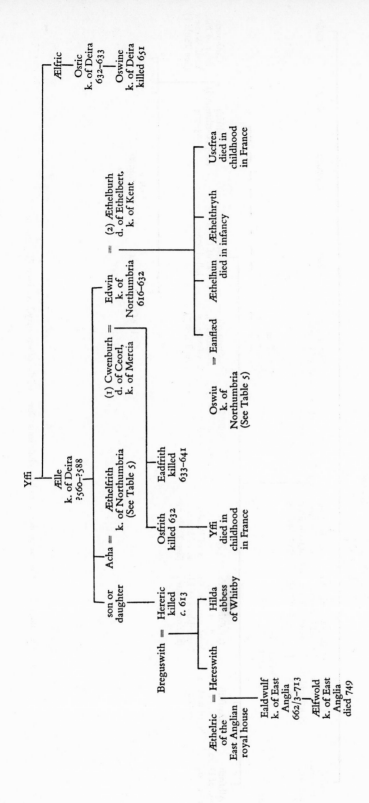

Table 4. The royal house of Deira.

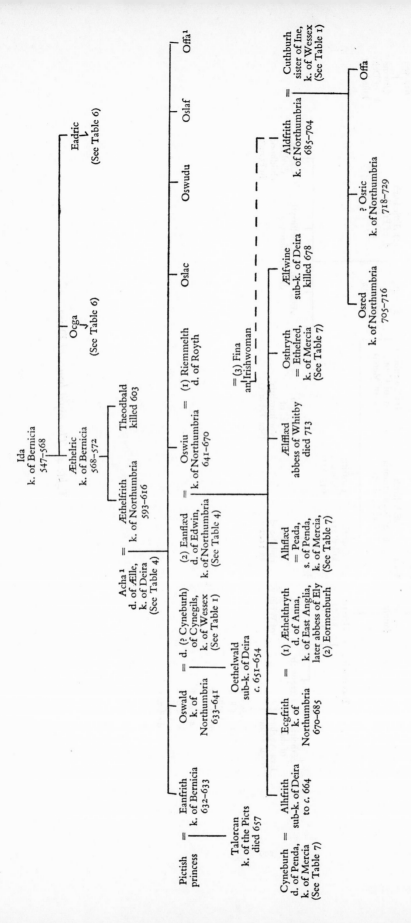

Table 5. The royal house of Bernicia: (a) main branch.

[1] Only Oswald and Oswiu can be shown to be Acha's sons. Some of the others may have been illegitimate.

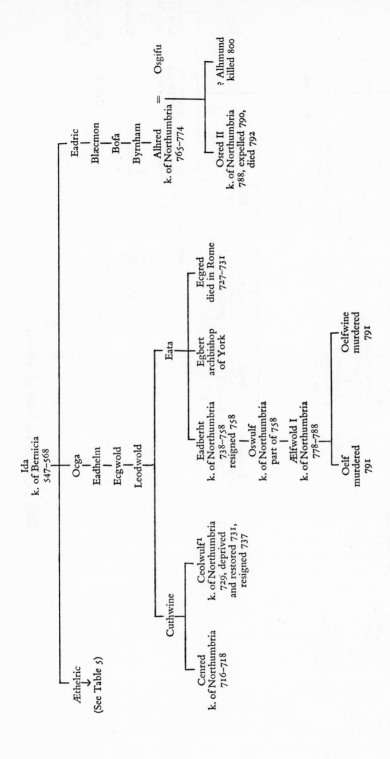

Table 6. The royal house of Bernicia: (b) subordinate branches.

[1] Annal 731 'A', 'B', 'C' makes Ceolwulf grandson, not son, of Cuthwine, by adding the name Cutha.

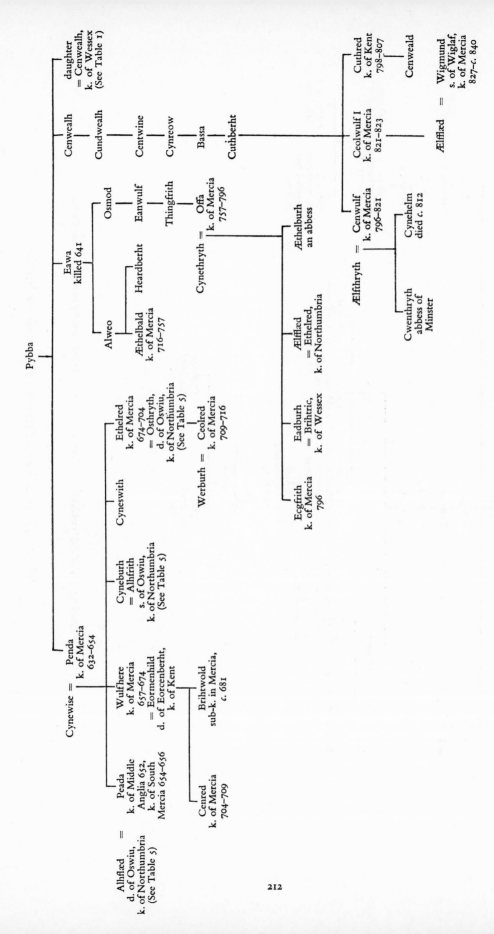

Table 7. The royal house of Mercia.

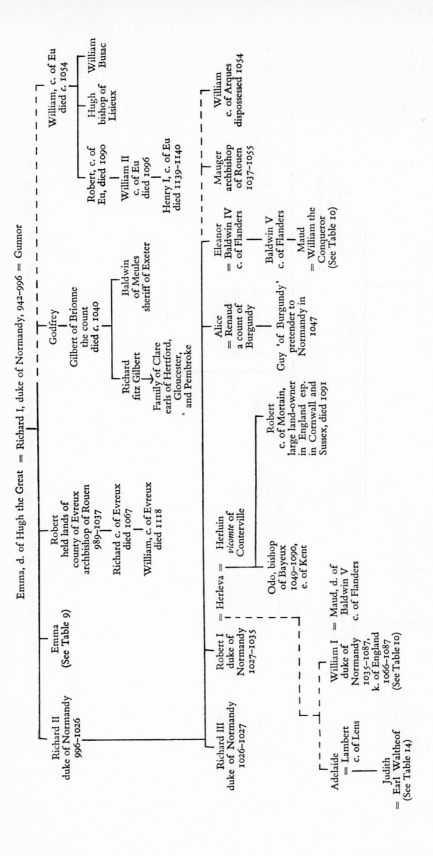

Emma, d. of Hugh the Great = Richard I, duke of Normandy, 942–996 = Gunnor

Richard II
duke of Normandy
996–1026

Emma
(See Table 9)

Robert
held lands of
county of Evreux
archbishop of Rouen
989–1037

Richard c. of Evreux
died 1067

William c. of Evreux
died 1118

Godfrey

Gilbert of Brionne
the count
died c. 1040

Richard
fitz Gilbert

Family of Clare
earls of Hertford,
Gloucester,
and Pembroke

Baldwin
of Meules
sheriff of Exeter

William, c. of Eu
died c. 1054

Robert, c. of
Eu, died 1090

William II
c. of Eu
died 1096

Henry I, c. of Eu
died 1139–1140

Hugh
bishop of
Lisieux

William
Busac

Mauger
archbishop
of Rouen
1037–1055

William
c. of Arques
dispossessed 1054

Alice
= Renaud
a count of
Burgundy

Guy 'of Burgundy',
pretender to
Normandy in
1047

Eleanor
= Baldwin IV
c. of Flanders

Baldwin V
c. of Flanders

Maud
= William the
Conqueror
(See Table 10)

Robert I
duke of
Normandy
1027–1035

= Herleva =

Herluin
vicomte of
Conteville

Richard III
duke of Normandy
1026–1027

Odo, bishop
of Bayeux
1049–1090,
e. of Kent

Robert
c. of Mortain,
large land-owner
in England esp.
in Cornwall and
Sussex, died 1091

William I = Maud, d. of
duke of   Baldwin V
Normandy   c. of Flanders
1035–1087,
k. of England
1066–1087
(See Table 10)

Adelaide
= Lambert
c. of Lens

Judith
= Earl Waltheof
(See Table 14)

Table 8. The Norman ducal dynasty and some of its connexions.

213

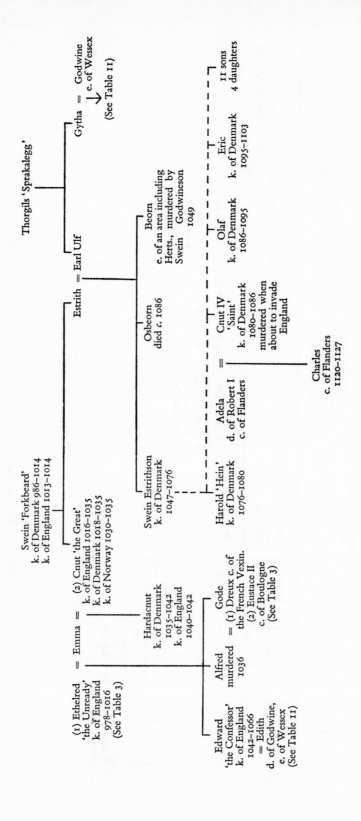

Table 9. The connexions of Emma, and the Scandinavian interest in the succession to the English throne.

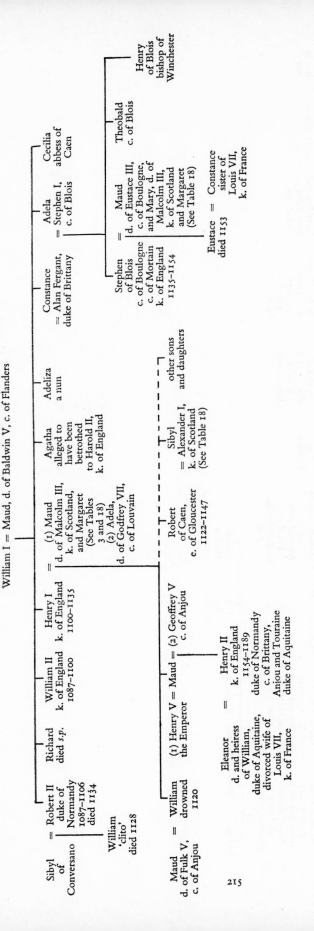

William I = Maud, d. of Baldwin V, c. of Flanders

Sibyl of Conversano = Robert II duke of Normandy 1087–1106 died 1134 | Richard died s.p. | William II k. of England 1087–1100 | Henry I k. of England 1100–1135 = (1) Maud d. of Malcolm III, k. of Scotland, and Margaret (See Tables 3 and 18) (2) Adela, d. of Godfrey VII, c. of Louvain | Agatha alleged to have been betrothed to Harold II, k. of England | Adeliza a nun | Constance = Alan Fergant, duke of Brittany | Adela = Stephen I, c. of Blois | Cecilia abbess of Caen | Henry of Blois bishop of Winchester

William 'clito' died 1128

Maud d. of Fulk V, c. of Anjou = William drowned 1120

(1) Henry V the Emperor = Maud = (2) Geoffrey V c. of Anjou

Eleanor d. and heiress of William, duke of Aquitaine, divorced wife of Louis VII, k. of France = Henry II k. of England 1154–1189 duke of Normandy, c. of Brittany, Anjou and Touraine duke of Aquitaine

Robert of Caen, e. of Gloucester 1122–1147

Sibyl = Alexander I, k. of Scotland (See Table 18)

other sons and daughters

Stephen of Blois c. of Boulogne c. of Mortain k. of England 1135–1154 = Maud d. of Eustace III, c. of Boulogne, and Mary, d. of Malcolm III, k. of Scotland and Margaret (See Table 18) | Theobald c. of Blois

Eustace died 1153 = Constance sister of Louis VII, k. of France

Table 10. The descendants of William I.

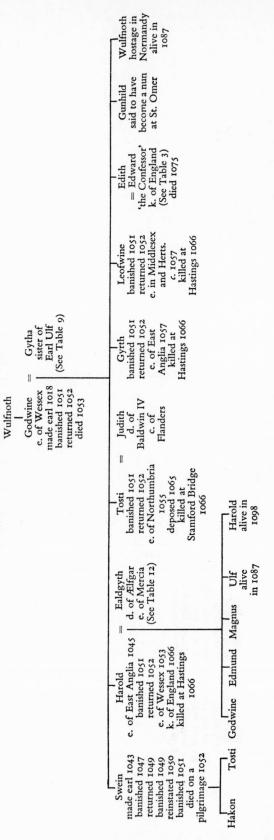

Wulfnoth
|
Godwine = Gytha
e. of Wessex   sister of
made earl 1018   Earl Ulf
banished 1051   (See Table 9)
returned 1052
died 1053

Swein
made earl 1043
banished 1047
returned 1049
banished 1049
reinstated 1050
banished 1051
died on a
pilgrimage 1052

Harold = Ealdgyth
e. of East Anglia 1045   d. of Ælfgar
banished 1051   e. of Mercia
returned 1052   (See Table 12)
e. of Wessex 1053
k. of England 1066
killed at Hastings
1066

Tosti = Judith
banished 1051   d. of
returned 1052   Baldwin IV
e. of Northumbria   c. of
1055   Flanders
deposed 1065
killed at
Stamford Bridge
1066

Gyrth
banished 1051
returned 1052
e. of East
Anglia 1057
killed at
Hastings 1066

Leofwine
banished 1051
returned 1052
e. in Middlesex
and Herts.
c. 1057
killed at
Hastings 1066

Edith
= Edward
'the Confessor'
k. of England
(See Table 3)
died 1075

Gunhild
said to have
become a nun
at St. Omer

Wulfnoth
hostage in
Normandy
alive in
1087

Hakon   Tosti   Godwine   Edmund   Magnus   Ulf   Harold
alive   alive in
in 1087   1098

Table 11. The family of Godwine, earl of Wessex.

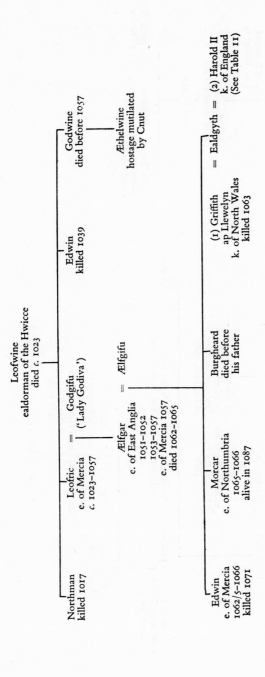

Leofwine
ealdorman of the Hwicce
died c. 1023

Northman
killed 1017

Leofric = Godgifu
c. of Mercia   ('Lady Godiva')
c. 1023–1057

Edwin
killed 1039

Godwine
died before 1057

Æthelwine
hostage mutilated
by Cnut

Ælfgar = Ælfgifu
c. of East Anglia
1051–1052
1053–1057
c. of Mercia 1057
died 1062–1065

Edwin
e. of Mercia
1062/5–1066
killed 1071

Morcar
e. of Northumbria
1065–1066
alive in 1087

Burgheard
died before
his father

Ealdgyth = (1) Griffith
ap Llewelyn
k. of North Wales
killed 1063

= (2) Harold II
k. of England
(See Table 11)

Table 12. The family of Leofric, earl of Mercia.

217

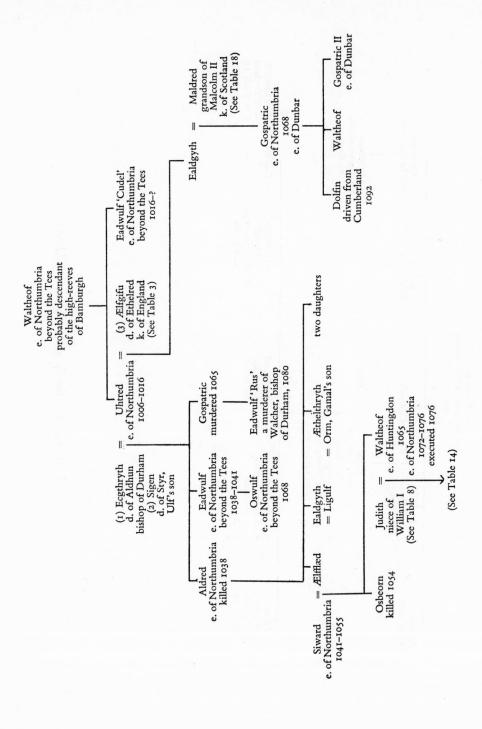

Table 13. The family of the earls of Northumbria.

Waltheof
e. of Northumbria
beyond the Tees
probably descendant
of the high-reeves
of Bamburgh

(1) Ecgthryth
d. of Aldhun
bishop of Durham
(2) Sigen
d. of Styr,
Ulf's son

= Uhtred
e. of Northumbria
1006–1016

= (3) Ælfgifu
d. of Ethelred
k. of England
(See Table 3)

Eadwulf 'Cudel'
e. of Northumbria
beyond the Tees
1016–?

Ealdgyth = Maldred
grandson of
Malcolm II
k. of Scotland
(See Table 18)

Aldred
e. of Northumbria
killed 1038

Eadwulf
e. of Northumbria
beyond the Tees
1038–1041

Gospatric
murdered 1065

Oswulf
e. of Northumbria
beyond the Tees
1068

Eadwulf 'Rus'
a murderer of
Walcher, bishop
of Durham, 1080

Gospatric
e. of Northumbria
1068
e. of Dunbar

Dolfin
driven from
Cumberland
1092

Waltheof

Gospatric II
e. of Dunbar

Ealdgyth
= Ligulf

Æthelthryth
= Orm, Gamal's son

two daughters

Siward
e. of Northumbria
1041–1055

= Ælfflæd

Osbeorn
killed 1054

Judith
niece of
William I
(See Table 8)

= Waltheof
e. of Huntingdon
1065
e. of Northumbria
1072–1076
executed 1076

(See Table 14)

218

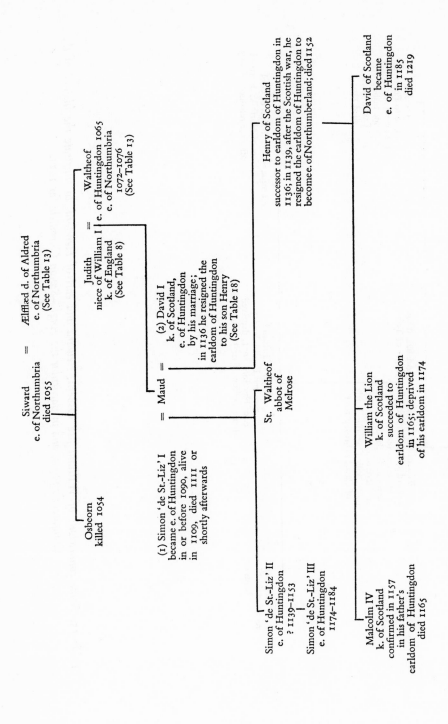

Siward
e. of Northumbria
died 1055

=

Ælflæd d. of Aldred
e. of Northumbria
(See Table 13)

Osbeorn
killed 1054

Judith
niece of William I
k. of England
(See Table 8)

=

Waltheof
e. of Huntingdon 1065
e. of Northumbria
1072–1076
(See Table 13)

(1) Simon 'de St.-Liz' I
became e. of Huntingdon
in or before 1090, alive
in 1109, died 1111 or
shortly afterwards

=

Maud

=

(2) David I
k. of Scotland,
e. of Huntingdon
by his marriage;
in 1136 he resigned the
earldom of Huntingdon
to his son Henry
(See Table 18)

St. Waltheof
abbot of
Melrose

Henry of Scotland
successor to earldom of Huntingdon in
1136; in 1139, after the Scottish war, he
resigned the earldom of Huntingdon to
become e. of Northumberland; died 1152

Simon 'de St.-Liz' II
e. of Huntingdon
? 1139–1153

Simon 'de St.-Liz' III
e. of Huntingdon
1174–1184

William the Lion
k. of Scotland
succeeded to
earldom of Huntingdon
in 1165; deprived
of his earldom in 1174

David of Scotland
became
e. of Huntingdon
in 1185
died 1219

Malcolm IV
k. of Scotland
confirmed in 1157
in his father's
earldom of Huntingdon
died 1165

Table 14. Some descendants of Siward, earl of Northumbria, and the descent of the earldom of Huntingdon.

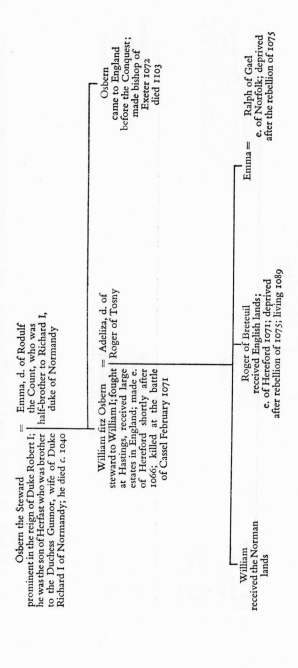

Osbern the Steward
prominent in the reign of Duke Robert I;
he was the son of Herfast who was brother
to the Duchess Gunnor, wife of Duke
Richard I of Normandy; he died c. 1040

= Emma, d. of Rodulf
the Count, who was
half-brother to Richard I,
duke of Normandy

William fitz Osbern
steward to William I; fought
at Hastings, received large
estates in England; made e.
of Hereford shortly after
1066; killed at the battle
of Cassel February 1071

= Adeliza, d. of
Roger of Tosny

Osbern
came to England
before the Conquest;
made bishop of
Exeter 1072
died 1103

William
received the Norman
lands

Roger of Breteuil
received English lands;
e. of Hereford 1071; deprived
after rebellion of 1075; living 1089

Emma =
Ralph of Gael
e. of Norfolk; deprived
after the rebellion of 1075

Table 15. Some connexions of William fitz Osbern, steward and earl of Hereford, to illustrate the history of the Conqueror's reign, and in particular the Anglo-Saxon Chronicle for 1075.

220

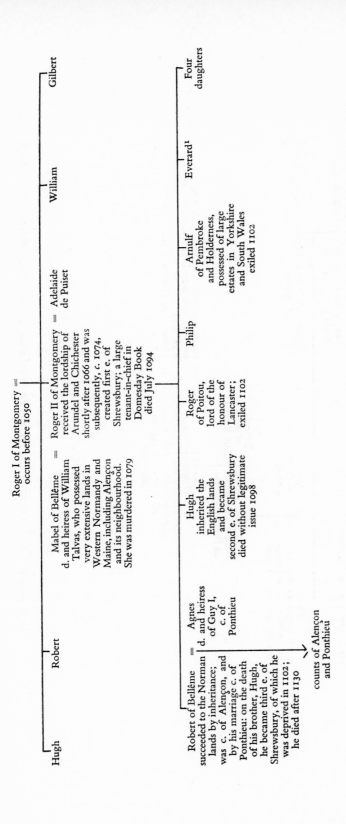

Roger I of Montgomery =
occurs before 1050

Hugh

Robert

Mabel of Bellême =
d. and heiress of William
Talvas, who possessed
very extensive lands in
Western Normandy and
Maine, including Alençon
and its neighbourhood.
She was murdered in 1079

Roger II of Montgomery
received the lordship of
Arundel and Chichester
shortly after 1066 and was
subsequently, c. 1074,
created first e. of
Shrewsbury; a large
tenant-in-chief in
Domesday Book
died July 1094

= Adelaide
de Puiset

William

Gilbert

Robert of Bellême
succeeded to the Norman
lands by inheritance;
was c. of Alençon, and
by his marriage c. of
Ponthieu: on the death
of his brother, Hugh,
he became third e. of
Shrewsbury, of which he
was deprived in 1102;
he died after 1130

= Agnes
d. and heiress
of Guy I,
c. of
Ponthieu

Hugh
inherited the
English lands
and became
second e. of Shrewsbury
died without legitimate
issue 1098

Roger
of Poitou,
lord of the
honour of
Lancaster;
exiled 1102

Philip

Arnulf
of Pembroke
and Holderness,
possessed of large
estates in Yorkshire
and South Wales
exiled 1102

Everard[1]

Four
daughters

counts of Alençon
and Ponthieu

[1] All the children of Roger II were by Mabel of Bellême except Everard.

Table 16. The family of Montgomery in connexion with its English lands before the rebellion of 1102, and with particular reference to the earldom of Shrewsbury.

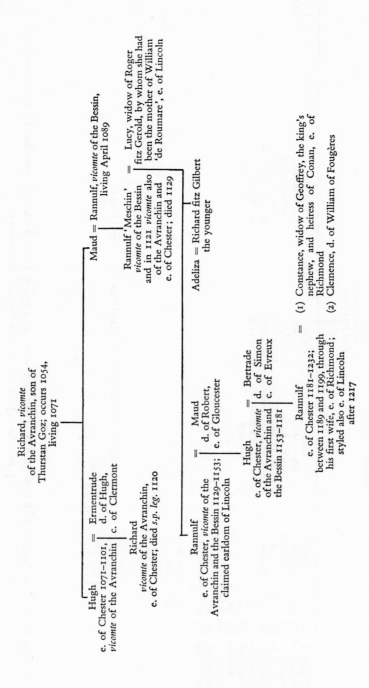

Richard, *vicomte*
of the Avranchin, son of
Thurstan Goz; occurs 1054,
living 1071

Hugh = Ermentrude
e. of Chester 1071–1101, d. of Hugh,
vicomte of the Avranchin c. of Clermont

Richard
vicomte of the Avranchin,
e. of Chester; died *s.p. leg.* 1120

Maud = Rannulf, *vicomte* of the Bessin,
living April 1089

Rannulf 'Meschin' = Lucy, widow of Roger
vicomte of the Bessin fitz Gerold, by whom she had
and in 1121 *vicomte* also been the mother of William
of the Avranchin and 'de Roumare', e. of Lincoln
e. of Chester; died 1129

Rannulf = Maud
e. of Chester, *vicomte* of the d. of Robert,
Avranchin and the Bessin 1129–1153; e. of Gloucester
claimed earldom of Lincoln

Adeliza = Richard fitz Gilbert
the younger

Hugh = Bertrade
e. of Chester, *vicomte* d. of Simon
of the Avranchin and c. of Evreux
the Bessin 1153–1181

Rannulf = (1) Constance, widow of Geoffrey, the king's
e. of Chester 1181–1232; nephew, and heiress of Conan, c. of
between 1189 and 1199, through Richmond
his first wife, e. of Richmond; (2) Clemence, d. of William of Fougères
styled also e. of Lincoln
after 1217

Table 17. The vicomtes of the Avranchin and the Bessin in relation to the descent of the earldom of Chester.

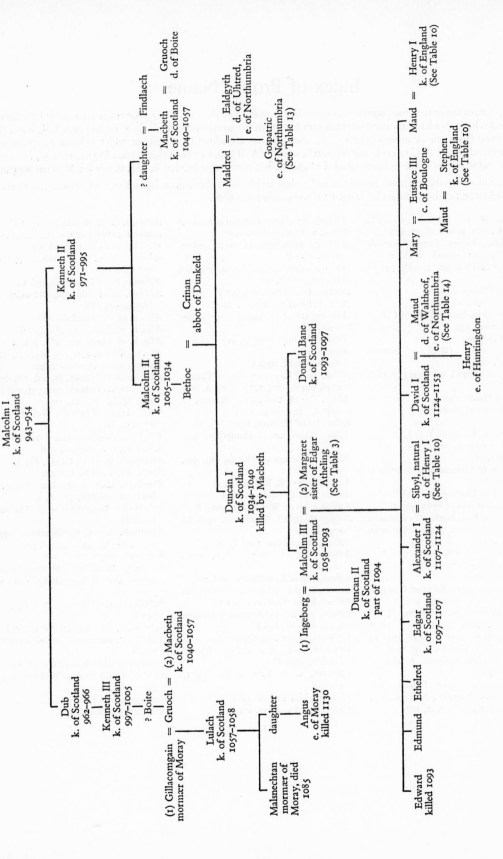

Table 18. The descendants of Malcolm I, king of Scotland.

Index of Proper Names

The references are to the annual numbers as given in the margin of the text, but a page reference is added whenever the annal is long. No letter is placed after the number when the name occurs in all the versions printed. If, however, it is missing from one or more versions of the annal, letters are added to indicate in which column or columns it is to be found. Thus, 47 C refers to the column headed C (A, B), and 47 D to that headed D (E); 1054 C, D means that the name occurs in the columns headed C and D, but not in that headed E. MR stands for Mercian Register.

The following abbreviations have been used: abp: archbishop; abt: abbot; bp: bishop; br: brother; c.: count; d.: daughter; e.: earl; f.: father; k.: king; r.: river; s.: son; w.: wife.